Broadcasting House when it was opened in 1932.

AUNTIE'S WAR

www.penguin.co.uk

Also by Edward Stourton

Absolute Truth
In the Footsteps of St Paul
John Paul II: Man of History
It's a PC World
Trinity: A Portrait (ed.)
Diary of a Dog Walker
Cruel Crossing

AUNTIE'S WAR

The BBC During the Second World War

Edward Stourton

Doubleday

LONDON · TORONTO · SYDNEY · AUCKLAND · JOHANNESBURG

TRANSWORLD PUBLISHERS
61–63 Uxbridge Road, London W5 5SA
www.penguin.co.uk

Transworld is part of the Penguin Random House group of companies
whose addresses can be found at global.penguinrandomhouse.com

First published in Great Britain in 2017 by Doubleday
an imprint of Transworld Publishers

A CIP catalogue record for this book
is available from the British Library.

ISBNs 9780857523327 (hb)

Typeset in 12/14.5pt Bembo Std by Jouve (UK), Milton Keynes
Printed and bound by Clays Ltd, Bungay, Suffolk

Penguin Random House is committed to a sustainable
future for our business, our readers and our planet. This book
is made from Forest Stewardship Council® certified paper.

1 3 5 7 9 10 8 6 4 2

To Freya

CONTENTS

CONTENTS

INTRODUCTION

N O ONE COULD HAVE accused the young Harman Grisewood of lacking ambition. When he was five he was asked what he would like to be when he grew up. 'The Pope,' he replied.

He never quite managed that, but he did the next best thing: he became the voice of the BBC.

Grisewood's road to the BBC was pure Evelyn Waugh. After Oxford he pottered off to Cyprus, where his father had, on impulse, bought an estate so vast that it embraced two villages. The venture foundered, so the young intellectual moved on to his great-uncle's palazzo in Malta and mooned about there in a funk about what to do with his life. Eventually he fled the gloomy ancestral grandeur, taking refuge in the Woodstock Road with a mentor from his Oxford days. 'Go to the BBC,' advised this *dilettante* family friend. 'They will give you enough for your needs. You will read them stories or act – or whatever it is they want. It won't be unpleasant.'

Grisewood duly got his first BBC work – as a jobbing actor – through an old friend from the Oxford University Dramatic Society; that is how these things were done then. In 1933, after an alarming interview with the BBC's founder, John Reith – the great man brandished a poker at the grate and demanded that Grisewood pronounce the word 'fire' – he joined the staff as an announcer.

Wilfred Pickles, another member of that elite corps of early BBC announcers, was roughly the same age, but he came from a very different

1

world. He was born 'in a small bedroom of the soot-blackened working class house, 24 Conway Street, Halifax, Yorkshire'. He began his adult life as a labourer, working for his builder father, but amateur dramatics provided an *entrée* to the Corporation's studios in Manchester.

In 1941 he was summoned to Broadcasting House in London to join the news-reading team; he was told that the minister of information, no less, felt 'the listeners are getting a little tired of the so-called Oxford accent'. His vow to keep his short, northern 'a's made headlines, and one newspaper speculated that he would begin his first bulletin with 'Here is the news, and ee bah gum this is Wilfred Pickles reading it.'

Val Gielgud, scion of a great acting family, came to know both Grisewood and Pickles, but his arrival at the Corporation was very much in the Grisewood style; there was, he confessed, 'a flavour both of undue influence and frivolity about my engagement'. The editor of the *Radio*

Harman Grisewood going through the schedules with Val Gielgud (on the right, pointing to the scheduling book) and Stephen Potter (left).

Times hired him as an assistant, 'not because he needed an assistant – no man needed assistance less – but because he was a friend of mine'.

But Gielgud's fate was, for a while, in the hands of young women like E. B. Champion, an eighteen-year-old who had just qualified at the London College of Secretaries. She took a job in the Accommodation Department of the BBC because it paid £2.5s a week – a few shillings more than the salary she had been offered at a firm of City solicitors. And when, with the approach of war, the Drama Department was evacuated to Evesham in Worcestershire, it was her job to find digs for the staff.

From the word go, Gielgud, who by this stage had moved to Drama, loathed his lodgings in this bucolic exile. 'My billet is vile,' he recorded in his diary on 7 September 1939. 'Its owners seem to regard one rather as if one was a medieval *condottiere*, likely to steal the silver and ravish the daughter as opposed to hoping for bed and breakfast.' A week later he escaped to London for the day and 'met my mother for lunch at the Ivy'. From his flat he collected 'a case of wine, a bottle of kummel, a thick overcoat, gloves, a coffee-pot, a huge electric torch which, set in solid rubber, can be used as a truncheon (!)' – the last item was perhaps for protection against the 'moon-faced rustics' he had found in Worcestershire. The country was not his thing at all.

E. B. Champion went on to a hush-hush job at Bush House, working for the BBC's sinister sister organization, the Political Warfare Executive – of which much more later. Gielgud and Grisewood both had successful BBC careers, but Wilfred Pickles became more famous than any of them. His radio show *Have a Go* ran for more than twenty years and attracted audiences of 20 million. He was what we would call today a genuine 'celebrity'.

Like most of Britain, the BBC of the pre-war years was rotten with class privilege and snobbery. But the memoirs and diaries of the men and women who came through the doors of Broadcasting House during the 1930s and 1940s provide a vivid spectacle of the whirlwind of war sweeping away all the old social certainties. One of the ambitions of this book is to trace the way the huge social and political changes of wartime Britain were reflected at the BBC.

But the BBC did not just mirror change; it was an agent of change too. The Second World War was Britain's first total war, in the sense that it engaged the whole nation and, because of the bombing campaigns, put millions of civilians on the front line. It was also the first big conflict of the broadcasting age, and those two 'firsts' are both critical to understanding what it was like to live through it.

Asa Briggs, the BBC's first official historian, described the BBC as a 'neglected' aspect of Second World War history. In *The War of Words*, the third volume of his magisterial BBC series *The History of Broadcasting in the United Kingdom*, he wrote 'most historians of the war have shared the view of some of the top civil servants during the war and have either left the BBC out of the reckoning or dismissed it perfunctorily'. Yet if you reflect on the Second World War moments that have formed our collective memory – Chamberlain speaking from Downing Street in 1939, for example; Dunkirk, the Blitz and the Battle of Britain; Churchill's fighting speeches; or D-Day – you will very quickly realize that the BBC was a presence in all of them, sometimes itself playing a critical role, often defining the way these events have come down to us.

The war forced Auntie to grow up very fast, so this is a critical period in her institutional history; and because she was the national broadcaster, she was, throughout this period of revolution, interacting with the general population, which itself faced huge changes under the pressures of war. The BBC in wartime was both a drama of its own and a central player in the national drama.

The Corporation had, for example, a very good Blitz, and that chapter is both a rich well of wider social history and a source of cracking war stories. For the staff, the most powerful symbol of the swirling social mobility at the Corporation was the Concert Hall (now known as the Radio Theatre), an art deco cavern in the basement of Broadcasting House which still looks very much as it would have done when the building was opened in 1932. In the worst days of the German bombing – in 1940 and 1941 – it was fitted out as a dormitory, with 'a discreet curtain of blankets . . . stretched across to divide the sexes'. Any member of staff required to remain in the building after dark could apply for a ticket to spend the night there, so it was, in a way, the very incarnation of the Blitz spirit, with everyone mucking in together.

The announcer Freddie Grisewood (Harman's cousin) remembered it thus: 'In this Hall, all those who were on late or early morning shifts passed fitful nights, on mattresses laid out on the floor with Army blankets to cover us.' He did not altogether approve of this close contact with his less exalted colleagues. 'Never in the whole of my experience,' he reminisced, 'have I heard such a varied assortment of noises issuing from the human frame. Snores, grunts, whistles, moans, occasionally deep sobs were mingled with sad sighs, and even snatches of song.'

But BH could provide a comforting sense of home from home, which made it worth putting up with this nocturnal racket. Douglas Ritchie, an assistant news editor at the time, remembered that 'I did not like the air raids very much, and after spending all night there and having breakfast as well, Broadcasting House seemed like a perfect air-raid shelter ... The minute I stepped outside the air raid used to boil up and usually there were German bombers directly overhead or a series of dog-fights. But Broadcasting House felt like a stone and I felt like one of those creatures that creep under stones.'

The Booker Prize-winning novelist Penelope Fitzgerald, another BBC veteran of the war years, was more sceptical of the apparently democratic spirit abroad, and detected the Old Adam of privilege at work. 'The first heroic or primitive period of the concert-hall had only lasted a very short while,' she wrote in her sly satire *Human Voices*. 'The grades quickly reasserted themselves ... Just inside the entrance, the old dressing rooms had been turned into separate cubicles for executives and senior newsreaders, but junior newsreaders (after one o'clock in the morning) and administrative assistants (on programmes of special importance) could claim to use any that were vacant.' In one of the novel's comic climaxes the senior announcer, sporting 'the correctly creased uniform of the BBC's Defence Volunteers', is denied his customary berth because a junior secretary from the Department of Recorded Programmes has gone into labour in one of the cubicles, having come adrift from her moral moorings in the louche social currents of Blitz-battered London.

Fitzgerald compared Broadcasting House to an ocean liner. 'Since the outbreak of war damp sandbags had lapped it round,' she wrote, 'but once inside the bronze doors, the airs of cooking from the deep hold suggested more strongly than ever a cruise on the *Queen Mary*. At night, with all its blazing portholes blacked out, it towered over a flotilla of taxis, each dropping off a speaker or two.'

The building was, of course, a particular target for the Luftwaffe. It was given a coat of camouflage paint – so that it looked more like a battleship than a cruise liner – and there was an armoured car parked outside, ready to take the duty newsreader to emergency studios in Maida Vale. BH, with its distinctive – you might even say eccentric – profile became almost as much a symbol of defiance during the Blitz as St Paul's Cathedral.

On 15 October 1940, at quarter past eight in the evening, a 500lb bomb fell through a window on the seventh floor and bored its way down through the building to the music library on the third. It did not immediately explode, but just after Bruce Belfrage had begun to read the nine o'clock news someone tried to move it, and it did. The audience heard a crump, but Belfrage continued to read the bulletin almost without a pause (he later admitted to needing a 'stiffener' when he came off the air). For the millions of listeners at home – many of whom would have suffered equally narrow squeaks during those harrowing weeks – here was an eloquent expression of what British phlegm really meant. The BBC's motto is 'Nation shall speak peace unto Nation', but during the war years the wireless also allowed the British people to talk to themselves, and a true 'national conversation' became possible for the first time.

During the 1970s and 1980s, revisionist historians set about debunking some of the great national myths that have grown up around the Second World War, but while researching this book I have been struck by just how much essential truth there is in those myths. It is undeniably the case, for example, that during the late summer and autumn of 1940, when any rational person would surely have concluded that the war was lost, the British people showed themselves to be capable of steadfastness and social solidarity to a quite astonishing degree.

The files of the Ministry of Information, which was responsible for civilian morale, bulge with evidence that the governing classes were positively astonished by the resilience shown by the great mass of the population in the face of a bombing campaign of unprecedented ferocity. George Orwell, clear-eyed and unsentimental as ever, concluded in 1941 that Britain 'is a land of snobbery and privilege, ruled largely by the old and silly. But in any calculation about it one has got to take into account its emotional unity, the tendency of nearly all its inhabitants to feel alike and act together in moments of supreme crisis.'

All myths are, of course, coloured by the passing of time. But when you strip the BBC back to its original 1940s hues the restored picture becomes, if anything, more striking and interesting than ever.

I quickly learned, for example, that the language we use about this subject today often meant something very different then. The words 'impartial' and 'independent' have long been associated with the BBC, and it is part of the Corporation's myth that those principles survived the war. The BBC of the 1940s was not – not even remotely – either of those things in the sense we use the terms now.

The idea of broadcasting 'impartially' about an existential Nazi threat would have struck most people you will meet in this book as absurd or shocking. There was of course a huge range of political opinion within the wider BBC family, but almost everyone agreed on the overwhelming need to defeat Hitler.

At one end of the spectrum there were the warrior correspondents like Charles Gardner, who was sent to France in the autumn of 1939 as part of a tiny BBC team with the British forces helping to defend the French frontiers during the 'Phoney War', the strange lull before full-blown hostilities began in May 1940. Richard Dimbleby was given the army to cover (the British Expeditionary Force, or BEF) and Gardner was assigned to the RAF's Advanced Air Striking Force.

Gardner's memoir boils with his frustration in the face of official censorship. It was not that he felt he was being forced to cover things up – far from it; he thought the censors were missing all sorts of opportunities for morale-boosting propaganda by restricting the way he reported the heroism and skill of our young knights of the skies. When the Germans attacked in earnest in the summer of 1940, he found himself trapped in the back of a car while a Heinkel strafed the street with machine-gun fire around him; he escaped in time to see the German plane shot down by a Hurricane, and confided to his diary, 'I must say that I viewed this with great pleasure. Not long ago I would have been disturbed at the unpleasant end of these Germans, but now I am as jingoistic and bloodthirsty as anyone.' By the end of 1940 Gardner had left the BBC and joined the RAF himself.

'Propaganda' is another of those words that need careful handling. As Gardner was delivering his final despatches from France in May 1940, the BBC's North American Service was just about to go on the air for the first time. The left-wing MP and writer Vernon Bartlett (a key figure in the BBC's pre-war history, of which more later) opened the service with the words, 'I am going to talk to you three times a week from a country that is fighting for its life. Inevitably I am going to be called by that terrifying word "propagandist". But of course I am a propagandist. Passionately I want my ideas, our ideas, of freedom and justice to survive.' Almost everyone involved with the Corporation would have said 'Amen' to that.

An extraordinary array of writers and intellectuals of the left contributed to the BBC's war effort; the hugely important German Service alone could count on Dick Crossman, the future *New Statesman* editor and Labour Cabinet minister, the great novelist Thomas Mann, and Hugh Carleton Greene, brother of Graham and future BBC director-general. And at the far end of the spectrum from Charles Gardner stood that intellectual and moral giant George Orwell. 'All propaganda is lies,' he declared, sternly and perceptively, in 1942, 'even when one is telling the truth.'

And yet even he spent two years writing and producing programmes for India in an attempt to shore up the links that bound Britain to her empire, which he detested. Orwell went to war with words because he understood that the values he cherished most were at stake in the struggle against fascism. 'Totalitarianism has abolished freedom of thought to an extent unheard of in any previous age,' he declared in a radio talk he wrote in May 1941, just after joining the

Corporation. 'If totalitarianism becomes worldwide and permanent, what we have known as literature will come to an end.' He finally left the BBC because he believed that 'in the present political situation the broadcasting of British propaganda to India is an almost hopeless task', not because he did not believe in the cause.

So much for the BBC's wartime 'impartiality'. Its 'independence' is an even more ticklish matter.

When war broke out, responsibility for the BBC was moved from the Postmaster General's office to the Ministry of Information – itself a curious and most un-British institution which we shall explore in Chapters Two and Seven. I have worked in countries where the broadcasters are run by a ministry of information – Iraq during the Saddam Hussein days, for example – and I always assume it means that they are the government's mouthpiece.

In the BBC's case a degree of independence was preserved by the survival of the Board of Governors as a kind of buffer zone between the Corporation and the Ministry, but on several occasions – especially in the very dark days of 1940, when invasion seemed imminent – there were powerful political voices arguing that even this fig leaf should be removed, and that the BBC should be brought fully under government control. It did not help that Churchill was initially sceptical about the BBC, which he felt had denied him the airtime he deserved during his wilderness years. He hated the tall and craggy Scotsman Lord Reith (whom he nicknamed the 'Wuthering Height') and seems to have had an equally low regard for Reith's wartime successor, Sir Frederick Ogilvie. Within a week of moving into Number 10, Churchill was demanding that Duff Cooper, his minister of information, come up with ideas for 'establishing more effective control over the BBC'. In the end the issue was – as we shall see – settled by a very British compromise, and the BBC's independence was preserved. But at times it was, as the Duke of Wellington put it about another famous battle, 'the nearest run thing you ever saw in your life'.

It was still, of course, the case that every BBC despatch had to be censored – both politically and for security reasons. And the BBC was, as an institution, directly involved in prosecuting the war in all sorts of ways. Its Monitoring Service, which began life in a few wooden huts at a Worcestershire country house in 1939, became a hugely important source of intelligence, and its transmitters were used in a very clever wheeze known as 'meaconing' – it involved re-transmitting German radio programmes to confuse enemy aircraft that were trying to use the BBC's transmitters as navigational aids. This is not the way a truly 'independent' organization conducts itself.

But through it all – and herein lies the great and mysterious miracle of the BBC's wartime story – runs a golden thread of truth-telling. In September 1939, R. T. Clark, the man in charge of the BBC's News Department, declared in a memo: 'It seems to me that the only way to strengthen the morale of the people whose morale is worth strengthening, is to tell them the truth, and nothing but the truth, even if the truth is horrible.' It set the BBC on a course that Penelope Fitzgerald described as 'the strangest project of the war, or of any war'. She writes, 'Without prompting, the BBC decided that truth was more important than consolation, and, in the long run, would be more effective. And yet there was no guarantee of this. Truth ensures trust, but not victory, or even happiness. But the BBC had clung tenaciously to its first notion, droning quietly on, at intervals from dawn to midnight, telling, as far as possible, exactly what happened. An idea so unfamiliar was bound to upset many of the other authorities, but they got used to it little by little, and the listeners had always expected it.' In the course of the war the ideal of truth-telling became, as she suggests, accepted as an obvious good in itself and, almost by accident, Britain acquired the most open, trusted and successful broadcasting culture in the world as a result. Unravelling the mystery of how that happened is another of this book's ambitions.

I use the word 'mystery' because the outcome we all take for granted today really was not certain. At about the time that R. T. Clark circulated his manifesto for the truth, the Ministry of Information sent a memo to the Home Office about maintaining civilian morale during air raids. It sheds a fascinating light on the official mind of the time. 'The people must feel they are being told the truth,' it begins, promisingly enough. 'But what is truth? We must adopt a pragmatic definition. It is what is believed to be the truth. A lie that is put across becomes the truth and may, therefore, be justified. The difficulty is to keep up lying . . . It is simpler to tell the truth and, if a sufficient emergency arises, to tell one big, thumping lie that will then be believed.' Dr Goebbels could not have put the matter better.

As anyone who has worked abroad for the BBC will tell you, the legacy of the war years lives today. The BBC still stands for something big and important in far-flung places, and I find myself constantly brought up short by the reaction to those initials around the world.

Auntie periodically insists that those of us who travel a lot attend what is called a HEFAT course – Hostile Environment and First Aid Training – at which we learn the sort of skills you hope you will never have to use; if you suffer a sucking chest wound from shrapnel, I'm your man. The courses are usually held in some hideous Home Counties mansion with dank shrubberies – rather the sort of place one can imagine being sent for special ops training during the Second World War, in fact – and the saving grace of this somewhat penitential experience is spending the evenings with members of the wider BBC family – something one would never otherwise do.

During one course, a young World Service presenter told me about his childhood in the Ugandan countryside. His school was so basic that he was instructed to arrive with a bucket of fresh mud for the walls every day, but he got hold of a copy of *Great Expectations* and Pip's story kept him going. He was so thrilled to have made it on to the BBC airwaves that he could hardly contain himself – he talked about journalism non-stop, with limitless curiosity and huge enthusiasm.

There was also a gentle Sudanese who said almost nothing until the class about what to do if you are arrested. He then shared the fact that he had spent six months in jail because he had broadcast something his government didn't like. There is a direct link between the idealism that inspires such people and the BBC's wartime record. This is a work of history, and emphatically not a book about the Corporation today, but, after more than thirty-five years working as a British broadcaster (not just for the BBC – the wartime legacy has formed our independent sector too) I do not mind admitting that I feel sentimental about this chapter of British history.

The nation where this sentimentality is most widely shared is

France. This is surprising – another of the mysteries I hope to unravel, indeed – because in 1940 the phrase 'perfidious Albion' really did reflect the way this country was seen by many French men and women, who believed their nation had been betrayed by Britain.

And we did, beyond any doubt, lie during those dark days in the run-up to the fall of France. The evidence of our duplicity during the evacuation of Dunkirk is, as we shall see, overwhelming. There may have been sound strategic reasons for our dishonesty, but if you were a French soldier left holding the line while your British comrades scrambled on to the safety of a ship, those reasons would not have meant much to you.

The BBC was not much help as a truth-teller on this occasion. It played a big part in mythologizing Dunkirk through broadcasts by Churchill and the writer J. B. Priestley after the event, but its reporting of what actually happened as the Germans closed in on the British and French forces bottled up around the port of Dunkirk was – for reasons I shall explore – late and partial (in both senses of the word).

And yet by the end of the war the BBC had acquired a quite extraordinarily high reputation in France. The army museum at Les Invalides in Paris contains a whole section devoted to the BBC, including a moving display of letters – sometimes addressed simply to 'La BBC, Londres, Angleterre' – that ordinary French men and women sent in to thank the Corporation for the way it kept truth alive for them during the years of Occupation.

The mystique has endured through all the ups and downs of post-war Franco-British relations. My colleague John Simpson recalls that in 1985 he was able to smuggle his camera crew into a debate at the French Assemblée Nationale because the deputy speaker was a former Resistance fighter. 'I owe so much to you,' he told John. When I was a BBC Paris correspondent at the end of that decade I was amazed by how easy it was to persuade top-flight French politicians to trot round to our offices in the Rue du Faubourg Saint-Honoré, and how often people mentioned the war when I introduced myself as a BBC correspondent. It was during my time in Paris that I first began to ruminate on some of the questions I shall try to address in this book.

I have also been inspired by sheer professional admiration – to the point of envy, sometimes – for the BBC broadcasters of the wartime era. *War Report*, which went on the air immediately after D-Day and continued, almost nightly, until the German surrender in May 1945, must surely rank as one of the greatest radio strands of all time. It was run from a former actors' Green Room in the basement of Broadcasting House, and the vividness of the reporting brought home how dramatically broadcast journalism had developed during half a decade of warfare. The programme's correspondents wrote the rule book we still use; all the qualities that make good radio today – clear, vigorous prose, the use of sound, an eye for the telling detail, a sense of occasion and a certain intimacy of tone – are there in abundance.

They were men (almost exclusively, although the first woman war correspondent, Audrey Russell, was appointed in 1944) of remarkable courage. Some of them became very famous – Richard Dimbleby, of course, more than any of them. Others are largely forgotten today. The name Guy Byam probably means nothing to you, but reflect on the fullness of the life packed into this brief notice from *The Times* of 12 February 1945:

> The United States Strategic Air Forces announced on Saturday that Guy Byam, a BBC war reporter, is missing since flying on a daylight bombing attack against Berlin on Feb 3. The Flying Fortress in which Byam flew to make a recording for the BBC was struck by anti-aircraft fire over Berlin. It lagged behind the rest of the formation, and later another Fortress reported hearing distress signals in the North Sea off the Frisian Islands. Byam's aircraft has not been heard of since.
>
> Byam had parachuted into Normandy on D-Day, jumped again with the 101st British Airborne Army at Arnhem, escaping by swimming the Rhine. He flew with RAF Bomber Command in an attack on the *Tirpitz*, and survived the sinking of HMS *Jervis Bay* after it was torpedoed.

All that, and he was only twenty-six when he died. His report on the retreat from Arnhem, delivered on 27 September 1944, is one of the most powerful despatches I have ever heard. 'They came out

General de Gaulle outside Notre-Dame at the liberation of Paris.

because they had got nothing left to fight with except their bare hands ...,' it begins.

I cannot resist quoting another remarkable report from this era. I have done a little war reporting myself – a very little, by the standards of this generation. Robert Reid's despatches about the liberation of Paris reveal the gulf that separates our work today from the experience of those doing the job during the Second World War.

One of the tricks in the HEFAT team repertoire involves a post-prandial stroll across the lawn. You can admire the pretty countryside, and chat with your colleagues and tutors as you walk, but the Home Counties peace is suddenly interrupted by a burst of automatic gunfire, and you are expected to dive under the nearest rhododendron bush. Once the game is over you very often find that, when seeking

The scene at the cathedral a few moments later when snipers opened up.

cover, you have rushed towards the source of the fire rather than away from it; it is surprisingly difficult to identify where bullets are coming from when you are taken by surprise. This lesson came to mind as I tried to imagine Robert Reid's experience of finding himself in the middle of a full-blown sniper attack inside Notre-Dame.

On 27 August 1944, as General de Gaulle arrived at the cathedral to celebrate the liberation of Paris, gunfire erupted from the rafters. Reid's recording of the event is interrupted as the firing begins, and he picks up like this: 'Well, that was one of the most dramatic scenes I've ever seen. Just as General de Gaulle was about to enter the cathedral of Notre-Dame, firing started all over the place. I am afraid we couldn't get you the noise of that firing because I was overwhelmed by a rush of people trying to seek shelter, and my cable parted company from my microphone. But I fell just near General de Gaulle and I managed to pick myself up ... He walked straight ahead in what appeared to be a hail of fire from somewhere inside the cathedral – somewhere from the galleries up near the vaulted roof. But he went straight ahead without hesitation, his shoulders flung back, and walked right down the central aisle, even while the bullets poured round him.'

The firing began again as the general left, and Reid modestly recorded, 'I don't mind saying that at the moment I'm just squatting cross-legged on the floor by the side of the cathedral making this recording . . . I didn't want to be too conspicuous standing up with the microphone in my hand.' At seventy years' distance we can only salute his *sangfroid*.

But I am getting ahead of myself; the BBC and its correspondents travelled a long journey before they reached the triumphant excellence of *War Report*. It is a journey that begins – improbably – with a cellist and a nightingale.

THE CELLIST AND THE NIGHTINGALE

T HE BBC BEGAN LIFE as the British Broadcasting Company in 1922, so Auntie was still a teenager when war broke out; but she was a teenager of the precocious kind who uses long words and follows settled habits. By the 1930s she already had her hallowed traditions.

One of them could be traced back to 1924 and a cellist called Beatrice Harrison. This distinguished soloist – Delius was among her fans – liked to play in her Surrey garden to the accompaniment of nightingales, and, fired with the passion of a great artist, she persuaded John Reith, the BBC's managing director (and later its first director-general), that the scene was worthy of broadcast. No one had ever attempted a live programme of this kind before, so when it went out successfully, on 19 May that year, it was regarded as a milestone.

This first ever wildlife outside broadcast proved so popular that the cellist and her nightingales became an annual spring fixture. 'There she would sit and play in the bosky gloom,' wrote Harman Grisewood, who was working as an announcer during this period. 'The fancy was that a bird would respond.' Reaching characteristically for a Keatsian allusion, he continued, 'When the engineers reported to the announcer on duty that full-throated ease was available on the line he would have to interrupt the programme and say "We now take you over to Bagley Woods to hear the song of the nightingale."' And Grisewood tells us that Beatrice Harrison and her birds were also, in the last anxious months of peace, earmarked for a critical propaganda mission.

Beatrice Harrison, playing for the nightingales in the 'bosky gloom'.

In February 1939 he and a BBC colleague flew to Berlin to assess the seriousness of the Nazi threat. They saw the 'yellow marked benches for Jews in the *Tiergarten*', listened for the click on the line as the Gestapo monitored their telephone calls, and observed the vast quantities of grain being stored in warehouses – a clear sign, they concluded, that the German capital was hunkering down for war.

Grisewood felt that the threat of war was underestimated in the higher reaches of the BBC. One of the Controllers caught him reading *Mein Kampf* while he was on an announcing shift and ticked him off, telling him that Hitler was 'just a vulgarian'. When he made his report on the Berlin trip to the director-general, he 'was disappointed that his reactions were not more marked'.

But Frederick Ogilvie, a gentle academic who had taken over as director-general from Sir John Reith the previous year, had, to use a phrase the BBC would later make famous, 'a cunning plan'. The

Corporation had recently begun German-language broadcasts. 'The proposal made to the Director General,' Grisewood reports, 'was that this bird-charming exploit of the lady cellist should be relayed to the Germans as a token of our peace-loving intentions ... To show me that the Germans were susceptible to "this sort of thing" I remember his repeating to me the lines of the song *Es sang vor langen Jahren / Wohl auch die Nachtigall ... Da wir zusammen waren / Da sang die Nachtigall* [Many years ago / There sang the Nightingale ... When we two were together / Then sang the Nightingale].' In his autobiography, written after the war, Grisewood adds, 'You may smile now, gentle reader, but it wasn't funny at the time.'

It would be unfair to suggest that the BBC entered the Second World War entirely unprepared – as we shall see, some aspects of wartime broadcasting (though not always the right ones) had been thought through with real imagination. But the Corporation of the 1930s was marked by a certain innocence, and it was much too wrapped up in its own doings to pay much heed to what was happening in Berlin. If the BBC Controllers had taken the trouble to read *Mein Kampf* instead of sneering at its author, they might have had a better sense of what a formidable adversary they would soon face.

Hitler devoted two whole chapters of the book to the importance of propaganda (and included, interestingly, praise for the way British propaganda had 'brilliantly' exploited the disintegration of morale among German troops during the First World War). The *Reichsministerium für Volksaufklärung und Propaganda* (Ministry for National Enlightenment and Propaganda) was the first new ministry the Nazis established when they came to power in 1933, and from its earliest days it was clear that radio would be at the heart of their project to control every aspect of German national life.

The minister for propaganda, Joseph Goebbels, believed the medium was 'the most modern and most important instrument of mass influence that exists anywhere'. He immediately set about securing control over the *Reichsrundfunkgesellschaft*, or RRG, the German equivalent of the BBC. At the beginning of the decade the RRG had been part-owned by nine regional broadcasting companies which had considerable freedom to decide their own programming.

The process of bringing it more directly under central government had already begun in the last year of the Weimar Republic, and Goebbels finished the job promptly. By the summer of 1933 100 per cent of the RRG's shares were held by the Propaganda Ministry.

At the same time, Dr Goebbels commissioned the development of a new, cheap radio to ensure that his message would reach as wide an audience as possible. The *Volksempfänger*, or 'people's receiver' (so the radio counterpart of the *Volkswagen* car), was launched in August 1933 and cost about half the price of most sets on the market at the time. It could not receive short-wave signals, and only Austrian and German stations were marked on the dial, which suited the Propaganda Ministry very well. An even cheaper version would be launched on the eve of war, with a design that invited the popular nickname *Goebbels-Schnauze*, or Goebbels' snout.

Two months after his appointment, Goebbels laid out his plans for radio in a speech to senior programme staff. With radio, he told them, 'you can make public opinion'. He appointed a new chief programme director, Eugen Hadamovsky, who declared, 'The men who are moulding the new German radio are fighters. They value radio as a key element in the political battle.' Radio, he argued, was the 'most powerful and most revolutionary weapon which we possess in the struggle for the new Third Reich'. It was an illustration of the broader point about the Nazi use of technology made by Albert Speer at his trial in Nuremberg in 1946. 'Hitler's dictatorship differed in one fundamental point from all its predecessors in history,' Speer famously observed. 'His was the first dictatorship ... which made complete use of all technical means for domination of its own country. Through technical devices like the radio and loudspeaker, eighty million people were deprived of independent thought. It was thereby possible to subject them to the will of one man.' Or, as Goebbels put it, 'It would not have been possible for us to take power or to use it in the ways we have without the radio.'

Hadamovsky even claimed that radio was, in some essential way, a Nazi medium. 'Only the National Socialist movement gave radio its proper sense,' he wrote. 'Radio is the characteristic means of expression of the National Socialist man and his *Weltanschauung* [philosophy of life]. It is the instrument that possesses all the internal and external premises to picture his new values; blood and soil, race, fatherland and nation.' Exactly what he meant by that volley of ideo-babble, who knows; but the Nazis very clearly saw radio as a political weapon before anything else. In the corridors of the Reichsfunkhaus, the striking modernist headquarters of German radio in Berlin, no one was talking namby-pamby nonsense about a mission to 'inform, educate and entertain'. This was not a radio culture in which Beatrice Harrison of Bagley Woods would have flourished, and truth-telling was scarcely a priority.

Hermann Rauschning, a senior Nazi who broke with Hitler in 1934 and fled to the United States, wrote several influential books which were avidly read in the late 1930s by those looking for clues to Nazi intentions. In one of them, Rauschning claimed that as early as 1933 the Führer told him, 'Artillery preparation for an attack as during the [First] World War will be replaced in the future war by the psychological dislocation of the enemy through revolutionary propaganda. The enemy must be demoralized and driven to passivity ... Our strategy is to destroy the enemy from within, to conquer him through himself. Mental confusion, contradiction of feeling, indecision, panic – these are our weapons.' Many years later the authenticity of Rauschning's conversations with Hitler was questioned, but that passage very accurately reflects what the Germans would attempt with radio propaganda in France, Belgium and the Netherlands in 1940. And throughout the 1930s the Nazis steadily built up their capacity to project their message abroad, beginning with short-wave transmissions to the United States within weeks of Hitler coming to power. 'In wartime,' the future Führer wrote in *Mein Kampf*, 'words are acts.'

So very early on the Nazi leadership had recognized that, as well as offering a powerful new tool of political control, radio had changed the nature of warfare.

With the benefit of hindsight, that seems obvious; but it wasn't at the time. The transformation was brilliantly – if somewhat breathlessly – articulated by Charles Rolo, an Anglo-American journalist who also worked for the British and American governments (a much commoner employment pattern then than it is now). His influential book *Radio Goes to War* was the first real trumpet call on the Allied side to summon public attention to the radio revolution. 'Spreading with the speed of light, it [radio] carries the human voice seven times round the globe in one second,' he wrote. 'When Hitler makes a speech in the Kroll Opera House in Berlin, listeners in America hear his words by short wave before his own immediate audience hears them.'

Rolo had been involved in propaganda work, and it was the propaganda potential of the medium that really excited him. 'Radio speaks in all tongues to all classes,' he gallops on. 'All-pervasive, it penetrates beyond national frontiers, spans the walls of censorship that bar the way to the written word, and seeps through the fine net of the Gestapo. It reaches the illiterate and the informed, the young and the old, the civilian and the soldier in the front line, the policy makers and the inarticulate masses. So great is the importance of radio today that the seizure of a defeated nation's transmitters has become one of the primary spoils of war.'

Stirring and perceptive stuff, but *Radio Goes to War* was published in 1943, in the heat of the conflict, a full decade after the Nazis had begun laying the foundations for their radio propaganda operations. Rolo notes that by the time his book came out there were more than 100 million sets in existence: 40 million in Europe, 55 million in the United States, 4 million in Latin America and nearly a million in Africa and the 'Near East', as it was then known.

Perhaps the BBC should have understood what all that would mean for wartime broadcasting as well as Dr Goebbels did; the Corporation was, after all, in the vanguard of the radio revolution. But Auntie's staff had plenty to distract them from the clouds gathering in Germany and, like most people in Britain, they were only too willing to look the other way. The BBC was doing amazing things in the early 1930s, and no one there wanted to think about war.

≈

Asa Briggs covered this period in the second volume of his official history, and he gave the book the evocative title *The Golden Age of Wireless*. The audience simply grew and grew. In 1927 (when the

BBC ceased to be a company and was granted the grander institutional status of a corporation with a Royal Charter) there were some 2.2 million licence-holders in Britain. The newly created Corporation was ambitious to push up the numbers. Each year it published its *Hand Book* – later known as the *Year Book* – which laid out its achievements and aspirations. 'Statisticians will continue to argue about "saturation points",' declared the 1930 edition. 'So far as the BBC is concerned, there is no saturation point short of "a wireless in every home".' And the number of licences did indeed climb relentlessly, even during the years of the Depression; it doubled, for example, between March 1929 and March 1933.

By 1939, 9 million households had radio licences, and the BBC estimated it had 34 million listeners (of a population of some 48 million). Siân Nicholas, who has written the best modern academic account of the BBC during this period, estimates that if the incidence of licence-fee evasion is taken into account the real figure for listeners may have been as high as 40 million. Those who could not afford a radio at home could often count on listening in the pub, or with a neighbour. 'By 1937,' Nicholas writes, 'George Orwell could assert with confidence "literally everyone in England has access to a radio".'

It was not quite true; there were pockets of resistance to the new technology. Some of the grander gentlemen's clubs in St James's and Pall Mall – probably the same ones that ban mobile phones today – did not allow this new-fangled invention into their venerable quarters until war actually broke out, and there was no radio in the Palace of Westminster until then either. During the 1930s those MPs who were 'anxious to hear a sports broadcast' would 'gather round the radio of a Member's car in New Palace Yard'. But in the course of the decade, radio matured into history's first mass medium.

Broadcasting House – which even today remains a powerful symbol of what the BBC stands for – opened in May 1932, and the Corporation declared a kind of *annus mirabilis*. 'The year 1932 saw the close of the first decade of British broadcasting,' proclaimed the *BBC Year Book*, 'a decade marked by a record of achievement which can have few parallels in the history of British public institutions.' It was just a few months before Hitler came to power. As he tightened his grip on German society in the years that followed, the BBC was – in a somewhat gentler way – becoming steadily more embedded in the fabric of British national life.

Val Gielgud – who became head of productions in 1929, with responsibility for all drama – felt that BH 'typified, in steel and concrete, and its central studio-tower of non-conductive brick, a new *professionalismus*'. The BBC published a long article lauding the building's up-to-the-minute technology and modernist architectural wonders, including a breathless statistical litany:

- The number of doors is 800

- The number of panes of glass in the building is 7,500

- The length of corridors is 1 mile

- ... The steam-raising capacity of the boilers is 12,000 lbs per hour.

- The number of radiators in the building is 840.

Someone had also calculated that 'The moisture given off in twelve hours by people in the tower, when it is fully occupied, would weigh one ton.' It is a revolting detail, but anyone who has worked in the BH studios will confirm that they can indeed be sweaty places.

Gielgud enjoyed the 'invigorating views across the rooftops of London', and noted that even when it opened the new headquarters was too small for the growing number of staff. 'The imagination of those responsible for broadcasting has never been able to keep pace with its growth,' he observed. There were two services, a National Programme (designed to do what its name suggests) and a Regional Programme, which varied across six geographical areas (Midlands, West, North, Scottish, Northern Ireland and Wales).

John Reith – the BBC's first director-general when the Royal Charter was founded – took a view of broadcasting that was informed by his muscular Christian morality. He believed people should make choices about what they tuned in to hear, and his ideal listener was the very opposite of the couch potato – or what was known at the time as a 'tap listener', someone who simply turned on the radio in the hope of finding something gushing out of it. In fact, he sometimes berated the listeners for failing to make their tastes known. The 1930 *Year Book* bemoans the lack of new talent appearing in vaudeville programmes. 'The public are in no way absolved from responsibility in this matter,' the *Year Book* declares, 'as long as they remain content to listen to rubbishy songs and remain satisfied with the poor standard of material offered by comedians.' These articles were always published anonymously, but that sentence has a distinctly Reithian tone.

So the BBC encouraged choice by offering a mix of programming – from variety and music to drama and speech. It lost some listeners to competition from commercial stations broadcasting from the Continent. Radio Luxembourg and Radio Normandie made especially significant inroads into the audience on Sundays, when Reith's sabbatarian instincts dictated sober fare; until 1938 nothing at all was broadcast on Sunday mornings apart from a service at 9.25, followed by the weather forecast. But by and large the British public found plenty to like when it twisted the dial to BBC frequencies.

Val Gielgud had never actually directed a radio play when he took over responsibility for the BBC's entire drama output, but his pioneering productions introduced theatre to millions of people who might never otherwise have experienced it. 'I think it is fair to claim,' he wrote, accurately if somewhat boastfully, 'that during the early nineteen thirties the prestige of broadcast plays and playing rose by leaps and bounds.' He had no fewer than seven drama studios at his disposal and broadcast a mix of classics (lots of Shakespeare, sometimes starring his brother John) and new material by contemporary writers like Noël Coward.

Music flourished too. Siân Nicholas writes that 'The explosion of public interest in serious music in the 1930s ... was widely credited to the BBC's encouragement of first-class live music broadcasts.' The BBC's own Symphony Orchestra was up and running in the first year of the decade, and was joined – in short order – by the Theatre Orchestra, the BBC Chorus (which became the BBC Choral Society in 1935) and the smaller Wireless Chorus (which later became the BBC Singers). During the General Election of 1935 another BBC ensemble, the Gershom Parkington Quartet, provided light music in the intervals between the announcements of results.

'The ever widening sphere of entertainment and of information that broadcasting brings within the reach of every home,' declared the 1934 *BBC Year Book*, 'cannot fail to enrich existence with a store of new interests and of new knowledge, which will surely be reflected in a fuller and a happier life, and in a better capacity to meet and face its problems.' For much of the 1930s, the staff at the BBC were simply having too much fun to worry about the grimly ideological, bellicose calculations behind the programme policy of Dr Goebbels and Mr Hadamovsky in Berlin.

≈

The one thing the Corporation did remarkably little of – in the early 1930s at least – was news.

That was partly because the newspapers tried everything they could to frustrate the flourishing of what they perceived as a commercial threat – and in the very early days the BBC, still finding its feet, was happy to compromise. 'We want to act in such a way,' declared one senior BBC official, 'that broadcasting may be an incentive to the public to buy more newspapers.' For the first four years of its existence the British Broadcasting Company – as it then was – agreed to an extraordinarily restrictive agreement which stipulated that it 'should only obtain its news for broadcasting through the agencies which worked for the newspapers, that such news should be broadcast as prepared by Messrs Reuters, and further that the first of two bulletins should not be broadcast earlier than 7.00 pm' – it was thought that anything earlier would discourage people from buying their daily paper.

It wasn't until 1927 that Reith negotiated an agreement with the newspaper proprietors and the big news agencies to edge things forward a bit by allowing the BBC its first news bulletin at 6.30 p.m. This was produced by a staff of just two sub-editors working at Savoy Hill, the BBC headquarters before the opening of Broadcasting House, and they were a tiny element in the much bigger BBC empire known as Talks. 'The talks department,' the 1928 *Year Book* explained, 'is responsible for the news service, the "bulletins" for farmers, gardeners, scouts, guides, wireless societies etc, running commentaries on important events, debates, talks on current affairs, critics' talks, and all the sporting, humorous, travel, literary and general talks.'

In 1930 'Special efforts were made to improve the presentation of news, so that items should be brief and simply worded.' An internal review of news services that year recorded that 'The BBC News staff was doubled, so as to provide two Editors and two Sub-Editors, working in two shifts. A Records Clerk and an office boy were added to the News Section.' The review concluded that 'The new arrangements have worked most satisfactorily, and have given the BBC much fuller powers of selection of news.'

But there were still no reporters – news from Westminster, for example, came in the form of telephone calls from the Reuters parliamentary correspondent – and the BBC laid claim to a slice of the news pie in the most tentative terms. 'The public is most anxious to know what is happening in the world,' declared the *Year Book*, 'and although the supply of news is mainly the task of the Press, there are certain duties which only a broadcaster can accomplish.' These were the days when the BBC could simply cancel a news programme if it decided there was nothing worth saying. 'Good evening, today is Good Friday,' one broadcast notoriously began. 'There is no news.' It was not until 1934 that a full-blown News Department was established and, as we shall see, it was some time before it grew into anything remotely resembling the kind of news machine that could cover a world war.

And news, as the Corporation discovered to its cost, could mean trouble.

Vernon Bartlett is sometimes described as the BBC's first foreign correspondent; for six years from 1927 he was the only regular broadcaster on foreign affairs. The way he writes about the experience in his autobiography takes one into a world that is in some ways completely familiar and in others completely alien.

Bartlett was hideously nervous during his first live broadcast ('I was just enough of a gentleman to get outside the building before I was violently sick on the pavement,' he recalled), but enjoyed the fame

27

once he had settled into the job, confessing that 'It takes a very long time before one ceases to experience at least a faint feeling of pleasure when the mention of one's name brings some such reply as: "Oh, you are the fellow who talks on the wireless."' And – a familiar experience to any broadcaster, this – he took relentless flak from members of the public with strong views on the pronunciation of foreign names. 'What a lot of bigoted and angry old men there are,' he wrote. 'Never did I receive so many insults as after one unfortunate talk in which, having read a French newspaper on the way to Broadcasting House, I pronounced the name of the capital of Afghanistan as a Frenchman would – "Kaboul" – instead of "Kabul", thus accenting the second syllable instead of the first. From the letters I received, I might have committed some crime too frightful to be mentioned.'

But unlike today's foreign correspondents, Vernon Bartlett was allowed to have views – indeed he was encouraged to do so. When he was first hired he was working as a civil servant in the London office of the Secretariat of the League of Nations, and this was considered a helpful qualification for the job rather than the reverse – today it would of course be out of the question to be employed by the BBC and, say, the United Nations at the same time.

Bartlett did not really report events in the sense in which we use the term today, but gave 'talks' which ran after the bulletins, and no one seems to have worried very much about what he said. 'In some ways I was given a freedom to express views which would be given me by no London newspaper,' he wrote. 'And at the same time I never escaped from the feeling that I should be dropped like a hot brick if I got the BBC into any trouble.'

In 1933 he did get the BBC into trouble, and was indeed duly dropped like the proverbial brick. His crime – and this is surprising, because he would later become a doughty campaigner against the evils of Nazism – was being overly sympathetic to Hitler. He knew Germany well, and reflected later that at the time 'I still hoped that all those young men who were enthusiastic members of the Nazi movement would be able to control it and to abolish from it those abominable intolerances and stupidities which have alienated so much opinion.'

The crisis came in October 1933 when Germany pulled out of the World Disarmament Conference in Geneva, a League of Nations attempt to tidy up the inconsistencies of the Versailles Treaty agreed after the First World War, and to reduce the international tensions which were so obviously growing in the early 1930s. The negotiations set the Germans – who argued that they should be allowed to escape the tight restrictions placed on their military strength at Versailles – against the French, while the British tried to mediate. 'The central political issue,' the British foreign secretary of the day, Sir John Simon, told the Commons, 'is how to reconcile Germany's demand for equality with France's desire about security . . . It is a most terrible problem charged with the most potent and persistent of all the historic influences which divide nations. That influence is Memory – the memory of invasion on the one and the fear it leaves behind, the memory of defeat on the other and the sense of humiliation it engenders.'

Failure was all but inevitable, and when Germany walked out of the talks it at the same time withdrew from the League of Nations altogether; with the benefit of hindsight, it is clear the moment was a significant milestone on the road to war. But in a speech justifying the decision, Hitler claimed that Germany was being treated unfairly by the other big powers – especially France – and Vernon Bartlett thought he made the case well. 'As I listened I thought of all the most moderate Germans I knew and how entirely they would support every argument that Hitler put forward,' he wrote. That was the tenor of that evening's talk, which went out after being cleared by a senior BBC official over dinner at the Langham Hotel, just across the road from Broadcasting House.

The government took a very different view, which was expressed in an uncompromising speech condemning Germany's action by Sir John Simon at the talks in Geneva. This was included in the news bulletin that had immediately preceded Bartlett's talk, so the contrast between the two was all too apparent.

In the midst of this grave international crisis the prime minister, no less, took the time to despatch a 'most serious complaint' from Downing Street to Portland Place. Ramsay MacDonald accused the

BBC of 'putting its foot in it' and said that it had 'caused me a great deal of embarrassment'. He had already been angered by one of Bartlett's broadcasts a couple of days earlier, which he described as 'propaganda for Germany' and 'absurd in its ignorance of the latest phases and its one-sidedness as a report of what had taken place'. The letter was despatched the morning after the Geneva talks had collapsed, and Mr MacDonald added, 'Last night, I am told, the comment when the news was broadcast was even worse, in tone and spirit.'

Bartlett knew the game was up. 'It was quite obvious that there was going to be a devil of a row,' he remembered. 'I, on behalf of the BBC, had taken a line which was a very strong, if indirect, criticism of the attitude of my own Foreign Secretary.' The way the BBC handled the matter is instructive. First they defended their man – a remarkably robust response went fizzing back to Downing Street from Portland Place. Then they fired him.

The manner of Bartlett's removal from the airwaves is an example to be relished by connoisseurs of the art. 'It was agreed at Broadcasting House that it would be easier for me to continue my talks if I were no longer a member of the regular staff,' he wrote. So he secured himself a job on a newspaper – the left-wing *News Chronicle* – having, he claimed, first consulted the BBC about the propriety of this step. 'Almost at once,' he recalled, 'I ... was told that, since I *was* on a newspaper, I could obviously not continue to broadcast.' Unsurprisingly, he thought this was shabby.

The BBC, however, managed to turn his departure to good account. In Parliament a couple of months later a brigadier-general from the shires launched a ferocious attack from the back benches on their foreign affairs coverage, calling the BBC bosses 'a small but all-powerful oligarchy' and citing Vernon Bartlett's talks on Germany as evidence for the prosecution. By way of defence, the Corporation pointed to Mr Bartlett's swift execution. Auntie could be clever and cold-hearted when she felt herself threatened.

This unfortunate affair was not mentioned at all in the relevant BBC *Year Book*, which came out a few months later – indeed it contains absolutely no allusion at all to the Corporation's news operation beyond a chapter with the enigmatic title 'News – A Fable'.

This tells the story of the news editor of an organization called the Ruritanian Broadcasting Corporation who puts out the following item in his General News Bulletin:

> In a speech in the Ruritanian Diet this evening M. Protomanoff, the Minister for Boviculture and Piggeries, said that the Government could not accept the scheme for the nationalisation of the pig industry. It was, he said, in direct contravention of the established policy of the Government, and nothing could induce him to proceed with such a measure. M. Deuterocarpoff, the Leader of the Opposition, criticised the Government's attitude, which he regarded as reactionary and out of tune with the spirit of the times. The Opposition, he added, would not rest until it had roused the whole of Ruritania to a sense of the Government's deficiencies.

The news editor retires to bed feeling well pleased with his day's work, only to find himself assaulted from all sides the following morning. The government condemns the item as a 'gaffe' which reveals the 'Oppositionist tendencies of the RBC', while the Opposition cites it as an example of 'the secret censorship which is at work in that reactionary and subservient organisation'. The communist newspaper complains that the broadcaster has failed to report a demand for the abolition of private property (*'The RBC is at it again!'*); the *Ruritanian Agricultural Daily* declares the report 'revealed the RBC's usual contempt for the farming industry'; and the *Ruritanian Evening Light* editorializes, 'We are sick of pigs. Cannot the RBC give us brighter news bulletins ...' All of them demand that 'the whole matter should at once be investigated'.

The news editor goes back to bed, this time with a splitting headache, and we are left – in the true spirit of a fable – with a moral: 'Those who are looking for bias can always find it, even when it is not there.'

Innocent times indeed. The days when concerns about the BBC's news policy bias could be brushed aside with such an entertainingly light touch would soon be gone.

THERE MUST BE EXPERTS
SOMEWHERE

GOVERNMENT PLANNING FOR A wartime BBC began in the mid-1930s. Much of it was concerned with the creation of a Ministry of Information, which, it was envisaged, would manage the BBC's relationship with the government. But the planning process was oddly desultory and furtive. The historian Philip Taylor suggests that this reflected a reluctance – which was perfectly understandable – to accept the dreadful reality that was looming on the horizon. 'Few people in British government circles,' he writes, 'were prepared to accept the idea that a Ministry of Information would be necessary. A Ministry of Information did, after all, mean war.' And he believes the furtiveness sprang from a fear that 'should the preparations become public knowledge, it might create a political outcry at home'. There was, Taylor suggests, 'still a great deal of suspicion about official propaganda in Britain'.

To understand British attitudes to propaganda in the 1930s, we need to take a step back in history to the first Ministry of Information, which was created in February 1918 – with the formidable Lord Beaverbrook at its head – to tidy up the various public information and propaganda bodies that had sprung up in the course of the Great War. It was not much loved, and disappeared again less than a year later, almost as soon as the war was over. The Ministry was discussed only once in Parliament – in August 1918 – but the debate is revealing.

The parliamentary charge against the Ministry was led by one

Leifchild Stratten Leif-Jones, a prominent Liberal backbench MP and famous temperance campaigner (his drinking habits earned him the nickname 'Tea-Leaf Jones'). 'The government have at last provided us with an opportunity, long desired, to put to them certain questions about the Ministry of Information,' he began. 'At present we know little about it, as it is not the creation of Parliament. It exists, and was announced to us through the Press, though up to the present we have been kept in the dark as to its constitution, its purposes, its methods, and its relation to other Departments of the State.'

The Ministry had recently provided an opportunity for one of those confected eruptions of moral outrage that the British press always enjoys so much: a junior official who took a party of foreign journalists on a freebie to Dublin had entertained them at shockingly lavish expense. '£31 of public money was spent in two days in drink and £5 in cigars,' Tea-Leaf told the Commons, adding (he was clearly enjoying himself), 'I have heard it criticised by wine drinkers as being an excessive amount, but . . . I am not an authority on these matters.'

The job of responding for the government fell to Stanley Baldwin, a Treasury minister at the time. He dismissed the Dublin-gate business with appropriate sobriety, and went on to make some bigger and more important general points about the Ministry's work. 'Propaganda,' Baldwin said, 'is not a word that has a pleasant sound to English ears . . . The Englishman dislikes talking about himself, and he dislikes advertising what he has done. If in England you say a man is a self-advertiser, it is looked on as one of the unkindest things you can say about him.' But he argued that the war had demonstrated the need for propaganda, both at home and abroad, because 'Public opinion today has far greater weight in the moulding of Governments and of policy in various countries than it ever had before.' And he suggested we had turned out to be rather good at it: 'there have been articles in some of the German newspapers,' he told the House, 'to the effect that admirable work is being done by English propaganda and suggesting that the Germans should organise themselves as efficiently.'

He compared what he called 'propaganda work' to 'anti-submarine work; work that is necessary . . . work as to which you cannot disclose to your adversaries how you are doing it'. Propaganda was, in other words, a necessary evil of modern warfare; we could do it better than anyone else if we put our collective mind to it, but we should hold our noses and avert our eyes while we were doing it.

Two decades later that – I think admirable – squeamishness resurfaced in the discussions about wartime propaganda in general and the management of the BBC in particular.

≈

The officials who were set to work planning for a new Ministry of Information were greatly hampered by the secrecy that was imposed upon them; there could be no open debate about exactly what kind of wartime propaganda would be useful and legitimate, and they could not consult the sort of academics and specialists who might have helped. One modern historian has dug out a wonderfully vivid illustration of the general chaos in the 'plea of one official who wrote, after being forced to consult an article on propaganda in the *Encyclopaedia Britannica*, "there must be experts somewhere".'

As far as the BBC was concerned, the planners did at least have an anchor in the form of one very clear public policy pronouncement, which came with the authority of Parliament: the publication in 1936 of a big official report into broadcasting by a committee under Lord Ullswater, a former speaker of the Commons. The Ullswater Report was a *tour d'horizon* across all aspects of the BBC's activities, but it included, almost as an aside, the observation that 'in serious national emergencies ... full government control' of the BBC would be necessary.

However, the committee offered no further thoughts on what this might mean in practice, and behind the scenes there were real concerns that the public might not like to see the Corporation taken over. A sub-committee of the Committee on Imperial Defence was set up to consider all this, and one of its earliest reports reflects this ambivalence: 'We are aware that whilst it is desirable as far as possible to maintain the independence of the British Broadcasting Corporation and to avoid it becoming, in the eyes of the general public, a Government Department, it is essential that during an emergency the Government should exercise effective control over its activities'.

Working out how that circle could be squared took up an inordinate amount of bureaucratic time and energy. Everyone agreed that the Ministry of Information was the right body to oversee the BBC, but since the Ministry itself was only notional at this stage – it remained a 'shadow' ministry until a couple of days after the outbreak of war – it was even more difficult to establish how the relationship might work. At a distance of eight decades, the debates about the appropriate structures for the Ministry of Information and the BBC seem surreal and impenetrable.

The official papers also reveal that they were, from time to time, enlivened by ambition, venality and low cunning. John Reith, the BBC's director-general, saw an opportunity to increase his own power. In a paper to the Imperial Defence sub-committee, he argued that in wartime 'The organisation of the broadcasting service should be simple and its relationship with the government direct, in order to facilitate quick decisions and their immediate execution.' He therefore proposed reducing the number of BBC governors to two, and giving those two seats on the Board to the director-general – in other words to himself – and his deputy. This would have meant he united the BBC's two most powerful positions in his own person.

The idea caused a Whitehall farce of the kind that made the BBC series *Yes, Minister* so successful many decades later. Reith's proposal would, of course, have meant sacking the existing governors. A new chairman, Sir Allan Powell, had only just accepted the job when he was told about the plan, and he was not a happy man. 'Sir Allan Powell came to see me yesterday,' recorded Sir Horace Wilson, one of the closest aides to the prime minister, Neville Chamberlain, in a Downing Street memo. 'He showed some perturbation as a result of a conversation he had had yesterday...' As the memo continues it becomes evident that 'some perturbation' is Civil Service speak for 'hopping mad'. 'There seemed to be two points in his mind,' Sir Horace concluded. '1 A feeling that his displacement might be taken to indicate that he was useless as a Chairman, at any rate in time of emergency, and 2 That he would suffer financial loss.' It is good to know that on the eve of war the top people at the BBC were worrying about what really mattered – clearly nothing could be of greater importance than the chairman's salary. Sir Allan need not have worried; it was eventually decided that in the event of war the Board of Governors should remain in existence but would consist of just two people, the chairman and his deputy. Sir Allan remained chairman until 1946, and kept his 'remuneration'. One of his notes to Sir Horace during this crisis suggests, in a scribbled PS, 'lunch at the Athenaeum'; perhaps they were able to celebrate with a glass of club claret.

≈

John Reith himself, in the meantime, had quit the field of battle, and it is impossible to overstate what a milestone his departure marked, because he had made the BBC very much in his own image. The socialist scholar Harold Laski painted a vivid picture of his commanding but sometimes infuriating character in a piece for the *Daily Herald* newspaper: 'His deep-set eyes look as though, at any moment, they may let loose a tempest. He is vehement, determined, aggressive, masterful. He works easily with you while you agree with him. When you disagree, no one can quite tell, least of all he, what will be the outcome ... There is a fanatic in him. It is one of his gifts and one of his limitations. It explains his power of work, his energy, his drive. But it means also that he carries about with him a bundle of dogmas – social, religious, ethical, political – and has a tendency to make them the measure of all things for all men.'

Reith's drive had enabled him to turn the BBC into what one American journalist called 'probably the finest broadcaster in the world', but it also meant he completely dominated the organization. 'At a conference,' Laski observed, 'he seems to talk as though he was in charge of the national well-being. He speaks with the urgency of a Pontiff. You too rarely hear from the admirable and efficient staff he has gathered around him. He gives the impression that the BBC pivots too exclusively upon his private sense of right and wrong ... He has gathered about him brains aplenty. But he has cramped their usefulness and their creative quality by being too dominating in his governance.'

It was not the sort of leadership likely to make for a smooth transition of power when the time came for him to leave. In the spring of 1938 Reith was asked to become chairman of Imperial Airways. Today that sounds like an odd job for someone in his position to consider, but airlines, like broadcasters, were at the forefront of the technological revolution that seemed to promise Britain such a bright twentieth-century future, and Imperial Airways was a national institution. What was more, the invitation to lead it came from none other than the prime minister, and after sixteen years at the helm of the BBC the director-general was restless for new pastures. He accepted and his appointment was duly announced in Parliament.

His departure from the organization that was so much his own was bound to be an emotional one, but he immediately received around a thousand letters and telegrams and was, according to his biographer Ian McIntyre, 'for a day or two buoyed up by what he called the "tremendous splashing" in the newspapers'. *The Times* declared, 'Sir John can leave Broadcasting House with the knowledge that his pioneering work, now brought to maturity, has not to wait for the approval of posterity.' Maurice Hankey, the Cabinet secretary, told him he had 'created one of the greatest organisations in the world, which will continue on your lines for centuries'.

Then came a blow that soured everything. Instinctively imperious to the last, Reith assumed that he would be intimately involved in the choice of his successor. The Board of Governors, to whom the task of appointing a new director-general fell, thought otherwise. When he was told that some members of the Board felt he should not be there during the final interviews for the job, he flew into the most dreadful rage and, by his own account, 'broke down'.

The following week one of the governors raised the fact that Sir John had never written a formal resignation letter, and he was asked to do so 'for tidiness sake'. This produced another volcanic eruption, expressed in the letter Reith wrote to the governors:

> Having tonight announced your betrothal to the attractive young suitor of your choice, were you fearful that the morning would find a dissolute old wretch on the doorstep demanding restitution of his rights?
> Now then —

> I resign
> I shall resign
> I have resigned.
> There it is – in all three tenses ...
> Is that sufficient?

Neither he, nor indeed the BBC, would ever be quite the same again. For both this was, in a way, the end of that prelapsarian Golden Age.

≈

It was perhaps a little unfair to describe F. W. Ogilvie as an 'attract-ive young suitor'. He was forty-five and the vice-chancellor of Queen's University Belfast, and the BBC governors had come to him rather than the other way round. In the 1930s no one used the word 'Establishment' as we use it today, but its modern sense aptly

Frederick Ogilvie, the new director-general.

describes the governors' approach to the appointment process. There was nothing vulgar like an advert inviting applications; instead the governors considered their own list, which included senior dons from the two grandest Oxbridge colleges – Christ Church, Oxford, and Trinity, Cambridge – a Treasury mandarin, the assistant editor of *The Times*, assorted peers and public servants. Ogilvie was recommended to the BBC chairman, Ronald Norman (brother of the chairman of the Bank of England, Montagu Norman), by the warden of All Souls College, Oxford.

Frederick Ogilvie's cleverness, kindness and patriotism were beyond doubt. His undergraduate years at Balliol College, Oxford, had been interrupted by the outbreak of the First World War and he immediately joined up, losing an arm in the notoriously bloody battle for Hill 60, near Ypres, in the spring of 1915. He had completed his degree as soon as the war was over, lectured in economics at Oxford for seven years and spent six as the professor of political economy at Edinburgh before moving to Queen's. He had written a book called *The Tourist Movement: an Economic Study.*

But no one seems to have given much consideration to the question of whether Ogilvie would be well suited to running an institution like the BBC in wartime – despite the fact that by the summer of 1938 even the most ostrich-like appeaser must have had some sense that war was a real possibility. Reith, who met him at an early stage of the selection process, described him as 'a man of fine character and outlook; of personal charm; thus far an exceptional candidate', but in his autobiography he claimed, 'I was quite sure he was not the man for the BBC.' Ogilvie had no experience of broadcasting and no public profile.

And perhaps, as Harman Grisewood's story about the nightingales suggests, he was simply too nice to run a vast national institution at a time of national crisis. Asa Briggs's verdict on Ogilvie is difficult to fault. 'Patience and a willingness to listen courteously and carefully to the views of other people were qualities he possessed in abundance,' he wrote, 'and, to some at least of his new colleagues he soon appeared in a favourable light – simple, friendly, unassuming. These very qualities, however – and some of them Reith did not possess – were limitations in the circumstances of the time. Managerial power was needed more than patience, and willingness to listen could suggest weakness instead of strength.' Harman Grisewood dismissed him in characteristically lapidary style, recording in his autobiography, 'Reith left the BBC in the summer of 1938 and a Mr Ogilvie was appointed, an academic from Belfast of whom few of us had heard. At Portland Place we felt very leaderless in those months . . . and for a longish time after.'

Reith's departure also exposed the reality that Auntie had acquired the vices of many organizations that grow very fast. The Corporation was getting bigger all the time, and as it increased in size the gap between those who ran it and those who made the programmes grew too. 'As the organisation expanded and the administrative machinery inevitably did likewise,' Val Gielgud observed, 'there was a growing tendency towards bureaucratisation, a proliferation of regulations, an irritating increase in delay between decision and action.' Even the director-general seemed impotent in the face of the burgeoning bureaucracy. When Ogilvie bumped into the band leader Jack Payne in a corridor in the Bristol offices, the DG complained, 'I believe that one of the minor tragedies of a gigantic organisation like the Corporation is its utter impersonality. Geographically and in organisation everybody is poles apart. If you want to talk business with another department it is not just a simple matter of telephoning; you have to write "memos" and have them passed from hand to hand.' Ogilvie declared he would like to 'build a big bonfire of these millions of inter-departmental memos – a bonfire which would blaze to the memory of red tape!'

But he never did. Sir Cecil Graves, one of his deputies (who had wanted the top job himself), bemoaned what he called 'the growth of departmentalism'. Heads of programme departments, controllers and assistant controllers locked horns in turf wars that now seem as strange and distant as the Schleswig-Holstein Question. 'It was,' Grisewood observed, 'a far from happy ship, and it was driving into the uncharted waters of wartime broadcasting'.

THE BOMBER WILL ALWAYS
GET THROUGH

WHEN THE PLANNERS IN Whitehall and Portland Place finally addressed the practical challenges of wartime broadcasting they were haunted by another Stanley Baldwin speech – his three terms as prime minister made him such an influential figure that the inter-war years used sometimes to be referred to as the 'Baldwin era'. The speech had been given back in November 1932, in a Commons debate on disarmament, just days after the German elections that paved the way for Hitler's rise to power. At the time Baldwin was serving as Lord President of the Council in Ramsay MacDonald's coalition, and had taken over the chairmanship of the Committee on Imperial Defence from the prime minister, who was unwell. It was the eve of Armistice Day, and in a powerful, reflective late-night oration – of a kind the Commons seldom hears today – Baldwin delivered his thoughts on modern warfare, and in particular on the threat from the air.

London had had some experience of air raids during the First World War. Zeppelin attacks began as early as 1915, and although they never reached anything like the intensity of the Blitz, they killed enough people and did enough damage to terrify the population. On the night of 8 September 1915, for example, a single Zeppelin broke through the capital's defences and dropped incendiaries and high explosives more or less at will. Thousands of Londoners – including the prime minister, Herbert Asquith, at Number 10 – watched from their windows as the searchlights sought out the vast airship and anti-aircraft guns pounded away; twenty-two people were killed and nearly ninety injured. Two years later Germany was able to attack the capital with high-altitude bombers for the first time. Its Gotha biplanes were powered by twin engines and had a wingspan of 72 feet – vast by the standards of the time. In June 1917 thirteen Gothas mounted a raid on London that killed 145 people. At a school in Poplar eighteen children were killed by a single bomb, which fell through the roof and exploded in the infants' department.

All this had had a profound impact on Baldwin's thinking. Aircraft technology had, of course, advanced considerably since the end of the First World War, and in his 1932 speech he warned that 'the speed of an air-attack, compared with the attack of an army, is as the speed of a motor car to that of a four-in-hand, and in the next war you will find that any town which is in reach of an aerodrome can be bombed within the first five minutes of war from the air, and the question is, whose morale will be shattered first?' And everyone remembered his chilling prediction that night: 'I think it is . . . well for the man in the street to realise that there is no power on earth than can protect him from being bombed. Whatever people may tell him, the bomber will always get through.'

All Home Front planning in the second half of the 1930s was based on that assumption. It was widely believed that a new war would begin with a massive aerial attack on civilians and that, sooner or later, the bombers would indeed 'always get through'. And in 1938 a group of psychiatrists produced a most alarming report for the Ministry of Health, in which they estimated that the number of psychiatric casualties of bombing would exceed those who were physically hurt by a ratio of three to one; this led to the conclusion that there would be 'between three and four million cases of acute panic, hysteria and neurosis during the first six months of war'.

The fear of bombing very nearly took the BBC off the air altogether. The Air Ministry was concerned that radio transmitters could be used by German planes as aids to navigation, and there was a long debate – conducted entirely in secret – over whether broadcasting would simply have to stop with the declaration of war.

The heroes of this saga were the BBC's engineering staff – working under the chief engineer, Sir Noel Ashridge – who came up with a very clever wheeze. They proposed concentrating all home broadcasting on two groups of medium-wave transmitters operating on a single wavelength. Any one of these transmitters could be closed down at short notice on the orders of the Air Ministry, but, because they were all broadcasting on the same wavelength, listeners in the areas affected would still be able to pick up a signal from a neighbouring transmitter and the broadcasting service could continue uninterrupted. The plan was finally accepted by a technical sub-committee of the Committee on Imperial Defence in July 1938. It did, however, involve merging the National and Regional Networks into a single network, and thus was born the Home Service. The Home Service later evolved into today's Radio Four, so when you listen to *The Archers* or *Today* you can, in a roundabout way, thank Hermann Göring and his Luftwaffe.

Paradoxically, the fear of bombing also strengthened the case for keeping the BBC on the air. Even the Air Ministry recognized that the Corporation might play a significant role in cheering people up when air raids produced the general collapse in morale that everyone expected. An internal BBC document entitled 'Memorandum of Protection against Air Attack' stated that 'It is not improbable that the fortitude of the population, particularly in crowded and urban areas, may be severely strained and any measures which may be taken to help maintain their morale will be of inestimable value. It is conceived that the broadcasting of programmes of music may be a valuable factor to this end, and [this] is another reason why great importance is attached to the maintenance of the broadcast service.'

So the BBC came up with a dispersal policy: at the outbreak of war most departments were to leave London for safer bases elsewhere in the country. It was a good time to own a spare stately home; all sorts of official organizations – especially those at the spookier end of the Whitehall world – were looking for what a BBC memo of the time identified as 'a mansion house in a good state of repair' for resettling staff away from the capital, and a number of vast and often unlovely country houses became part of the war effort. In March 1939 the

Corporation acquired Wood Norton Hall near Evesham in Warwickshire. Lost in woodlands in deep countryside, the building was judged to be suitably difficult for enemy bombers – and indeed anyone else with malicious intent – to find. But not everyone liked it. The Drama Department was earmarked for evacuation to Evesham, and Val Gielgud took a dim view of its practicality. 'Wood Norton Hall is the appropriate setting for a nightmare,' he wrote. 'Once home to an exiled Duc d'Orleans, it sprouts *fleurs-de-lys* on everything from the weather-vane to the bath–plugs, and has a bear pit in the garden. To my horror one may not smoke in it . . . Parquet floors are not a good base for typewriters.' Despite the *fleurs-de-lys* and the parquet, Wood Norton Hall would become one of the largest radio stations in Europe, broadcasting 1,300 programmes a week, and there is a BBC presence in the grounds to this day.

Other big departments were to go to the Whiteladies Road offices of the BBC in Bristol, and the city was later selected for the strangest of all the projects inspired by that Baldwin doctrine that the bomber would 'always get through': the construction of an underground headquarters, a fortress designed to ensure that broadcasting could continue even in the most extreme circumstances. The engineers first looked at a disused tunnel on the Bristol–Avonmouth railway line, and the great conductor Sir Adrian Boult was sent in with the full BBC Symphony Orchestra to test the acoustics. These proved satisfactory, but by the time the BBC actually got round to beginning the project the bombing had begun in earnest and the tunnel was already being used regularly as an air-raid shelter. The Corporation then turned to a tunnel near the Clifton Suspension Bridge, which had originally been dug in the late nineteenth century for a funicular railway, carrying passengers up the cliff face above the River Avon. The railway enterprise had long since gone bankrupt and the tunnel had been empty for six years. Four large chambers were dug along its slope, one for transmitters and communications equipment, one as a studio (with an upright piano to save space), one as a recording room (which was said to have 'enough recorded programmes stored away in its lockers to maintain a radio service for weeks') and one as a control room.

You can still visit – by special appointment – the Clifton Rocks Tunnel. It is sadly diminished: there is no sign now of the powerful diesel generators, which stood ready to take over if the mains were cut; the eighty telephone lines that fed into the control room; or the vast stores of food and water designed to sustain a full broadcasting team for three months. But it remains eerily atmospheric, and the odd relic – a huge gas door, the treads on the stairs designed to muffle the sound of feet during broadcasts – underlines what an amazing and meticulous engineering achievement it was.

This rabbit warren under the cliffs was fully manned, day and night, from the moment of its completion right up until the end of the war, and all BBC programmes from the west of England passed through its control room. But the studio remained silent, waiting for the invasion that never happened. The BBC war correspondent Frank Gillard (who began his broadcasting career at Bristol) published a piece about it in the 1946 edition of the *Year Book*. 'The tunnel,' he wrote, 'was ready to shoulder its full responsibilities at any moment. But that moment, of course, never came. The Rocks Tunnel was never put to the supreme test. But it remains a monument to the thoroughness of the BBC's technical preparations for whatever emergency the war might bring . . .'

≈

The pre-war efforts to improve the BBC's news operation were to prove of more enduring value than this feat of engineering.

Richard Dimbleby was far from being the only BBC correspondent of the period with a claim to greatness – as we shall see, Frank Gillard was certainly another – and the way his reputation has endured owes as much to his post-war career as the voice of great state occasions. But nothing can diminish his unique role as a founding father of modern broadcast news. He brought it off with a piece of shameless cheek.

Dimbleby first applied to join the BBC in the spring of 1936. After his interview, several weeks passed without a word from Broadcasting House, so this ambitious young man wrote a long letter to the BBC's chief news editor telling him how to run his department.

'I am daring to make a suggestion concerning the news bulletins which you may care to consider,' he wrote. 'Naturally I should very much like to assist with it myself.'

The letter was polite, but its vision was bold, and it is worth quoting at some length:

> It is my impression, and I find that it is shared by many others, that it would be possible to enliven the News to some extent without spoiling the authoritative tone for which it is famed. As a journalist, I think I know something of the demand which the public makes for a 'News angle', and how it can be provided. I suggest that a number of members of your staff – they could be called 'BBC Reporters' or 'BBC Correspondents' – should be held in readiness, just as are the evening paper men, to cover unexpected news of the day. In the event of a big fire, strike, or public commotion, railway accidents, pit accidents, or any other major catastrophes in which the public is, I fear, deeply interested, a reporter could be sent from Broadcasting House to cover the event for the bulletin.
>
> At the scene, it would be his job, in addition to writing his own account of the event, to secure an eye-witness (the man or woman who saw it start, one of the survivors, a girl 'rescued from the building') and to give a short eye-witness account of the part he or she played that day. In this way, I really believe that News could be presented in a gripping manner, and, at the same time, remain authentic.

Dimbleby pointed out that the newspapers were already 'enlivening news by the infusion of the human element', and he also cited the example of a newsreel series called *The March of Time*. 'In this, as you may have seen,' he wrote, 'the practice followed is not only that of showing the news, but telling why, and how, it happened. That is what I suggest the BBC could do with great success . . .' Dimbleby added a comment that seems designed to flatter the organization he hoped to join: 'It does seem to me that in the future and particularly in the event of a national emergency, the BBC will play a vital part.'

At a time when the BBC had no reporters at all and took pride in the cool colourlessness of its news bulletins, this was revolutionary stuff. It was also, in the deferential social climate of the 1930s, an extraordinary piece of *hutzpah*. Unsurprisingly, the chief news editor, John Coatman, did not immediately set about implementing the pushy young man's blueprint, but neither did he file the letter in the dustbin; a copy still exists in the BBC's Written Archives at Caversham, a prophetic document foreshadowing the wartime radio revolution in which its author would play such a significant part.

Dimbleby finally joined the BBC staff in the autumn of 1936. After his first broadcast, the deputy director-general, Sir Cecil Graves, rang the newsroom to complain that he had begun the piece with an inverted sentence and should never be allowed on the air again. Six months later – the broadcasting ban having been lifted after a decent interval – he was able to show what his style of reporting could achieve when East Anglia was inundated by what became known as the Fens Floods. Dimbleby spent nearly a fortnight reporting the story, using the BBC's mobile recording unit – a converted laundry van – to great effect, 'interviewing farmers and housewives, bargees and river authorities, councillors and policemen; recording gurgling pumping stations, rowing boats, motor barges, sloshing water and pouring rain'.

One of the subs in the newsroom, Michael Balkwill (who had won the Newdigate Prize for poetry at Oxford, and knew a thing or two about good writing), noticed a quality that was to mature in Dimbleby's war reports and which is one of his legacies to radio journalism – his attention to detail. 'He did not deal in vague descriptions of "hundreds of acres inundated in the grim fight against encroaching waters",' Balkwill observed, 'he found out and explained in his reports what the complete situation really was – and explained it in terms of exact locations, comparative water levels, pumping stations and sluice gates, with proper use of technical terms . . .'

In 1938 the BBC's engineers managed to develop the first recording car. Recordings were still made on wax discs, but the equipment was smaller and lighter, and the car was a much nimbler and more efficient version of the old converted laundry van. Dimbleby's fellow reporter Charles Gardner described the vehicle as 'an ordinary saloon car with specially designed recording gear on the back seat.

The whole apparatus is driven from batteries stored in the boot, and it is quite possible to take everything out quite quickly and install it in any place that might be desirable. The normal crew for a recording car is one of three men – the commentator or producer, the engineer who actually makes (or "cuts") the record, and a recording expert, who places the microphones and afterwards plays the discs in the programme.' This technical advance proved every bit as significant as the editorial revolution in the newsroom. 'It is no exaggeration to say,' Dimbleby wrote, 'that the whole vast network of BBC News recording has developed from the introduction of that solitary vehicle.'

≈

The autumn of 1938 brought the first real test of whether the BBC and its news operation were up to the challenge of a national emergency. The Munich Crisis blew up in September 1938, a matter of weeks after the departure of John Reith and the arrival of Frederick Ogilvie.

Like most of the international flashpoints of the 1930s, this terrifying game of diplomatic chicken had its origins in the Versailles Treaty signed in the aftermath of the First World War. Czechoslovakia, one of the new nations created out of the ruins of the Austro-Hungarian Empire, had been granted territory which included some 3 million ethnic Germans. The Sudetenland, as it became known, was a powerful symbol of what many Germans saw as the injustice of the treaty, and in 1937 Hitler began stirring up trouble there. Ethnic German demands for autonomy from Prague reached such a pitch – very much with his encouragement – that in August 1938 he mobilized the Wehrmacht (the German armed forces) and demanded the right to annex the Sudetenland within a month. The prime minister, Neville Chamberlain, flew to Hitler's mountain eyrie of Berchtesgaden on 15 September to try to negotiate a resolution, and for the rest of the month Britain was on a war footing.

At Broadcasting House sandbags were packed around the entrances and the building was fitted with gas doors. Trenches were dug around the Corporation's transmitters, which were placed under guard. The number of news bulletins was increased so that listeners could follow every twist and turn of the negotiations in Germany, and the BBC began broadcasting public service messages about evacuation plans for children and the distribution of gas masks. One announcement warned people of the dangers of misusing their masks: 'It is even stated that some people have been testing gas masks in gas-ovens or by motor-car exhaust pipes! This misuse of the masks carries its own punishment, but as this is quite likely to be unintentional suicide the suggestion is . . . made that masks should be kept for the gases they are designed to deal with . . .'

It took three prime ministerial trips to Germany before an agreement was reached with Hitler, and the deal gave the German leader almost everything he wanted. On 30 September, Britain, France and Italy signed that famous piece of paper which Chamberlain claimed would guarantee 'peace in our time'. His arrival at Heston Aerodrome (next door to what is now Heathrow) after his final meeting with Hitler was broadcast live by the BBC, with Dimbleby commentating. 'This morning I had another talk with the German Chancellor, Herr Hitler,' the prime minister told the nation over the airwaves, 'and here is the paper which bears his name upon it as well as mine . . . We regard the agreement signed last night and the Anglo-German Naval Agreement as symbolic of the desire of our two peoples never to go to war with one another again.' Everyone heaved a sigh of relief; the gas doors came down at BH and the sandbags were removed from the entrance hall.

History has judged Chamberlain harshly for his role in the Munich Crisis. By March the following year Hitler had gobbled up the whole of what had been Czechoslovakia, and Munich is generally seen as the nadir of Chamberlain's appeasement policy. The BBC, on the other hand, felt that it had done rather well during the crisis. A somewhat self-congratulatory internal memo declared: '. . . the BBC was commended afterwards on all sides for its efficient news service and for its steadying effect on anxious listeners . . .' There is a note in the BBC files recommending a pay rise for R. T. Clark, who was now the chief news editor, as a reward for the way he had handled things. According to the internal review, 'The News Bulletins became the most important sections of the programme to a world-wide audience during these anxious days, and the calm voice of the BBC announcer evoked special comment from abroad, in contrast to the excited accents of the American announcers and the extreme anti-Czechoslovakian propaganda from Germany.'

That theme was taken up in the *Listener*, the now-defunct BBC magazine which published an eclectic weekly mix of talk scripts, reviews and think-pieces. In an editorial a week after the Munich Agreement was signed, it declared that '. . . broadcasting has . . . emerged from the crisis as one of the determining factors. It has played a two-fold part; firstly in informing the public both of the facts and of the atmosphere of the problems facing the nation; secondly, in giving directions and guidance what to do, and so maintaining the spirit of unity and self-discipline.'

The editorial also foreshadowed the way broadcasting would itself become a battleground, the forum for a clash of values that would help define what the war was about when it came. 'Those who listened, for instance, to the broadcasts of Herr Hitler's speeches at Nuremberg and Berlin could,' said the *Listener*, 'even if they knew no German, have been left in no misunderstanding of the atmosphere in which the German attitude to the international problem was evolving; and, by contrast, nothing could have been more effective in clarifying our own minds and simplifying our emotions than the tone of voice of Mr Chamberlain's own broadcast to British listeners. What a contrast in broadcasting technique – between the fiery oratory delivered in the *Sportspalast* before cheering masses of followers, and the calm talk from the quiet room in Downing Street addressed to small groups of listeners round the family hearth.'

THE SOUND OF RIPPING PAPER

Munich led directly to two developments that were to loom large in Auntie's wartime story.

During the crisis the Corporation broadcast news bulletins and Chamberlain's speeches in German, French and Italian. It was a challenge to find foreign-language speakers with the right skills at short notice – the files record that 'Difficulty in finding a suitable German announcer was increased by the desirability of avoiding either a man with a Jewish or Viennese accent, or one who was known to be strongly anti-Nazi and liable to be discredited in Germany' – but the broadcasts were judged to have been effective, and they were 'stabilised after the crisis into a regular service'. This became the nucleus of the European Services, which were to play such a vital role during the German occupation of most of the Continent.

The second development is a little more difficult to pin down, but it appears that at some point during the Munich Crisis the government called on the services of a man called Sir Campbell Stuart, a veteran of the propaganda operation against Germany during the First World War. With another war now looking likely, he was instructed to begin planning for the same task again, and in the months that followed Stuart worked up a secret propaganda unit under the auspices of the Foreign Office. It became known as 'Department EH', a reference to its offices in Electra House, the London headquarters of Cable and Wireless. No one in the BBC knew of its existence at this stage, and its story remained one of the closest-kept secrets of the war until very recently. But Department EH would, in time, be given a significant role in deciding policy for the BBC's European Services.

After the excitement of Munich, the BBC's domestic services settled back into their usual routine, and to the audience Auntie appeared to sail through the spring and summer of 1939 as if nothing was amiss.

≈

It is often forgotten that the BBC ran a remarkably successful television service in the late 1930s. 'Vision sets', as they were called, were expensive – nearly £100 each in the very early days, or several thousand pounds in today's money – and the signal could be received only in London. Unsurprisingly, the market moved slowly at first: in January 1937 only 400 sets had been sold, and the figure had risen to no more than 2,000 by the end of the year. But things picked up as the service improved; by the outbreak of war some 20,000 homes had television, and in August 1939 the *Wireless and Electrical Trader* magazine reported breathlessly on a television-industry convention at which delegates were confidently told to expect the sale of 40,000 sets within the next six months.

Some of the programming listed in the pages of that year's *Radio Times* sounds a little tame by today's standards. On 4 August, for example, the Saturday-afternoon schedule included the offer 'Elizabeth Cowell and Edward Halliday will take viewers for a stroll round the west side of Kensington Gardens, and interview owners of model boats and aeroplanes by the Round Pond'. But much of it is surprisingly familiar. In May the 'Scanner' column in *Radio Times* promised that 'With the coming of summer (which should mean more settled weather and good light) television outside broadcasts are featuring more prominently than ever in the programmes ... The next big occasion for the mobile unit will be the Chelsea Flower Show.' The writer added, rather charmingly, 'everything worthwhile will be shown to viewers, except the colour of the flowers'. June brought coverage of Trooping the Colour, just as it does today; new camera angles were promised for Wimbledon at the end of the month; and in

August, on the Monday and Tuesday of the last full week of peace, the BBC broadcast live coverage of the final Test Match of the West Indies tour at the Oval. The commentator was one Aidan Crawley, who would soon be flying night patrols over the Channel and, after a glamorously swashbuckling war, would become a Labour minister and later the first editor-in-chief of ITN.

≈

Later that same week, a small family drama was played out at Victoria Station which was to have profound consequences for the BBC.

On 26 August, a thirty-three-year-old fascist activist and adventurer called William Joyce and his wife, Margaret, said goodbye to family and friends and boarded the boat-train for the Continent. Even the porters knew war was coming by this stage; Joyce's biographer, Mary Kenny, records that 'The porter carrying their luggage made some joke about the "Berlin" ticket labels: "Blimey, that's a peculiar place to be going just now!" "Oh, I expect everything will blow over all right," replied William.'

Joyce had been something of a star in the British fascist firmament of the late 1930s, and through his far-right connections had established that he would be welcomed in Germany with open arms – or so he thought. The couple arrived in Berlin in glorious sunshine – what the Germans then called 'Hitler weather' – and set themselves up in a hotel. But the promise of immediate German citizenship and a good job turned out to be illusory, and their Berlin contact warned them they might face internment as enemy aliens instead. Frightened, they changed their minds about the whole enterprise and tried to get home, but it was too late; the staff at the British embassy were too busy packing up for their own hasty departure to help anyone else.

The Joyces were rescued by one of those glamorous British bohemians who seem to have been attracted by Hitler's brilliance. Dorothy Eckersley came from a literary family with leftish traditions – she was the daughter of a suffragette and a cousin of Virginia Woolf – and, by the time she turned up in Berlin in 1939, had a rackety past: she had toured America as an actress, borne two

53

William Joyce, aka Lord Haw-Haw, just before leaving for Germany – looking the part of a Hitler fan.

children out of wedlock and was on her second marriage. But she still had the sort of social connections that made a difference in the 1930s, and when Joyce sought her out in desperation – the two had met in fascist circles in London, and he remembered that she was in Berlin – she was only too pleased to help. She got him some work in the German Foreign Office, which soon led to his notorious career as Lord Haw-Haw, Nazi Germany's most effective radio propagandist.

Given the trouble he was shortly to give the BBC, there's a nice irony in the role the Corporation had played in bringing his saviour to Berlin. Dorothy was the wife of Peter Eckersley, once the BBC's chief engineer; he had been perhaps Reith's closest collaborator and was described by Asa Briggs as having 'more ideas about broadcasting than any other man in the country'. But Peter and Dorothy both divorced to be together, and that sort of thing just would not do in Reith's BBC: the director-general's fierce Christian morality was central to the corporate ethic. In 1929 Eckersley, despite his brilliance, was forced out of his job.

It was after this traumatic wrench that the couple began the rightward drift into fascist politics which would land Dorothy in Germany on the eve of war. Peter had been left behind in London, where the authorities were keeping a close eye on him. In November 1939 a confidential report by the Metropolitan Police on his alleged pro-fascist activities offered the view that 'Eckersley's attitude to this country changed after the Archbishop of Canterbury got him the sack when his first wife divorced him – sack from the BBC.' Dorothy was not to know this, but launching the future Lord Haw-Haw on to the airwaves was the best revenge against the Corporation she could possibly have taken for its shabby treatment of her husband.

≈

The immediate cause of the Second World War was – appropriately – a radio station. On the evening of 31 August 1939 a *Sturmbannführer* (or major) of the National Socialist Security Service, the *Sicherheitsdienst*, or SD, dressed up as a Polish officer and led a party of convicted criminals – also wearing Polish uniforms – in an attack on a German radio station in Upper Silesia, which the Versailles Treaty had required Germany to cede to Poland. They seized it and broadcast a few patriotic Polish messages, then the criminals (who had been promised amnesty in return for their participation in this deadly farce) were mown down by machine-gunners, leaving a pile of corpses as the evidence Hitler needed to justify hostilities. German troops crossed the Polish border shortly before six the following morning.

At 10.00 a.m. that day – 1 September – Department EH was mobilized and its members were told they should make their way to the Sugar Loaf Hotel in Dunstable, where they were to ask for a Mr Gibbs Smith – which was an alias for a senior member of Campbell Stuart's department. From there they were taken to the Riding School at Woburn Abbey, the home of the Duke of Bedford, which was to be the department's headquarters for much of the war and became known as Country Headquarters, or EH CHQ. The department's official history gives the following account of its duties, which is worth quoting at some length as an illustration of the eccentric and often dysfunctional nature of British intelligence and propaganda operations at the outbreak of war:

> The work of Department EH was divided into: planning; editorial functions including drafting leaflets; secret activities through a department in neutral countries (these were the placing of agents for the collection and dissemination of propaganda); intelligence, including issuing and editing intelligence documents; liaison duties with the Political Intelligence Department of the Foreign Office and the Foreign Office; with the MoI and the BBC with particular reference to the guidance of the BBC German Service; with the Services including liaison with the Air Ministry in regard to leaflets; with the Secret Service Departments, ie with C and D; with the MEW and the Refugee Organisations through a sub-department ... ; with the French Departments responsible for propaganda to Germany through the EH Paris office under Mr Noel Coward.

A brief acronym guide may help. The MoI refers to the Ministry of Information, which thought it was running the BBC and, at this stage, may not even have known that Department EH existed, far less that it also claimed some authority over the BBC. C was the head of MI6, or SIS as it was more commonly known then, and Section D was the bit of MI6 that would eventually morph into the Special Operations Executive, or SOE, which would itself be divided into SO1 and SO2. SO1 was concerned with covert propaganda (so its functions overlapped with those of Department EH), and SO2 was charged with sabotage (and therefore covered some of the same ground as the Ministry of Economic Warfare, or MEW).

The Noël Coward who rounds off this bewilderingly bureaucratic passage is indeed the same Noël Coward who wrote *Hay Fever* and the lovely lust-song 'Mad about the Boy', and his appearance here is a reminder of what a whacky world these folk inhabited. Another member of the Woburn team was Vernon Bartlett, the BBC foreign correspondent we met in Chapter One; he later complained that he had been headbutted by one of the ducal llamas on the estate.

BBC Television went off the air without warning at noon on the same day, 1 September. There was no announcement to tell the viewers why the switches at Alexandra Palace had been thrown, nor were they given any indication of when normal service might resume; in fact they were, as E. S. Turner puts it in *The Phoney War on the Home Front*, left to '[twiddle] their knobs in a vain effort to tune in the advertised attractions: a cabaret show, Mantovani, a visit to the zoo and variety.'

Television could never have survived the war; it was too expensive and reached too few people. The problem of preventing the signal being used to guide enemy bombers had not even been addressed, and by closing the service the BBC freed up dozens of technical staff to focus on radio. It is tempting to speculate whether we would have today's rich radio culture if the television service had been kept going and the Second World War had been a picture war as well as a sound war.

Only that morning Val Gielgud had been working on a production of Somerset Maugham's *The Circle*, his first full-length play for television, which was due to be broadcast on Sunday, 3 September. He was rehearsing in a mews off Marylebone High Street, and as the Alexandra Palace transmitters closed down he took a telephone call which informed him that the BBC had gone into the 'emergency period' – he remembered the moment well, because just as he put down the receiver 'the office messenger arrived with various "properties" for the play, including two tennis racquets and a number of balls'. They were never needed; the last voice to be heard on pre-war British television was that of Elizabeth Cowell, the announcer and presenter who had, less than a month earlier, taken the viewers on that stroll by the Round Pond in Kensington Gardens.

≈

The Ministry of Information still existed only in its 'shadow' form at this stage – it did not move into its grand headquarters in the Senate House of London University until the following week. But

on the day of Hitler's invasion of Poland there was a meeting of
the Home Publicity Division. The vexed question of civilian morale
in the face of an overwhelming bombing campaign – which
everyone still expected – was raised once again. According to the
minutes:

> Lady Grigg said that the most comforting thing . . . at least where
> women were concerned, was a cup of tea and get together to talk
> things over.
>
> This was agreed to be a most valuable suggestion. Ways for
> carrying it into effect . . . were considered. It was decided that
> some . . . widely spread method was required and that an appeal
> should be made to householders to supply tea to anyone in their
> neighbourhood who needed it during or after an air-raid.
>
> Professor Hilton . . . referred to the value of sugar for steady-
> ing the nerves . . .

In Broadcasting House staff were busy opening their instructions
for wartime broadcasting. Jean Seaton, who succeeded Asa Briggs as
the Corporation's official historian, wrote in her article 'The Day We
Went to War' that 'The Second World War was heralded in the BBC
by the harsh sound of ripping paper . . . On all sides, up and down the
Corporation's hierarchy, in Variety, and in Music, in Children's and in
News, in the Music Department and all over the Secretariat and in the
all-important, yet invisible to the public, Engineering department,
people tore open envelopes.'

The critical set of instructions known as 'Document C' had taken
months to draw up. It was a very precise, step-by-step guide for
synchronizing the National and Regional Networks and placing the
BBC on a war footing. The senior control room engineer at
Broadcasting House was told to expect a telephone call with a code
word from Number 10 or the War Office. He should then open an
envelope in the Control Room safe and, if the code word matched
the one he had been given over the phone, he should initiate the
process of synchronization. The programme output that would follow
on the newly established 'single home programme' was based on the

assumption that normal life might have been brought to a standstill by Baldwin's bombers; most of it, instructed Document C, 'will be information, announcements and news, issued only on the instructions of the Ministry of Information or received on the direct line from Central War Room, the latter to have priority at all times. Continuous gramophone records will be provided other than when announcements or news are radiated'.

That evening the BBC's listeners heard the following announcement: 'Within the next two hours you will be asked to adjust your sets to a wavelength of 391 metres or 449 metres – that is to say, to the wavelengths of Scottish Regional or North Regional. From that time on broadcasting throughout the United Kingdom will, until further notice, be confined to those two wavelengths.' They were also given notice of the vastly increased diet of news they could expect: 'There will be news bulletins at 7 am, 8 am, 9 am, 12 noon, 1 pm, 2 pm, 4.30 pm, 6 pm, 7.30 pm, 9 pm, 10.30 pm, and 12 midnight. In addition there may be news announcements at the following hours: 10 am, 11 am, and 3 pm, 4 pm, 5 pm, 7 pm, 8 pm, 10 pm, 11 pm, 1 am, 3 am, and 5 am. If announcements are going to be made at 1 am, 3 am, 5 am, they will be preceded by a five-minute interval signal – Bow Bells.'

War was, of course, declared in a radio broadcast. At 11.15 on the morning of 3 September, Neville Chamberlain spoke again from Downing Street. 'This morning the British Ambassador in Berlin handed the German Government a final Note,' he told the nation, 'stating that, unless we heard from them by 11 o'clock that they were prepared at once to withdraw their troops from Poland, a state of war would exist between us. I have to tell you now that no such undertaking has been received, and that consequently this country is at war with Germany.' The broadcast was listened to by those 'small groups of listeners round the family hearth' up and down the country. Almost immediately the sirens went off in London. It was a false alarm; the bombing Blitz so confidently predicted by Baldwin would not be launched for another year. But the world's first radio war had begun.

And Beatrice Harrison's nightingales were, as things turned out, to make their small mark on its history after all. In 1942 the traditional live broadcast of their music was interrupted by the drone of nearly 200 Lancaster and Wellington bombers, and they were abruptly taken off the air by the switch censor; the broadcast could have given sharp-eared German spies a clue that the raid was coming.

CETTE DRÔLE DE GUERRE

CHARLES GARDNER WENT TO war with all the gaiety of a young cavalier. 'My plane for "destination unknown"', he wrote, 'was due to leave Heston at 10.00 in the morning, so I duly elevated myself early at the Langham Hotel to find a *Radio Times* photographer outside to add my picture to the rogues gallery of BBC War Correspondents.' Dressed in a 'completely bogus' uniform (with 'British War Correspondent' in gold on his shoulder tabs and a gold 'C' for 'correspondent' as his cap badge), he draped himself over a car in front of Broadcasting House for the camera.

A BBC driver chauffeured him down to Heston Aerodrome, where he discovered that the secret location from which he was to cover the doings of the AASF, the RAF's Advanced Air Striking Force, was Reims, the capital of champagne country – so not a bad billet for a young man in search of adventure. Like Boot in Evelyn Waugh's wonderful satire *Scoop*, he had come prepared with sundry journalistic accoutrements, including a sleeping bag (or 'flea bag', as he called it) and a camp bed, but he found himself putting up at the Lion d'Or, 'a typical French hotel of the better class', where the champagne flowed like beer in an English pub and '"Deux Coupes Marianne" after a couple of days supplanted in my ears the English familiarity of "Two brown ales".'

Richard Dimbleby, also deployed to France to cover the British

Expeditionary Force, had, as the senior man, first call on the only available BBC recording car, and he had smuggled it over the Channel on a ferry the week before war was declared, hiding it in an underground garage in Paris. Gardner had no recording equipment and no studio, and would have to travel to Paris to file his reports. So the office authorized him to spend £30 on a five-year-old 9 h.p. car called a Mathis for the journey. He christened it Harold.

The only thing missing was a real story.

≈

The AASF was made up largely of Fairey Battles, light bombers sent to support the French *Armée de l'Air*, which was shockingly under-equipped. The Faireys were powered by the legendary Merlin engine, which later won such glory in Spitfires and Hurricanes, but while the fighters had to carry only a pilot, the Fairey Battles were flown by a three-man crew, and the extra weight made them slow and vulnerable to attack. More to the point, however, the Faireys of the AASF were not allowed to carry any bombs – their duties were almost entirely restricted to reconnaissance, and the only thing the RAF dropped over enemy territory at this stage was propaganda leaflets.

Noël Coward, Department EH's man in Paris at the time, took a pretty dim view of these as an offensive weapon: 'Their subject matter was concerned mainly with the fact that war was wicked and peace was good and that the Nazis had better beware because the Allies were very strong indeed and prepared to fight to the death to defend the democratic way of life. All this was admirable, although a trifle inaccurate and more than a trifle verbose.'

The Chamberlain government's lack of fighting spirit in the autumn of 1939 was reflected in a famous story about the air minister, Sir Kingsley Wood. When it was proposed to him that the Black Forest should be bombed because it was full of munitions dumps, Sir Kingsley is reported to have 'turned down the suggestion with some asperity. "Are you aware it is private property?" he said. "Why, you will be asking me to bomb Essen next!"' The story is told by General Sir Edward Spears, who hated what he called 'Munichers' (and also, from time to time, the BBC), so it should be treated with a little caution, but the

Charles Gardner, in his 'completely bogus' uniform, interviews officers from the AASF – his engineer is recording in the car.

view that Britain was 'pulling its punches' at this stage of the war was widespread.

'The "no bombs" order was obviously a political one,' Gardner wrote later, 'and this reluctance of ours to take up the offensive was one of the things which gave rise to the many "peace" rumours which were flying about at the time.' This was the Phoney War – *drôle*, the French called it, like an off-beat joke – when, for fully eight months, the Allies and the Germans ranged against one another along the Western Front did little more than jab and feint. The correspondents in Reims, while enjoying the champagne, were soon chewing the elegant carpets of the Lion d'Or in frustration. Gardner recalled that 'Most of our spare time – which was almost all day – was given over to discussing the war. What we all wanted to know was: "Why hadn't the balloon gone up?" A question which, if we had but known it, we were to go on asking right up to May 10 [when the big German attack in the West began].'

At the Château de Polignac, the AASF headquarters, Gardner noticed a couple of striking posters. One showed Hitler peering round a corner and carried the legend:

> He wants to know your unit's name,
> He wants to know from whence you came.

Another showed 'a girl in *déshabillé* on a couch, saying goodbye to a satisfied-looking soldier who was just leaving her. The words underneath read:

> A maiden loved – an idle word,
> A comrade lost, and Hitler served.

The press office was nearby, in premises belonging to a manufacturer of farm machinery, 'a charming landlord with large stocks of champagne which he sold cheaply'. There was a bottle on the table when Gardner called in for his introductory visit, and a 'good time was had by all'. But Gardner very quickly became frustrated by what he regarded as the blinkered attitude of the censors who had to approve all his copy for broadcast; they kept trying to kill the stories he felt would have greatly boosted morale on the Home Front.

He cites one 'first class story' of a 'scrap' he learned about from the pilots of a squadron of Hurricanes. One of them had chased a German Dornier and hit it so many times that two of the three-man crew bailed out. The Hurricane pilot then flew alongside the damaged German plane to 'take a "look-see",' and, observing that its pilot was huddled over the wheel – apparently either dead or wounded – he left it to crash. But the German pilot was in fact 'only foxing'. As soon as the Hurricane had overtaken him, he 'stood up, and with one hand on the wheel, reached forward to the front gun and shot our plane up so much that it had to land'.

The Dornier was also forced to crash-land and the pilot was taken prisoner, but the officers of the Hurricane squadron felt he had put up 'such a good show' that he deserved a party. He was granted parole and invited to the mess for a knees-up.

In the middle of the celebrations the young German broke down in tears and had to leave the party. He explained that 'for most of his thirty one years he had been taught to hate the British and, just before setting out on his last flight, he had been assured that, if he was captured alive, he would be tortured and killed. To find, instead, that he was treated as an honoured guest had been too much . . . he went back to the mess and made a speech on those lines and, eventually after a few drinks, he went on his way in a mellow condition.'

Gardner felt this was such a terrific tale that it should be printed on the propaganda leaflets being dropped over Germany. The Air Ministry took a very different view, first resisting the idea that it should be published at all, and then insisting that everyone's copy about the incident should go through the laborious process of being submitted to its Intelligence Department in Whitehall.

Gardner found another tasty morsel in what he called – in a piece of tightly written copy he filed to London – 'the amazing adventure of the two young British pilots who landed in Germany to ask the way'. The flight lieutenant and flying officer in question were return-ing from a perilous long-range mission over Poland (dropping leaflets, not bombs) when they began to run short of fuel after battling with a headwind. They landed in a field in what they thought was France, turned off the engines and unloaded the guns, then left the plane to meet 'a group of peasants' walking towards them. On being asked whether they were French, one of these locals 'replied in a strong German accent, but very politely, "*Non Monsieur, c'est l'Allemagne, la frontière est à vingt kilomètres*," and obligingly . . . pointed out the direc-tion in which France lay.' The two men legged it, fired up the engines and escaped by the skin of their teeth. They did not try landing again until an advertising hoarding for a popular French drink reassured them that they were on the right side of the border.

It took 'a day and a half of rowing' before this engaging tale could be told. At first it was banned outright, and when word finally came through that the story could be published it was 8.40 in the evening, so Gardner missed the all-important nine o'clock news. The pilots were not happy either; the story that was eventually allowed to pass the censors made no mention of their epic flight – the longest of the war so far – and, they felt, it seemed to suggest they were a couple of incompetents who had simply got lost while flying circuits.

Another grouse that united pilots and correspondents was the official ban on naming any of the air crews. Gardner wanted to celebrate the bravery and skill of the ace pilots who were already showing that the RAF could be more than a match for the Luftwaffe. He particularly admired a twenty-one-year-old New Zealander called Cobber Kain, but even when Kain was awarded a Distinguished Flying Cross – and the announcement was published in the London papers – Gardner could not identify him in his broadcast.

Tensions with the AASF over the way the Air Ministry censored the correspondents eventually became so acute that the press corps – Gardner included – went on strike for a week and refused to provide any coverage, an amazing thing to do in time of war. Fortunately, it was glorious weather, so Gardner and a couple of his fellow correspondents climbed into Harold and motored out to the Reims golf course in the grounds of a lovely medieval chateau.

≈

Richard Dimbleby was suffering similar frustrations with the army, and was leading an altogether less comfortable life than Gardner. When he and his recording-car team reached the headquarters of the British Expeditionary Force at the bleak northern French town of Arras, they found its main hotel full of officers, so they had to book into a cheap hotel with 'no heating, little hot water, poor food and lumpy beds'. His first despatch was delivered after the army organized a facility for the accredited – today we would say 'embedded' – correspondents to test the mood among the troops. Dimbleby declared that 'I and my colleagues have come back to our billets impressed to the point of amazement by the cheerful optimism of the British Army.' The censor was no doubt delighted to read that, and the story was fine as far as it went. But that was about as interesting as things got.

Dimbleby did eventually manage to talk himself into a temporary attachment with the French Army so that he could take the recording car down to the Maginot Line. The French had built this network of forts after the First World War as a first and, so they believed, impregnable line of defence. In the summer of 1940 the Germans simply outflanked the Maginot Line, but at the time of Dimbleby's visit most people on the Allied side assumed it would be the flashpoint where the Phoney War would turn real. Dimbleby's despatch conveys a sense of the wild front-line freedom which anyone who has reported a war will recognize. He walked into a deserted village where he found this scene:

> ...outside the houses pigs and hens were roaming together. There was manure piled high on the pavement ... Outside one house lay a young pig that had clearly been dead for some time. I stepped over it, pushed open the door and went into the living room ... In the room at the back there was an unmade bed. There was the remains of a fire in the kitchen. The living room had been left in a state of turmoil; drawers had been pulled out and the contents spilled onto the floor. It was covered with letters, newspapers, old photographs and bills. There were some dead flowers from an upturned vase, and alongside them a large brown envelope with a German inscription on it addressed to the owner of the house. It contained a brightly coloured catalogue, and offered for sale some beautiful spring bulbs from Cologne.

Every radio reporter I know would be proud of those sentences. They are brisk, clear and vivid. The bulb catalogue is a small master-stroke, a mundane but poignant detail that immediately evokes an ordinary life interrupted by war. We all look for that kind of detail today, but reporters like Dimbleby and Gardner were inventing the genre. Those 'small groups of listeners around the family hearth' who heard the broadcast back in Britain would have been transported straight to this strange no-man's-land where two armies faced one another in sullen inaction.

Dimbleby also, according to his son Jonathan, succumbed to a temptation which we have all felt from time to time but which is now gravely frowned upon: encouraging someone to start a fight so that you can get some decent 'actuality', as we call it these days. Longing to 'get the sounds of war on disc', he spent much of his time at the Maginot Line 'trying to persuade the French to open fire'. The problem with this recording technique is that it tends to provoke the other side into firing back, as the French soldiers pointed out to him. Wisely, they repeatedly refused the request. Dimbleby did eventually manage to record the sound of the big guns of the Maginot Line, only to be criticized in the British press for sensationalism. And he found the French censors just as obdurate as their British counterparts. In his despatch from the Maginot Line he was forbidden to say that he was in France.

By the spring of 1940 the hyperactive Dimbleby had become thoroughly bored and abandoned the Western Front altogether. He persuaded the BBC to send him to the Middle East, where the chance of finding some action seemed better. An Imperial Airways Flying Boat flew him across the Mediterranean to Cairo, taking him away from what eventually became one of the biggest stories of the war, the fall of France.

≈

Dimbleby's boredom in France was as nothing to the boredom afflicting the Home Front – indeed, at the time the Phoney War was, in Britain, often referred to as the Bore War.

Fun in Britain was officially banned the day war was declared. 'Notoriously,' writes E. S. Turner in *The Phoney War on the Home Front*, 'at the start of the war, the only places of public resort permitted to stay open were the churches and the public-houses.' The Home Office, expecting that great wave of bombers, closed down cinemas and theatres everywhere (except, rather weirdly, for the Welsh seaside town of Aberystwyth, where the chief constable of Cardiganshire granted the Pier Cinema an exemption). Music halls were closed down too and chorus girls were evacuated to the countryside, where they were taught 'to milk cows, with the aid of rubber teats and canvas udders'.

George Bernard Shaw denounced this Cromwellian assault on places of spectacle and entertainment as 'a master-stroke of unimaginative stupidity' in a letter to *The Times*. 'What agent of Chancellor Hitler is it who suggested that we should cower in darkness and terror?' the great man asked. Shaw argued that 'all actors, variety artists, musicians and entertainers of all sorts should be exempted from every form of service except their professional one'. Given how long the Bore War lasted, that suggestion was probably wiser than it seemed at the time.

All sorts of other traditional British pleasures were under assault too. Football pools were banned for the first two and a half months of the Phoney War, and even when the complete ban was lifted the stakes were limited to £1 for established players and 5 shillings for new ones. A writer in the *Field* magazine lamented that 'War is upon us at the very moment of cub-hunting', and there was much agonized debate in the pages of *Horse and Hound* about whether hunting should continue at all during hostilities. One correspondent argued that abandoning the chase would 'be hailed by the Nazis as a sign that things are not going too well here', another wrote to say that 'Anyone hunting today is helping the enemy and retarding our war effort' and

Auntie does her bit for the war effort: women queuing to join the Women's Auxiliary Air Force after a BBC appeal for WAAF recruits in the second week of war.

that feed for horses could more profitably be used for cattle. 'Sacred relics of cricket were being moved from the Long Room at Lord's,' writes E. S. Turner. 'The singing boys of St Paul's were singing in Truro Cathedral ... The last motor race had been run at Brooklands.' Culture was in retreat everywhere you looked. Kenneth Clark, the young director of the National Gallery (and later presenter of the landmark BBC television series *Civilisation*), packed up the pictures in his care and despatched them to a quarry in Wales before taking up a new job at the Ministry of Information. And with severe petrol rationing, even the pleasures of the open road were limited.

Those seeking enjoyment and relaxation had really very few options, and as they sat at home behind the blackout curtains the wireless was an obvious place to turn. But the service they found on the BBC – now of course reduced to a single network – had been designed for crisis conditions created by a massive aerial attack, and it was a very starchy diet: endless news bulletins – when there was not nearly enough news to fill them – and exhortations from government spokesmen. As staff in Variety had been instructed in a departmental memo, 'Immediately following the outbreak of war, all existing arrangements will be cancelled and the lighter side of broadcasting will consist almost entirely of commercial records, eg dance music.'

Tom Hickman, in his book *What Did You Do in the War, Auntie?*, identifies this as the period when the Corporation acquired its nickname. 'The radio did not inform,' he wrote, 'it hectored and, like a spinster aunt, it fussed ... Now the sobriquet began to enter the language and it was not born of the affection it later engendered.' All sorts of people vented the frustration they felt about the Bore War by attacking the BBC, and during those uneasy months through the autumn and winter of 1939 and into the spring of 1940, poor Frederick Ogilvie, the director-general, was assailed on every side – by the listeners, by backbench MPs, by ministers and opposition leaders, by the spooks out at Woburn Abbey and, the BBC files reveal, by a procession of clergymen, dowagers and members of the peerage who felt they knew how to run things better than he did.

Those endless records played between the news and the public service announcements were interspersed with live performances by the organist Sandy MacPherson on the instrument in the Radio Theatre below Broadcasting House. MacPherson's usual home was a show called *Sandy's Half-hour*, but in the early days of war he had to perform for rather more than thirty minutes – he notched up an impressive forty-five sessions in a fortnight, in fact. The BBC correspondent Frank Gillard thought he was making it up as he went along. 'Poor man, he really did seem to be chained to his instrument,' he said later. 'It seemed to me that he was playing without musical scores, because it wasn't the usual polished performance, I can tell you.' And even when things began to settle down a little, the dispersal of non-news departments to the supposed safety of their refuges away from London inevitably interrupted the wonderful flow of creativity on to the airwaves that had earned the BBC such a secure place in the public's affections before the war. 'What was expected to be *blitzkrieg* turned out to be more like an *ersatzkrieg*,' lamented John Watt, the director of Variety, from exile in Bristol, where his department was struggling to recover its peacetime form.

Listeners were soon writing in to say they 'would rather face the German guns' than endure any more of MacPherson's heroic efforts. A poll in October 1939 suggested that 35 per cent of the public were dissatisfied with the BBC output, and the press, of course, was merciless. 'For God's sake, how long is the BBC to be allowed to broadcast its travesty of a programme?' demanded the *Sunday Pictorial*. 'Puerile,' declared the *Sunday Chronicle*. A backbench Tory MP demanded 'a thorough clearing out' of BBC staff and their replacement with 'men attuned . . . to the needs of war, with new ideas and a fresh outlook'.

MY ETON GRANDSONS TOLD ME ...

T HE AUTHORITIES IN GERMANY and Britain took very different views about listening to foreign broadcasting. In the first week of war, Goebbels came up with a 'Decree on Extraordinary Radio Measures' which created a new legal concept: 'radio crime'.

'In modern warfare the opponent does not only use military means but also methods which influence national morale and are intended to undermine it,' the preamble declared. 'One of these methods is radio. Every word which the opponent broadcasts is of course a lie and intended to damage the German people. The Reich Government knows that the German people are aware of this danger and, therefore, expects that every German will have the sense of responsibility to consider it a matter of decency to refrain from listening to foreign broadcasts.'

Those citizens who 'lack this sense of responsibility' were threatened with penal servitude, or, in less serious cases, a straightforward prison sentence and the confiscation of their equipment (of course). If they were also found guilty of 'intentionally disseminating information gleaned from foreign radio stations which is liable to threaten the defensive capability of the German nation', they could even face the death penalty.

These were not idle threats. William Shirer, the Berlin-based American correspondent who provided one of the few sources of independent reporting from Germany in the early days of the war, included the following in a despatch in January 1940: 'At Stuttgart, a special court sentenced a 58-year-old German to two years in the penitentiary for having listened to a foreign radio station and then passed on the news to his friends where he worked. Some of the Berlin papers are moved to publish editorials tonight praising the sentence.' Shirer added an anecdotal coda to the piece: 'In this connection, I was informed today of a case in which the British Broadcasting Corporation some time ago broadcast the names of German prisoners taken. Eight people wrote to one woman they knew to tell her that they'd just heard her son was safe. But this story had an unexpected sequel. She denounced them to the police, and all were arrested.' The paragraph was cut by the censor before his broadcast.

The British government knew that they could never have got away with this kind of thing – nor, to be fair to the Ministry of Information, is there any evidence that they particularly wanted to. For most listeners in Britain a 'radio crime' might have been an apt description of what poor Sandy MacPherson was doing with his organ, but the idea that you could be sent to prison for tuning in to a dodgy station on your dial simply would not wash. Indeed the radio manufacturers openly promoted sets that had the power to pick up foreign stations. 'Get Europe under your thumb! What is Rome thinking? Let's see what fairy tales Germany has tonight', declared one ad, while another promised '. . . *uncensored* shortwave war news and *entertaining* programmes! Germany, Italy, Russia, USA – are you listening to all these? The rest of the world is transmitting in English day and night. The short waves are important these days. Don't miss the world's news.'

Faced with the dreary stuff emanating from Broadcasting House, many listeners sought solace in this enticing-sounding radio world beyond our shores. One of the most popular foreign stations before the war had been Radio Normandie, a commercial station that began life as Radio Fécamp and had been established by a successful Normandy businessman (the family also manufactured the liqueur Benedictine, and created the charming myth that the drink's secret formula had been discovered by monks). Radio Normandie was easy to receive across the Channel, and for much of the 1930s had been seen by the BBC as a dangerous rival and a threat to its monopoly.

In September 1939 Radio Normandie was closed down along with most French commercial stations in accordance with an agreement between the French and British governments, but a small part of the network kept broadcasting away from near the port of Fécamp itself, and proved extremely popular with the thousands of British troops stationed in France with the BEF. The broadcasts greatly concerned the RAF, who believed the station could be used by German bombers as a navigational aid – the old problem that had led to the synchronization system back at home. The campaign to get the station closed became Noël Coward's one moment of real glory in his brief career as a propaganda spook.

It is not clear why Sir Campbell Stuart, the head of the black propaganda unit Department EH, decided that Noël Coward was just the man to run his Paris operation, but the great writer and wit was flattered by the invitation and relieved to escape the job of 'entertainments officer' in the navy which he suspected was heading his way. Campbell Stuart gave him a viscount as an assistant, saying that this rank would impress the French (Coward remarked that 'if the French were so Debrett-minded, it would be better to get a marquis or even a young duke, if there were any available') and despatched him to the French capital with a list of suitable contacts and funds for a nice flat near the Place Vendôme. The Ritz was still functioning and it was fun to be in the swim. 'The Secret Service virus was epidemic in Paris,' Coward wrote in his autobiography. 'Everybody was up to something ... The most unexpected people would arrive suddenly from London, wrapped in mystery and wearing strange, secretive smiles.'

When Coward was told about Radio Fécamp he went to work with a will, pulling out all the stops in his search for the right contacts to get the station closed down. To his horror, he discovered that a senior French politician had a financial interest in the station, and despite his best efforts Fécamp was allowed to continue on its merry way. 'I learnt,' he wrote later, rather primly, 'that men of considerable responsibility, can, when financial interests are involved, behave with shoddy evasiveness.'

Coward eventually tried some evasiveness of his own: he invented a story that the press were about to publish a 'scandal of horrifying proportions' about Fécamp, which would 'not only cause grave inter-Allied disunity, but would almost certainly unseat the government', and delicately insinuated this bombshell into the ear of the French prime minister's *chef du cabinet*. In early January 1940 Fécamp was finally taken off the air. Noël Coward and two of his collaborators celebrated 'by giving ourselves an excellent dinner and then going on to hear Edith Piaf sing in her night-club'. They had – unintentionally perhaps, since their overriding concern was security and not broad-casting competition – done good service to the BBC by finally killing off a long-standing rival in the battle for listeners.

The Corporation faced an altogether more serious challenge from 'Station Bremen and Station DXB on the 31 metre band', as the famous call-sign, broadcast from Hamburg, had it. Lord Haw-Haw is one of the oddest anti-heroes in the history of radio: a traitor, a genuine star at a time when the BBC was still dominated by the cult of anonymous authority, by turns funny and sinister, brilliant and strange. William Joyce was not the only British voice on Germany's propaganda station, and in Radio Bremen's early days the term 'Haw-Haw' was sometimes used generically, a more vivid shorthand than the 'G.B.E.' (German Broadcasts in English) of BBC memos. But Joyce's voice had a distinctive timbre, a curious – and slightly camp – nasal quality. For many people that drawled prelude to his performances – 'Jairmany calling, Jairmany calling, Jairmany calling ...' – became the defining sound of the Phoney War.

'In no other war had the British enjoyed the novelty of being cajoled and hectored by renegades in their own sitting-rooms,' writes E. S. Turner. 'Mostly those who listened to Lord Haw Haw excused themselves on the ground that he was the best entertainer on the air. Others listened so that they might be in the conversational swim the next day. Others again argued they ought to hear both sides and that, after all, Haw-Haw sometimes told the truth. Even those who scoffed the loudest gave credence and currency to the misinformation he circulated.'

He could certainly entertain. Take this sally, aimed at the Ministry of Information with its endless and often repetitive public service announcements: 'The British Ministry of Misinformation has been conducting a systematic campaign of frightening British women and girls about the dangers of being injured by splinters from German bombs. The women have reacted to these suggestions in alarm, by requesting their milliners to shape the spring and summer hats out of very thin tin plate, which is covered with silk, velvet, and other draping materials ...' This of course was before the Blitz, when it was still possible – just – to make jokes about bombs. It is such an oddball piece of humour that it almost seems to belong to the surreal style of much later comedians like the Pythons, and when you hear it the clipped delivery makes it odder still.

Another of Haw-Haw's favourite targets was Winston Churchill, at this stage first lord of the Admiralty. He was already a hated figure in Germany because of his pre-war attacks on Hitler and the Nazis, and the tone of anti-Churchill German propaganda in the early weeks of war was caricatured in a BBC memo as 'Churchill disguised as a rowing-boat, his jaws dripping with blood and port as he goes around torpedoing American ships'.

The one area of the Phoney War that was not phoney at all was the war at sea. SS *Athenia*, with 1,400 passengers on board, was torpedoed and sunk within hours of the declaration of war, and the initial German naval campaign was so successful that by the end of 1939 Britain had lost 422,000 tons of shipping. This grim picture provided Haw-Haw with plenty of scope for taunting Churchill, who was, after all, responsible for naval operations. In the first month of the war the navy's most modern aircraft carrier, HMS *Ark Royal*, was withdrawn from U-boat hunting after a near miss from a torpedo, so Haw-Haw made a habit of peppering his broadcasts with the question (asked in his archest tones), 'And where is the *Ark Royal*?' And his station broadcast an unpleasantly satirical version of the popular song 'Stormy Weather'. It was spoken in a sibilant German accent, but with just enough of a lilt to evoke the melody of the original, which was played in the background with the distinctive big band sound of the 1940s. 'Mr Churchill's latest song,' it began:

Don't know why, can't blockade the sky
Stormy weather
Since my ships and German planes got together
I'm beaten every time
Stormy weather
Life is bare – blooming misery everywhere
Stormy weather
Just can't keep my poor ships together
They are sinking all the time – oh blimey
They are sinking all the time ...

Joyce was not simply a cynical propagandist; he really meant what he said – some of it, anyway. Certainly his resentment of the British upper classes – the 'upper nation', as he called them – seems to have been genuine. 'It is an unforgettable experience to watch the entrance to a London theatre in the evening; pre-war, of course,' he said in one broadcast. 'Limousine after limousine with extravagantly clad women and their male companions, stepping out of cars like condescending gods and goddesses, whilst the dull and silent crowd composed of members of the lower nation looks at this brazen display of wealth and leisure. The sight almost reminds one of conditions in the declining Roman Empire, and one is at a loss to say whether the impudence of the upper classes or the meek tractability of the lower is the more astonishing. The upper nation of the Mayfair type of snob feeds on the lower nation whom it robs. How long is this going to last?'

When the Blitz began and the Home Front war turned serious, Joyce appeared in a more sinister light, but during the slightly hysterical calm of the Phoney War he seemed somehow to hit the right notes. His biographer, Mary Kenny, describes him as a 'kind of left-wing Fascist' and says he 'brought cheekiness, boldness, and even satire, mocking the "swells" in a way that hadn't been heard on British airwaves before ... He also possessed something not previously identified: a "radio personality". Other broadcasters had better speaking voices, finer elocution, etc., etc., but he had this "radio personality" which meant those who heard it never forgot it.'

The Ministry of Information published a poster to discourage people from listening to Haw-Haw:

WHAT DO I DO ... if I come across German or Italian broadcasts when tuning my wireless?

    I say to myself: 'Now this blighter wants me to listen to him. Am I going to do what he wants?' I remember that German lies over the air are like parachute troops dropping on Britain – they are all part of the plan to get us down – *which they won't.* I remember that nobody can trust a word of what the Haw-Haws say. So, just to make them waste their time, I switch 'em off or tune 'em out!

To no avail. For a while the Haw-Haw cult 'went viral', as we might say today. After a particularly successful Haw-Haw broadcast – in which he made merry at the government's expense over the introduction of rationing – the distinguished theatre critic and man of letters Harold Hobson wrote to *The Times* that 'The dear fellow is ... a figure of national popularity. He is the hero of a *revue*; he is the subject of a well-known song; that ineffable voice of his, Cholmondeley Plantagenet out of Christ Church, has an irresistible fascination.'

The fact that at this stage no one knew who he was only added fuel to the flames. 'The British press went Haw-Haw mad,' writes Kenny. 'Who *was* Lord Haw-Haw? A German schoolmaster? ... A British student in Germany? Perhaps a Scot? Was there a hint of Irish brogue?' Whether his upper-class accent was authentic or not was the source of much speculation. The novelist Rose Macaulay took issue with the claim that Lord Haw-Haw's voice was 'aristocratic, upper-class, haw-haw, and so forth'. She accepted that Haw-Haw spoke excellent English, but challenged the judgement of her fellow literary lion Harold Hobson; 'surely not,' she declared, '"Cholmondeley Plantagenet out of Christ Church".' One cannot help reflecting that this obsession with the nuances of Haw-Haw's accent rather rammed home his point about what a class-conscious place Britain was.

Haw-Haw was particularly adept at broadcasting in a manner that suggested he knew what was happening from secret sources. 'It was his custom to refer to local conditions in Britain,' writes E. S. Turner, 'to impending evacuations and requisitionings, in such a way to suggest that he had received his information from agents on the spot, when in fact he had obtained it from reading the British press.'

In the febrile atmosphere of the Phoney War, Haw-Haw rumours took on a life of their own and people were quick to believe them even when they were not true. Perhaps the most famous example of this was the widely held belief that Haw-Haw showed off his omniscience by correctly revealing that a particular church or town clock in Britain was running fast or slow, even though there seems to be no evidence that he ever did any such thing. A High Court judge – the Rt Hon. Sir Herbert du Parcq – mentioned over lunch with a senior BBC friend that he had been the subject of a Haw-Haw broadcast, and asked for a copy of the transcript from the Monitoring Service. After consulting the files, the BBC wrote to inform him that '. . . there is no trace of his ever having mentioned you'. The note added, 'It does show how much inaccurate talk there is about what the gentleman in question says.'

By the end of 1939 the Haw-Haw phenomenon had created a vague but powerful sense of unease in high government circles in London. On 5 December 1939 General Pile, the head of Anti-Aircraft Command, sent a long letter to the War Office expressing his concern about the impact of the broadcasts, and citing the kind of anecdotal evidence that is particularly difficult to counter. 'I feel quite sure the soldiers are interested in these broadcasts,' he declared, 'because at a canteen in London where my wife works and where every night our own official news can be heard on the wireless, no soldier takes any notice of it, he continues to play his game of darts or draughts or whatever it may be. When, on the other hand, someone tunes into Lord Haw-Haw, the whole room gets up and gathers round the wireless.' He took the view that the Haw-Haw broadcasts were 'nothing less than an attempt to foment a social revolution'.

A week later Frederick Ogilvie, the BBC director-general, received a note from the War Office that began, 'We are getting a disturbing amount of reports from Public Relations Officers at Commands and from other sources which indicate that the Hamburg broadcasts in English are becoming a definite factor affecting public morale in this country. The transmissions are, I think you will agree, ingenious, and though the British public's first reaction was one of amusement, I am not sure that the constant re-iteration of Lord Haw-Haw is not having a bad effect.' The memo suggested that putting P. G. Wodehouse on the air to mock Haw-Haw might be an effective remedy – a suggestion full of irony, since six months later Wodehouse was captured by the Germans and persuaded to broadcast for them instead. The note ends with the politely bullying tone that often characterized relations between Whitehall and the BBC during this period: 'It is not for us to teach the BBC its business, but I think you ought to know that we do take a rather serious view of the Hamburg propaganda.'

Ogilvie really did not need reminding of the seriousness of the Haw-Haw phenomenon. A BBC report on Christmas Eve 1939 estimated that the audience for some broadcasts from Radio Bremen was 'as large as that for the 9.00 pm Home Service News Bulletin'. And the director-general's in-tray was overflowing with suggestions about how to counter the threat this posed to Home Front morale.

Several of them came from members of that 'upper nation' that Haw-Haw had been attacking so effectively. Viscount Coverdale – who communicated his views via a senior official at the Foreign Office – suggested that 'the moment the German ceases speaking an English voice should continue the talk, putting points right, keeping the same vein of humour, using the same technique'. He added helpfully that 'I know the possessor of an exact replica of that German voice who would broadcast well the material provided – most of which would perforce be written on the spot by someone of wit and intelligence.'

The Countess of Harrowby, writing from Sandon Hall, Stafford, chose to deliver her thoughts via the good offices of Sir Stephen Tallents, an official who held senior jobs at both the BBC and the Ministry of Information, because, as she wrote to him, 'when I was a girl I knew your mother and her family quite well, and probably saw you as a small boy'. She revealed that 'My Eton grandsons told me they looked upon him [Haw-Haw] as the best amusement of the day, but there are possibly other people who take him more seriously,' and

that, shockingly, 'a member of my own Red Cross party here says a
woman friend of hers in the Potteries District has been <u>completely</u>
won over, and another said doubtingly (having listened to him the
night before) "you don't know who to believe, do you?"' The
Countess's idea for meeting the Haw-Haw challenge – which echoed
Lord Coverdale's – came from a 'clever friend' who suggested 'that it
would be a good thing if the BBC could collect some very sound
"quickwits" who could slip in a good answer occasionally, for Haw-
Haw sometimes pauses sufficiently long for this, and of course as
nothing kills like ridicule he might be made to look ridiculous . . .'

One Percy Goff, who ran a large farm in Yorkshire, wrote to
let the BBC know that 'with over forty years close contact with the
working classes I am appalled at the accumulating and increasing
interest taken by them in this swine's broadcasting'. He added, 'Even
my own maids and charwomen are becoming tainted.' Generals and
vicars also felt themselves to be among Haw-Haw's targets, and piled
in with a will. One senior officer reminded Ogilvie that they had met
on prize day at the Scottish public school Glenalmond. 'I wonder
whether it would be worthwhile if in our foreign broadcasts the most
obvious lies were answered,' he wrote, adding, rather unhelpfully, 'I
may not have noticed if they are or not, as I only understand French.'
A letter from Canon Rogers of The Rectory, Birmingham, proposed
that Haw-Haw should be defeated by literary satire. It was accompanied
by a spoof script based on Oscar Wilde's essay 'The Decay of Lying'.
In the original, two characters called Vivian and Cyril engage in a
Socratic dialogue denouncing the 'worship of facts' and praising deceit in
a characteristically paradoxical Wildean way. Just the ticket, suggested
the canon, to serve as a vehicle for mock-praise of Haw-Haw.

And of course the newspapers got in on the act too. There were
ferocious leaders. 'How much longer are British listeners going to
tune in to that English-speaking cur with the persuasive voice of a
confidence trickster?' thundered *Everybody's Weekly*. 'Let the B.B.C.
jam his broadcasts until such time as we have won the war and he can
state his case before being put up against the wall.' And there were
personal letters to Ogilvie: the news editor of the *Sunday Express*, one
J. L. Garbutt, suggested something similar to Lord Coverdale's solution

and requested that if Ogilvie adopted this brilliantly original idea he should, to show his gratitude, give the story to the paper as an exclusive.

The BBC's response to this avalanche of advice was cool, considered and evidence-based. Reading the internal memos about the Haw-Haw question and the correspondence with government departments that followed, you can watch the concept of truth-telling as a weapon of war being worked through in a methodical way. On 19 December 1939 Sir Richard Maconachie, the BBC director of talks, attended a meeting to discuss Haw-Haw at the Ministry of Information. 'It was agreed,' he noted in a subsequent memo, 'that it was especially desirable for Left Wing refutations to be given to Haw-Haw broadcasts, as these broadcasts were directed chiefly to our Left Wing.' Maconachie pointed out that if the BBC began broadcasting extreme left-wing propaganda it was likely to make itself extremely unpopular with Neville Chamberlain's Conservative-dominated government, and he could not resist adding a waspish parenthetical swipe at Professor John Hilton, a Cambridge academic who was the Ministry's director of home publicity. The memo continues, 'It is significant of Professor Hilton's inexperience that he entirely accepted my point as a "new and striking one!"'

Maconachie suggested to the meeting – and this certainly would have been 'new and striking' at the time – that the influence of German propaganda might already be on the wane because 'events had occurred to expose its falsity'. He cited the enormously import-ant destruction of the German pocket battleship *Graf Spee* on 17 December.

Graf Spee had been a serious menace to British shipping in the first few weeks of war, roaming the South Atlantic and capturing or sinking merchant vessels more or less at will. But she was eventually run to ground by a British battle group off the coast of Uruguay, and after a bruising battle her captain scuttled her at the mouth of the River Plate. This, Maconachie declared, was the best possible answer to the claims of German naval supremacy made by Haw-Haw and his kind. It was only a couple of days since the ship had gone down, but Maconachie argued – bravely, in the circumstances – that it might prove a 'turning point'.

A few days later – on Christmas Eve – Maconachie developed his ideas in another memo, advancing three arguments against responding directly to Haw-Haw broadcasts. It would, he suggested, contribute yet further to Haw-Haw's public profile; it would be impossible for the BBC to stop responding once it had begun; and people would be likely to assume that anything that was *not* directly denied was true. He also pointed out that the idea of an immediate rebuttal – of the kind Lord Coverdale had suggested – was impracticable. 'The really effective reply, as to all false propaganda, is given by facts,' and he again cited the scuttling of *Graf Spee* by way of example. 'Since the reply of facts is a "long term" system of refutation,' Maconachie wrote, 'the success of false propaganda with any audience which has access to facts is essentially a "short term" affair. It is thus reasonable to suppose that the influence of G.B.E. [German Broadcasts in English] on the British audience will decline rather than increase with the lapse of time.'

That same day Frederick Ogilvie wrote to Sir Campbell Stuart – who would certainly have felt that this was his turf – in similar terms. 'News is what people principally look for at present, from China to Peru, and it is on its news service that the prestige of any station (and country) finally depends,' Ogilvie argued. 'And the Haw-Haw question merely makes it all the more important that the BBC's news service should be allowed to maintain its standards of truthfulness and speed. It will be a very sad day for this country if people at home and abroad begin to say "The BBC seems to be keeping back unpleasant news. What is the British government trying to hide" . . . the best defence is attack, and it should be attack on British terms, not Haw-Haw's.'

It was smart footwork. Haw-Haw's success was, in part, an indictment of the BBC's failure to hold its listeners, yet here was the director-general using 'the Haw-Haw question' as a way of defining BBC values. And an institution that only a few years earlier had had nothing to speak seriously of by way of a news-gathering operation was now placing news at the heart of its mission.

The BBC soon had some hard evidence to back up its position. In mid-December the Corporation had – at the request of the Ministry of Information – begun a survey to determine the extent of

Haw-Haw's impact on public opinion. Thirty-four thousand people were interviewed (these were general interviews about listening habits with Haw-Haw questions thrown in), 750 questionnaires were filled in by a 'representative sample' of listeners, there were a further 5,000 interviews with a specially selected group, and the survey also collated 'correspondence with the BBC, both solicited and unsolicited'.

The results – which were sent to the Ministry of Information in March – revealed that at the end of January 1940 one in six adults was listening regularly to Lord Haw-Haw's station in Hamburg. But it also noted that during the same period four in six were listening to BBC news. More significantly, Lord Haw-Haw's audience was on the slide; according to the report, 'the number of listeners to Hamburg in the last days of February was approximately two-thirds those who listened in the last week of January'. So Maconachie turned out to be right.

The report was candid about the reasons for Haw-Haw's success: 'The blackout, the novelty of hearing the enemy, the desire to hear both sides, the insatiable appetite for news and the desire to be in the swim have all played their part, both in building up Hamburg's audience and in holding it together. The entertainment value of the broadcasts; their concentration on undeniable evils in this country; their news sense; their presentation; and the publicity they have received in this country, together with the momentum of the habit of listening to them, have all contributed towards their establishment as a familiar feature of the social landscapes.'

But it also turned up some intriguing and important evidence about Lord Haw-Haw's audience. It was not, it turned out, made up of 'maids and charwomen'. The survey revealed that: 'All types of person are to be found among Hamburg's public ... Those whose families have been broken up by war, and whose money incomes have gone down, listen no more to Hamburg than do people not so affected ... The one outstanding feature in the Hamburg audience is an interest in public affairs ... Careful study reveals, in the view of those who listen regularly to Hamburg, an unmistakable consistency. But this consistency is not one which would be in any way encouraging to the Hamburg propagandists. It exists only because the people who listen regularly to Hamburg tend to be those who are most interested in public affairs. Such people realise, without promptings from Hamburg, that some parts of the Empire are not united on the issue of the war, understand the reasons for rationing, are willing to give Hitler credit for certain pre-war achievements in the social field. On certain points they evidently hold views which the enemy wishes to encourage, and may even have encouraged. But there is little evidence that they would not have held those views in almost as great a measure if Hamburg had not broadcast in English.'

Ogilvie and Maconachie do seem to have missed one important lesson of the Haw-Haw phenomenon. H. V. Hodson, another Oxbridge don at the Ministry of Information, dropped a note to Ogilvie after one of their meetings to clarify his views. 'I ask myself why people listen to the Bremen broadcasts,' he wrote, and '... it is surely because of the personality that is conveyed in these bulletins and talks. To me the personality is repulsive, but I feel you will agree that most of those who listen to Hamburg-Bremen do so because it is Lord Haw-Haw, with his insidious and fascinating style.' Hodson suggested there was something here from which the BBC could usefully learn. 'I do not intend that the objectivity of the BBC News Bulletins should be tampered with, nor that the anonymous presentation of these bulletins by an announcer should be altered in any way,' he continues, 'but I do suggest that there is all the difference in the world between the forthright, vigorous and human presentation of the news ... and the rather inhuman, though clear and precise, reading of readymade bulletins.' The BBC was not yet ready for celebrity news presenters and reporters, but Hodson's advice was prescient: the war would create them.

≈

At the end of March 1940 Frederick Ogilvie sent Sir Kenneth Lee, the Ministry of Information's senior official, a report on handling the 'new armament of war', which radio had clearly become during the first six months of declared hostilities with Germany. Despite all the problems the BBC had been through during that period, he was clearly in bullish mood, because he broached the sensitive issue that had made Charles Gardner's life so difficult during those months:

official foot-dragging in the release of news. Ogilvie did it gently, however. And, as Noël Coward said of those propaganda leaflets, the way he conveyed the message was 'more than a trifle verbose'. He wrote, 'To us at least it seems – and I hope that, after reading this memorandum, it will also seem to you – that the great issues at stake demand a real change of outlook ... It seems, for example, that the Service Departments should take most earnest account of the outstanding opportunities for victory or defeat in the world's mind which radio commands; that even such honourable reluctances as spring from a desire to reserve statements for a first hearing in Parliament, to spare the feelings of the bereaved, or to preserve the traditional reticence of serving officers and men, may in the national interest have to yield to the paramount necessity of so delivering the British case that it may catch the ear of the world before the enemy has had time to forestall and distort it.'

Auntie still had a long way to go before catching up with Dr Goebbels in her understanding of what radio could do during war, but at least she now had her running shoes on.

MR CHURCHILL SHOULD SLEEP
IN HIS BOOTS

MANY OF THE BEST wartime Whitehall stories come from the pen of Harold Nicolson. A man of parts — he was a diplomat, Tory MP, belletrist, BBC broadcaster and later governor — he is best remembered for his diaries and letters. On 14 September 1939 he wrote to his wife, Vita Sackville-West, at the family home in Kent, with the gossip from London:

> The Opposition is getting somewhat restive, especially about the Ministry of Information. The latter has been staffed by duds at the top and all the good people are in the most subordinate positions. The rage and fury of the newspapermen knows no bounds. John Gunther [an American writer], for instance, told me that he had asked one of the censors for the text of one of our leaflets which we dropped on Germany. The request was refused. He asked why. The answer was, 'We are not allowed to disclose information which might be of value to the enemy.' When Gunther pointed out that two million leaflets had been dropped over Germany, the man blinked and said, 'Yes, something must be wrong there.'

The Ministry of Information is brilliantly satirized in Evelyn Waugh's *Put Out More Flags* (one of Waugh's characters, a Mr Bentley, says that his work there 'mostly ... consists of sending people who want to see me on to someone they don't want to see'), but the organization was, as Nicolson's story suggests, often beyond the reach of satire. Its location in the monumental splendour of London University's Senate House in Bloomsbury's Malet Street was no doubt congenial to the many intellectuals and writers who were drafted in to work there. But from its earliest days it suffered the legacy of that general squeamishness and confusion about propaganda that made pre-war planning so difficult. No one quite knew what it was for.

Ian McLaine, in his authoritative study *Ministry of Morale, Home Front Morale and the Ministry of Information in World War II*, describes its original structure like this: 'the fourteen divisions of the department were organised in four groups: censorship, news and press relations; "publicity" – that is to say propaganda – covering home, empire and foreign countries; production of publicity material; and administration.' But bits of these functions kept falling off while others were added on, so that 'It continually changed shape, now contracting, now expanding, convoluting itself and thoroughly confusing MPs, the press, the public, and, not least, the officers of the department themselves.'

The first minister of information, a Scottish judge called Lord Macmillan, told the House of Lords that 'I have had considerable difficulty in ascertaining what are its [the Ministry's] functions'. The principles he laid out for it on the outbreak of war sound eminently sensible; in a speech in the first week of September 1939 he ruled that 'All British information should be truthful and objective ... Dissemination should be speedy and widespread' and the 'suggestion of the Government spoon-feeding the public' was to be avoided. But he admitted in his autobiography that he had no idea why he had been given such a 'controversial political office' and he did not last long. Nor did his immediate successors; there were no fewer than three ministers of information within the first year of the Ministry's existence, and a departmental wit came up with the ditty 'Hush, hush, chuckle who dares,/Another new minister's fallen downstairs'.

The senior civil servants regularly resigned or were fired too, and while the Ministry attracted some very talented staff from outside Whitehall, many of them quickly became disenchanted with their employer. Some were incredibly rude about it. Kenneth Clark, the art historian, served there first as the head of the Film Division and later in the very senior role of controller of home publicity, and he described the Ministry as 'a perfectly useless body', taking the view that 'the war would have been in no way affected if it had been dissolved and only the censorship retained'. The great John Betjeman – whom Clark hired to work as his deputy at Film – was among those who referred to it as 'The Ministry of Aggravation' or 'Minnie'.

It certainly aggravated the BBC. The Ministry was the embodiment of what we now call the nanny state, and understood itself as a mixture of national cheerleader and policeman, keeping everyone's spirits up, but also telling them how to behave. The stream of exhortation and instruction that emanated from Senate House earned a memorable rebuke from the Labour frontbench spokesman and parliamentary wit Aneurin Bevan. 'Is the Minister aware,' he asked in the Commons towards the end of the first month of the war, 'that the impression is now universal that if the Germans do not manage to bomb us to death the Ministry of Information will bore us to death?' The Ministry regarded the BBC as the main vehicle for disseminating all this dullness, and the 'nanny ministry' must take a large share of responsibility for the 'interfering auntie' image that the Corporation acquired during the Bore War.

'So far as propaganda on the Home Front is concerned,' the Ministry's director of broadcasting relations instructed the controller of programmes at the BBC in February 1940, 'the backbone of our effort should be directed towards the counteraction of apathy – presumably by taking every opportunity of showing people that a real war is being waged, even though the Military situation is static, and by showing that they are themselves participating in it by collaborating in anti-gossip, road safety, food measures and the like.' He added – as if that wasn't enough to be getting on with – 'I should be most grateful if you would pay particular attention to anti-gossip and road safety in the coming weeks, to be followed by food, evacuation and the economic situation as time goes on.'

All decent programme-makers hate being told what to do, and the only thing they detest more than instructions is vagueness. Ministry memos combining the two poured into Broadcasting House.

Vagueness – also directed at the controller of programmes – arrived later in the spring, as the military situation in France began to look more worrying. 'Will you do all you can to ensure that the News bulletins are followed by cheerful and cheering programmes as far as is possible. I am well aware of the programme planning arguments against such an arrangement, and of the difficulty of defining a "cheerful" programme. Nevertheless, I do ask your cooperation in this respect, particularly in the early morning programmes.'

And even at this moment of national crisis there was time for the trivial and tedious. A few days later another note arrived at Broadcasting House from the Ministry – this time from a different official in the Broadcasting Division:

ECONOMY IN PAPER

As you know I have asked for some notice to be given to the need for economy in paper, not as a campaign, but an occasional repetitive theme.

Our regional Information Officers report that trades-people all over the country are finding it difficult to get their customers to co-operate in the matter of delivery of goods, wrappings and so on. Could you tie the two things together on the general paper saving issue?

The Ministry's headquarters in Malet Street were only a short walk from Broadcasting House, but the note was of course sent in duplicate – to 'Controller (Home) and Assistant Controller (Programmes)' – and generated the consumption of yet more paper in the form of BBC memos about how this directive should be implemented.

The broad censorship arrangements laid down by the Ministry of Information were, however, on the face of it at least, benign, and certainly most un-Goebbels-like; responsibility for general (as opposed to military) censorship of BBC broadcasts was delegated to the BBC itself. The Ministry took the view that 'the executive work of the security censorship of broadcasting in this country will best be carried out by the BBC staff engaged in the moral and political censorship required in peace'.

The controller of programmes was designated chief BBC censor, and a system of switch censors was introduced: during every programme there was a member of BBC staff on hand who could shut down transmission immediately if he or she judged that the rules were being infringed. The BBC's management took its duties as a censor very seriously, and the system of course relied heavily on the goodwill of the staff, most of whom seem to have cooperated without complaint. A memo from Val Gielgud to some of his senior colleagues in the first week of war instructed them that 'Your guiding rule should be common sense, together with the greatest discretion and an extreme sense of individual responsibility.' Quoting the controller of programmes – now also the chief censor – he gave them a rule of thumb: 'If in doubt, and if there is time, refer. If in doubt, and there is no time for reference, delete.' There is very little evidence of deliberate breaches of the censorship guidelines, and when someone did push the envelope a bit the malefactor seems to have been regarded as 'naughty', a bad schoolchild rather than a subversive enemy of the state.

The BBC's news services, however, were covered by slightly different and tighter rules, and the Ministry explicitly stated that 'It is more important that BBC news should comply with all the requirements of the "security" censorship than that statements published in a newspaper should do so.' The way the Ministry understood the BBC news operation is instructive. The censorship structure was laid out in a document drawn up before the outbreak of war – while the Ministry of Information was still in its 'shadow' and secret form – and it states that:

> The BBC News Services will be made up of:
> a) statements issued by the News Division of the Ministry, which will have been approved by the Control Division before they leave the Ministry; of these some will be for verbatim publication, while editors would be permitted, at their discretion, to cut down or alter others.
> b) material obtained elsewhere, e.g. from News Agencies – which might or might not have been censored by its Control Division before it reaches the BBC.

In other words, the Ministry was working on the assumption that it would be the main source for what the BBC broadcast and could therefore exert enormous influence over what went on the air. The idea that the BBC might develop an independent news-gathering operation simply does not seem to have occurred to anyone – and of course when this document was drawn up the BBC 'news-gathering machine' meant Gardner and Dimbleby zooming merrily round the country in their recording cars.

The guidelines about what should not be broadcast for security reasons were laid out in what were known as Defence Notices (later more commonly referred to simply as D Notices). These were buttressed by a system of so-called 'stops', which could be used to prevent the broadcast of specific items of news. There was a broadcasting liaison team at the Ministry of Information to provide 'advice' to BBC news staff if they were uncertain about a particular point, and a number of BBC people were transferred to the Ministry to ensure that the system ran smoothly. It all looked as sensible and civilized as the circumstances allowed.

But while the Ministry of Information had responsibility for censorship, it did not have the real power it needed to manage the system efficiently, because the departments running the armed services were allowed to keep the right to decide what was of military significance. So on almost any story that really mattered, the navy, army or air force decided what could be published or broadcast.

The most notorious example of the chaos this could cause afflicted the newspapers much more seriously than the BBC. On 11 September 1939 – less than two weeks into the war – the news that the British Expeditionary Force had arrived in France was revealed in a Paris radio broadcast. The War Office had until then kept the lid on the story but, since it was reasonable to assume that the Germans were able to hear what was said on a French public radio station, they agreed to lift the ban on the news and the papers duly wrote it up for their morning editions. However, just before midnight the secretary of state for war, Leslie Hore-Belisha (of Belisha Beacon fame), decided the papers were providing too much detailed information and re-imposed the ban.

Rear Admiral George Thomson, the chief censor at the Ministry of Information, recalled the ensuing nightmare in his memoirs: 'The newspapers like the word "sensation". Here was one for them. Not only had a considerable number of telegrams containing the news been already despatched overseas, but the main editions of the newspapers had already been printed and a large number of newspapers for breakfast-table reading next morning were already in the trains on the way to Scotland, Ireland and the provinces.' The police were sent to Fleet Street to stop the presses rolling, bundles of early editions were hauled off trains, and 'even motorcars were held up in the street, any newspapers found being confiscated'.

Three hours later the secretary of state reversed his own decision, and the ban was lifted again. It was, writes Ian McLaine, 'the very stuff of farce and, quite naturally, the fury of the press was directed at the censorship authority responsible which, however much it tried to point out privately that the ultimate power of censorship did not reside where it should, was obliged to bear the blame.'

Things became so difficult that for a while during the early months of the war the Ministry of Information's censorship duties were hived off to a separate Press and Censorship Bureau – which required one reorganization of the Ministry's structure when censorship left and another when it returned six months later. So when the BBC director-general, Frederick Ogilvie, sent his report on wartime broadcasting to Sir Kenneth Lee at the Ministry in March 1940, he was all too well aware of what a sensitive question censorship had become. And he also knew that his real target was the service ministries, not the people under siege at Senate House.

But the case for a change in approach to censorship was still worth making, and the BBC made it well. The Corporation came up with a litany of case histories which, they argued, demonstrated that, by delaying news, the services had handed an advantage to the enemy. Perhaps the most serious 'case study' cited in Ogilvie's report was the handling of the German air raid on Scapa Flow earlier the same month.

The great deep-water harbour in the Orkney Islands had been chosen to serve as Britain's main naval base in part because it was so far from any German airfields, and the raid by fourteen Ju–88 bombers was certainly a nasty shock. But it was not a major defeat. HMS *Hood*, a battle cruiser, was hit by a bomb which killed four officers, but she was still able to sail to the Clyde for repairs. A twenty-seven-year-old islander became the war's first civilian victim of an air raid, and a nearby aerodrome was damaged. But the way the story was, as we would say today, 'spun' made it seem like a much more serious reverse than it was.

The raid began at 7.50 on the evening of 16 March and was over by 9 p.m. At 3.40 a.m. on the 17th, the German Zeesen propaganda radio station broadcast the news in English for an American audience. At 7.15 that morning – nearly twelve hours after the raid took place – the Admiralty rang the BBC and asked the News Department not to broadcast the news until they had published their own account of what had happened. An internal BBC document details the way the story then came out:

> 10.22 Reuter quoted a German High Command communi-qué message which was read over the German radio early in the morning.
>
> 10.24 B.U.P. [British United Press agency] reported the German communiqué.
>
> 12.00 noon A statement was issued by the Admiralty describing the raid and explaining that it took place at 7.50 pm on 16th March.
>
> 1.00 News of the raid given out on the home news bulletin.

The memo also states that the BBC newsroom knew about the raid before seven o'clock that morning, so they had been forced to sit on the story for more than six hours. It then goes on to detail the way the Germans gained a significant propaganda advantage by getting their version of events in early – especially in the all-important American newspaper market:

> 17th March: American Sunday morning papers published the exaggerated claims given at 3.40 am in the German news in English to America.
>
> 10.30 pm The Germans broadcast with sound effects a

fantastic [as in unreal, rather than very good] account of the raid on Saturday night, claiming direct hits on 'Hood', 'Repulse', 'Renown', and an unnamed cruiser. They also said that airbases were bombed.

19th March: *The New York Times* carried a headline: 'Scapa Flow loss put at six warships'. A despatch from Washington stated that the United States State and Navy Departments had no official details, but 'It seems that the German official version is more nearly accurate than the British official one.' The same newspaper carried a leading article stressing the significance of the Scapa raid and arguing that the Germans had gained 'the most important victory of air power over naval power since the outbreak of war.'

In their final submission to the Ministry of Information, the BBC added to this catalogue of woe the fact that 'A suggestion made shortly after this raid that the London representative of the American broadcasting stations, for whom the BBC provides technical facilities, should be allowed to fly to Scapa Flow and contradict from personal observation the German misrepresentations of the raid, was refused by the competent Government authorities.' Altogether it made, the BBC argued, a strong case for what their report to the Ministry of Information described as 'two urgent needs': the earlier release of news, and 'prompt provision of authoritative commentary on news'.

It was clever of the BBC to argue that clumsy censorship, by encouraging people to tune to German stations to get their news, was aggravating what we can broadly call 'the Haw-Haw problem'. And Scapa Flow was a good case study for the BBC to cite, as the incident had generated plenty of public concern independent of the Corporation's efforts. The *Daily Telegraph* described it as an illustration of the way 'German propaganda is being assimilated in the United States', and noted that both the *New York Times* and the *Washington Post* 'accepted the German version without question', while *The Times* in London condemned the 'painfully meagre and uninformative' way the incident was reported in Britain. The *Evening Standard* opined that 'The old saying that a lie gets half-way round the world before truth can get its boots on should be hung up in the offices of every Government department. And since many of these raids take place at night Mr Churchill should sleep in his boots . . . Delay and suppression encourage rumour, and rumour will run errands for Dr Goebbels but never work for us. Sealed lips are as dangerous as careless talk.' And Lord Snell, the Labour leader in the House of Lords, complained that the British public 'are worthy of better treatment than that', and attacked what he called 'this slothful method which compels us to accept our information from outside and, possibly, tainted sources'.

But the BBC case does not seem to have impressed the service ministries one whit. The Admiralty, the villain of the Scapa Flow debacle, was especially notorious for its surly attitude to news in general and the broadcasting world in particular. Winston Churchill, first lord of the Admiralty for the early months of the war, had already informed the Ministry of Information that 'it was for the Admiralty or other department to purvey to the Ministry the raw meat and vegetables and for the Ministry to cook and serve the dish to the public. If the Admiralty could have had their way they would have preferred a policy of complete silence.'

It did not help that Churchill hated the way the BBC covered war news; at a Cabinet meeting in December he 'deplored the unrelieved pessimism of the BBC broadcasts which unfailingly open with a long account of ships sunk'. Even the Ministry of Information's chief censor, the retired admiral George Thomson, was struck by the reluctance of his old service to engage with the idea that news or broadcasting might have an impact on the nation's morale. 'The Admiralty never varied,' he wrote. 'It was seldom, if ever, that any naval news of real interest or importance was allowed to come out, unless from the lips of the Prime Minister or the First Lord of the Admiralty, until so long afterwards that any interest in the event had vanished.'

≈

Churchill was making life difficult for the BBC mandarins in another sphere too – partly because he was, as the war would vividly demonstrate, such a brilliant broadcaster. On 1 October 1939 he gave a talk to mark the end of the first month at war (it was in fact a month since the invasion of Poland rather than the declaration of war, but a mere detail like that was not going to trouble the great man). It was a

Sunday evening, and he was given the prime slot after the nine o'clock news bulletin. He warned of the possibility of a long war, but promised victory. 'How soon it will be gained,' he declared, 'depends on how long Herr Hitler and his group of wicked men, whose hands are stained with blood and soiled with corruption, can keep their grip on the docile, unhappy German people.' He threw in one of those quotable phrases we still use today, describing Russia as 'a riddle wrapped in a mystery inside an enigma'. And he took full advantage of the chance to stick up for the navy, which he said was hunting U-boats, 'I shall not say without mercy, because God forbid that we should ever part company with that – but at any rate with zeal and not altogether without relish'. It was vintage stuff, and even Churchill's long-standing rival, Chamberlain, thought it 'excellent' as he listened in Downing Street.

Unfortunately, it also stirred up a hornet's nest of inter-departmental and inter-service rivalry. At the War Office – which was responsible for the army – they felt their branch of the services deserved just as loud a shout as the navy, and the secretary for war, Leslie Hore-Belisha, demanded to be given a Sunday-evening broadcasting slot of his own. The BBC director-general, Frederick Ogilvie, had to appeal to the minister of information to stop the unseemly squabbling: 'A disquieting practice has been growing up in the last few days, by which Departments of State, in making arrangements with our Talks Department for broadcast talks by their respective chiefs, seek to prescribe to our Talks Department the precise day and hour at which the talk is to be given.' He pointed out that there were still strong sabbatarian feelings in some sections of the audience, especially in Scotland and Wales, and that this made Sunday broadcasts especially sensitive. 'If the Army is to have a Sunday evening just because the Navy did,' he wrote, 'what about the Air Force and possibly other services? We should soon find our Sunday evenings exclusively devoted to military reviews ... I am quite confident that this would not be congenial to the bulk of listeners.'

This row within the government's own ranks was the harbinger of a wider dispute brewing at Westminster. Once it became apparent that the outbreak of war was not going to be followed by massive bombing raids and an overwhelming national emergency, party politics settled back into something like business as usual, and prominent figures on all sides began to argue about how much airtime they should have and when they should be able to broadcast.

In late November the senior Labour politician Herbert Morrison – whose grandson Peter Mandelson was to be such a legendary master of the art of media management – wrote to the chairman of the BBC governors to complain that he had been denied a Sunday slot and given one on Monday instead – only to find that Sunday had gone to the prime minister. This, he suggested, amounted to 'something in the nature of sharp practice'. He added a more general whinge. 'While I am writing, I may say that I feel that in the News also I have not been fairly treated,' he wrote, citing two of his speeches which had been ignored by the News Department while 'every opportunity is taken to broadcast the statements of leading political figures on the other side'. And he signed off with a sarcastic – and very unfair – swipe at Ogilvie and his team: 'I appreciate that if the BBC has become a mere Government organ and if you are subject to political censorship from above, it is not your fault, but if that be so I think it should be publicly stated so that all of us, including the House of Commons, should know where we are.'

The following day Sir Walter Citrine, the general secretary of the Trades Union Congress, weighed in in similar terms. He had been asked to give an evening talk, but instead of accepting the invitation he used it as an opportunity to complain about the fact that he had not been asked before. 'It appears to me as a slight on the Trade Union Movement that they have been neglected so long and that no attempt at contact has been made with them,' he declared, denouncing the offer of a slot as 'completely inadequate'. The BBC recognized that in the early days of the war it had – understandably, in the circumstances – given government ministers more airtime than it would usually have done, and it was anxious to correct the balance. But attempts to mollify Sir Walter seemed to be to no avail. 'The Trade Union Movement has been ignored,' he responded to the BBC's renewed invitation a few days later, 'and I do not feel prepared to accept an invitation to give one of these talks until I am satisfied that the Trade Union Movement is given its fair part to play in talks of such a national character ... there has been a lamentable omission on the part of the BBC.'

Hore-Belisha's determination to secure himself a Sunday slot became almost obsessive. He cast it as a matter of public interest: 'One's sole aim and desire in this matter are to give the public that information and determination which are so necessary for the conduct of this war,' he wrote to Ogilvie. But his endless 'racket' (as a BBC memo described it) was driving everyone to distraction. On 2 December the senior BBC mandarin Lindsay (later Sir Lindsay) Wellington circulated his views: 'My capacity for giving advice on the competitive antics of Mr Hore-Belisha is almost exhausted. In all seriousness I do not think I have anything fresh to suggest. In my view we should not merely resist, but should bluntly refuse to allow him to broadcast on Sunday, December 17th.' Even the home secretary thought his Cabinet colleague was being tiresome, urging the BBC to continue 'to refuse Sunday to Hore-Belisha and [saying] that this refusal would have the Prime Minister's blessing'.

The BBC tried to introduce some kind of system to stop the rows. It proposed that Sundays should be reserved for the prime minister, and that Wednesday evenings should alternate between government ministers and 'Opposition and other non-Government leaders'. Every other Saturday evening would also be reserved for politicians, 'four for members of the War Cabinet and two for the leaders of the Labour and Liberal Oppositions'. This prompted a furious response from the Labour leader, Clement Attlee. '[O]n matters of controversy,' he wrote to Ogilvie, 'the Opposition should have equal rights to the Government. We are the official opposition. We cannot admit the claim of the Liberal Party to an equality ... they are only a tenth of our numbers.' The Ministry of Information may have been doing its best to persuade the country to pull together, but the politicians clearly were not listening.

Churchill treated all this manoeuvring with complete insouciance. The first lord of the Admiralty apparently felt he should be able to ring down for a broadcasting slot rather as if he were ordering breakfast in a good hotel. A puzzled BBC memo between Christmas 1939 and the New Year recorded that 'One of Mr Churchill's secretaries telephoned to say that Mr Churchill would be glad to broadcast on January 13th or 14th ... the secretary couldn't say whether the invitation emanated from us or if the suggestion was the First Lord's own ...' Further investigation revealed that the proposed broadcast was entirely Churchill's idea and that the BBC had made no approach to him at all. To its credit the Corporation informed him that his desired slot was already booked and he would have to wait.

≈

The New Year brought little comfort for Professor Ogilvie. The propagandists of Department EH were on his case too, furious about the way the directives they issued from Woburn Abbey about broadcasts to Germany were, as they saw it, being ignored when they reached Broadcasting House. According to the official history of the Political Warfare Executive (as Department EH became), 'complaints against the BBC included unwillingness to cooperate evinced by delay in answering suggestions; unwillingness to carry out weekly directives; complete lack of direction of BBC bulletins and *Sonderberichte* [as EH rather pompously insisted on calling its special reports] as a whole; insufficient attention to BBC news bulletins: foolish items being included with downright inaccuracies on many occasions'. Ogilvie trooped out to Bedfordshire for a meeting in the Woburn Riding School 'in which EH criticisms were ventilated'.

But perhaps the oddest encounter the director-general had to endure during this period was a visit from his predecessor. John Reith was appointed to succeed Lord Macmillan as minister of information in the first week of 1940 and called on Ogilvie the following month. It was the first time he had stepped through the portals of Broadcasting House since his ill-tempered and lachrymose departure from the DG's office a year and a half earlier. Ogilvie took care to write up a detailed account of the meeting, which he began by presenting Reith with a copy of the 1940 *BBC Year Book,* 'inscribed with greetings and best wishes from the Old Firm'.

Reith was back on his past forceful form and proceeded to instruct his successor on how he should be running the shop. 'He said with great emphasis that, in his view,' Ogilvie recorded, 'nothing would be better calculated to raise the Morale of the Home Front ... than a daily series of talks at about 9.00 pm of a "heartening kind", hitting at Haw-Haw, telling cheering stories of bravery in the fighting services or at home, etc. He put it as a personal and urgent request from him to me that this should be done as soon as possible.' Reith – who is often regarded as the father and protector of the BBC's independence – then launched into what sounds very much like an argument for an outright government takeover of the Corporation. 'He said he had always felt that it would be simpler for the BBC to be taken over, and that this would make things easier for the BBC,' Ogilvie noted. As evidence, Reith cited the General Strike of 1926, saying that it would have been 'much easier at that time if the BBC had been taken over'. This surprised Ogilvie, as he – in common with most historians – had thought that the strike was 'an important turning point in broadcasting history, and that the BBC had then succeeded to some extent in reflecting not merely the government's point of view but the national issues at stake'.

Ogilvie stood his ground, and responded to the onslaught with what we might today call a restatement of Reithian values. 'Democracy was one of the issues at stake in this war,' he declared, 'and the BBC in its present setting could do much, and was doing much, to reflect freedom of opinion both to this country and the world.'

Reith left the meeting stating that he 'had only been exploring the position in a personal, not an official, way'. Ogilvie was sensible to have kept a minute, but as things turned out he need not have worried too much: within a matter of weeks the real war had begun, and Reith was to be one of its first casualties (professionally rather than physically), dumped by Churchill almost as soon as he moved into Downing Street.

SO MANY GOOD-BYES

CAPTAIN DAVID STRANGEWAYS, AN adjutant with the Duke of Wellington's regiment stationed near Lille, was woken early on the morning of 10 May 1940 by an orderly clerk shouting, 'David, sir, David.' He was about to give the man a bleary rebuke for this informal mode of address when he remembered that 'Operation David' was the code name for the army's planned response to a German offensive. The balloon had – as Charles Gardner might have put it – finally gone up.

The Coldstream Guards were apparently made of cooler stuff. Another young officer, James Langley, was woken that same morning by his servant, Guardsman Birks, with the words, 'Good morning, sir. Here is your tea. Your bath is ready. It is a fine morning. The Germans invaded France, Belgium and Holland at dawn. Major McCorquodale has cancelled today's training programme and there will be a meeting of all officers and platoon commanders at 8.15 in the company office.' He should have added Luxembourg to the list – no amount of *sangfroid* could obscure the fact that the way Hitler ended the Phoney War – with a quadruple invasion – was daring and dramatic.

'Considering that the Allies had been at war with Germany for over eight months,' writes the historian Andrew Roberts, 'it is astonishing that the *Wehrmacht* achieved such surprise as it unleashed *Blitzkrieg* in the West, especially as only a month earlier it had equally suddenly invaded Denmark and Norway.' And the Germans moved at a breathtaking speed. Within three weeks Lieutenant Langley would be fighting a desperate rearguard action to protect the evacuation of the British Expeditionary Force at Dunkirk.

The government in London was in the midst of a paralysing crisis. Two days earlier Chamberlain had narrowly survived a 'no confidence' vote in the House of Commons, called over the widespread dissatisfaction with the government's handling of the crisis in Norway. Faced with the cruel evidence that he had lost the support of many in his own party, the prime minister tried to put together a National Coalition, but Labour refused to support him and he realized he would have to go. The choice of his successor hung in the balance: would it be Lord Halifax, the arch-appeaser and Chamberlain's favourite, or the maverick warrior Winston Churchill? Eventually Halifax withdrew, partly because he did not believe he could command the support of Parliament from the House of Lords. At 5.00 p.m. on 10 May, Labour's agreement to join a coalition under Churchill came through in a phone call and he was summoned to Buckingham Palace. As he was being driven back to Downing Street after his audience with the king, his bodyguard, Inspector Thompson, congratulated him but warned, 'You have an enormous task ahead.' Churchill responded, 'God alone knows how great it is. I hope it is not too late. I am very much afraid that it is. We can only do our best.'

Charles Gardner was back on strike. In early May the RAF introduced a new set of censorship regulations to make life even more difficult for the press corps at AASF. They were banned from visiting aerodromes except during breaks in operations, and then only to collect background material, and were forbidden to interview pilots about operational matters. Gardner had recently acquired his own recording car, but he was now specifically prohibited from taking it to aerodromes (at any time, apparently) and could not record any kind of interview with a pilot without permission from the RAF's headquarters in France, which was nearly 100 miles from his base. All scripts also had to be submitted to HQ for censoring before they were recorded, which meant a round trip of some 200 miles and guaranteed that 'there was no earthly chance of getting the script back for the same night's News'.

Everyone downed tools – again with the support of their employers. This time, instead of playing golf, Gardner took advantage of the opportunity to spend some time with his wife, Eve, and their young son. In common with several correspondents attached to the AASF, he had flown them over from Britain earlier in the spring. He and a colleague rented a shared cottage for their families, where, in 'those last days of sunshine', they 'mowed the lawns … wore grey flannels, and did all the escapist things which men will do when they don't want to stop and think'. Faced with the prospect of enforced idleness while the strike was on, Gardner rented a flat in Versailles for a week's family holiday. They arrived on the morning of Friday, 10 May, just as the news of the German offensive came through.

The grumbles that had provoked the strike suddenly seemed trivial. Gardner returned to his duties immediately, leaving Eve metamorphosed from happy holidaymaker to 'a lonely and deserted wife in a strange foreign town'. He remembered waving goodbye from the street. 'An old French woman who was passing,' he recalled in his memoir, 'turned round and said in English, "Ah – there are so many good-byes being said today – so many. Good luck young man."'

By this stage Gardner had his own studio near the main AASF base in Reims. The engineers had constructed it on the top floor of an elegant house belonging to a French general, and its windows looked down over a large garden and a summer house. Gardner described the facilities in a letter to the *Radio Times*. 'We have,' he wrote, 'some nice pictures of French aeroplanes, a visitors' book, a map of the front, a bottle of ink, and some essentials like amplifiers, telephones, and batteries, which the engineers have grouped very neatly against one wall.' An RAF orderly had painted 'Silence, BBC on the Air' above one of the doorways, and 'We have even run to an outside warning light, so now all we want is a commissionaire outside and a daily memorandum from someone about the waste of paper-clips to make us think we are back in Portland Place.'

On 14 May he made a small piece of radio history at the studio. The German air raids were now close enough to hear, and during his broadcast that day 'an air raid started outside, and I was able to take the microphone to the window and let the listeners hear the crash of bombs'. That same evening he learned that the German advance had reached a point some 20 miles away, and on 15 May the AASF abandoned Reims altogether. Gardner had to leave his cosy little studio – with its now useless map of the front – behind. He managed to get Eve and their son on board a ship home from Le Havre, while he hooked up with the rest of the press corps in Paris.

Gardner was a very fine broadcaster – he had an ear for good sound, an opportunistic nose for a story and, like Dimbleby, a vivid, direct writing style. But his despatches from the front during the chaotic weeks of May 1940 reflected the world as he – and, of course, his listeners – wanted it to be, not the world as it actually was. And although it would be quite wrong to suggest that he lied or deliberately exaggerated, a comparison between his despatches and the diary he kept in the run-up to the fall of France shows quite clearly that he was not reporting what he actually saw and felt.

On 22 May, for example, he found himself mooching around Paris with the rest of the boys from the AASF press corps. 'After everybody's been hanging about this town, getting depressed-er and depressed-er,' his entry for the day begins, 'we have at last found out where the remains of the AASF have beaten it to. As I write this, the place is so secret that I can't even put it down here.' Realizing that there might be no communications or living quarters at the new base (it was Troyes, south of Reims), the group agreed a rota system for collecting material. 'In the meantime,' Gardner wrote, clearly in very black spirits, 'Major Barrett Wilson has been making enquiries about the number of war correspondents who are flowing about the streets looking dismal, and has put out a suggestion that in future we should go around with bright smiling faces.'

Gardner records that what he called 'this smiling face order' was passed on to the press corps 'just as we buy a paper and read that there's fighting in Cambrai. We were all sitting in the Colisée at the time, and how we roared with laughter! When we hear that Paris is taken, doubtless we'll have hysterics . . .' Later that same day he added, 'Cambrai has fallen. Excuse me while I have a good laugh.' And the more he and his colleagues discovered, the bleaker their collective mood became: 'We gather that the evacuation of Reims was unbelievably chaotic. Even the efficient gunners had to leave their guns behind (having first removed the breech blocks).' He went on, 'No one knows how long the AASF is going to stay put. Everyone is under six hours' notice to get out. The aerodromes are established, but only just – and anyway we've precious few aircraft to put on them. I'll never forget Hurst [a colleague] walking about an empty Reims Champagne on the first day of that Sedan break-through, saying "bomb the b——s, bomb the b——s, but for Christ sake, what with?"'

But Gardner's BBC despatch that day told the story rather differently:

> For the last two days the extension of the German advance has been throwing more and more work on the bombers of the Royal Air Force, but both the machines from home and from the Advanced Air Striking Force have been flying and attacking almost incessantly. To give you one example, a squadron leader in one of the units has been up practically the whole time since the start of the invasion. He has led raid after raid after raid after raid – and he has done it so well that in all that time his squadron has lost only three machines.

You could, at a push, argue that that passage is consistent with the cry of despair at the end of the diary entry I have quoted above, but the relentlessly upbeat tone continues:

> Our fighter squadrons are carrying on their almost incredibly good work. A pilot from a squadron which is now famous throughout the whole of the Air Force in France, and which – if we could have revealed its number – would have been famous now throughout the world, has not long ago been given his DFC [Distinguished Flying Cross] – the second in his unit. Well, he's just reappeared after being shot down. He bailed out at 500 feet – and he was lucky, because his parachute opened in time, and though he did drop heavily, he got away with an injured shoulder.

That last sentence definitely crossed the line. Flying Officer Orton was also badly burned before bailing out (a fact we know Gardner was well aware of, since it is recorded in his diary). And so the positive spin continued, despatch after despatch, as the defence of France crumbled and the British Expeditionary Force was bottled up around the Channel port of Dunkirk.

Getting to Troyes became increasingly dangerous and unproductive, and communications closed down so completely that Gardner could only get his despatches to London from Paris by cabling the copy via New York. He decided to 'clear out and get to London', having first packed the recording car and its engineers on to a Bristol Bombay from Le Bourget airport. In one of his last despatches, Gardner told the audience, '[I]n the past few weeks you have heard and read many stories from here of the work of our fighter squadrons in France. In various despatches we have described fights and incidents, which may not have been, of themselves, of paramount importance – but all the same, it was these incidents which added up – all together – into the superiority, man for man, and machine for machine, which the Royal Air Force has established.'

Even if it had been incontestably true that the RAF could more than match the Luftwaffe 'man for man, machine for machine', it was, as Gardner well knew, by this stage almost beside the point. The Allies were hopelessly outgunned in the air over France. Just before he left Paris, Gardner bumped into a Hurricane pilot he knew well, who was on a day's leave; 'he told me that earlier on in the week they'd all been flying half-asleep, and had had to keep their eyes open with their hands,' Gardner wrote in his diary, 'so exhausted were they by dawn-to-dusk fighting odds at ten, twenty, and even fifty to one.' Not a hint of that was passed on to the audience.

Charles Gardner reproduced both his diary and his despatches in a short memoir, called simply *A.A.S.F.* He makes no apology for the disparity between the stories he reported to his listeners and the reality he recorded privately, and why should he? He was a patriot, and he had been broadcasting at a time when his country was, in his words, 'facing the most disastrous loss in its history, and was badly shaken'. When the book was published – later in 1940 – the threat of invasion still hung in the air.

≈

The press corps with the British Expeditionary Force fared no better than their colleagues with the AASF. They were swept away from the front with the retreating British forces, never got a sniff of the action and quickly lost all sense of what was happening around them. The *Mirror*'s man, Bernard Gray, recalled that on 20 May he found himself at a loose end in Boulogne with a colleague from the *Manchester Guardian* and Kim Philby, later notorious as a Soviet spy, but at the time a correspondent for *The Times*. They suggested to their liaison officer that they should be allowed to go to Le Touquet for a game of golf. 'Le Touquet?' said the officer in charge. 'Of course, old boy. Delighted for you to go, normally. But it's a bit difficult at the moment you know. The Germans are there.'

Bernard Stubbs, who had replaced Richard Dimbleby as the BBC's man with the BEF in France, slipped home from Boulogne a few days before the Dunkirk evacuation. He brought with him a 'BEF News Bulletin', which had been given to him by the army's General Headquarters (GHQ) in France. Stubbs read it on the air from London on the Forces Programme on 22 May, and it is worth quoting at some length because it is the nearest the BBC came to painting a true picture of what was happening in France:

> There is no pause, no breathing space. It would be impossible, even if it were prudent, to give any definite statement as to the actual position. There is no actual position, no definite front line. This war is not like the last. It must not be pictured in terms of the last war. This battle is not being fought at the pace of the infantryman marching his three miles an hour, but at the pace of the fastest moving vehicle that man's ingenuity can devise. Today there is no fixed line. There is not even a single front. There are a dozen isolated fronts. A dozen different battles are being fought. Rumour follows upon rumour. Frequently Germans are reported to have been seen in a town thought to be many miles behind our lines. But the presence of one mechanised unit in such a village does not mean that the German line of attack runs through it. Far from it. There is no fixed line ... This is open warfare. These advanced units are cavalry patrols. That and no more than that. As often as not they are lost patrols.

It is impossible to draft any fixed position. There is no fixed position; there is no fixed line.

By night and day, ceaselessly, relentlessly, with unabated energy, with unabated courage, the Allied forces are hitting back against their enemy. The situation is serious still, but it is not desperate. We are in the field, and we are hitting hard, blow for blow, and bomb for bomb.

This surprisingly frank assessment was an aberration, and the Ministry of Information instituted an investigation to find out how it had come to be authorized. In a note six days later the BBC reassured the Ministry that 'In the event of a bulletin suddenly being sent to us it will not be radiated until it has been cleared by your official.' A Ministry official has added a handwritten note: 'There seems to be every possibility of G.H.Q. bulletins conflicting with War Office and M of D [Ministry of Defence] bulletins.' It did not happen again.

The departure from France of Stubbs, Gardner and their colleagues meant that there was almost no first-hand reporting of the evacuation of Dunkirk, one of the biggest stories of the war. One British freelance journalist – the writer David Divine – succeeded in crossing to France three times on a 35-foot boat that was rescuing British soldiers, and Charles Martin of Pathé was taken over by the navy with his camera, but that was it – the BBC had to rely almost entirely on what they were told by official sources.

Many at the time would no doubt have argued that this was a very good thing. It obviously made sense to keep the Germans guessing about what was up for as long as possible. There was also good reason for being less than frank with the French, even though they were our allies; their priority was, not unnaturally, the defence of French territory, not escaping across the Channel. The case for keeping the British people in the dark would be more difficult to make, but of course in the world's first radio war you could not tell your audience at home the truth without it reaching the enemy too. The way the Dunkirk evacuation was kept secret until the actual operation was almost over is really remarkable. The full picture of what happened remained undisclosed for even longer, buried beneath the Dunkirk myth which quickly took hold.

The navy began sending ships over to Dunkirk on the afternoon of 26 May, a Sunday, and Operation Dynamo, as it was officially known, formally began just before 7.00 that evening, with an Admiralty order to Admiral Ramsay, who was to run things from Dover. The order shows just how pessimistic the Admiralty was about what could be achieved: '. . . it is imperative for "Dynamo" to be implemented with the greatest vigour, with a view to lifting up to 45,000 of the British Expeditionary Force within two days, at the end of which it is probable that evacuation will be terminated by enemy action'.

By the time that deadline was up, the operation was, as things turned out, still in full swing, and there had been no mention of it at all on the radio or in the press. The BBC's bulletins on the 28th were preoccupied with King Leopold of Belgium's decision to surrender, which was being widely condemned in both Britain and France as an act of betrayal. The 6.00 p.m. bulletin reported that morning's French War Communiqué, which said, 'The military situation has become graver in a manner unexpected in the north, as a result of the capitulation of the King of the Belgians, whose army was engaged at the side of the French and the British. The latter are facing up to the situation and continuing to fight. On the rest of the front there is nothing important to report.'

The reality covered by 'nothing important to report' included a ferocious German air assault on Dunkirk and its civilians, which is vividly described in Nicholas Harman's influential work *Dunkirk: The Necessary Myth*:

> The German air force had blocked the port. Now, on the second day of the British Evacuation, they smashed the town behind it. Two thousand tons of high-explosive bombs threw buildings into the streets and ripped open the roofs of houses. Into the rubble dropped thirty thousand incendiary bombs, little flaming horrors weighing just one kilogramme each, designed to lodge in the rafters and set a fire where the inhabitants could not quench it. The water mains had burst the previous day. There was nothing

the fire brigade could do. On this day died one thousand of the three thousand civilians killed during the evacuation of this miserable city ...There was nobody to bury the dead ...

The air raids also took a terrible toll on the nerves of the British troops waiting their turn to embark on navy ships. A lieutenant in the Royal Horse Artillery described the scene in a cellar where he and a group of men had taken shelter: 'By four in the afternoon our nerves were becoming a little frayed. One of the NCOs (wearing last war ribbons) was crying quietly in the corner and several men began to make queer little animal noises – rather like homesick dogs. This was understandable because, as the raids repeated, they seemed to have a kind of cumulative effect on one's system; after a while the mere thought of a raid was worse than its reality.'

There was, needless to say, no mention of any of this in BBC bulletins, and while the civilians and soldiers wilted under the onslaught from above neither the name 'Dunkirk' nor the word 'evacuation' had been used on the air. On 29 May the BBC reported only that 'It was learnt in London today that the BEF has withdrawn some miles towards the coast', but added that its 'exact whereabouts cannot be stated at the moment.' The 9.00 p.m. bulletin added the stirring news that the king had sent a message of encouragement to Lord Gort, the commander-in-chief of British forces in France, and the broadcast included the following truly amazing statements: 'The Allied forces have not lost cohesion, and their morale is high. The French military spokesman said this morning that Dunkirk was not in immediate danger ...' There was a mention of the air war, but not in terms that anyone engaged in the desperate battle would have recognized: 'Bombers of the Royal Air Force continue to give our troops all the support in their power; this evening a formation of fighters shot down 22 enemy aircraft without loss to themselves.'

By this stage the French were beginning to understand what their British allies were up to. The first suggestion that the BEF might come home appears in a telegram from Anthony Eden, the secretary of state for war, to General Lord Gort, on 25 May. It implied that the matter would be discussed at a meeting between Churchill and his

French counterpart, Paul Reynaud, the following day, and instructed Gort: 'In the meantime it is obvious that you should not discuss the possibility of the move with the French or Belgians.'

On 27 May, with the evacuation already well under way, Eden sent Gort an absolutely clear instruction: 'Your sole task now is to evacuate to England maximum of your force possible.' Yet when, a day later, Gort showed the order to the French General Blanchard – who, under the agreement between France and Britain, was technically his superior – the Frenchman was 'horrified'; Blanchard, it seems, still had not given up on the idea of defending Dunkirk and then counter-attacking, and he had heard nothing from the French government to make him think differently. It is not clear whether this confusion arose because the British government deliberately deceived Paris or because the correct position got lost on the French side in the 'fog of war', but it caused terrible tension between the Allies for the remainder of the operation and contributed mightily to the belief that 'perfidious Albion' betrayed France in her hour of need. The stories that later circulated – some of them true – of British soldiers pushing their French brothers-in-arms into the sea as they struggled aboard ships did not help.

At a meeting of the War Cabinet late on the evening of 28 May, Alfred Duff Cooper, whom Churchill had appointed to replace John Reith as minister of information, raised concerns about the impact the news from France might have when it eventually became widely known. The Cabinet minutes record that he 'suggested that the public should be given some indication of the serious position in which the BEF had been placed', adding that 'There was no doubt that the public were, at the moment, quite unprepared for the shock of realisation of the true position.' Churchill demurred, replying that 'the seriousness of the situation should be emphasised, but he would deprecate any detailed statement or attempt to assess the results of the battle, until the situation had been further cleared up.'

So even in London, at the heart of government, the full truth about what was happening remained an amazingly successfully guarded secret. Harold Nicolson had been given a junior ministerial position at the Ministry of Information when Duff Cooper was appointed, so being 'in the know' was part of his job. But twenty-four hours after that meeting of the War Cabinet he confided to his diary: 'We are creating a Corunna Line [a reference to the Peninsular War against Napoleon] around Dunkirk and hope to evacuate a few of our troops.' By this stage a third of the British troops in France had already been brought home.

The sharp-eared may have picked up on the hint of official nervousness about the peril Britain was facing in an item at the end of the news bulletin that night: 'New regulations for the control of all aliens in this country over sixteen were announced today by the Home Secretary. From Monday next, June 3rd, no alien may have or control a bicycle, motor vehicle, sea-going craft or aircraft, without police permission. No alien may be absent from his residence during night hours without a police permit.'

The following day, 30 May, the BBC at last used the word 'evacuated' for the first time. Listeners were told that there was 'a battle now raging' near the French coast, and that 'The troops not immediately engaged have been evacuated with the assistance of the Royal Navy.' Then the spin began. The pencilled additions and crossings-out on the BBC news scripts provide the odd intriguing hint of the way the censorship process was working, but there is no particular reason to think that there was a great divide between the views of Auntie's men and the men from the Ministry. Everyone was reeling from the enormity of Britain's defeat, and searching desperately for explanations.

The lack of a really clear 'line' is reflected in uncertainty about whether to portray the Germans as ruthless killers or bone-headed incompetents. One bulletin reported that returning British soldiers 'bitterly condemned the German airmen for machine-gunning civilians and bombing hospitals', but later included a story to illustrate the 'blind obedience of the German soldiers and their lack of ability to think for themselves'. While the French still held the town of Rethel (near Reims), the BBC newsreader intoned, '[A] German policeman suddenly arrived on a motor-bicycle armed with a white baton, gloves and a guide book. He said that he had come to direct the traffic there, but instead found himself a prisoner.'

British troops, by contrast, were praised for their 'valour' at every opportunity, and every straw of comfort was clutched. 'Another striking fact,' declared the BBC, 'and another blow to German propaganda, is that this evacuation is proving once again the importance of sea power. The Germans, with not much of their navy left, proclaim that sea power is useless and that air power has taken its place. Nevertheless, the German airforce has been unable to prevent the re-embarkation of our troops ...'

A recurrent theme of the bulletins was that the good discipline and orderly behaviour of British soldiers was all the more remarkable because of the very testing circumstances of their withdrawal. On 31 May the BBC reported: 'The Germans have claimed on more than one occasion that, in the face of their pressure, the British army was fleeing from them in disorder. This is, of course, a fantastic libel. The fact is that there is no military operation so difficult as a retreat, and that re-embarkation at the end of a retreat requires more skill, more courage and more discipline than anything else in war. When it is remembered that all this is being done by our men, for the most part on open beaches, without any possibility of concealment, it is perfectly obvious that there could have been no disorder and certainly no question of the BEF running away from its enemies.' After the words '... is being done' someone (presumably the censor) has added the pencilled parenthesis 'and done successfully'.

When this bulletin went out, Lieutenant Langley, the Coldstream Guards officer who was so politely informed of the German offensive by his batman on the morning of 10 May, was fighting a rearguard action so desperate that his commanding officer had begun threatening to shoot his own officers and men. On Sunday, 1 June, a captain from a company to his right in the line informed Langley and his superior, Major Angus McCorquodale, that he was planning to retreat. Langley recalled, 'Angus merely said "I order you to stay put and fight it out ... You see that big poplar tree on the road with a white mile stone beside it? The moment you or any of your men go back beyond that tree we will shoot you."' Langley's account of what then happened is chilling – and jars horribly with the picture the BBC was painting for those at home. Major McCorquodale told him to find a rifle and prepare to shoot to kill. 'We had not long to wait before the captain appeared,' Langley goes on, 'followed by two men. They stood for a long time by the tree and then the captain walked on. Both our rifles went off simultaneously: he dropped out of sight and the two men ran back.' Lieutenant Langley had a portable radio with him, and in his autobiography he records the merriment of the front-line troops when they tuned in to the BBC and heard a report that was entirely at odds with what they knew to be true. Langley was badly wounded – he lost an arm – and taken prisoner (he later escaped and became a significant figure in MI9, the intelligence unit formed to help Allied escapees get out of Europe).

Thanks to the extraordinary courage of men like Langley (and many of his French brothers-in-arms), Operation Dynamo did achieve an astonishing result. Some 220,000 British troops and more than 110,000 French troops escaped to Britain. But Langley was not alone in worrying about the way the story was presented by the BBC. A much more senior officer, Admiral Ramsay, who had commanded Operation Dynamo, included in his final report a damning observation about the reporting of the air war over Dunkirk: 'The formations of our own fighters when operating over the area were so outnumbered that it was no surprise to the observer to note that more British machines were shot down than were enemy, and feelings of disgust were engendered on listening to the BBC report of the same evening, which recounted the opposite story.' As Nicholas Harman notes in *Dunkirk: the Necessary Myth*, 'The men in the front line could recognise a falsehood when they heard one.'

Harman's book was published in 1980, four decades after the great drama on the beaches of Dunkirk, and in his introduction he writes that he had 'expected – perhaps naively – that it would retell in modern form the uplifting story on which I was reared', only to find that 'as I proceeded the simple truths began to slide away'. His book became an attempt to demythologize the myth. But his subtitle – the *The Necessary Myth* – is important. 'It was, of course,' he writes, 'the wish and duty of the press to support the government and the soldiers in their fight against an enemy whose evil could hardly be doubted.' Those working on the BBC news bulletins certainly felt that too, as did those, like Gardner, who had been embedded with the services.

Towards the end of his book Harman concludes, 'The harsh

reality of defeat, the confusion and squalor of the beaches and the harbour, were immediately transmuted for public opinion at home and abroad into an episode of glory.' The BBC was absolutely central to that metamorphosis, and it was achieved with the help of two of the greatest broadcasters in history.

And in the summer of 1940, no one had any time for seminars on media ethics.

A BETTER MARGATE

T HE OPENING OF *The Good Companions*, the novel that made J. B. Priestley rich and famous, could not have been written before the age of manned flight and cinema. The reader is plucked up and made to hover high above the 'knobbly backbone of England, the Pennine range'. A long, swooping pan (which lasts some two and a half pages) takes him down past 'These windy moors, those clanging dark valleys, these factories and little stone houses' to the town of Bruddersfield, a fictional version of the Bradford Priestley came to know as a child in the 1890s. We eventually alight amid a 'tide of cloth caps', thousands of men and boys who have 'just seen what many of them call "t'United" play Bolton Wanderers'. And we are immediately in a very particular pre-war English environment.

The two men whose voices carried Britain through the desperate summer of 1940 came from utterly different worlds. Winston Churchill was born in the ducal palace of Blenheim and bore one of Britain's noblest names. Priestley entered the world in a terrace of two-up, two-down workers' cottages, the son of a schoolmaster. His mother – who died when he was two – came from what he described as 'the clogs and shawls back o' t'mill working class'. Today history heaps ever greater honours on Churchill's head, while Priestley's reputation is (the occasional revival of his play *An Inspector Calls* notwithstanding) much diminished. Yet at the time of Dunkirk, Priestley was probably as well known as Churchill, and certainly the better loved of the two.

The Good Companions came out in the summer of 1929, and by Christmas that year the publishers were shipping 5,000 copies a day out of their warehouse to keep the shelves stocked. His 'giant jackpot, this gold gusher, this genie out of the bottle' propelled him to the status of national treasure, which he enjoyed throughout the 1930s. Churchill, by contrast, was much distrusted when he became prime minister, especially by members of his own tribe. 'Although he was an aristocrat by birth,' wrote the historian Sir David Cannadine, 'Churchill was widely believed to be not really a gentleman at all. On the contrary, he was often described as a highly gifted, but undeniable, cad.'

But both men were patriots, and one of the miracles of that summer was the way they articulated a similar sense of what that meant in 1940, even though they came − originally at least − from different sides of Haw-Haw's divide between 'the upper nation of the Mayfair type of snob' and the 'lower nation whom it robs'.

Priestley learned his love of country the hard way − in the trenches. He joined up in September 1914, just over a month after the beginning of the First World War, and was sent to France a year later. He was wounded within a few weeks of going up into the line (a rifle grenade dropped in his dugout, killing one man and wounding four), but was soon back on duty as a fighting soldier. In June 1916 he was buried alive by a trench mortar; when he was dug out he was partly deaf and began to run a high fever, and this time his condition was sufficiently serious for him to be sent back home to convalesce. On his release from hospital he applied for a commission, and returned to France in 1918 as an officer − only to be gassed in the last weeks of war and shipped home again. Unsurprisingly, all this had a profound effect on him. 'I seem to know intimately more dead men than living ones,' he wrote later. 'To think about an old playing field is to see a crowd of ghosts.'

But he was blessed with optimism and, as that magnificent overture to *The Good Companions* suggests, he had a keen sense of modernity, which included an early appreciation of the importance of radio, 'the staggering power and effect of broadcasting', as he called it. In 1940, when his radio fame was at its height, he claimed a place as a

J. B. Priestley, a prophet of 'the staggering power and effect of broadcasting', at the microphone.

prophet of the medium. 'I have been hard at it getting through to the public mind,' he wrote, 'in one way and another, for about twenty years, but as a method of communication this broadcasting makes everything else seem like the method of a secret society. So long as you don't go on too long and the listeners are not tired of you, a mere whisper over the air seems to start an avalanche.' And he added – offering a glimpse of his pricklier side – 'Unfortunately the only people who do not seem aware of this terrific power of the broadcast word are the War Cabinet, who still do not realise that in the BBC we have something as important to us in this war, which is quite unlike previous wars, as an army or navy or air force.'

There is certainly evidence that he spotted the threat posed by Nazi broadcasting earlier than most. He was a compulsive traveller, frequently taking trips around the country and relying heavily on what he found for his journalism – one of his best-known non-fiction books, *English Journey*, is subtitled 'a rambling but truthful account of what one man saw and heard and felt and thought during a journey through England during the autumn of the year 1933'. He undertook one of these national pulse-finding peregrinations during the Phoney War autumn of 1939, and afterwards reported in the *News Chronicle* that 'At least three persons out of four I have spoken to during these last few weeks have been influenced by Nazi propaganda.' The Nazis had, he argued – accurately, as we have seen – 'several years ago' set out to persuade the world to accept their 'dangerous half- and quarter-truths as whole truths'. And he accused British officialdom of a lack of real commitment to the whole area of propaganda and morale: 'our persons in authority may assent to the statement that this is a war in which public morale is all important, may readily agree that our own people must be heartened and neutrals kept well-informed and friendly, but … in their heart of hearts they do not believe these things.' And, like so many others, he took a pop at the Ministry of Information. 'Its chief fault,' he declared, 'is that most of the people at the top are organisers, who know how to run a department but do not know much about the public mind, whereas the men in control ought to have been persons who understood what they were trying to serve. What is wanted in that Ministry is a little less Lincoln's Inn Fields and a little more Gracie Fields.'

The BBC's *Postscripts*, which were to make Priestley even more famous as a broadcaster than he already was as a novelist, were introduced to meet the Haw-Haw challenge. These short talks – around ten minutes long – were scheduled immediately after the news on Sunday evenings – a prime slot, and Haw-Haw's Sunday-evening shows were pulling in huge audiences. The early *Postscripts* were given by a witty Irish lawyer and writer called Maurice Healy, and Priestley took over in the aftermath of Dunkirk. Quite whose idea it was is not clear. Priestley's second wife, Jane, claimed it as her own; she wrote that she persuaded him to 'go to the BBC, who were very glad to give him a programme'. He later said simply, 'I had gone to the BBC and said I would like to do some broadcasting. I had often done broadcasting in the Savoy Hill days' – a reference to the BBC's home before Broadcasting House. However it came about, it was an inspired piece of casting. Priestley's life and career had equipped him particularly – perhaps uniquely – well to play the role of 'one ordinary Englishman talking to other ordinary Englishmen'. His war record, his northern roots – still discernible in a gentle Yorkshire accent – his instinct for the public mood and his seriousness about the propaganda war are all reflected in the genius of these radio gems. Even his penchant for sentimentality – which some literary critics identified as a flaw in books like *The Good Companions* – was put to good effect at a time of heightened national emotion.

His first *Postscript*, which remains one of the best known, was, as he put it, 'a testing sample', and was broadcast not on a Sunday, but on Wednesday, 5 June, in the immediate aftermath of the Dunkirk evacuation. It is a piece of alchemy; within days of the terrible disaster of defeat, Priestley has already begun the rewriting of history. 'What strikes me about it [Dunkirk],' he told his audience, 'is how typically English it is. Nothing, I feel, could be more English than this Battle of Dunkirk, both in its beginning and in its end, its folly and its grandeur.' He concedes that Britain's failure in France was a 'blunder', but that is dealt with in just a few lines, and he picks up like this: 'let's do ourselves the justice of admitting that this Dunkirk affair was also very English (and when I say English I really mean British) in the way in which, when apparently all was lost, so much was gloriously retrieved. Bright honour was almost "plucked from the moon". What began as a miserable blunder, a catalogue of misfortunes and miscalculations, ended as an epic of gallantry. We have a queer habit – and you can see it running through our history – of conjuring up such transformations. Out of a black gulf of humiliation and despair, rises a sun of blazing glory.' There, in a few short sentences, is the Dunkirk myth made concrete. Priestley articulated what millions of people up and down Britain desperately hoped was the true interpretation of the Dunkirk debacle. And he added for good measure, 'This is not the German way.'

In 1933, flush with the royalties from *The Good Companions*, Priestley had bought Billingham, a manor house on the Isle of Wight – complete with ghosts, a secret passage and a butler. So he was familiar with the paddle-steamers that plied their trade along the south coast. Many of these were among the flotilla of civilian boats and ships that helped to evacuate the British Expeditionary Force from Dunkirk, and Priestley squeezed them for every drop of sentiment, making them the heroes of his broadcast. He hovered close to downright hamminess, but stayed the right side of the line by acknowledging how near he came to overdoing it. '[T]here was always something old fashioned, a Dickens touch, a mid-Victorian air, about them [the steamers],' he said. 'They seemed to belong to the same ridiculous holiday world as pierrots and piers, sand castles, ham-and-egg teas, palmists, automatic machines and crowded sweating promenades. But they were called out of that world – and, let it be noted they were called out in good time and good order. Yes, these "Brighton Belles" and "Brighton Queens" left that innocent foolish world of theirs – to sail into the inferno, to defy bombs, shells, magnetic mines, torpedoes, machine-gun fire – to rescue our soldiers.'

It was six months since Priestley had complained that the Ministry of Information required 'a little less Lincoln's Inn Fields and a little more Gracie Fields', and he must have enjoyed his private joke at the end of his Dunkirk broadcast: 'Among the paddle steamers that will never return was one that I knew well, for it was the pride of our ferry service to the Isle of Wight – none other than the good ship "Gracie Fields". I tell you, we were proud of "Gracie Fields", for she was the glittering queen of our local line, and instead of taking an hour over her voyage, used to do it, churning like mad, in forty-five minutes. And now never again will we board her at Cowes and go down into her dining saloon for a fine breakfast of bacon and eggs. She has paddled and churned away – for ever. But now – look – this little steamer, like all her brave and battered sisters, is immortal. She'll go sailing proudly down the years in the epic of Dunkirk. And our great-grand-children, when they learn how we began this War by snatching glory out of defeat, then swept on to victory, may also learn how the little holiday steamers made an excursion to hell and came back glorious.'

It was prophetic stuff – both in its tone and in the sense that his prediction has turned out to be true. Priestley knew very quickly that his 'testing sample' had been a success. As he made his way out of Broadcasting House after the programme he bumped into a 'very prominent broadcaster' and noticed that the man 'was weeping'.

The *Postscripts* that followed in June and July are little short of sublime. Priestley enjoyed the fruits of his financial success, and the grittiness of his Bruddersfield background had been tempered by the Arcadian pleasures of rural English life at Billingham. 'I don't think there has ever been a lovelier English spring than this last one, now melting into full summer,' he told his audience on 9 June. 'Sometimes, in between listening to the latest news of battle and destruction, or trying to write about them myself, I've gone out and stared at the red japonica or almond blossom, so clear and exquisite against the moss-stained old wall – and have hardly been able to believe my eyes; I've just gaped and gaped like a bumpkin at a fair through all these weeks of spring.'

The following weekend found him on look-out duty with a group of Local Defence Volunteers – 'a parson, a bailiff, a builder, farmers and farm labourers ... a hurdlemaker ... together with a woodman and a shepherd' – and he reported that they were united in a spirit of *Dad's Army* defiance: 'As we talked on our post on the hilltop, we watched the dusk deepen in the valleys below, where our women-folk listened to the news as they knitted at the hearth, and we remembered that these were our homes and that now at any time they might be blazing ruins, and that half-crazed German youths, in whose empty eyes the idea of honour and glory seems to include every form of beastliness, might soon be let loose down there.' With their unabashed patriotism and clever 'tying up of the big war theme to the small, homely things', the *Postscripts* drew vast audiences; between 30 and 40 per cent of the adult population tuned in to hear Priestley every week.

It is, of course, very difficult to say how much difference Priestley's broadcasts made to the military equation in 1940; morale cannot be as easily measured as Spitfire production or bomb casualties. But Graham Greene gave his fellow author a place above all Britain's military leaders and most of its politicians. Priestley, he declared, 'became in the months after Dunkirk a leader second only in importance to Mr. Churchill. And he gave us what our other leaders have always failed to give us – an ideology.' Greene had no particular reason to like the great postscripter; Priestley had taken him to court over what he argued was a defamatory portrait of himself in Greene's novel *Stamboul Train*.

That 'ideology' would later get Priestley into trouble with the Churchill government, for Priestley was determinedly, indeed sometimes radically, left-wing. But in the summer of 1940 the need

Listening to the wireless ... in pubs ...

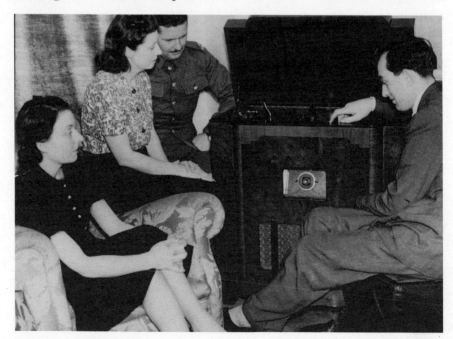

in homes ...

in the field . . .

even across the garden wall.

for national unity trumped everything. Churchill's War Cabinet included five Labour ministers, and Priestley celebrated the cross-party spirit in a characteristically oblique fashion in his broadcast of 7 July. He had been in the Commons to watch Churchill take questions, and reported a 'tiny thing' that had 'heartened and inspired him'. When the prime minister passed the senior Labour Party minister Ernest Bevin, he gave him 'a little dig in the ribs'. As he did so, Priestley said, 'there flashed across his face, a sudden boyish, mischievous, devil-may-care grin. And I said to myself "these are the men for us"... Mr Churchill, a man in his sixties who has driven himself as hard as he could since Omdurman, who has held high office for more than thirty years, and upon whose shoulders now rests perhaps the fate of Europe for centuries, could in this grave hour to which he has done full justice in his private decision and his public utterances, let slip that wonderful, lightning grin which was like a miraculous glimpse of the inner man who, like so many formidable men, is still a boy at heart, still full of devilment.' He ended this *Postscript* by quoting Shakespeare's Henry V: 'The game's afoot;/Follow your spirit; and upon this charge/Cry: God for Harry, England and Saint George!'

The following month the BBC asked Priestley to contribute to a document providing 'Hints to Broadcast Speakers' which the Corporation proposed to circulate to the widening circle of wartime on-air contributors. The idea had been suggested by Priestley himself, and he took some care over the task. When he sent in his thoughts he noted that 'I have no copy of these remarks of mine, so leave them in your tender care.' It is fortunate that they have been preserved in the BBC's Written Archives at Caversham; they have survived the test of time admirably, and I would commend them to anyone running a broadcasting training course today.

Priestley understood the intimacy of radio broadcasting. 'As you are addressing individuals or, at the most, small groups,' he wrote, 'platform effects and please-give-me-your-applause tricks are worse than useless. Rather careful conversation will be, for most speakers, the mark at which to aim.' He also understood that addressing an audience at home was quite different from orating at a public meeting and, remarkably for an author of his generation, he had a sure instinct for the spoken, as opposed to the written, word. 'The writing should be as simple and direct as possible,' he advised, 'and except when the speaker is aiming deliberately at a special effect, long sentences, with many relative clauses, and elaborate syntax generally, should be avoided.' The informality of this spoken medium dictated a different stylistic discipline. 'In the early days of broadcasting, when too much stress was laid in the studio on the fact that coughs, etc. would be heard by millions, it was difficult to relax at the microphone,' Priestley wrote, 'but now it is realised that ease is all important. Little accidents – a cough, a slip, etc. – don't worry audiences half as much as a strained manner does. The trick of successfully converting a script into effective radio speech depends chiefly on variety of pace.' There was a great deal of artifice – craft skills, if you like – behind Priestley's apparently artless broadcasts.

Priestley also understood the way radio – much more than television – can so mercilessly reveal the personality of those who attempt it: 'The microphone immensely magnifies insincerity or the least suggestion of condescension. Therefore the speaker should try to say what he really thinks and feels, and also give the impression that he is earnestly addressing his equals rather than affably condescending to his inferiors.' Above all, he appreciated the democratic character of the medium. He warned that 'Pompous openings, in the manner of many after-dinner speakers, should be avoided, for there is a pleasure in turning a knob and thereby extinguishing some apparently self-important personage.' This clear-eyed recognition of punter-power was written less than three months after Churchill told the War Cabinet that it would be best to keep the public in the dark about the reality of Dunkirk.

The list of 'hints' the BBC produced drew heavily on Priestley's note. It began with the observation that 'anyone with previous experience of writing or public speaking has much to unlearn before he can achieve success at the microphone.' Its list of dos and don'ts includes the following:

– avoid foreign words and inversions

– use transitive rather than intransitive verbs

127

– use direct rather than indirect constructions

– use active rather than passive words

– use short rather than long sentences

– use concrete rather than abstract nouns

One of my earliest jobs in television was what was known as 'chief subbing' – turning the material producers wrote to introduce their films and reports into something the newscaster could read without getting horribly tangled. It would have been very much easier if the production team had all read and absorbed these simple guidelines.

≈

The BBC document quoted above makes the very Priestleyesque point that, 'As the typical listener is the individual at his own fireside, the standard style of broadcast speech must be the colloquial form of speech in which one man talks to another in his home.' But it adds an important qualification: a recognition that there was one broadcaster who matched Priestley's popularity that summer, and did it by breaking all the rules. 'Some broadcasters,' the BBC guide continues, 'employ the rhetorical style and the grand manner. In this case the radio audience is envisaged, not as separate individuals, but as members of a community, and the speaker claims the right and authority to address them as such. When this claim is accepted by the radio audience, and the speaker has the necessary qualities, this form may be very effective, but it is an extremely difficult one for most speakers. The present Prime Minister is a notable exponent of this style, but those who lack his instinct in turning a phrase would be well advised not to follow him along this dangerous path.'

Evelyn Waugh was as rude about Churchill's broadcasting as his fellow Catholic novelist Graham Greene was admiring about Priestley's. In characteristically contrarian style, Waugh dismissed the prime minister as 'simply a "Radio Personality"'. But the barb was well wide of the mark. Churchill was absolutely not a 'radio personality' in the way Priestley was; he made no concessions at all – certainly in the early days – to the particular demands of the medium and, although he came to appreciate its power, he never fell in love with the microphone in the way that Priestley did. He was an old-fashioned parliamentary orator, and his rhetorical roots were planted firmly in the nineteenth century.

Churchill first learned the power of words by observing and admiring the speeches of his father, the brilliant but mercurial Victorian Tory Lord Randolph Churchill. As a teenager in the early 1890s – before Priestley was even born – young Winston developed a habit of watching Commons debates from the Visitors' Gallery, and saw that parliamentary titan William Gladstone in action during his final years in office. Gladstone – famously described by his rival Benjamin Disraeli as a 'sophistical rhetorician, inebriated with the exuberance of his own verbosity' – would sometimes speak at heroic length; his budget of 1853 was an uninterrupted marathon of four and three quarter hours. In addition to parliamentary epics of this kind, political oratory in the Victorian era often involved addressing vast public meetings – without, of course, any form of electronic amplification – and required immense physical stamina as well as a flair for the dramatic phrase that would whip up emotion and keep a crowd hooked.

Half a century after his schoolboy trips to the House of Commons, Winston Churchill was still drawing on what he learned there, and that Victorian rhetorical tradition is reflected in some of his most famous orations. His Dunkirk speech, for example, which was delivered on 4 June 1940, the day before Priestley's *Postscript* about the 'little pleasure steamers', is written in just the sort of sonorous Ciceronian periods for which Gladstone strove, yet his peroration – which must be one of the most famous passages of oratory of the twentieth century – caught the mood of that summer perfectly:

> We shall fight on the beaches, we shall fight on the landing grounds, we shall fight in the fields, and in the streets, we shall fight in the hills; we shall never surrender, and even if, which I do not for a moment believe, this Island or a large part of it were

subjugated and starving, then our Empire beyond the sea, armed and guarded by the British Fleet, would carry on the struggle, until, in God's good time, the New World, with all its power and might, steps forth to the rescue and the liberation of the old.

'Long sentences, with many relative clauses, and elaborate syntax generally, should be avoided,' said Priestley. 'Avoid ... inversions,' said the BBC style guide, which seems almost prissy when you put it next to this magnificent stuff. Churchill remained defiantly grandiloquent. Richard Dimbleby, in a 1953 essay on 'Churchill the Broadcaster', wrote, 'I was asked once what it was, in a nutshell, that made Churchill so outstanding at the microphone, and I replied, "The fact that he breaks every accepted rule of broadcasting." This is true. He drops his voice where he should raise it, he alters the recognised system of punctuation to suit himself (some of his scripts were virtually unintel-ligible to anyone else), he speaks much of the time with anything but clarity. Yet such is his power as an orator, and such his feeling for the public pulse, that during the war years he was sure of a silent and appreciative audience of millions, following every word and phrase with relish.'

Churchill's brilliance as a broadcaster is central to the way Britain looks back on its Second World War story, especially during that summer of 1940, when so much hung in the balance. 'He will always be remembered by the people of Britain for the way in which he spoke to them in their homes when death was near,' Dimbleby wrote in his retrospective essay. It is one of those 'facts' about the conflict with which we have grown up.

And the myth is so powerful that it has distorted the historical record. The Dunkirk speech, for example, was delivered in Parliament, but never actually broadcast by Churchill himself. It was, of course, reported and quoted on that night's news, but the recording we now know was made by Churchill in 1949 for a disc of his speeches produced by Decca. And yet really quite quickly people began to imagine they had heard him giving the speech on the BBC. The historian Richard Toye, in *The Roar of the Lion*, his analysis of Churchill's wartime speeches, has dug out vivid diary entries written at the end of the war by people who were convinced they had heard a Churchill broadcast: 'Nella Last remembered shortly after the war that when she "heard that husky, rather stuttering voice acclaiming we would fight on the beaches, on the streets" she felt "her head rise as if galvanised and a feeling that 'I'll be there – count on me, I'll not fail you.'"' Even the great broadcaster Ludovic Kennedy was let down by his memory of the Dunkirk speech, writing 'when we heard it, we knew in an instant that everything would be alright'. Marmaduke Hussey, who was the BBC's chairman for ten years from 1986, was convinced he had heard the speech on the radio when he was a schoolboy at Rugby, and wanted to use the anecdote in a speech of his own; the staff at the Caversham Archives had considerable difficulty in persuading him that this could not have happened.

Churchill's next great parliamentary performance was broadcast – not live from the Commons, which would have required the formal approval of the House, but as a prime ministerial statement immediately before the nine o'clock news that evening. The date was 18 June, just after the collapse of the French government and just before the Pétain regime that replaced it signed an armistice with Hitler. The peroration, restating the government's determination that Britain should stand 'alone, if necessary' against Hitler, is every bit as famous as the Dunkirk speech a fortnight earlier:

> If we can stand up to him [Hitler] all Europe may be freed, and the life of the world may move forward into broad, sunlit uplands; but if we fail then the whole world, including the United States, and all that we have known and cared for, will sink into the abyss of a new Dark Age made more sinister, and perhaps more pro-longed, by the lights of perverted science. Let us therefore brace ourselves to do our duty and so bear ourselves that if the British Commonwealth and Empire lasts for a thousand years men will still say, 'This was their finest hour.'

The words brought loud cheers in the Commons, but there is evidence that the radio broadcast may not have had quite the success that history and myth have claimed for it. The indefatigable diarist Harold Nicolson, who was serving as a junior minister in the Ministry of Information at this stage of the war, complained about the prime minister's lack of broadcasting skills. 'How I wish Winston would not talk on the wireless unless he is feeling in good form,' he wrote in his journal. 'He hates the microphone, and when we bullied him into speaking last night, he just sulked and read his House of Commons speech over again. Now, as delivered in the House of Commons, that speech was magnificent, especially the concluding sentences. But it sounded ghastly on the wireless. All the great vigour he put into it seemed to evaporate.' And there were mixed reviews from the public. The following day's report from Mass Observation (the research organization the government turned to for a sense of the public mood) stated that 'his delivery was frequently criticised. Some suggested he was drunk, others thought that he was tired. It would seem that the delivery to some extent counteracted the contents of the speech.'

Whatever Churchill's feelings about the microphone – and, indeed, about the BBC – he does seem to have come to a real appreciation of the value of broadcasting to the nation. On 14 July he delivered another morale-boosting address, building on the Dunkirk spirit inspired by his speech of 4 June. He declared that 'we would rather see London laid in ruins and ashes than that it should be tamely and abjectly enslaved', and he warned that the war would be a long haul. It was not one of his truly memorable orations – although it did include the clever idea that the people of Great Britain were engaged in 'a War of the Unknown Warriors' – but this time he clearly hit the right note. The Ministry of Information's Home Intelligence Reports stated that 'Reports from all Regions agree that the Premier's speech last night won universal approval,' and the historian Richard Toye concluded that 'For the first time we can find evidence of a Churchill speech evoking mass popular enthusiasm and boosting morale and optimism throughout society.'

Sunday, 14 July 1940 also stands out as a rare moment when the BBC's listeners were able to hear its two most popular performers, Churchill and Priestley, almost back to back; Churchill's speech ran up to the nine o'clock news and Priestley's *Postscript* immediately followed the bulletin. The contrast could not have been more striking. While

Churchill was statesmanlike and sonorous, Priestley was on his chattiest journalistic form. He described a visit to the seaside resort of Margate, eerily empty because of the fear of a German invasion: 'Everything was there: bathing pools, bandstands, gardens blazing with flowers, lido, theatres; and miles of firm golden sands all spread out beneath the July sun. But no people! – not a soul.' And somehow, without letting the conceit behind the piece get out of hand, he managed to turn the experience into a message of hope: 'This Margate I saw was saddened and hateful; but its new silence and desolation should be thought of as a bridge leading us to a better Margate in a better England, in a nobler world.' Not many writers or speakers could get away with a call for 'a better Margate' without slipping into bathos.

The audience for the nine o'clock news that night – which certainly reflected the appeal of the speakers who preceded and followed it – was put at 64.4 per cent, nearly two thirds of the adult population. The mental image we all have of families and folk in pubs gathered around the radio is one piece of our national myth that absolutely does stand up to scrutiny.

WAR NOISE, BELLS, GUNS, SIRENS ETC

T HE MILLIONS WHO TUNED in to the nine o'clock news that Sunday
evening heard another piece of radio history: an eyewitness
account of an engagement in what Churchill had already named the
Battle of Britain. Charles Gardner's report was delivered in tones of
breathless excitement: 'For now the Germans are dive-bombing a
convoy out to sea: there are one, two, three, four, five, six, seven German
dive-bombers, Junkers 87s. There's one going down on his target now.
Bomb! No! Missed the ships. It hasn't hit a single ship; there are about
ten ships in a convoy, but he hasn't hit a single one and there, you can
hear our anti-aircraft going at them now. There are one, two, three,
four, five, six – there are about ten German machines dive-bombing
the British convoy, which is just out to sea in the Channel.'

This was raw reporting, a far cry from the measured Churchillian
periods that preceded it or the nicely turned Priestley phrases that
followed. As Spitfires piled in to defend the British convoy, Gardner
provided a moment-by-moment commentary from his recording car
on the sea front. The recording of course had to be cleared before it
could be broadcast, but this as-live description of an aerial dog-fight
was unlike anything the audience had heard before. Many people
compared Gardner's style to that of a commentator at a football
match – but he was, of course, watching men fighting and dying.
'Somebody's hit a German and he's coming down with a long streak,
coming down completely out of control, a long streak of smoke, and

Tin hats on – covering the Battle of Britain, August 1940.

the man's bailed out by parachute. The pilot's bailed out by parachute. He's a Junkers 87, and he's going slap into the sea, and there he goes. SMASH. A terrific column of water and there was a Junkers . . .' And a little later: 'Oh, we've just hit a Messerschmitt. Oh that was beautiful! He's coming right down. I think it was definitely that burst got him. Yes. He's come down. You hear those crowds? He's finished! Oh, he's coming down like a rocket now. An absolutely straight dive. Let's move around so we can watch him a bit more. Here he comes, down in a steep dive, the Messerschmitt . . . No, no, the pilot's not getting out of that one.'

Not everyone liked it, and there were letters to *The Times* complaining that, as one correspondent put it, 'The BBC standard of taste, feeling, understanding, and imagination is surely revolting to all decent citizens.' Veterans of the First World War were prominent among the critics. 'As a pilot in the last War,' wrote a certain R. H. Dawkins from a vicarage in Carlisle, 'will you allow me to record my protest against the eye-witness account of the air fight over the Straits of Dover given by the BBC. Some of the details were bad enough; but far more revolting was the spirit in which these details were given to the public. Where men's lives are concerned, must we be treated to a running commentary on a level with an account of the Grand National or a cup-tie final?'

There was so much public debate that the BBC's Listener Research Department conducted an emergency survey over the following weekend, sending out questionnaires to 220 of the listeners they regularly consulted ('Honorary Local Correspondents') and a further 30 to 'industrial welfare workers recommended by the secretary of their professional society as being likely to report intelligently'. The results illustrate the BBC's remarkable reach and influence. Over 90 per cent of the correspondents and all but one of the welfare workers had heard Gardner's report (which had been repeated on Monday, the 15th). The survey report stated that, 'Not a single Correspondent or welfare worker said that he or she had not heard the subject discussed, and the vast majority made it plain that spontaneous comment had persisted for several days. A number of Correspondents, especially those in factories, say that it was the only topic of conversation on Monday morning and that it was exhilarating to have something to talk about instead of rumours.'

The survey reflected some of the reservations expressed on the letters page of *The Times* (another veteran of 1914–18 said he felt 'slight nausea' at the 'descriptions for public entertainment of brave men going to their doom'), but the overall reaction was overwhelmingly positive. A big majority of both local correspondents and the selected welfare workers said the broadcast had been greeted with 'Widespread appreciation with no criticism.' A few plumped for 'Widespread appreciation with some criticism,' while the category 'Widespread criticism and no appreciation' attracted just three ticks from the local correspondents and none from the group of welfare workers. The survey results suggested that newspaper reports of controversy about the broadcast had been largely confected by the papers themselves. 'A number of Local Correspondents say that the only criticism they came across was in the press, and that they could find no support for the press protests when they made enquiries from their colleagues, friends, customers etc,' the document reported. And it concluded that 'There can be no doubt that this broadcast was enormously appreciated, that it gave a great fillip to morale.'

Charles Gardner's vivid reporting style was, of course, the most obvious quality that attracted listeners (some admitted being ashamed that they had found it so exciting), but another hugely important factor comes through the Listener Research Report. There was a widespread feeling that telling a story as it happened made it much more difficult to put a propaganda gloss on the truth. 'The evidence is overwhelming that the appetite for first-hand accounts that are known not to have been doctored is enormous,' the BBC's researchers concluded, and they reported that 'a number of replies say that the realism of the account did much to restore faith in the standard news reports of one British plane being the equal of a greater number of German planes'. A housewife from the Midlands told them, 'It may go a long way to clear the doubt from a lot of people's minds about our pilots taking on the odds they are doing, as quite a few think the reports are cooked.'

Charles Gardner's over-optimistic reporting of the air war in the run-up to Dunkirk may have contributed to that cynical mood, but his broadcast on 14 July seems to have helped restore a degree of faith in Auntie. And the director-general, Frederick Ogilvie, defended both the style and the content of the report in his own letter to *The Times*: 'The business of news broadcasting is to bring home to the whole public what is happening in the world and, at a grim time like this, to play some part in maintaining civilian morale. British fighting men do not wage war with long faces ... Theirs is a spirit of cheerful realism, and, in a total war, is it not also the spirit of the nation as a whole?'

The episode had a sad and, in view of the way Gardner's report reinforced the Corporation's commitment to truth-telling, ironic postscript. It turned out that it included a terrible reporting blunder. The Junkers 87 that he saw 'going slap into the sea' was in fact a British Hurricane. The pilot he watched bailing out was picked up by the navy, but died of his injuries the next day.

≈

As the BBC mandarins managed the fallout from Gardner's report, they were having to dodge flak on another flank as a result of that

remarkable evening of broadcasting on 14 July. Priestley's Margate
Postscript had included a passage that might – at a stretch – be described
as 'militarily sensitive'. As he drove down to the almost-empty seaside
resort he described the scene along the way: 'there were things that
weren't quite what they first appeared to be – if you see what I mean,'
he said. 'The Bren guns seemed to be getting mixed up with the
agricultural life of north Kent. The most flourishing crop seemed to
be barbed wire. Soldiers would pop up from nowhere and then vanish
again – unless they wanted to see our permits. Some extra-large
greenish cattle, quietly pasturing underneath the elms, might possibly
have been tanks. It was a rum sort of farming round there.'

The Germans must surely have been aware that Britain was preparing its coastal defences, and it is difficult to see what of value they
would have learned from these brief sentences. But the Ministry of
Home Security – which had been established in 1939 to create a civil
defence system – was concerned that 'Priestley's broadcast last Sunday
was very revealing both on the evacuation schemes and on the general
preparations of the East of Kent ...', and that, more generally, 'by taking not one but two or three talks on the wireless it is possible to
gather a great deal of information which ... it is not necessary or
advisable to give to the Germans'.

Sometimes official complaints on issues like this must have been
difficult to answer with a straight face. During a live show the
comedian Arthur Askey ad-libbed a reference to the unusually hot
summer, saying, according to the official account, '"I've never known
such weather in Manchester" or words to that effect'. This prompted
a complaint from the Ministry of Information, on the grounds that all
references to weather were banned from the airwaves because they
might help the Germans plan their air raids. 'I have a report on Arthur
Askey's mention of the weather on Saturday week,' a senior BBC
figure wrote back carefully, 'and find it was an extempore gag. I am
having him written to and reproached, and told that it helps the
enemy make their weather maps.'

Everyone's nerves were on edge that summer, and it must have
been a frustrating time to serve in the armed forces or a fighting
ministry. Britain was hunkering down, bracing itself against the

possibility of invasion, and in the European theatre only Bomber Command had the reach to take the war to the enemy. Most of the population were reduced to the role of spectators as 'the Few' battled it out in the skies above them.

At the BBC, Val Gielgud was so vexed by his sense of being a powerless bystander that he 'spent all of one day on a trip with a commentator and a recording van scouring southeast England in search of the Battle of Britain'; he was rewarded by no more than a glimpse of 'one ninety-second dog-fight at some fifteen thousand feet'. He had, by this stage, escaped Evesham and its *fleurs de lys* and moved back to London, but he found Broadcasting House as jittery as anywhere. 'I caught a violent cold from sitting on guard with a shot-gun in the Control Room at Broadcasting House for five hours and a quarter in a draught of refrigerated air,' he wrote in his diary. 'One is becoming acclimatised to living almost literally from one day to the next, in the hope of proving that if hopes are dupes fears can also be liars.'

So perhaps it is not surprising that, in this febrile atmosphere, people began to imagine things. In early June the Air Ministry complained that the BBC had provided valuable information to the enemy in its coverage of a bombing raid over Sussex. The Ministry claimed that, while 'the exact location where the bombs were dropped was not mentioned', an interview with a chicken farmer the following night had given the game away, because 'The chicken farmer's name was mentioned, and it appears that to anyone in the know this gave an exact identification of where the bombs had dropped, because this particular man was as well-known in poultry circles as, say, Suttons amongst gardeners.' At the bottom of the BBC memo recording this complaint someone has scribbled 'this was not done by News', and a wider search of the BBC's output produced no evidence that any such interview was ever broadcast. Some days later a BBC mandarin solemnly reported that he had been through 'Talks, News, Empire and Variety – and Schools and Children's Hour' and found 'absolutely no trace of an interview at the microphone with the farmer whose farm was bombed'.

The Admiralty was next up to the plate with a grievance: the captain of a warship had reported that its crew were confused by the broadcasting of the bugle call 'alarm to arms'. There was another trawl through programmes that went out on the relevant day, again to no avail. To keep the sailors happy, however, a memo was circulated with the instruction that producers should 'Please exercise the greatest care in the use of bugle calls in our programmes. Some calls such as the "Alarm" should never be used, and even harmless calls should be used with discretion so as not to lead to misunderstanding.' There is another scribbled note on this memo, this one eloquent of exasperation: 'this is rather nonsense, isn't it?'

Nonsense or not, the flap over the possibility that the BBC might inadvertently damage the war effort by broadcasting something revealing or confusing very nearly led to a formal change in the censorship regime. On 25 July the influential Tory MP and soldier Duncan Sandys sent a memo to Downing Street expressing his concerns about 'the absence of any arrangements for censoring, from a security point of view . . . the News Talks given by the BBC'. He also raised the way announcements from government departments were being broadcast. '[T]he individual items published by one department appear quite harmless,' Sandys wrote, 'but when taken in conjunction with announcements from another department are found to give away important information.' Sandys was Churchill's son-in-law, and his memo was sympathetically received. A high-level meeting was convened on the prime minister's authority, and a senior BBC official was sent along to bat for the Corporation.

In the end the fuss ran out of steam, because Sandys's crisis meeting concluded that it was simply 'impractical' to submit absolutely everything to strict military censorship in addition to the civil censorship that was already in place through the usual BBC system. It was merely agreed that 'Civil Departments might be reminded of the special need for care in framing announcements in the absence of any military censorship', and 'the same injunctions should be given to the BBC censor in relation to broadcast talks'. But the episode underlines the fact that both the government and the BBC were having to improvise. This first real radio war threw up all sorts of unexpected challenges and, as we have seen, Britain's governing classes – in contrast to the Nazi Party – had not developed a real strategy for radio's wartime role.

That very serious reality could produce comic results – or at least results which look comic in retrospect but probably did not feel that way at the time. In June the government banned the ringing of church bells except as an alarm; in the event of a German invasion, bell-ringing was to be the means of spreading the news across the country. The memo-blizzard this unleashed at the BBC is preserved in a most enjoyable file in the Corporation's Written Archives entitled 'War Noise, Bells, Guns, Sirens etc'.

The first challenge was to enforce a ban on music containing bells, lest one of these send the country into an invasion panic. So it was ruled, for example, that 'Tchaikovsky's 1812 Overture in its original scoring (i.e. with bells) is banned for security reasons'. Unfortunately, the BBC was insufficiently ruthless in rooting out bell-ringing from its gramophone archive; some months after the ban was introduced, the News ran a little short one evening and the duty announcer reached for a record to fill the gap, only to find that it included an unmistakable violation of the bell-ringing ban. After a lengthy post-mortem, a shame-faced BBC boss was forced to admit that 'The record was placed in the Miscellaneous Emergency Rack by Miss White of this department. Although it had not been heard, on the face of it it appeared to be a perfectly normal record of the Fodens Motor Works Band playing "John Peel", and in a thing like that one doesn't expect peals of bells.'

A huge amount of bureaucratic time and energy was spent debating what was permissible in the bell-ringing arena. Could producers use a single tolling bell? They could: 'a toll is permissible but not a peal', they were told. Could they use bells on the short-wave broadcasts of the overseas services? No, they could not, because the risk of misunderstanding was too great. One producer suggested a concert of hymns sung to the sound of hand-bells, and wanted his boss to seek government permission; the BBC mandarin in question turned this down on the grounds that a concert of hymn-singing and hand-bells would be a dreadful racket and not at all suitable for broadcast.

Another producer got into a tangle over his adaptation of Hugh Walpole's novel *The Cathedral*. In an anguished memo he describes the challenges he faces in getting the 'atmosphere and feeling' of cathedral life right. 'A lot of this could of course be done with distant organ and choir effects,' he writes, 'but there is a further complication in that the action takes place at the time of Queen Victoria's Jubilee, and one dramatic scene should be played to the accompaniment of great public rejoicing and celebrations, when normally speaking all the church bells in the town would be ringing a triumphant peal.' He was told to be 'very discreet in his use of bells'.

Internal debates of this kind continued at the BBC for nearly three years, and it was not until April 1943, when the threat of a German invasion had become remote, that the bells edict was revoked and the Fodens Motor Works Band's rendition of 'John Peel' could once again be broadcast without posing a threat to national security.

≈

Every so often the paper-trail that tells the story of BBC–government relations in 1940 is interrupted by an eruption of exasperation. 'I felt very much inclined to stand the racket and tell MI7 [the censorship and propaganda section of Military Intelligence], the War Office and everyone else concerned to go to blazes,' wrote one senior BBC executive, after being forced to make last-minute changes to a play because the script had got lost somewhere in Whitehall. But there is no real evidence that those at the top of the BBC felt they were being pushed around unduly, or that what they saw as their basic mission of truth-telling was being compromised. The fall of France had made the Home Front the front line; that put the BBC's bosses absolutely in the thick of things, and many of them greatly enjoyed the experience.

For example, we find Sir Richard Maconachie, the BBC Director of Talks who had made such an effective case for prompt and accurate reporting the previous December, now enthusiastically endorsing and contributing to government propaganda efforts. 'There is to be a broadcast campaign, anti-gossip and anti-rumour, in the form of short interjections by announcers,' he wrote on 5 July, and he sent out a plea for help to his colleagues. 'For this purpose, pithy wisecracks and slogans are wanted. <u>Will everyone please think some out over the weekend.</u> Examples: "Mouths shut and hearts high", "Keep Hitler guessing and the bombs missing" and "Long tongues mean a long war".'

The views of junior members of staff were more nuanced. Marjorie Redman joined the Corporation as a secretary on *Children's Hour*, contributing the odd story or poem to the programme to supplement her earnings. In 1931 she moved to the *Listener* and secured a position there as a sub-editor. Her war diary is a reminder that most BBC staff experienced the summer of 1940 first and foremost as anxious ordinary citizens, and her account of the momentous events unfolding around her is leavened with engaging anecdotes about the foibles of her BBC colleagues. On 17 June she records that 'Morning papers say French government has resigned. Marshall Petain has become Prime Minister,' and she continues, 'Miss Playle feels in this hour of stress company of some kind she must have, and takes me off to lunch. She is convinced for some reason that should the Germans land in England one of their first acts would be to put her up against a wall and shoot her. "Of course, you'll be alright," she adds to me kindly. Cannot think why, unless she has been sending some of her famous memoranda to Hitler.'

Like Priestley – and Arthur Askey – Miss Redman was struck by the poignant contrast between the brilliant British spring and summer and the horror of the unfolding war. On Sunday, 23 June, she notes down the humiliating terms of France's armistice with Germany, and then adds, 'after lunch go for glorious walk through forest; tea at village; walk back another way, I decide not to return to town until tomorrow, and sit on balcony in warmth of June evening, reading Helen Waddell's *Peter Abelard*, and feel drenched in loveliness, and in sadness that everything isn't as lovely as it looks.'

Miss Redman kept her diary throughout the war, and her entries for the summer of 1940 are especially striking because of her reflexlike doubt about the veracity of anything she was told by official sources, including much of what was said by her own employer. On the day that Italy declared war on the Allies, she records that 'Mr Duff Cooper, in the 9 o'clock news, tries to prove that this is almost a help to us, and I cannot help remembering the old Dutchman who at dinner said the BBC told many lies, and that there was something amiss with a people which had to be buoyed up with untruths.' At around the same time she notes, 'Miss Mearing told me that her father (vicar) has been issued with "Hints for Sermons" by the Ministry of Information. Feel if they are going to interfere in our spiritual instruction they are as bad as the Nazis.' And on 1 July she interrupts her diary entry to listen to the nine o'clock news, reporting afterwards that 'It is slipped in casually in the middle that the Germans have occupied the Channel Islands.' There was, it seems, plenty of healthy scepticism on the shop floor of Broadcasting House.

When, in August, Marjorie Redman saw a 'confidential memorandum' which stated that 'Fascists, Communists, conscientious objectors and pacifists are not to be allowed at the microphone', she made the shrewd observation that it was 'particularly aimed at pacifist parsons and their sermons'. The Church of England was, of course, even more of an 'establishment' institution than the BBC, and it could not be ignored. But in senior BBC circles, its clergymen seem to have had a reputation for trouble-making. And other denominations could, from a BBC perspective, be even more tiresome; one senior Methodist even suffered the indignity of being taken off the air by the switch censor.

The Reverend Henry Carter OBE was asked to give a talk on the Empire Service, and the script he submitted included some sharp commentary on inequality in Britain. 'Out of every hundred men, women and children in Britain,' he wrote, 'one man and one boy own nearly a quarter of the wealth that should be available to meet the needs of them all. That is only another way of expressing Professor Colin Cark's verdict that 1½ percent of the population holds 25 percent of the wealth of the country. And at the other end of the social scale, he shows that no less than one fourth of the children of the nation are in the very poorest economic groups. These are the facts for Britain.' This passage was judged to be so shockingly left-wing that it would have been an 'obvious present to Haw-Haw', who of course had made great play of Britain's class divisions, and it was excised from the script – with, we must assume, the Reverend's consent. But while he was broadcasting the switch censor noticed that

Carter was departing from the script he – the switch censor – had been given and, concluding that the distinguished clergyman was about to reinsert the offending passage, hit the censor button, sending a long silence into the imperial ether. It turned out to be a mistake; the reverend gentleman had simply inserted a 'couple of linking sentences' to make the junction work after his talk had been cut back, and these had not been passed on to the switch censor. No matter; OBE or not, the clergyman was judged to be 'rather politically minded' and it was decided that 'Carter, without being banned, should not be invited to broadcast again' – an altogether more elegant way of silencing a turbulent priest.

Though there was no formal change in the censorship system that summer, there is no question that the existing rules were more tightly applied, and it certainly became more political. Britain was standing alone – as Churchill took every opportunity to remind the country and the outside world – and was desperately seeking new allies in the struggle against Hitler. This made anything the BBC broadcast about foreign governments an extremely sensitive issue, so 'guidance' poured in from the Foreign Office as well as the Ministry of Information.

In late June, for example, staff in the BBC News Department received a 'Confidential memorandum' informing them that 'The Foreign Office this morning call attention to a complaint from Sir Stafford Cripps, HM Ambassador to Moscow, that the personal references to Joseph Stalin in Empire News 6.00 pm G.M.T. are likely to prove disastrous. H.M. Ambassador points out once more that the BBC is inevitably regarded as a Government mouthpiece. He considers it absolutely necessary to remove unnecessary grounds for misunderstanding and suspicion, and the Foreign Office strongly support this view.' At the time Stalin was Hitler's ally, and Churchill had despatched Stafford Cripps to Moscow in the hope of wooing him. Cripps, a former Labour minister, had Marxist views which, it was thought, were likely to appeal to the Soviet leader. Everyone knew how vital it was to keep a channel of communication open with the Russians, and the BBC had no hesitation in passing on the Foreign Office advice. 'Editors are urgently requested by the F.O.,' the memo continues, 'not to make any allusions whatever in their broadcasts, especially at the present moment, that could possibly have a prejudicial effect on our relations with Russia.' No one, it seems, fussed unduly about editorial independence.

≈

The BBC had become a weapon of war, and the way the war came to the Home Front in the summer of 1940 brought home for the first time what that really meant. One consequence was that Auntie had to keep the lid on stories about herself. Some of the Corporation's installations did not officially exist, so when, for example, an unfortunate engineer was 'accidentally electrocuted' at the Fraserburgh station in July 1940, the BBC took the view that 'as our station there is secret it was very important that no reference to the accident appeared in the press'. And at around the same time we find a BBC mandarin noting solemnly that 'My attention has been drawn to a book called "The Log of Not Quite a Lady" by Ursula Bloom, in which she mentions paying a visit to the BBC at Evesham. I don't know whether this is an infringement of the D Notice, but it appears to be bordering on it.'

The German occupation of Europe and the threat of invasion also posed new threats to the BBC's foreign staff, who were becoming more essential than ever as the importance of the language services grew. The BBC took the view that 'The publication of the names of the BBC's foreign staff in the Press is contrary to the interest of national security on the grounds that once their identity becomes known, they can more easily be approached by foreign agents anxious to use the BBC as a means of communicating with the enemy. Such staff are not only open to bribery, but special pressure can be brought to bear on those who have relatives in countries occupied by the enemy.' The government agreed, and a new D Notice was duly issued to the papers.

And censorship requests between the BBC and the Ministry of Information went in both directions. Information about the synchronization system that allowed the BBC's transmitters to stay on the air kept leaking out in the press. On 25 June the *Daily Telegraph* casually mentioned that 'Normally a number of stations are syn-chronised on common wavelengths to baffle bomber pilots using direction-finding gear', and the *News Review* stated confidently that 'The basis for Sir Noel's [Noel Ashbridge, the BBC's chief engineer] hush-hush machine is believed to be a series of transmitters. Pro-grammes are switched over from one to another. This would explain the sudden changes in volume which sometimes puzzle the listeners.' On both occasions the BBC wrote to the Ministry of Information, complaining about these infringements of censorship regulations and asking the Ministry to take action. The BBC's operating methods had become a state secret – a most peculiar position for an organization dedicated to the dissemination of information.

IRREVOCABLE WORDS

THE AMERICAN RADIO CORRESPONDENT Eric Sevareid was based in Paris for the Columbia Broadcasting Service (CBS) when war broke out and, like Charles Gardner, he managed to reach Britain ahead of the German advance in May 1940. In London he bumped into some old friends and colleagues from his Paris days, spotting 'French faces' in the crowds along Piccadilly, and on the first Bastille Day after the fall of France – 14 July, which was also the day of Gardner's ground-breaking dog-fight broadcast on the south coast – Sevareid 'wandered idly into Whitehall to observe the French parade, and was fascinated by what I saw'. Instead of the massed ranks that would normally have turned out for this great assertion of national pride and Republican values, he found 'a couple of lines of French sailors, airmen and soldiers, stretching for no more than a city block. Just a handful . . .' This modest gathering was being inspected by 'the towering general with the improbable nose' who 'strode stiffly among the ranks, never opening his tightly compressed lips, glaring, almost, into every pair of rigid eyes' and 'had the portentous air of a general surveying a great army'. He was struck by the scene, despite the way it teetered on the edge of absurdity. 'Somehow you could not feel sentimental, nor could you smile,' he wrote. 'You had the impulse to remove your hat and stand rigidly at attention yourself. This was impressive; it gave one to think.'

It is impossible to exaggerate the precariousness of Charles de

Gaulle's position in the summer of 1940. 'I was nothing when I began my task,' he recorded in his *Mémoires de guerre*, 'not even the shadow of a force or an organisation could I call upon. In France itself, I could count on neither following nor fame; abroad, neither credit nor standing.' His only assets were a fierce faith in a 'certain idea of France', an equally settled faith in the way that idea was entwined with his own destiny, Churchill's friendship, and the BBC. 'The first thing I had to do was to raise the colours,' he wrote, 'the radio was at hand to do that.' Winston Churchill, he continued grandly, 'placed the BBC at my disposal'.

Without the BBC, de Gaulle might never have become the great national hero and world-class leader he was, and the movement we now call the French Resistance would almost certainly have taken much longer to emerge as a real force. It would also have had to operate in a very different way, because the BBC's personal message service became a cornerstone of contacts between London and the men and women in the field. Edward Tangye Lean, a BBC broadcaster who in 1943 published *Voices in the Darkness: The Story of the European Radio War*, recalls a wartime conversation with André Philip, who became de Gaulle's commissioner for labour after escaping to London from France. 'The Underground resistance movement was built up by the BBC,' Philip told him. 'At the beginning it was everything. We needed help from outside, and the BBC gave that help.'

It is questionable whether Charles de Gaulle was even entitled to call himself a general when he arrived in London. He had been given the temporary rank of brigadier-general (in English usually referred to simply as a 'brigadier') after leading successful actions during the French retreat just before Dunkirk. After France's capitulation in mid-June, the Vichy government formally demoted him to his permanent rank of colonel, and compulsorily retired him, referring to him thereafter as 'retired Colonel de Gaulle'. It is true that he served as a member of the French Cabinet, but he had been appointed on 6 June 1940 – so less than two weeks before he fled the country as a rebel. A temporary rank and less than a fortnight as a government minister provided the slightest of foundations for his extraordinary claim, in his famous *Appel* (appeal, or call to arms) on the BBC on 18 June, to be the true embodiment of the French state.

De Gaulle was appointed to the French government after writing to the prime minister, Paul Reynaud, at the beginning of June, offering himself quite shamelessly as France's only possible saviour in her hour of need, 'a new man, a man of the new kind of war', who could bring 'renewal' to the country. De Gaulle pre-emptively dismissed any talk of junior government jobs and declared that the only position short of ministerial rank he would consider was the command of all four of France's armoured divisions. 'Allow me to say without modesty,' his letter concludes, 'that after twenty days experience under fire, I alone am capable of commanding the corps, which will be our supreme resort. Having invented it, I state my claim to lead it.' Reynaud, who liked de Gaulle and seems to have been quite unfazed by his hubris, made him under-secretary of state for war and almost immediately despatched him to London on a mission to persuade Churchill to commit more RAF squadrons to the battle for France.

De Gaulle and his party flew from Le Bourget Airport on the morning of 9 June. He had never been to London before, and the city was still enjoying its pre-Blitz summer. De Gaulle recalled that 'the English capital had a look of tranquillity, almost of indifference. The streets and parks full of people peacefully out for a walk, the long queues at the entrances to the cinemas, the many cars, the impressive porters outside the clubs and hotels, belonged to another world than the one at war … It was plain, in any case, that to English minds the Channel was still wide.' De Gaulle lunched at the embassy and then made his way to Downing Street, where Churchill gave a vintage performance, 'talking an extraordinary language, half French, half English', and walking up and down so briskly that one member of the French party 'had the feeling of being at a tennis match' as he watched the prime minister stride from one side of the room to the other.

Churchill refused to send more planes to fight in France – arguing, rightly, that they would soon be needed to defend Britain itself – but he made a profound impression on his guest. De Gaulle found a man after his own heart, 'made for action, fitted to take risks, to play his part bluntly and without scruple', and he came away from the meeting more convinced than ever that 'Great Britain, led by such a fighter, would never flinch.'

That conviction underpinned the steady determination de Gaulle displayed as French defences collapsed before the German advance. The day after his meeting with Churchill, the French government abandoned Paris and moved south, and on 11 June Churchill flew to France for a meeting with the French Cabinet at the town of Briare on the banks of the River Loire. The French again pushed for more planes to be sent to France, and Churchill again refused. De Gaulle sat next to Churchill at dinner and was once more impressed – and seems to have done his best to impress Churchill in return. In the account he gave in his *Mémoires de guerre* he indulged his weakness for writing about himself in the third person: 'He himself [Churchill], no doubt, went away with the feeling that de Gaulle, though without means, was no less resolute.' They met again two days later at Tours when Churchill, still desperately fighting to stiffen the resolve of the French government, shuttled back to France, and throughout these tense days de Gaulle fought to persuade Paul Reynaud that the fight must, at any cost, continue; he had even studied the possibility of evacuating half a million men to North Africa with the help of the British Navy.

By the time the two met again – at lunch at the Carlton Club back in London on Sunday, 16 June – they were co-conspirators. Their last gamble in their campaign to keep France in the war was the offer of a political union between France and the United Kingdom. This highly imaginative and sweeping scheme had been dreamed up by the French political economist Jean Monnet, who was based in London at the time (he would go on to be one of the founding fathers of the European Union), and received the post-prandial approval of the British Cabinet that Sunday afternoon. De Gaulle telephoned Reynaud with the news, and Churchill lent him a plane to take him back to Bordeaux, where the French government had withdrawn.

But the gesture was too late. When Reynaud placed the project before the French Cabinet, Marshal Philippe Pétain, who, as the hero of France's victory at Verdun during the First World War, wielded enormous moral authority, dismissed the idea of what he called 'union with a corpse'. The Cabinet refused its support, Reynaud resigned and the French president, Albert Lebrun, invited Pétain to form a government. As de Gaulle put it in his *Mémoires de guerre*, 'That meant certain capitulation.' So the drama was all over by the time his plane touched down at Bordeaux at 9.30 that night. In his memoirs, de Gaulle claims he knew immediately what to do: 'My decision was taken at once. I would leave as soon as morning came.'

But it cannot have been that simple. Ten years later he told the novelist André Malraux that the moral dilemma he faced 'was appalling'. The government of which he had been a part had collapsed, so he had no standing as a minister. The new government was led by a man whose views he had fought at every turn, but it was still the legally constituted government of France and leaving would be an act of open rebellion. 'Uprooting, exile, misunderstanding, scandal' is the way the French historian Jean Lacouture describes the path he chose: 'his action contained countless cruel or dangerous implications and it might turn essential friendships and allegiances from him . . . it was a paroxysm.'

Late that night, Sir Edward Spears, whom Churchill had sent to France as his personal representative, and the British ambassador paid a final call on Paul Reynaud. In the sepulchral gloom of the building where the French government had set up temporary shop, they found an 'overwrought' de Gaulle hiding behind a pillar; he insisted that he was about to be arrested by the new government and that he must leave as soon as possible. It was agreed that, first thing in the morning, he would return to London aboard the plane that had brought him to Bordeaux, and in his memoirs de Gaulle recalled that this was achieved 'without any romantic adventures or difficulty'. Spears, however, described an elaborate deception designed to disguise their plans. De Gaulle, he recorded, insisted on stopping on the way to the airport to instruct his officials – who were apparently unaware of the change of regime – to make a series of appointments for him. He accompanied Spears to the airport on the pretext of saying goodbye to him, and kept up this pretence for their chauffeur until, at the very last moment and with the propellers already turning, he and Spears hooked hands and he was hoisted on to the taxiing plane. The only person to accompany him was his ADC – a young cavalry officer called Geoffroy Chaudron de Courcel – but, as Churchill put it later, he 'carried with him, in that small plane, the honour of France'.

The party landed briefly in Jersey to refuel, and reached Heston early on the afternoon of 17 June. Spears gave his French guests lunch at his club, and at 3.00 p.m. de Gaulle went on to meet Churchill in Downing Street. The prime minister was working in the garden – it was a balmy summer afternoon – and when de Gaulle outlined his plan to address the French nation via the BBC Churchill immediately agreed. However, the two also shared the view that the broadcast should be delayed until after Marshal Pétain had made the new French government's position clear – it was, after all, still just possible that the old warrior would have a change of heart.

But Pétain's radio address later that afternoon put the matter beyond all doubts. 'I give to France my person to assuage her misfortune,' the Marshal declared. 'It is with a broken heart that I tell you today it is necessary to stop fighting.' France was to give up even before negotiating terms. The Germans made the French sign an armistice in the same railway carriage in which Germany had been forced to accept the one ending the First World War. France was to be divided between a German-controlled 'Occupied Zone' in the north and west, and a so-called 'Free Zone', which would be run by Pétain's government from the spa town of Vichy.

The news of the French capitulation came as a shattering blow to Frenchmen and -women in London. Pierre Maillaud, a London-based correspondent for the Havas news agency (he would go on to become one of the stars of the BBC's French Service) felt his misery mocked by the city in its summer glory. 'As our country drove towards disaster and isolation without us,' he wrote, 'the liveliness of the streets, the brilliance of the day reflected in the city's windows, the buzz of the crowds – from whom we were now cut off by our internal distress – all seemed like a provocation, impossible to bear. The parade of red buses which swung across the verdant screen of Green Park seemed like a jarring display of cheerfulness at a wake.'

Jean Oberlé, another London-based correspondent who would become a BBC regular, attended a press conference at the Ministry of Information, but was overwhelmed with emotion and had to leave. He recorded that 'a woman, an English journalist, took me by the arm and said "Don't cry ... we will free your beautiful country."' As he crossed the Senate House courtyard the porter emerged from his lodge and clapped him on the back, urging him to 'Keep your head up sir, and all will be well!'

De Gaulle began work on his address on 17 June after seeing Churchill, and on the 18th de Courcel arranged for a family friend working at the French embassy to come and type it up. As he pored over the text that afternoon – smoking heavily and scribbling corrections – de Gaulle was quite unaware of a last-minute twist in the plot which very nearly derailed his encounter with destiny altogether. The War Cabinet met that day with Chamberlain rather than Churchill in the chair – the prime minister was working on his own great 'finest hour' speech, which he delivered in the Commons later that afternoon – and Item 11 of the Cabinet Minutes records that:

> The Minister of Information [Duff Cooper] said that General de Gaulle had communicated to him the text of a broadcast which he wished to make saying that France was not defeated and inviting all French soldiers to rally to him.
> The War Cabinet agreed that, while there was no objection to the substance of the broadcast, it was undesirable that General de Gaulle, as *persona non grata* to the present French Government, should broadcast at the present time, so long as it is still possible that the French Government would act in a way conformable to the interests of the Alliance.

Churchill got this news while he was working on his speech, and he despatched Sir Edward Spears to track down every member of the War Cabinet and to persuade them to reverse their collective decision. A helpful footnote has been added to the Minutes: 'The members of the Cabinet were subsequently consulted again individually, and it was agreed that General de Gaulle should be allowed to broadcast . . .'

The BBC was told only that evening that 'a French general called de Gaulle' would appear to make a broadcast. When he turned up at Broadcasting House he was escorted to Studio 4B by Elisabeth Barker, one of the few women who had managed to fight some way up the

BBC hierarchy, and she later remembered being struck by both his height and footwear; he was, she recalled, a 'huge man with highly polished boots, who walked with long strides, talking in a deep voice'. It was – and still is – the custom to ask guests to say a few words so that the engineers can adjust their equipment for a speaker's voice level, and this ritual is usually accomplished by suggesting someone give an account of their journey to the studio or that morning's breakfast; de Gaulle simply boomed 'La France,' and, according to Elisabeth Barker, 'he stared at the microphone as though it were France and as though he wanted to hypnotize it. His voice was clear, firm and rather loud, the voice of a man speaking to his troops before a battle. He did not seem nervous but extremely tense, as though he were concentrating all his power in one single moment.'

It was a brief address, and the *Appel* came at the end: 'I, General de Gaulle, now in London, call upon the French officers and soldiers who are on British soil or who may be on it, with their arms or without them, I call upon the specialised workers in the armaments industry who are or who may be on British soil, to get in contact with me. Whatever happens, the flame of French resistance must not and shall not die.'

Part of the thrill of live broadcasting – even at my less elevated level of daily news work – is the knowledge that once your words are out of your mouth you cannot get them back. 'As the irrevocable words flew upon their way,' de Gaulle wrote later, 'I felt within myself a life coming to an end – the life I had lived within the framework of a solid France and an indivisible army. At the age of forty-nine I was embarking upon an adventure, cast beyond the settled patterns of my life by fate.'

In his memoirs de Gaulle states that he made his broadcast at 6.00 p.m., but Asa Briggs, in his official BBC history, insists the address was trailed in the eight o'clock news and went out at 10 p.m.; a programme chit filled out by the conscientious Miss Barker – who recorded that the general was paid 'no fee' for the broadcast – confirms the later time. Some of de Gaulle's biographers have challenged the BBC record, and some have argued that he pre-recorded the broadcast at six and left it to be transmitted later. This odd wrinkle in such a well-told story perhaps reflects the fact that at the time very few people understood the significance of the broadcast. The BBC's engineers famously – and to de Gaulle's great irritation – did not bother to commit it to a disc (or, if they did record it, lost it later). The version we are familiar with today was, like some of Churchill's speeches, recorded much later.

The Corporation's bosses realized quite quickly that their new guest was a figure of consequence – when de Gaulle turned up for his next broadcast he was given a glass of sherry in the director-general's office, and Miss Barker was later reprimanded for failing to wear stockings when she was part of the original welcoming party – but, as Asa Briggs puts it, 'the first de Gaulle speech was a landmark mainly in retrospect'. And it seems likely that it reached only a relatively small audience; while writing his history Asa Briggs interviewed a senior BBC official who 'lived in France for twenty years after the war before she met anyone who had actually heard this first broadcast'. In

Elisabeth Barker, who escorted General de Gaulle on the evening of his BBC appeal for resistance in France.

Britain that night's news was, of course, dominated by Churchill's 'finest hour' speech.

But Pierre Maillaud, the French news agency correspondent who earlier that day had felt such a painful sense of alienation as he watched London's cheerful summer colours and her bright double-deckers, did hear the broadcast and responded immediately. At nine on the morning of 19 June, he and a journalist friend made their way to the Mayfair flat that served as de Gaulle's first London base. De Courcel ushered them into the great man's presence, and they spent ten minutes discussing the need for an international campaign to counter German propaganda about France. As they left, Maillaud's companion described de Gaulle as 'puffed up', but Maillaud himself felt inspired. 'The call of June 18th was a beginning,' he wrote; 'it broke the dead silence that had descended over France.' He noted that he and his companion had found de Gaulle 'surrounded by Frenchmen. Others had gone to see him before us that morning, others followed us. More would come … the gesture had been made, the impetus had been created.' Maurice Schumann, who would become de Gaulle's principal BBC spokesman, described the broadcast of 18 June as an 'act of disobedience' – in the sense that it was a rebellion against the new French government – but 'first and foremost an act of obedience to History.'

Despite the would-be resisters whom Maillaud met milling around de Gaulle's flat that morning, the idea that the general represented a government-in-exile would, for a good while to come, remain a preposterous presumption – at the very most we would today call it a 'virtual-reality' government. And not everyone shared Churchill's enthusiasm for de Gaulle. The War Cabinet concerns which nearly scuppered that critical first broadcast were not laid to rest for some time, and they were felt even more strongly in the United States, which maintained full diplomatic relations with the Vichy regime right up until the German occupation of the whole of France in 1942.

Any wobble in policy towards France in Whitehall or Washington was bound to have an impact at the BBC. Six days after de Gaulle's *Appel*, a Foreign Office-inspired memo was circulated within the BBC reporting, 'We are … advised to avoid pushing General de

Gaulle too much personally at the moment.' Three days later yet another 'confidential memorandum' went round with the information that 'The FO remind us that any criticisms of Pétain and his Government had better come from the French themselves rather than from us or our press . . . we have had indications from Washington that it would have an unfavourable effect if we were to throw stones at Pétain.' That very same day the Ministry of Information was on the phone to inform the BBC that the 'Line to take re Pétain Government is still that it is a helpless tool in German hands.'

But Churchill's support for de Gaulle held true, and with it came access to the BBC's airwaves. De Gaulle gave no fewer than eight broadcasts in the second half of July, and the fact that he was taken seriously by the BBC was critical to his credibility in those early days, because the Corporation had already established a place in French affections.

≈

The BBC option had been available to listeners in France since the autumn of 1938, when the Corporation had begun broadcasting news bulletins in French, German and Italian in response to the Munich Crisis. But according to the French historian Dominique Decèze the BBC 'habit' only really took hold with the Phoney War a year later, and it was the result of the French government's failure to provide an adequate broadcasting service of their own.

Before invading France in June 1940, the Germans blitzed the French airwaves with propaganda, and their star turn was a man called Paul Ferdonnet. The son of a schoolteacher from the western French city of Niort, this 'French Haw-Haw' broadcast from transmitters designed to reach and niggle the soldiers stationed along the Maginot Line. 'While you moulder at the front, those in reserved occupations who've stayed behind to work in factories and enjoy the cushy jobs are sleeping with your wives,' Ferdonnet told them, and 'the English will fight to the last Frenchman'. The fault line between French and English interests was a seam he especially enjoyed mining. 'France, he said, could only lose by her association with England,' reported Tangye Lean in his near-contemporary account of the propaganda war during this period. 'She might sink to the level of a colony, plainly would do if the treatment of the two armies was an indication. The English soldier was not only clothed better; he was paid better, and never failed to buy up the available women in his particular plot of France.'

By way of a response to this onslaught on the airwaves, the French government appointed the distinguished dramatist and novelist Jean Giraudoux to direct the Information Bureau, and charged him to go on the air himself to explain the war. It was a disaster. '[T]he writer simply could not reinvent himself as a radio man,' Decèze writes, 'his "affecting homilies" were no match for Ferdonnet's merciless hammer-blows.' And the French radio authorities were well behind the BBC in learning the value of accurate reporting. That, at least, was certainly the view of the BBC itself; an in-house study in the spring of 1940 concluded that 'French radio had never established a reputation for veracity'. Faced with the unappealing alternatives of listening to 'the traitor of Stuttgart' or a home service they did not trust, more and more French listeners turned to the BBC.

In November 1939 the British consul in the city of Nantes noted that there was a 'growing number of French people listening to the news in French on the BBC, finding it fuller and more interesting than the news they find on French stations'. An internal BBC document in March 1940 concluded that 'Even the soldier who writes to the BBC in the hope that someone can be found to send him English cigarettes, the schoolboy wishing to correspond with an English or Canadian girl, or the crank who sends his latest treatise on the cure for all human evils, give evidence that the BBC in France has a large audience.' And the Corporation's initials, the document recorded, had become part of French public discourse. 'Miscellaneous references to the BBC are to be found in Paris and provincial newspapers,' it states, 'the editors of which generally expect their readers to know the meaning of the initials BBC, although the *Soleil Marseillais* gives C (P) [Controller, Programmes] the engaging title of *directeur des Rapports Publics de la Big Broadcasts Corporation*'.

The reasons given for BBC-listening included 'the frankness and truthfulness of the news'; French listeners said they 'find it more detailed than other news sources, appreciate the sense of humour of the editors and many prefer it to news from French sources'. And the lesson the BBC had learned in its attempts to counter Lord Haw-Haw's influence at home – that truth is the most effective answer to propaganda – was reinforced by the messages it received from France about Ferdonnet. '[T]he traitor used to have the advantage of announcing our losses before everyone else,' wrote one listener. 'Now that your broadcasts are heard his effectiveness has been dealt a heavy blow and his lies disgust us. We only wanted to know what was happening and that is why we listened to him.'

A touching letter addressed to the BBC by the father of a *poilu* – the French equivalent of a Tommy – at about this time brings home how successfully Auntie had projected her protective persona to her French audience. 'Please could you arrange for my son Joseph to be replaced in the French Army by one of your soldiers,' he wrote, 'so that he can come back and help run the farm, which I cannot keep going without his help?'

The BBC's auntie-like image in France was greatly enhanced by the way it responded to the evacuation of so many thousands of French troops from Dunkirk. The majority were shipped straight back to France to fight, but those who remained in Britain – including, of course, the wounded – were completely cut off from their families. On 29 June the *Daily Mail* reported that 'Around a hundred French soldiers, currently being looked after in British hospitals, were able to talk to those close to them in France during a French programme on the BBC.' Thus was born the BBC's personal messaging service, which, under the direction of a Miss Audrey Anderson, would, between the summer of 1940 and the end of February 1944, despatch nearly 2,000 reassuring messages to families and friends in Occupied Europe.

Many of them were sent in as scribbled notes to be read by BBC announcers. 'I managed to escape falling into the hands of the *Boches*, and I am happy to find myself here, in a free country. Raymond Deplanque' was one such. Sometimes they were closer to the kind of Valentine's Day notices you still find in *The Times*. 'Jean is thinking about Monique,' read one. The early messages, transmitted in the uncertain weeks after the fall of France, are especially affecting. A small bundle pinned together in the BBC's Written Archives bears the legend 'Christmas 1940?' Some of these were evidently read by the senders themselves. 'Good evening Mother, good evening my beloved younger sister, do you recognise my voice?' began one. 'Yes, this really is Paul wishing you a happy Christmas.' Another exiled Frenchman wrote, 'I can picture the little crib of holy angels around which we always gather, and it makes me think of that happy Christmas of 1939, when we were together. What a year it has been! What a sad Christmas this is! We shall spend it in London, perhaps beneath the bombs, but there will be hope in our hearts, and the gulf that separates me from you does not prevent me from wishing you a good Christmas.'

Today, of course, listener phone-ins and the like are part of the small change of radio broadcasting, but in 1940, in the middle of a war that had torn so many families apart, the impact was electrifying. 'How glad Dad was to hear your voice on the wireless,' wrote a 'peasant from Cantal' to a wounded French soldier in Britain. 'He was over at A's and they heard you very well, and understood easily. It came through very clearly. There were about 15 or 20 of them and they all understood. François went to tell Justine the next day but someone else had already told her. B. heard you too and so did someone else in Tessières – we all think it's wonderful.'

In time these personal messages would, of course, become the foundation for a highly sophisticated and complex communication system between London and the French Resistance, which would play a significant role in the preparations for D-Day and the liberation of France. But the first time anyone raised the possibility that the messages might be used to transmit code, it was seen as a threat, not an opportunity. The Ministry of Information raised the security risk of what it called the 'Radio Agony Columns' in a memo to the BBC in early December 1940. 'The position is that MI5 are concerned about the content of such messages, not from the news point of view but in case they conceal messages in code,' it stated, and it informed the BBC that 'MI5 are therefore prepared to sanction this particular form of broadcast provided that each message passes the routine scrutiny of the Chief Telegraph Censor' (who had the job of censoring ordinary mail).

As the message system settled into a regular feature of the French Service – when the number of de Gaulle's Free French in London grew, so too did the demand for this way of making contact with home – Miss Anderson and her team developed a rigorous security procedure. 'No message could be transmitted until fifteen days after it had been received,' she stated in a 1944 record of the service, 'and except in urgent cases no one could send more than one message a quarter.'

At the beginning of June 1940 a BBC appeal for listeners' letters was read out before news bulletins on the French Service. 'Letters from our listeners are always welcome,' the announcement began, 'if only because they prove to us that we are not speaking into a void.' The appeal asked for guidance on whether transmission times were suitable for workers in factories and in the countryside – the BBC bosses were concerned that the broadcasts were not reaching a working-class audience – and stated that 'All information on the extent of our audience in a particular place is equally precious.' It gave the Corporation's postal address as simply 'BBC, London'. The German occupation of a large part of France later that month of course made it more difficult for post to get across the Channel, but the postal service between Britain and the southern, Vichy-run zone went on working right up until the Nazi occupation of the whole country in November 1942.

Some of the fan mail that got through must have been deeply affecting for the BBC staff who read it. 'We listen to you, we believe you, we love you,' wrote one young woman, while a listener in Ax-les-Thermes, in the Pyrenees, declared that BBC programmes were 'a beacon of great hope amid the darkness of the armistice'. A demobilized French soldier recorded that 'weeping women kneel around the wireless set and men turn away their heads to hide the tears in their eyes, but if England announces a victory, there is applause and cries of "Bravo!"' If jamming made the programmes difficult to hear, he went on, 'heads come close together and ears are pressed to the set'. Some letters even got through from the area of France occupied by the Germans, and a twenty-two-year-old woman from a Paris suburb declared that she turned to the French Service news because 'only there will I find truth'. She added that she would sometimes lock herself in her room and listen to English-language programmes with her eyes closed. 'I don't understand them,' she wrote, 'but it does me good because I feel it is a friendly voice.'

The correspondence was closely monitored by the BBC's Intelligence Unit, both for evidence of the mood in France and to build up a picture of the way the audience were responding to the BBC's broadcasts, and there was plenty to encourage the analysts during those anxious summer days of 1940. Just after France signed the armistice with Germany, for example, a listener from Béziers in the south-west of France wrote with thanks for 'the good cheer your programmes bring to those French who remain eager for freedom and will not accept the fate of being eaten with "Hitler sauce" (neither the German nor the French version), those of us who cherish in our hearts, along with an impotent rage towards our bad shepherds, the hope of liberation.'

Two days later, from Grasse in the Alpes-Maritimes region, came more thanks and the wish that 'the English should know that, whatever happens, all our hearts are with you . . . and we are ready to dedicate whatever last strength remains to us to the common struggle.' At the end of the month the writer of a letter 'somewhere in the Midi' (most of the letters were, for obvious reasons, anonymous) praised Churchill's offer of union between France and Britain and told the BBC that it was 'the only friendly voice in the world' when all was 'emptiness and shadows'. Plainly the spirit of resistance was alive and well – if largely hidden – in parts of France, and the listeners wanted the world to know it; some of them begged the BBC to read out their letters of praise and defiance on the air.

The postbag also provided evidence that de Gaulle's broadcasts very quickly fired people's imagination; a letter sent just a few weeks after his first address refers to the growing popularity of his Cross of Lorraine as a buttonhole, and his disembodied but forceful presence on the airwaves seems to have transformed him into an almost mythical figure. A girl from the Savoie region wrote to tell him that 'Every time I dream of you I always see you clad in magnificent rose-coloured silk and girt with a golden belt.' Another group of young women eulogized him in devotional terms: 'You are the truth, you are hope – without you we should have no more hope.' Traveller's tales reached Britain of de Gaulle being compared to Joan of Arc; Tangye Lean writes, '[T]he BBC at this time could more fairly be compared with the voices heard by Joan than with her corporeal self. As another traveller who passed through France remarked, "Do you know that no one in France knows what de Gaulle looks like?" He was a voice, a slow, majestic, lofty voice, which invested final syllables with the values due in poetry and celebrated battle for the nation's sake as an absolute good.'

It would never have worked as well on television – radio lets you dream.

C'EST MOI, CHURCHILL,
QUI VOUS PARLE

T HE BBC'S ROLE AS go-between in the burgeoning three-way relationship between de Gaulle, the people of France and the British government hit a very rough patch indeed after the events of 3 July 1940.

At seven that morning, Admiral James Somerville delivered an ultimatum to Admiral Marcel-Bruno Gensoul, who commanded the French fleet anchored in the port of Mers-el-Kébir, near Oran in French Algeria. The French Army had been shattered by the German invasion in June, but France's navy remained a powerful and well-equipped force, and Churchill was determined that it should not fall into German hands. Somerville's ultimatum – delivered on Churchill's instructions – began with a preamble which recalled the days of chivalry: 'It is impossible for us, your comrades up to now, to allow your fine ships to fall into the power of the German enemy. We are determined to fight on until the end, and if we win, as we think we shall, we shall never forget that France was our Ally, that our interests are the same as hers, and that our common enemy is Germany. Should we conquer we solemnly declare that we shall restore the greatness and territory of France.'

To 'make sure that the best ships of the French Navy are not used against us by the common foe,' the British ultimatum offered the French admiral these options: to bring his fleet over to Britain and remain in command to continue the war against Germany; to sail it to

British ports and turn it over to British control; or to lead the fleet to the French West Indies where it could be 'demilitarised to our satisfaction'. But the ultimatum ended with a clear warning: 'If you refuse these fair offers, I must with profound regret, require you to sink your ships within six hours. Finally, failing the above, I have orders of His Majesty's Government to use whatever force may be necessary to prevent your ships from falling into German hands.'

Just before six that evening, after a day of fruitless negotiation, the British opened fire, and within a quarter of an hour they had put the French fleet out of action. Some 1,300 French officers and men were killed, and a further 350 were injured. The British lost two dead. The historian Andrew Roberts notes that 'The fratricidal nature of the action at Oran was underlined by the fact that the commander of the French fleet, Admiral Marcel Gensoul, had commanded a force at the outbreak of war that included HMS *Hood*, one of the ships that fired upon his fleet at Oran six months later.'

It was widely thought that Churchill ordered the attack partly to convince Washington of Britain's determination to prosecute the war, and his principal private secretary, Eric Seal, wrote that Churchill 'was convinced that the Americans were impressed by ruthlessness in dealing with a ruthless foe; and in his mind the American reaction to our attack on the French fleet in Oran was of the first importance.' It was, of course, also a gift to the Anglophobes in Marshal Pétain's new government, and those in France who believed that Britain had abandoned her French ally in her hour of need at Dunkirk took it as further evidence of British perfidy.

The BBC propaganda machine – and that is the appropriate phrase on this occasion – went into overdrive. 'Your blood has run for the Germans,' began the 5 July edition of the French Service programme *Ici France*. Admiral Gensoul, argued the anonymous author of the talk, had sacrificed French lives simply to 'secure the right to give his force up to the Germans, help Germany and perpetuate the slavery of France'.

The Vichy regime responded to Mers-el-Kébir by bombing Gibraltar and cutting off diplomatic relations with London, and when he announced the rupture the new French foreign minister, Paul

Baudouin, revived the well-worn canard that 'France was dragged into the war by Britain, which declared war first.' This was seized on by the BBC scriptwriters. On the evening of 6 July the French Service compared Baudouin to the treacherous French propagandist Ferdonnet: 'the last time we heard it said in French that France was dragged into war by England, the words came from the mouth of the traitor of Stuttgart,' the broadcast declared. And it ramped up the anti-Vichy rhetoric, playing cleverly with the new regime's pretensions to stand for the Catholic faith, hard work and family values: 'Will you defend our Faith beneath the German boot, beneath the dictatorship of Hitler's neo-paganism, which has been condemned by all Christianity's great voices? As for our families, will you defend them in the shadow of the swastika, which our wives and children know because they have seen it on the fuselage of the planes which even as recently as yesterday were pouring bullets and death down upon them? ... Will you really preserve the dignity of French labour by delivering our workers, our artisans and our peasants, their hands and feet tied, to the man who, in the middle of the twentieth century, has claimed the rights of a master race, that is to say the Germans?'

But no amount of this rhetoric could disguise the fact that Mers-el-Kébir was, in de Gaulle's own words, 'an axe blow to the hopes' of the Free French in London, and it placed the general in an extremely awkward position. To support the British action would of course damage his standing in France, but to condemn it would mean a break with his British hosts, on whom, as he well understood, he was so heavily dependent. After some agonizing, he decided that 'the salvation of France trumped everything, even the fate of its ships, and that the path of duty still lay in continuing to fight'. On 8 July he made another broadcast on the BBC, and in his memoirs he paid the British government a pretty compliment for its continued willingness to give him a platform. '[T]he British government,' he wrote, 'on the advice of the Minister of Information, Duff Cooper, had the finesse to allow me to use the BBC microphone for my purpose, however disagreeable for the British the terms of my statement may have been.'

De Gaulle's comments were carefully calibrated. He condemned the British attack in robust terms – indeed he stated that every French citizen must feel 'pain and anger ... in the depths of our beings' because of it – and he urged the British people to spare French feelings by avoiding any celebration of 'this hateful tragedy' as if it were a great naval victory. But he also acknowledged the likelihood that the fleet would one day have fallen into German hands, and might have been used against Britain or, indeed, the French Empire, which remained outside German control.

One of the ships hit at Mers-el-Kébir was *Dunkerque*, the pride of the French Navy, which had been completed just a couple of years before the outbreak of war. 'I would rather,' de Gaulle declared, 'know that our *Dunkerque*, even our beautiful, our beloved, our powerful *Dunkerque*, was wrecked at Mers-el-Kébir than see it one day, under German control, bombarding British ports, or indeed Algiers, Casablanca, Dakar.' He told his audience that 'In insisting that this drama is what it is – by which I mean something deplorable and detestable – but at the same time preventing it from becoming a source of moral opposition between the English and the French, all clear-sighted people in both countries are fulfilling their patriotic part.' And, he added, 'Those English who reflect on these matters must surely realise that no victory is possible for them if the soul of France passes to the enemy.'

Noel Newsome, the BBC's European news editor, was just the kind of reflective ally de Gaulle had in mind. Mers-el-Kébir may have temporarily slowed the flow of volunteers rallying to General de Gaulle, but it does not seem to have interrupted the dizzying speed with which Newsome and his team fashioned the BBC's French Service into a formidable weapon in the war of words. Newsome had joined the BBC at the outbreak of war from the *Daily Telegraph*, where he had used his editorship of the foreign pages to campaign against Chamberlain's appeasement policy. He became an evangelist for his new medium, believing the BBC had a vital role to play in the war effort; 'all news and views ... must ... serve the one real and fundamental propagandist aim of helping us to win this war as rapidly as possible,' he wrote in a memo in February 1940.

A further memo he sent out in early July 1940 – around the time of the Mers-el-Kébir crisis – was even more robust. The BBC, he wrote, should focus on 'our moral and material capacity not only to defend ourselves but to strike at the enemy' and 'our moral and material fitness to keep alive in conquered Europe the spirit of resistance to conquest by brute force and eventually to lead to a great uprising of the peoples against a morally and spiritually bankrupt tyranny whose actual material strength is waning.'

≈

The BBC was full of strong and colourful characters during this period, but the head of the French Service also deserves special mention, not least because he was held in so much affection by his French colleagues. Darsie Gillie had been the *Manchester Guardian's* correspondent in Paris before the war, and in June 1940, as the implications of the fall of France became so dramatically clear, he was extracted from an RAF squadron to take over the rapidly expanding service. The French historian Dominique Decèze describes him thus: 'devoted to France with a touching love, he knew her literature, the riches of her countryside, her history and her arcane politics. He wrote French beautifully but spoke it execrably'. He would often take the French side against his English colleagues – Newsome believed that all the European Services should pump out the same message, while Gillie argued that each service should tailor its output to the demands of its particular national audience – and was given to histrionic displays after the ensuing rows. A French member of his staff wrote that 'he would fulminate, shaking his long arms and endlessly striding around the corridors ... then take down a copy of Virgil and declaim the Latin verses in a loud voice as a way of putting the politics of the place behind him.'

Newsome and Gillie presided over a breathless expansion of the French Service to meet the crisis that followed the fall of France. In September 1939 the BBC had been broadcasting two fifteen-minute daily news programmes in French; that was increased to three with the outbreak of war. By the end of May 1940 – at the time of the Dunkirk evacuation – the number of daily bulletins had risen to five, but the diet was still restricted to news. Eight months later the French Service was providing a mix of news, entertainment and current affairs, which made it something very close to a 'network' in the modern sense of the term. The daily schedule looked like this – for some reason the BBC schedulers liked to start the broadcasting day in the middle of the night:

- 23.45–00.00   News

- 05.15–05.30   News

- 05.30–05.45   Programme

- 10.45–11.15   Programme

- 11.15–11.30   News

- 13.15–13.30   News

- 15.15–15.30   Programme

- 17.15–17.30   News

- 17.30–18.00   Programme

- 19.15–19.30   News and de Gaulle

- 19.30–20.00   News and Programme

- 21.15–21.30   News

To its French listeners the service sounded like an integrated whole, but it was in fact made up of three distinct elements, each controlled in a different way. The French Service news was an entirely BBC affair, produced by the news desk and subject to the editorial and censorship regime that applied to the BBC in general, but read by French speakers. The early-evening bulletin – broadcast at peak listening time – was followed by five minutes given over to de Gaulle's Free French, a regular slot that was a direct result of Churchill's order, on the morning after Mers-el-Kébir, that 'everything should be done to help General de Gaulle achieve his ends'. De Gaulle argued for three fifteen-minute slots in the course of the week, but the BBC persuaded him that he would be better served by a five-minute segment every evening. Churchill had ordered that the Free French should be allowed to treat the airtime as their own, and they were, within reason, given *carte blanche* to use it as they liked.

On big occasions de Gaulle himself would step up to the microphone, but more usually the Free French slot, which was introduced by the slogan '*Honneur et Patrie*' (For our honour and our country), was given by the young French journalist Maurice Schumann, who made his mark as a talented broadcaster with a very effective defence of the British action at Mers-el-Kébir on 9 July, the day after de Gaulle's own broadcast. The BBC team who looked after Schumann judged his voice to be too high-pitched and excitable, and tried to persuade him that he needed to drop his register with the help of a kind fib: they told him he would have more chance of penetrating the German jamming if his tone was deeper. Squeaky-voiced or not, Schumann would give more than 1,000 radio talks between July 1940 and the D-Day landings in 1944, and he became – perhaps even more than de Gaulle himself – the voice of Free France.

The third and final item on the French Service menu was the riskiest and, as things turned out, the most inspired. *Ici France* was broadcast after *Honneur et Patrie*, and it was the most obviously 'propagandist' element in the French Service mix. The programme staff answered to Newsome and Gillie, and through them it received directives from the political warfare team who were spinning their propaganda messages out at Woburn Abbey. But the programme content was driven above all by the principle that the French Service – unlike its German and Italian counterparts – was broadcasting to an ally who had been temporarily mislaid, and not a nation which had been lost for ever to the enemy. That allowed the slot to live up to its second and long-running title: in September 1940 it was rebranded as *Les Français parlent aux français*, and the French audience needed to feel that they really were being addressed by their fellow citizens.

The man recruited to run the programme, Michel Saint-Denis, reached Britain after serving as a liaison officer with the British Army during the Dunkirk evacuation. He had worked as a theatre director and actor before the war, and was a powerful physical presence, 'of medium height, broad shoulders and firm loins, fine of foot and with elegant hands. He had a round head and a straight nose, and in his youth he had been nicknamed "the Greek",' wrote one member of his team; 'he adored women, especially actresses'. Saint-Denis moved into his office in Broadcasting House in early July, the first French staff member of the BBC.

Shortly after setting up shop, Saint-Denis asked his friend Jean Oberlé – the French journalist who had burst into tears at that Ministry of Information briefing on the day of France's capitulation – to come into the studio for a recording. 'The Germans are going to use France's radio stations to mess with the heads of compatriots,' he told him; 'the only way they will hear the truth is to listen to London'. He had written a Bastille sketch and wanted Oberlé to play one of the parts. Oberlé, who was an artist as much as a journalist, did not really approve of radio, and thought Saint-Denis's sketch 'mediocre', but he was impressed with the way Saint-Denis 'advised, inspired and encouraged the beginners that we all were'. After the recording they went out to lunch together at a Swiss restaurant in Great Portland Street and Oberlé signed up to the programme team.

Saint-Denis's analysis of the way the Germans planned to use French radio was correct. Article 14 of the armistice Pétain's government signed with Germany on 22 June dictated the closure of Radio Paris and handed control of all radio transmissions from France to the occupying power. On 27 June the BBC announced on the French Service that its transmissions to the Unoccupied Zone of France were being jammed by the French government, which had, only ten days earlier, been its ally. The Germans immediately took over the broadcasting system in the Occupied Zone and also began jamming at the end of June.

On 5 July the Pétain regime was allowed, with Hitler's personal blessing, to re-open the transmitters in the southern part of France which it controlled, and at the same time the Germans began broadcasting from Radio Paris, along with the stations in Rennes and Bordeaux. Radio Strasbourg was simply incorporated into the Reich's network. All these stations began to pump out anti-British propaganda. The response from *Ici France* was wonderfully savage and direct. 'I don't know whether, like me, you have heard it [Radio Paris], but

I can tell you that this soulless voice is like a wound to the ears,' it began, '. . . the German voice mimics Radio Paris, but do not for a moment think it will stop there. They've taken care to warn us. The Germans have made it known that they plan to make the French capital the heart of their movement, their activities, their inspiration. They have even claimed power over its gaiety. Really, really, I promise you, they have used the word gaiety . . . as if the French people could ever become gay again under the eye of some German sergeant, beneath the threat of the Gestapo. It is inevitable that one fine day the order will go out: "From tomorrow, Parisians must be gay."'

Michel Saint-Denis would become a master of this kind of savage irony. He took the *nom de guerre* Jacques Duchesne, and the team he assembled in his small office on the ground floor of Broadcasting House lived up to the most enjoyable British prejudices about our French neighbours. All of them broadcast – and so became famous in France – under false names. Pierre Maillaud, whom we met in the previous chapter, joined under the pseudonym Pierre Bourdan, which was taken from a village in the Berry region of central France. Oberlé describes him as having 'The eye of a dreamer . . . with something melancholy in his look,' and reports that he 'adored wine, and declared that a man needed several litres a day before he could think clearly. He smoked like a chimney, hundreds of English cigarettes which turned his fingers yellow.' Jacques Cotance, who had established a pre-war pseudonymous fame by publishing poetry under the name Brunius, 'proclaimed himself an atheist, wrote poems in surrealist revues, concerned himself with cinema and left-wing thinking, all of which made him a kind of aesthete', and 'affected a certain carelessness in his dress'. There was the tall, handsome Yves Morvan – Jean Marin on the air – who 'feared nothing, drank like a Breton fisherman, was always amiable and courteous', and there was Maurice van Moppès, *aka* Momo, a brilliant but sometimes wayward cartoonist, musician and wordsmith. Oberlé reports that Duchesne would sometimes chase Momo round the studio brandishing a cane when the latter came up with a dud rhyme or a clunky slogan.

The team was put together under great pressure, and they quickly felt at home in Broadcasting House. They were guided by 'two young women, both Cambridge graduates, Miss Glock and Miss Reeves, one a red-head and the other a brunette, who would help us choose between the numerous texts given to us and to record them', and supported by a group of secretaries who 'all spoke kindly of France, where they had sometimes spent their holidays, which had left them with memories of scent bottles and the beaches of the Channel'. The BBC suits rather disapproved of the team's creative habits, but they put up with them; a memo on office accommodation noted that 'It has to be remembered that the French work in a kind of rookery atmosphere of chatter and debate – this may not be desirable, but it is the way they work best, and there is nothing to do about it.'

Some of the glittering Gauls became favourites on the smart social scene, and Tangye Lean has an engaging description of his first meeting with Duchesne/Saint-Denis, at a dinner party. The two found themselves together under a table with their ears pressed to the radio as the evening's French broadcast began. 'Now and then he turned towards me to emphasise with a nod some neat turn of phrase, once he banged his fist at a delayed cue,' Tangye Lean writes. '"We could turn it up a little, yes?" he said with an uneasy glance, because the clatter of plates was now louder than the jamming. I turned it up. "Do you think," our host suddenly said, "you could turn that off – we are finding it hard to hear ourselves dine." A look of complete wretchedness spread over my companion's face, but was followed by an inspiration. "Upstairs!" he said. "There's another set."' Only at the end of the encounter did the Frenchman reveal his true identity, and Tangye Lean reflected that 'Perhaps the main reason for the excellence of *Les Français parlent aux français* was precisely this enthusiasm of its organiser. With a message to give and enough theatrical experience to invent original ways of giving it, half an hour's propaganda became more exciting in his hands than any other radio I have ever heard.'

Sometimes a section of the broadcast would be given over to a kind of riff between members of the team, an apparently spontaneous and informal conversation which was in fact laden with propaganda messages. For example, on 14 July, that first Bastille Day after the fall of France, three of them discussed the parade that had drawn the American broadcaster Eric Sevareid to Whitehall:

Oberlé: . . . It was an astonishing ceremony. There was a whole
    guard mounted by French soldiers, sailors, all sorts of tanks.
Duchesne: That's all very well, but what do you want the people
    of France to do about it all?
Bourdan: Not much, obviously, but they can hope.
Oberlé: And did you hear Churchill's speech? I found that really
    reassuring.
Duchesne: For me it's clear; in all his speeches he has shown
    himself a man who understands France and loves it.

Pro-British messages like that were scattered throughout the conversation. A little later, Duchesne reminisced about his experiences on
the beaches of Dunkirk: 'I saw English soldiers under bombardment.
I can tell you that their conduct – what I saw of it – was magnificent.
They wanted to fight and the only thing that made them suffer was
having to retreat.' This kind of comment was, of course, designed to
counter the anglophobe slurs being put about by the Vichy regime –
the broadcast was less than two weeks after Mers-el-Kébir – but the
message was attractively packaged and the dose of propaganda was
subtly administered. And above all, it came from French lips.

Sometimes the conversation was a real *jeu d'esprit*. A broadcast in
early September, for example, was built around the conceit that the
broadcasters had established a new version of the Académie française
to deal with the way the French language had been distorted by
Germany's victory. 'Let's take the word "Armistice",' they said to
explain the game. 'Before 1940 an armistice meant a day of celebration,
but now it is a day of national mourning.' Each of them drew words
from a hat in turn, and discussed their new meanings:

Van Moppès (pulling a name from the hat): The word is
    'occupation'.
Duchesne: Occupation, occupation, hang on, that rings a bell.
Bourdan: Gentlemen, let's have a look in the *Petit Larousse* – it
    always gives good advice. Oblique (as in angle),
    obscurantism . . . occult . . . here we are, occupation:
    'Occupation: the action of keeping oneself busy, the
    action of making oneself the master of, of establishing
    oneself in . . .'

Oberlé: That's all meaningless.
Bourdan: 'The action of seizing something, of keeping
 something.'
Oberlé: Your *Petit Larousse* is useless.
Bourdan: I accept there's a lot of nonsense here, but could
 we not keep 'Occupation: the action of occupying or
 of occupying oneself'?
Van Moppès: Lace-making and dominoes, those are occupations.
Oberlé: At the moment the Germans have got lots of
 occupations.
All: Not bad. Very good, in fact.
Duchesne: A bit of a joke, but let's put it to the vote . . . hands
 up . . . definition accepted.

Duchesne's fictional academy also redefined 'liberty' as 'a word that has been provisionally suppressed', and Vichy as 'capital of France. As in: the Vichy government governs France, but only two-thirds of it', a reference to the way Germans had divided up the country.

Alongside this kind of clever word-play there were witty slogans, often sung to catchy tunes, which could be picked up and repeated within France. '*Depuis Strasbourg jusqu'à Biarritz / La radio est aux mains des Fritz*' (From Strasbourg to Biarritz/The radio is in Jerry's hands) was soon common currency all over the country, as was a brilliantly simple couplet, sung to the tune of 'La Cucaracha', which reminded everyone who controlled broadcasting there: '*Radio Paris ment, Radio Paris ment, / Radio Paris est Allemand*' (Radio Paris lies, Radio Paris lies/Radio Paris is German). Van Moppès' ditties were so popular that they were collected into a pamphlet called *Chansons de la BBC*, which was illustrated by the cartoonist composer himself. Copies were dropped into France by British planes, and they bore on the back cover the legend 'The songs you have heard on the radio are brought to you courtesy of your friends in the RAF.'

≈

In his definitive record of French Service broadcasting, the distinguished Resistance historian Jean-Louis Crémieux-Brilhac looked back on this period as a golden age: 'French radio from London would never be at once so frank and so spontaneous, and brought to the air with so much vitality,' he wrote, 'as it was during those tragic months in 1940 and 1941 when the outcome of the war was so far from being settled.' Some of the material can seem a little leaden on the page when read today, but to those who heard the broadcasts in the first months of the German occupation they must have been electrifying. It was the darkest hour in France's history, yet here was a team of broadcasters who could be funny about it. Many people in France felt so shattered by the speed of Germany's victory that they simply did not know what to think, and there was intellectual protein in the French Service diet too. Bourdan had specialized in foreign affairs before the war and was assigned to produce commentaries on the day's news; Oberlé believes he invented the news commentary *genre*, and that he was its 'most brilliant' exponent 'on any radio, French or foreign'. The BBC's foreign intelligence assessments reported a consistently high appreciation of his analysis. 'General praise of "*Les Français parlent aux Français*" is frequent,' recorded one Europe Intelligence Report. 'Pierre Bourdan, the "Statues of Paris" programme and the talks by chaplains of the Free French Forces have been particularly appreciated.'

The BBC's foreign intelligence reports were produced monthly, and they were based on a mixture of listeners' letters and information – sometimes no more than anecdotal – which reached Britain with escapees and refugees from Occupied Europe. The first really meaty analysis of the impact of Germany's victory on French listening habits is laid out in the report produced early in September 1940. 'The first conclusion is that the BBC has not lost its audience,' it stated confidently, 'all efforts made to discourage listening to London have so far very largely failed ... The evidence is conclusive; French officers who have escaped from invaded districts, American journalists, and their correspondents, agree.' This was put down partly to a German failure to be consistent in the enforcement of their listening ban. 'In Normandy,' the document reported, 'the German authorities have been threatening suspected listeners with the confiscation of their ration cards,' but 'In Bordeaux, a neutral traveller who had observed general listening all over occupied territory, heard the "French hour" from London turned on loudly in restaurants; German officers who were present did not interfere.' Jamming, however, was seen as a real threat, and not just because it made it difficult for French listeners to pick up the output; the BBC regarded the mere fact of its continued broadcasting into France as a kind of national virility symbol and the authors of the September 1940 intelligence report argued that 'belief in British weakness . . . may grow if the BBC signal, a real proof of British power and confidence, is wiped out each night by interference.'

The fact that letters continued to arrive at the BBC was itself an important indication of the mood in France. As the Vichy regime became more repressive, communication with London became hazardous, and an intelligence report in early 1942 noted that 'Even those who have the ingenuity and pluck to write are to some extent intimidated'; but the flow never dried up altogether, and there is evidence that people were willing to go to great lengths to get their messages to the BBC.

A number of letters preserved in the BBC Written Archives carry a scribbled note recording that they were received via a British embassy in a neutral country (especially Portugal and Switzerland) and some of those from the Occupied Zone included mysterious references to the way they were smuggled across the so-called 'demarcation line' that divided German-occupied France from Vichy territory. One listener who had managed to escape into Vichy told his 'Dear Friends at the BBC' that he had been 'charged, on behalf of a group of listeners in the occupied zone, to express our gratitude and admiration for the magnificent work you have undertaken', and a student from Toulouse wrote, in self-consciously elegant French, 'I know from the BBC's daily programmes that many messages reach you every day; I am sure they get to you by all sorts of methods, including, no doubt, the most roundabout routes; may this poor letter one day carry to those who fight on our behalf the purest homage from their suffering brothers.' Rather charmingly, another student – from Marseilles – declared that he and his friends were planning a huge party when the day of liberation came, and he explained that he was writing to invite the team of *Les Français parlent aux français* to join them; the letter was sent in November 1941, so he was getting his invitation in touchingly early.

The letters became an increasingly valuable source of intelligence about what was happening in France. When anything that might be useful in military terms came the BBC's way, Emile Delavenay, a French scholar and journalist who had been brought in to oversee the BBC's French intelligence work, would pass it on to a contact at the War Office. And his reports noted criticism as well as praise; his September 1940 offering quoted a letter which included the admonition 'You do not repeat often enough over the radio the reasons why you withdrew your troops from France and all the reasons which led to your preferring to continue the struggle alone. I do not think I am exaggerating when I say that half the French people is hostile to you because there are things they do not understand.' The document notes that 'Great Britain is still accused of indifference to French sufferings, of "stabbing France in the back" at Oran; she is still taken to task for her unpreparedness, for her past leniency to Germany, for having "wished that Frenchmen will be killed in her defence".'

The same European intelligence report reflects the complexity of French opinion about Marshal Pétain and their country's new government. Many letters attacked 'the gang of Vichy', but the report notes that 'No voice is raised against the Marshal himself' and quotes a letter which declared, 'We do not like to hear you speak slightly of Marshal Pétain, whom we respect and admire. He is bearing the heaviest part of the sacrifice of which we all must bear our share.' The following month's report noted a change in mood so that 'even the prestige of the Marshal no longer puts him above criticism', but adds, 'Not that the recent conclusions reached last month concerning the inadvisability of attacking him need be modified. Recent such correspondence shows that any such attacks are bitterly resented by many.' All this could, of course, be fed back to the BBC's programme-makers, and it was another 'first' for radio: never before had Britain at war been able to enjoy a constant flow of information and opinion from behind enemy lines.

By the time the October 1940 intelligence report was circulated, the analysts reflected a growing sense of self-confidence. '[A] Lisbon report that "there is not a Frenchman in the occupied territory who does not listen to English broadcasts" may be too optimistic,' they declared, 'but all sources confirm that our audience is increasing, and that in spite of penalties imposed by the Germans, the French civil population in the Paris district find great moral support in the BBC French programmes.' Even Churchill appears to have been impressed by what the BBC had achieved, because he decided to broadcast on the French Service himself.

On 21 October, Duchesne was summoned to Downing Street to help the prime minister with the translation of his speech. After a lunch of roast beef – which was interrupted by an air raid – the two of them got to work over a bottle of brandy, and, in an affectionate BBC broadcast many years later, the Frenchman recalled that Churchill's love of a fine phrase was not, as it were, lost in translation. 'He could not express himself fluently in French,' he remembered, 'but he understood the qualities of our language well enough to have a sense of whether it reflected his English, which was highly coloured, colloquial and eloquent all at the same time'. Churchill was especially pleased with a phrase he had come up with to describe the techniques of the Gestapo, 'the scientific low-cunning of a ruthless police force', and complained that Duchesne's translation ('*la bassesse et la ruse*', or baseness and trickery) was too abstract. Was there not a suitable word beginning with 'c', he asked, perhaps '*la basse et ignominieuse crafterie scientifique*'? The prime minister was disappointed to be told this was nonsense, but he brightened up when 'we thought of "*rira bien qui rira le dernier* [he who laughs last will laugh longest]" for all will come right,' and 'he was delighted when he suggested himself that his first call to the Resistance Movement should end with a sentence which he had read all over France during the war of 1914–18: *Les oreilles ennemies vous écoutent* [Enemy ears are listening to you].'

Churchill snatched a catnap while the speech was typed up in the style of all his speeches – in big letters and laid out like free verse, with breaks in the script dictated by rhythm rather than grammar – and then presented himself for a rehearsal, pink from a hot bath and wearing his blue siren suit. His French accent was famously off-key – de Gaulle is reported to have said that he learned English so that he could understand Churchill speaking French – but he enjoyed playing up his Englishness, and while rehearsing the speech he told Duchesne that 'If my French is too good they will like me less.' However, he applied himself diligently during Duchesne's lessons in pronunciation and 'relished some words as if he was tasting fruit'. Faced with the challenge of broadcasting in a foreign language, Churchill abstained from his usual evening consumption of brandy.

The broadcast was to be made from the Cabinet War Rooms, the underground bunker complex between the Foreign Office and St James's Park, and when the time came for the prime minister and his party to leave Downing Street for the waiting microphone there was another air raid in progress. Duchesne recalled that 'we crossed Downing Street running behind him; the anti-aircraft guns were firing from very close by and the shell bursts over our heads were followed by the whistling showers of falling splinters'. They crossed the grand courtyard of the Foreign Office, dashed down Clive Steps at the end of King Charles Street and disappeared underground.

Today the War Rooms are a tourist attraction, but in 1940 they were a closely guarded secret, and Duchesne was dazzled by the Bond-like world where the machinery of government hummed away in subterranean safety. Churchill's room was furnished with a camp bed and a table covered with battle plans. The prime minister settled comfortably into his chair in front of the microphone, but there was nowhere for Duchesne to sit when he introduced him. Churchill 'looked about him,' Duchesne recorded, '. . . and said "On my knees." Leaning back in the armchair he tapped his thigh. I inserted a leg between his and there I was, seated partly on the arm of the chair and partly on his knee.'

Duchesne had to sustain a good two minutes perched on the prime ministerial thigh while he read his introduction, then he discreetly extricated himself and left the microphone to Churchill, who first delivered the speech in English. When the time came to begin the French version, the prime minister ad-libbed an opening: '*Français, c'est moi, Churchill, qui vous parle*' (People of France, it is I,

Churchill, speaking to you). And off he went. He stumbled once or twice, but very few British prime ministers since his time could have managed almost fourteen minutes of near faultless French, even with the advantage of Duchesne's expert tutoring.

Churchill quoted the prayer on a French coin: 'God protect France'. He told his audience that he had walked alongside them for thirty years, in peace and war, and when he warned them of Hitler's ambitions he used one of those French words that can get English tongues into a terrible tangle: the 'Nazi gangsters' were, he said, bent on the '*anéantissement*' – annihilation – of everything French, 'army, navy, air force' – a big pause for emphasis here – 'religion, law, language, culture, institutions, literature, history, traditions'. He ended with a '*Vive la France*'.

Today we think of Churchill as a kind of British Bulldog, but Duchesne records that during their lunch together he broke down in tears when he spoke about what was happening to France, and his sensitivity to French culture and French national pride shines through this broadcast. In greatness it ranks alongside the 1940s speeches in the Commons which are so much more familiar to a British audience.

When it was over, Churchill loaned Duchesne his armoured car for the journey back to Broadcasting House and the following day Lady Churchill invited the Frenchman to lunch at a French restaurant near Covent Garden. She told him her husband had been well pleased with the way the evening had gone.

Some of the stories that reached the BBC's Intelligence Unit from France may have been more myth than reality, but there's an enjoyable anecdote about the way Churchill's speech was received which pops up in a number of sources, including Tangye Lean's book. He reported that on the morning of the speech 'a form-master in a *lycée* near Paris told his assembled pupils that it was no ordinary day. "We are going to hear the leader of the Allied Forces," he said. "The broadcast will be badly jammed, so will each of you take down every sentence you can hear properly? We will piece it together tomorrow." Next day they succeeded in reconstructing the speech in full.'

IMPREGNABLE FORTRESS
OF STUPIDITY

AT THE END OF August 1940, British bombers attacked Berlin over three consecutive nights, and on 4 September Hitler promised the German people that he would retaliate in kind. 'When they declare that they will attack our cities in great strength,' he told them, 'then we will eradicate their cities.' Three days later the Blitz began: on Saturday, 7 September, 350 German bombers, protected by the same number of fighters, attacked London's docklands, igniting a fire so vast and intense that it is said to have done more damage to the capital than the Great Fire of 1666.

Until then the Luftwaffe had concentrated on destroying airfields, and the switch to civilian and commercial targets was to prove a costly mistake; it gave the RAF a breathing space to repair its runways and its planes, and on 15 September two massive Luftwaffe attacks were driven back with heavy losses (some sixty German planes were brought down, while the RAF lost fewer than half that number). It was a decisive victory, and 15 September is now celebrated as Battle of Britain Day. Two days later Hitler postponed Operation Sea Lion, the planned invasion of Britain, indefinitely.

But the Blitz intensified. On 7 October the Germans switched their efforts to bombing during the hours of darkness, and on the night of 15 October 380 bombers hit London, killing 200 people and injuring 2,000. The casualties at Broadcasting House were among them. Marjorie Redman spent the night in north London. 'Last night not so bad in Hampstead,' she wrote in her diary, 'though did not sleep till the All Clear at 5.30. But other parts of London apparently had a dreadful time. Mass raids, the paper says, for first time. It is full moon and they'd dropped incendiary and h.e. [high explosive] bombs everywhere. Miss Playle had all her windows blown out; Miss Street-Porter had to leave her flat in middle of the night, and was nearly blown up as she walked down the road. I find on arrival at Broadcasting House that a bomb went into the 5th floor, on the Portland Place side, at 8.05 last night, and exploded at 9.02, killing six or seven people. Bruce Belfrage was reading the news when it went off. He paused, but continued – rather breathlessly – to the end. There is a gaping hole in the side of the building, but, except that the telephones are not working, most people are able to use their offices and get on with their jobs as usual.'

In the spirit of 'getting on as usual', Miss Redman records that in her lunch hour she popped out to buy some boots for winter, a prudent step 'before Purchasing Tax is put on next week', and her diary for the day ends with a reminder that 'politics as usual' continued at Westminster, despite the surrounding mayhem. 'Churchill declines to make statement on our war aims,' she wrote. 'Will only say we are fighting to survive. Feel if, after nearly 14 months of war and all the suffering of the civilian population, we do not know what we are fighting for, it is a poor do.'

This was a reference to an exchange in the Commons that afternoon between the prime minister and the left-wing Labour MP Sydney Silverman, who repeatedly pressed Churchill to 'take an early opportunity of stating, in general terms, our aims in this war, so that this country may take its rightful place as the leader of all those, wherever they may be found, who desire a new order in Europe, based not upon slavery to Germany but upon collective justice, prosperity, and security.' Churchill stonewalled; 'the time has not come when any official declaration can be made of war aims beyond the very carefully considered general statements which have already been published,' he said.

Silverman came back twice, accusing the government of giving 'the quite false impression that we are fighting this war merely to retain the status quo', and appealing to Churchill 'to assure those who think with us all over the world that we are ready to lead the fight for the better world which we all want.' The prime minister would not be moved. 'We are, among other things, fighting it in order to survive,' he told the Commons (which was still, just, meeting in the Palace of Westminster, but would soon be forced by the bombing to decamp to Church House across the road), 'and when our capacity to do that is more generally recognised throughout the world, when the conviction that we have about it here becomes more general, then we shall be in a good position to take a further view of what we shall do with the victory when it is won.'

This was one of the great fault lines of wartime politics. It helps explain Labour's extraordinary General Election victory in 1945, and it has also led to one of the most enduring myths about the wartime BBC: that Churchill had J. B. Priestley sacked by the Corporation because of his left-wing views. The prime minister believed that only winning mattered, and was determined to resist being drawn into what he saw as a distracting debate about a New Jerusalem in a post-war Britain. Priestley was very firmly aligned with those on the left who thought that the British people deserved some reward for the courage they had shown over the summer. 'That reward should have been,' he wrote later, 'the pledge and passionate assurance that we were not fighting Hitler in order to return to an idiotic state of things THAT WOULD INEVITABLY PRODUCE MORE Hitlers, that a new Britain would become the cornerstone of a new world order, that the bad old days of greed, selfishness, privilege, plutocratic government, unemployment, distressed areas, bad housing, and all the rest were gone for good.' And he echoed Sydney Silverman's comments about the danger that Britain would be perceived as 'fighting this war merely to retain the status quo'. 'Nobody outside this country wants to fight for rich English Tories,' Priestley wrote in the *News Chronicle*.

During the summer of 1940 Priestley was, as we have seen, as anxious as Churchill to evoke a spirit of national unity. But as the autumn advanced, and with a long winter of bombing in prospect ('as the blackout hour crept towards the afternoon', was the way Priestley strikingly put it), his *Postscripts* moved into more sensitive political territory. The first concerns were raised within the BBC itself – and in a very BBC-ish way. In early September the head of talks, Sir Richard Maconachie, sent a memo round his senior colleagues asking them to reflect on Priestley's position. 'He has definite views, which he puts over in his broadcasts,' he wrote, 'and is, I think, exercising an important influence on what people are thinking. These views may be admirable or otherwise, but the question which I wish to raise is one of principle – whether any single person should be given the opportunity of acquiring such an influence to the exclusion of others who differ from him, merely on the ground of his merits as a broadcaster, which are, of course, very great.'

Maconachie was right to flag the risk. A month later Priestley broadcast a *Postscript* that enraged many in the Tory Party. He began – characteristically – with an anecdote, a story of how difficult it had become to find hotel rooms in provincial towns. The reason, Priestley concluded, was that country hotels had been booked up by idle folk rich enough to escape the London bombs, and his script moves swiftly up through the gears from irritation to vituperation and cosmic rage. 'A large proportion of the people who are able to live in comparative peace, security and quiet consists, not of persons recovering from overwork, strain or shock, but those persons who don't know what to do with themselves,' he said.

This reflection becomes a springboard for a more general attack on the class system: 'This has, for a long time now, been a country in which there are far too many pleasant, able-bodied persons who, because of some system of private incomes or pensions and all kinds of snobbish nonsense, are condemned to yawn away their lives, forever wondering what to do between meals; in startling contrast to other people who wonder how to get it all done between meals. This is certainly true of certain types of women, who have been made so comfortably secure by timid parents that they have been shut out of the whole adventure of living.' And the *Postscript* ends with a good belt of just the sort of 'New Jerusalem' rhetoric that was bound to get up Tory noses. 'We are at present floundering between two stools,' Priestley declared, 'One of them is our old acquaintance labelled "Every man for himself" ... The other stool, on which millions are already perched without knowing it, has some lettering round it that hints that free men could combine, without losing what's essential to their free development, to see that each gives according to his ability, and receives according to his need.'

The following day the BBC's home controller, A. P. Ryan, was called into the Ministry of Information headquarters at Senate House for an uncomfortable meeting. Colonel Scorgie, a senior Ministry official, told him that 'he had had several telephone calls saying that last night's talk was calculated a) to set the rich against the poor b) to annoy country districts'. Scorgie also pointed out that the BBC's Monitoring Service had picked up a propaganda broadcast which 'quoted Priestley's radio speech of yesterday as showing how rich Englishmen could be found tucked well away from the AA guns and the German bombs'. Ryan, who was a brilliant bureaucrat, replied that Priestley 'is an individualist, and insists on speaking what is from time to time in his mind, and would rather go off the air than be cut about'. He warned that Priestley 'is very conscious of being criticised for political reasons, and, if he were put off, would undoubtedly not go without raising Cain in the press'.

This was no idle threat. An internal BBC report that morning revealed that Priestley still had overwhelming support among the listeners, with an average weekly audience of 11 million, although it also noted that there had been 'a falling off lately in correspondence about him addressed to the BBC, and an increase of criticism on political grounds'. Ryan managed to persuade the meeting that 'We cannot treat a prima donna like a third row chorus girl,' and the matter was allowed to drop. One of those present was the Tory MP and diarist Harold Nicolson, in his capacity as a junior minister at the Ministry. He offered the view that Conservative Central Office would attach great weight to 'the argument that if Priestley was silenced on political grounds eleven million people would want to know the reason why'. Given the subject of the meeting, it is perhaps worth noting that Nicolson was one of two officials present with a taste for living in castles – the other being the art historian Kenneth Clark.

The suggestion that Priestley should end his run of *Postscripts* in fact came from Priestley himself. A week after the Senate House meeting he wrote to Ryan from the Midland Hotel in Manchester to say that 'I want to have a complete rest from broadcasting quite soon'. As well as producing his weekly *Postscript*, he had been broadcasting regularly to the United States, which often involved working late at night, and he wrote that this had 'left me very tired, and possibly for that reason, I am becoming increasingly impatient with the silly little censorships of my script and lack of any real co-operation with the authorities (I am still referring to overseas)'. That final parenthesis is important. Priestley's complaint about censorship related to his work as a broadcaster to foreign audiences, and at no point in the letter does he complain that his Home Service *Postscripts* have been interfered with by the censor or anyone else; he simply states that he thinks it sensible to leave the Home Service 'while the going's good and they are not tired of me'.

Priestley's last *Postscript* of the run was broadcast on 20 October, and he began by rehearsing the reasons for stopping he had given to Ryan. 'The decision was mine,' he stated emphatically, 'and was in no way forced upon me by the BBC.' But he added 'another rather more subtle reason'. He reminds his listeners that 'I began these postscripts just after Dunkirk; got going with them during those blazing summer weeks when France collapsed and we were threatened with imminent invasion, and world opinion began to think we were doomed. We knew very well that we weren't doomed, and our people began to show what stuff they're made of, and the sight was glorious ... That was the high mood of the summer and I can only hope that I went some little way towards expressing it.'

The war, Priestley suggests, entered a new phase with victory in the Battle of Britain; 'this period, I think, came to an end with the defeat of the German Air Force over England by the R.A.F. and the failure of Goering's terror tactics to break the morale of the people of London,' he told his audience on 20 October. 'We're now entering a new period, and I think it should be interpreted for you on Sunday nights by a new postscripter, and preferably a speaker who feels the same sense of exultation about this period that I did about the earlier one.'

The Blitz still had another five months to run, and victory was, of course, fully four and a half years away, but it was a sharp judgement – both about the progress of the war and about his own position. Priestley was straining at the leash to fight on a new political front, and he surely knew that the BBC could not provide him with a permanent platform to attack the prime minister. He could not resist a bilious swipe at his opponents before saying goodbye. His final paragraph begins, 'I make no apology to those listeners who, out of their impregnable fortress of stupidity, have assured me of their hostility. I can only assure them that I propose to go on disliking more and more everything they stand for.'

Priestley's fans simply would not believe that he had not been sacked. Marjorie Redman's diary gives us a flavour of the gossip doing the rounds at the BBC. 'Learn that Priestley was removed from broadcasting mostly by intervention of Margesson, Conservative Chief Whip,' she wrote. 'Don't wonder – he said so many things that needed saying, such as that it was disgraceful that people who had money but did no useful work should be able to escape from London and book up all hotels etc., so that people who are worn to death by bombing could find nowhere to stay. And other outspoken things.' It seems she and her colleagues at the *Listener* had already had dealings with David Margesson over the book *Guilty Men*, an attack on Chamberlain and his fellow appeasers that had been published under a pseudonym in July 1940. 'Same man, Margesson,' she wrote, 'objected to *Listener* reviewing "*Guilty Men*", which indicted several members of Conservative Party, eg Chamberlain, etc., as being responsible for our being at war.'

Many listeners were equally convinced that there were dirty deeds being done. A BBC memo on 25 October recorded that 1,600 letters had already come in following Priestley's final *Postscript* five days earlier. 'Of these,' it reported, 'about 1300 were addressed directly to Mr Priestley by name and, almost without exception they expressed appreciation of the series as a whole and regretted that it had come to an end. A considerable number of the correspondents appear to suspect the BBC of bringing pressure to bear on Mr Priestley to wind up the series (some of them said they detected a "sadness" in his voice) and a good many others were disappointed in him for not taking a firmer stand against the "fortress of stupidity" of which he complained in his final broadcast.' C. B. D. Vernon of the left-wing *New Statesman and Nation* magazine wrote to say that, 'We refuse to believe that this decision came entirely from Mr Priestley,' and that it was 'very alarming to suspect that some influence has been brought to bear on Mr Priestley – or that the attitude of certain circles in this country has brought to an end this very fine series of talks. There were indications in last night's talk which suggest this.'

While Priestley continued to state publicly that he had given up his Sunday slot of his own accord, he was not at all averse to stirring up suspicion that he had been badly treated. A week after his valedictory *Postscript*, he published a piece in the *Sunday Express* under the headline 'The Difficulties I had to Fight'. 'You begin to suspect,' he wrote, 'that perhaps we are not all in the same war when, doing a job of this kind you find yourself day after day being obstructed instead of being encouraged. You want to describe something and are told shortly you cannot describe it, and are not even vouchsafed a reason. It is as if you are a naughty child. Then your text is absurdly mutilated on censorship grounds, though many of the corrections are nonsensical. You almost suspect yourself of being an enemy agent . . . Sometimes, weary and exasperated, you feel like a man compelled to walk across a field of glue.'

These comments – like those in his note to A. P. Ryan – related specifically to his work for the Overseas Service, but the piece was clearly designed to evoke a more general sense of sinister behaviour by 'the men high up' (Priestley's loaded phrase), who, he writes, do not understand the value of public opinion and 'wish to be left alone to fight some secret little war of their own. And they either cannot, or they will not, understand what this other huge conflict, in which public opinion counts for all, is about.' In a barb that must have stung, he contrasts the attitude of the British governing classes with those of the leading Nazis, who 'never make the mistake of under-estimating the importance of constant efforts at persuasion'.

Priestley followed up this sally with a piece in the *News Chronicle* in which he cast himself, rather than the BBC, as the true champion of free speech. 'I must point out what few listeners appear to know,' he wrote, 'namely, that in wartime the BBC is controlled, so far as policy and opinion are concerned, by the Ministry of Information, which in its turn is controlled by the War Cabinet. As talks such as the Postscripts are regarded as semi-official, there is, of course, far less freedom of opinion in them than there is in newspaper articles. All those listeners who urged me "to say more" can be told now that I stretched the censorship as far as it would go.'

In early November Harold Nicolson memorably described Priestley as a 'sly demagogue', who, he confided to his diary, retired 'in the guise of a martyr whereas if only he had been given five or six more talks he would have retired in the guise of a bore'. Priestley was certainly not above slyness; at about the time Nicolson recorded this judgement, the recently retired postscripter suggested a plot to the senior BBC official Sir Stephen Tallents. 'I feel strongly that you and Ogilvie [the director-general] ought to press the claims of broadcasting upon the government as hard as you possibly can,' he wrote, 'and if I resign temporarily from all my broadcasting jobs, it seems to me that I make your case easier to fight; for though often regarded as a "difficult man" (actually I am not, and am very conscientious about any job I undertake to do), the fact remains that, apart from the PM himself, I am probably the most popular broadcaster on both the home and overseas programmes and therefore I can present you with a good case.' Tallents wrote a polite letter back declining to be drawn into this game.

Churchill's minister of information, Duff Cooper, sent a note to Priestley 'to let you know what an admirable public service I feel your talks to have rendered', but the relationship between the two men was marked by flashes of really quite violent antipathy. When the possibility that Priestley might return to the airwaves was discussed later in the year, the minister told one of his civil servants that 'Priestley was a second-rate novelist, who had got conceited by his broadcasting success'. There may have been an element of envy at play here, as Cooper had literary pretensions of his own and could not claim anything like Priestley's success as a writer. But it was certainly true that Priestley's fame as a broadcaster had made him more difficult to deal with, and one of the BBC officials involved in managing the increasingly cantankerous postscripter recorded that 'Priestley seems to have a personal resentment against the Minister.'

If the two men had been able to get beyond their mutual dislike, they might have realized that, on some of the really big issues that concerned them both, they were of similar mind. Cooper was every bit as convinced as Priestley that Churchill should be persuaded to spell out the government's war aims – indeed this was something of an article of faith in the Ministry of Information generally. In his book *Ministry of Morale*, Ian McLaine writes that 'There was throughout the period under discussion [the summer of 1940] an uneasy feeling in the Ministry that unless the government made a firm pledge of post-war social reform the people would not be persuaded to give all their energies to the war effort.' The matter was discussed at a meeting of the Home Morale Emergency Committee in the immediate aftermath of Dunkirk, and the Ministry's senior civil servant declared that 'our aim should be to redress grievances and inequality and create new opportunities'. The officials were particularly concerned that the British public might react favourably to a peace offer from Hitler if they were not given more of a sense of what they were fighting for. The job of drafting an appropriate set of principles was given to two of the Ministry's grandest grandees – the castle-dwellers Harold Nicolson and Kenneth Clark. They were told – apparently without any sense of irony – to 'include the abolition of privilege and equality of opportunity'.

Duff Cooper, who would have the job of selling these ideas to Churchill, warned that the Ministry ought 'not to go too far in the matter of proclaiming a "revolutionary" doctrine', but the memorandum that went to the Cabinet at the end of July contained passages that could have come straight out of a Priestley *Postscript*. 'We should proclaim that we intend to make a better world at home,' it advised, 'in which the abuses of the past shall not be allowed to reappear. Unemployment, education, housing and the abolition of privilege should form the main planks of such a platform.' Cooper hoped that the presence of Labour ministers in the Cabinet would give the proposal a following wind, but Churchill remained immovably opposed to anything of this kind. The idea was, in the best Whitehall tradition, shunted off into a committee, which eventually produced a 'discussion paper', but Duff Cooper had fought as hard as he could for just the sort of war aims statement that Priestley was calling for.

And Cooper would certainly have endorsed Priestley's view that 'the men high up' were not interested in the propaganda war. He was full of enthusiasm for his job when he was appointed by Churchill in May 1940, but he soon discovered that many senior figures in the services, the War Cabinet and, above all, at Number 10 were largely indifferent to the work of his Ministry. It eventually sapped his will; Harold Nicolson wrote that 'Duff is not really on very good terms with the P.M. And does not wish to press difficult requests on him. He hopes to live from day to day without trouble from authority'. Francis Williams, who joined the Ministry of Information from the *Daily Herald* newspaper in the spring of 1941, recalled that by then his minister 'preferred talking over lunch to doing anything ... he was almost wholly ineffectual'.

The Priestley problem bubbled away throughout the autumn of 1940. Despite the widespread public suspicion that he had been 'bumped off by the BBC', he had not, in fact, stopped broadcasting for the Overseas Service, and in early December he caused another ruckus when he referred to Blitz life in Britain as 'wildly and solidly abnormal – almost crazy'. The following day the BBC's Monitoring Service picked up a German propaganda broadcast in which the announcer quoted this remark, and added that Priestley's talk betrayed real doubt about whether the United States would ever come to Britain's aid. 'I find it very interesting to hear Priestley calmly telling the British people what we have been telling them for months,' the announcer continued. 'Why is he doing it? Because Churchill realises that the bad news has at length to be broken, and prefers to leave the breaking of it to a good-natured and quite popular novelist, rather than depute a political personage to convey the dismal tidings' – so at just the moment the rumour-mongers in Britain were accusing Churchill of conspiring against Priestley, the Germans were accusing the two of them of conspiring together.

Duff Cooper did not find the incident at all funny, and a sharp memo was despatched from the Ministry of Information to the BBC demanding that all the paperwork related to the broadcast be sent over. The minister also wanted a note on whether Priestley really was of great value as an overseas broadcaster. 'He has not always been easy to handle,' the BBC admitted, but Auntie still insisted that 'Priestley's talks in the Voice of Britain have been the outstanding success with audiences overseas, especially, but by no means exclusively, in the USA. Thousands of appreciative letters, addressed to him and to the BBC make this clear.' One BBC mandarin rather cattily suggested that the real reason for Cooper's irritation was personal vanity; he was a regular target in German propaganda broadcasts, and the Monitoring Report which recorded the German references to Priestley also included 'Unflattering references to the Minister'. The memo went on, 'We naturally do not suppress such unflattering references and I hope he would not wish us to do so.'

After several weeks of fractious negotiations – involving the BBC, the Ministry of Information and Priestley himself – it was agreed that he would broadcast a new series of six *Postscripts*, beginning on 26 January 1941. Priestley was able to drive a hard financial bargain. He was paid 10 guineas a throw for his first season of *Postscripts*, and that remained the going rate for the postscripters who followed him after his run ended; now for the new series he was to be paid 50 guineas each – over £2,000 in today's money – and he was offered a further 15 guineas for the right to reprint the scripts in the *Listener.*

At the final meeting to settle the deal, the BBC director-general, Frederick Ogilvie, A. P. Ryan and Sir Walter Monckton, the director-general of the Ministry of Information, convened early and 'before Priestley came in' agreed how the new series would be censored. The BBC would have responsibility for ensuring that Priestley did not violate any 'formal censor Stops', and any 'policy points' would be forwarded to the Ministry of Information. But they must all have understood that their power to control what Priestley said would be limited, and, sure enough, the very first of the new run was the political equivalent of one of Göring's incendiary bombs. Monckton sent the script back to the BBC with a weary-sounding note. 'I have no doubt that this broadcast will produce a large measure of criticism,' he wrote, 'but I doubt whether there is any of it which we can actively interfere with.'

Priestley opened with a nasty swipe at those who had filled his chair in his absence: 'like you I've been delighted by the charm and persuasiveness of the various speakers, no matter whether they'd learnt the trick of it in the law courts or Shaftesbury Avenue [one of them was a lawyer and another an actor]. The matter could be more easily criticised than the manner.' He then climbed on to his favourite hobby-horse and charged full-pelt back into the fray, arguing once again that the government should declare itself for a new post-war order of things: 'What we want is a short, clear creed, acceptable to the decent common man everywhere, that will act like a trumpet-call; and then we must proclaim it every hour of the day and night, sending it thundering through the ether, showering it down in millions of pamphlets, painting it indelibly on walls, until even the Nazis them-selves see it written in letters of fire everywhere and their huge crazy empire of blood and terror suddenly cracks and totters, and crashes to its doom'.

This was too much for Churchill, who sent a memo to Duff Cooper complaining that Priestley was making 'an argument utterly contrary to my known views'. Tory backbenchers were up in arms too, and the minister of information also had to face an angry deputation from the 1922 Committee. To his credit, Cooper did his best to resist the pressure, assuring the prime minister that the BBC would 'give Priestley a rest' once his six contracted *Postscripts* had been completed.

In his book *Priestley's Wars*, Neil Hanson writes that 'It is incon-ceivable that Priestley was not aware of the prime ministerial displeasure and, whether by coincidence or not, the following broadcasts were less confrontational in tone and dealt with "safer" subjects like the national diet.'

Priestley was also coming under fire in the right-wing papers by this stage, and while the BBC postbag suggested he still enjoyed widespread support from the audience – the broadcast that irritated Churchill so much prompted 'over a thousand appreciative letters and about 200 from people who do not like him' – he provoked violently negative reactions from some sections of the audience. One listener described his work as 'smug patronising class-conscious stuff and platitudinous balderdash', and another offered the view that, 'Were Mr Priestley a Nazi agent he could do no better work for our enemies.' A study by Listener Research concluded that, 'It would not be fair to say that Priestley's appreciative public has declined, but his critics are more numerous and seem to have formed themselves into a more solid body of opinion with common grounds for complaint.' A. P. Ryan managed to negotiate two extra *Postscript* slots for Priestley (in addition to the six he had originally agreed), but he was finding it increasingly difficult to resist pressure from the Ministry of Information.

The censored script of Priestley's penultimate *Postscript* survives in the BBC files, and the way it has been cut about underlines how sensitive these broadcasts had become. The subject was the Merchant Navy; he had taken it on at the government's request, but he used it to return to his call for the promise of a better future. Where his original script has the socialist-sounding 'We owe these men decent social justice,' the censor has written, 'We owe these men a square deal.' Where Priestley has 'We've no right to be praising men one year and then letting them rot a year or two later,' the censor has replaced 'letting them rot' with 'ignoring them'. Priestley's text continues, 'At which, somebody mutters impatiently "yes, yes, yes, but we can attend to all that kind of thing later". Well, perhaps we can, though we never have done yet.' That might have been taken as a pop at Churchill, and was excised altogether. A couple of lines of Kipling have been introduced by the censor, and a note in the margin suggests this will make the message seem less 'political'. And where Priestley wrote of 'the old neglect and shabbiness and greedy jobbery', the censor has insisted it be reduced to 'the old neglect'.

Priestley's last *Postscript* was broadcast on 23 March 1941. A few days later he wrote to A. P. Ryan, 'You may be right in assuring me that political pressure has nothing to do with this move. But I do assure you that although it will certainly please some people and in that respect probably make your life easier, it remains, simply from the point of view of broadcasting, a rotten move.' This was ungrateful. He had, thanks to Ryan's efforts, been given two extra programmes, but he had apparently come to think of the Sunday-evening slot as his by right, and he was, as an internal BBC memo put it, 'smouldering – and sometimes blazing – with a perfectly sincere consciousness of an alleged injustice done to him'.

His letter to Ogilvie a couple of months later suggests that he became more, not less angry as time went by, and – this is still a common delusion among successful broadcasters – he had come to believe that his own career and the health of broadcasting culture were one and the same. 'I think you are allowing the most successful talks feature you have ever had to be deliberately wrecked, and this at a time when such a feature is of immense value to the BBC and the nation,' he told the director-general. 'But that is not all. I must also point out that I have been treated with shocking cynicism.' Priestley claimed – a 'shockingly cynical' untruth of his own – that he had never been told his broadcasts would be limited to six, and in an astonishingly disingenuous piece of footwork, declared, with an air of injured innocence, that his talks 'were not political, never mentioned a politician or a political party, contained no political arguments and instances'.

Nothing has come to light to suggest that Winston Churchill insisted that Priestley should be silenced, and Nicholas Hawkes, Priestley's stepson, who interrogated the evidence in depth for his book *J. B. Priestley's Postscripts*, could find no smoking gun. But there is equally no doubt that Priestley's run of *Postscripts* was brought to an end for political reasons. Ian McLaine refers, approvingly, to George Orwell's view that 'the Ministry of Information achieved the suppression of "undesirable or premature" news and opinion by participation in a conspiracy of the governing classes, which had always succeeded in preventing public discussion of anything thought to be uncongenial', and Priestley's suspicions that, as the *Daily Herald* put it, 'Powerful influences have been working against him' were well founded.

It is also true, however, that insiders like Ryan fought hard to keep him on the air, and Maconachie, one of the great guardians of Auntie's conscience, was right to question his monopoly on the uniquely popular *Postscripts* slot. And although it is possible to cast this episode as a conflict between power and free speech, it was all rather gentlemanly. No one was locked up, tortured or murdered as they might have been in Nazi Germany.

At the beginning of June 1941, still smarting from what he believed to be his shabby treatment, Priestley told Basil Nicholls, the BBC's controller of programmes, that 'I have been told, with what truth I don't know, that with ordinary folk up and down the country I am next in popularity to Churchill, an odd and rather embarrassing position for a private individual to find himself in.' The modesty is less than convincing. 'What happens when I go about, getting material for my Picture Post articles, rather confirms this,' Priestley continues. 'I was visiting miners last week, and the managing director of one big group of collieries assured me that my visit had done them all more good than anything that had happened for months and months.'

In the same letter Priestley takes the opportunity to vent his antipathy towards Val Gielgud, who had recently declined the offer of a Priestley play for broadcast. 'To my astonishment, there was much humming and ha-ing, and talk of not being suitable for broadcasting, etc.,' Priestley writes, 'and so I have asked for the script to be returned, and have told Gielgud that I do not propose to make any further suggestions to his department.' It appears that Gielgud has sinned in this regard before, and Priestley declares that 'It does seem to me unfair to the more serious listening public when a serious new play by me is not accepted at once, at a time when the public is not being offered much good new stuff.' He insisted that 'I like Gielgud personally' and that his remarks are 'off the record', but he feels that Nicholls should know his view that Gielgud 'tends to suit his own tastes too much in his choice of drama material'.

Later that year Priestley was back on the Home Service with a series called *Listen to My Notebook*. It was not a great success, and he seems to have blamed everyone but himself for the failure. 'Throughout the series I was truly appalled by the lack of publicity,' he complained, 'and the apparent inadequacy of the BBC to inform the public that this series, which after all was breaking new ground in several directions, was in existence at all.' He moaned about 'stuffy and unhealthy' studio conditions, was scathing about the BBC actors who performed some of his material ('unless carefully checked they are apt to give routine ham performances') and objected to being required to put the programmes together at the Manchester studios ('From my point of view, Manchester has nothing to recommend it, being far from London, hard to get about at night, unpopular with actors because of its bad lodgings, etc'). He is grumpy about the time wasted on the wrong effects records, and argues that the time he was given for rehearsals was inadequate. Finally he claims that he and the production team felt unloved, and would have liked 'a little more personal encouragement to the players and technical staff' in the form of 'a visit from a higher official, a compliment or two, and occasional drink and sandwich'.

This complaint landed on Val Gielgud's desk. The rebuke he delivered in response was magisterial – perhaps word had reached him that Priestley had been dripping his gossipy venom into the ear of the controller of programmes. 'Difficulties with studios, lack of rehearsal and effects have been commonplace to our work for so long,' wrote the head of drama, 'that it is a little difficult to take with any extreme seriousness this sort of whimper from someone who is having his hand held and a hot water bottle applied to his feet throughout.' He defends his actors and dismisses the idea that Priestley's programme was 'breaking new ground'; in Gielgud's view, 'The programmes as a whole seem to me to reflect very little more from Priestley than a continuous picking of the brains of the Features Department.'

And then there is this: 'Finally, I think Priestley's last paragraph is grotesque. As you know, he declined anything in the way of criticism or supervision. He objected strongly to the occasion on which other people and myself listened to one of his rehearsals. He cut me dead at a range of six feet in the Monseigneur [hotel] twice when I went there in order to be present at transmissions, and in general his manners were deplorable. Why he should expect, when he chooses to behave like this, that he should not only be given a free run to the microphone but also pats on the back and lumps of barley sugar, is frankly beyond my comprehension. For a man of such ability and such a record of successes, this document of his does not stand out as particularly creditable, either in its sense of proportion or in its sense of humour.'

Priestley was, however, right to say that his departure from *Postscripts* was, 'simply from the point of view of broadcasting, a rotten move'; the BBC never found anyone else who could make the slot work so well. They tried almost every writer you can think of from the period, and the files are full of gossipy comment on some of our greatest literary figures. T. S. Eliot is described as 'rather a difficult man, but might say something very interesting to the highbrows and the young on the necessity for identity', while the historian Arthur Bryant is dismissed because of his 'Mystical style; unattractive to this audience'. George Bernard Shaw gets a good rating – 'Brilliant, Excellent matter, very stimulating, Fireworks. Speaks very fast' – while the crime writer Dorothy L. Sayers is given a more nuanced 'Opinions divided. Great possibilities. Not as tiresome as she makes out'. Arnold Toynbee is described as 'Fluffy, able to simplify usefully'; this judgement was credited to a certain G. Burgess – the notorious Cambridge spy did a wartime stint with Auntie.

And the search for new postscripters threw up some truly eccentric results. The BBC's Wales Office in Cardiff sent in a suggestion for a talk on 'the complete and sudden transformation of a hillside of Bracken into a very fruitful, large potato patch in the course of comparatively few weeks. To be given by the County Agricultural administrator in West Wales', and one on '"Growing my Linseed Crop" on ground that had been grassland for many years. To be given by a lady farmer in West Wales'. There is also a scribbled note putting forward the name of a certain 'Mrs Miniver'. This surely was desperation; Mrs Miniver was a fictional character, the eponymous heroine of a book (and later a Hollywood film) about Blitz life in Britain.

FIREFLIES IN A SOUTHERN
SUMMER NIGHT

I N EARLY 1941 PENELOPE FITZGERALD wrote to an Oxford friend with
a vivid picture of BBC life in the Blitz. 'The BBC is not exactly
tedious,' she observes, 'in fact it is rent with scandals and there are
dreadful quarrels in the canteen about liberty, the peoples' convention,
&c, and the air is dark with flying spoons and dishes. Miss Stevens
poured some tea down Mr Fletcher's neck the other day . . .' Amid this
ideological ferment, the work of sustaining the nation's spirits goes
solidly on. 'We are doing a programme called "These Things are English",' Fitzgerald reports, 'with the funeral of George V, beer, cricket,
people singing in the underground &c. I think the people singing are
only expressing their own fierce triumph in getting the better of the
London Transport Passenger Board.' And she adds, with characteristically subversive wit, 'We had a mock invasion the other day. We were
overpowered in 5 minutes as the officers in charge of the defence forgot their passes and couldn't get into BH.'

Her wartime-BBC novel *Human Voices* was published nearly four
decades later, by which time she had won the Booker Prize and what
became known as the Myth of the Blitz was entrenched deep in
Britain's soul. The book both questions and strengthens the myth; it
reflects the frailty of the characters caught up in the terrible trial of
mass bombing, but it also explores their capacity to survive and to
preserve certain values. In her notes for the novel she put down 'BH
in wartime is improbably dedicated to putting out the truth. It also

keeps its old character – patriarchal & in that sense democratic: the lowest of the tribe may speak to the king. BBC people are affected by the character of BH and still more so as the vast building, sandbagged & darkened, becomes a kind of fortress.' Hermione Lee, Fitzgerald's biographer, argues that 'The BBC was perfect material for her because ... it hovers between the absurd and the heroic.'

There are two heroes. Jeff Haggard, the director of programme planning (or, as he is constantly referred to, in the best BBC style, DPP), who is dedicated to upholding Auntie's tradition of truth-telling, and his friend 'Mac', an American correspondent sent to London by his radio network to 'find out the reaction of the British people to attack from the air'. Dressed in 'a tin hat and his blue formal suit with a press armband', he roams Trafalgar Square in search of 'the ordinary man' and joins poker games with Londoners taking shelter in tube stations. He tells Haggard he has been instructed to 'do Britain, the Last Ditch'.

Mac is described as someone for whom 'everything is possible, except to leave things as they are', and his character draws heavily on a real restless roamer of London's Blitz-battered streets: Edward R. Murrow of CBS, who also had a penchant for Savile Row suits and sported his tin hat on his nightly patrols. There is a much-told Murrow anecdote that he stopped his car in the middle of an air raid so that one of his colleagues could win a wager by reading a newspaper by the light of burning buildings, and in *Human Voices* we find Mac 'reading the *Evening Standard* by the light of a small fire on the pavement caused by an incendiary bomb'.

Murrow was a myth-maker twice over. If Priestley could claim to have been the voice of Dunkirk and the Battle of Britain, Murrow could make a similar claim with regard to the Blitz. For America he defined the period. 'You burned the city of London in our houses,' the poet and American public servant Archibald MacLeish told him. 'You laid the dead of London at our doors and we knew the dead were our dead – were all men's dead – were mankind's dead – and ours.' In his early London days he was not, of course, as well known in Britain – although he often broadcast on the BBC as well as on CBS. But he very quickly became an emblematic figure in Blitz history.

Some of his fellow American correspondents published memoirs of the Blitz within months of it ending, and Murrow, young though he was, emerges as a kind of father figure, 'talk[ing] about the world in a shrewd, critical and yet understanding way' as they watched the waves of German bombers come over.

He was a third-party witness who confirmed what the British people endured and validated their courage, and his words can be every bit as evocative as classic Blitz images like the dome of St Paul's floating above clouds of fire. The day the Blitz began, 7 September, for example, caught him on a trip to the Thames Estuary with two other American correspondents, Vincent Sheean and Ben Robertson. 'Before eight, the siren sounded again,' he told his audience once he had made it back through the chaos to Broadcasting House. 'We went back to a haystack near the airdrome. The fires up the river had turned the moon blood red. The smoke had drifted down until it formed a canopy over the Thames; the guns were working all around us, the bursts looking like fireflies in a southern summer night. The Germans were sending in two or three planes at a time, sometimes only one, in relays. They would pass overhead. The guns and lights would follow them, and in about five minutes we could hear the hollow grunt of the bombs. Huge pear-shaped bursts of flame would rise up into the smoke and disappear. The world was upside down. Vincent Sheean lay on one side of me and cursed in five languages; he'd talk about the war in Spain. Ben Robertson of *PM* lay on the other side and kept saying over and over in that slow South Carolina drawl, "London is burning, London is burning."'

And Murrow also has near-mythic status as the founding father of American broadcast journalism, the patron saint of those rigorous standards of accuracy, objectivity and impartiality that have traditionally been associated with the news divisions of the big American networks. His contemporaries found it natural to identify him with the word 'truth'. Here, for example, is the first impression he made on his CBS colleague Eric Sevareid: 'a tall, thin man with a boyish grin, extraordinary dark eyes that were alight one moment and sombre and lost the next. He seemed to possess that rare thing, an instinctive, intuitive recognition of truth.' His reporter's credo – which he declared

Edward R. Murrow: 'he seemed to possess that rare thing, an instinctive, intuitive recognition of truth'.

in a broadcast on 1 September 1939, as Germany's invasion of Poland got under way – has been passed on to generations of journalism students: 'I have an old-fashioned belief that Americans like to make up their minds on the basis of all available information. The conclusions you draw are your own affair. I have no desire to influence them and shall leave such efforts to those who have more confidence in their own judgement than I have in mine.' Yet this was a huge fib – all the more shocking, perhaps, from someone who set such store by truth. Murrow absolutely did want to influence the views of his listeners; he was completely dedicated to Britain's cause and did everything he could – aided and abetted by the BBC – to convince the American people that they should come to fight by Britain's side. So there is a most intriguing paradox at the heart of the Murrow myth.

Murrow's first encounter with Auntie was somewhat discouraging. As a young radio executive working for CBS in New York, he picked up the significance of 'a small item in the Chicago *Daily News* to the effect that a Mrs E. A. Simpson had filed for divorce against Mr Simpson, in the Suffolk town of Ipswich'. This was the first published hint of the love affair between Wallis Simpson and Edward VIII, which was to cost Edward the throne. The relationship was well known among European elites, but the story was, notoriously, initially suppressed in the British press and by the BBC. In the mid-1930s CBS, like the BBC in its early years, devoted very few resources to news, but Murrow argued strongly that a story of such magnitude would bring in listeners. He managed to convince the network bosses, but because all broadcasting from Britain went through Broadcasting House he also had to persuade a reluctant BBC to help, and the Corporation had played a central role in covering up the story. One of his colleagues recalled that 'We were on a bit of a sticky wicket; the BBC was very uncooperative; they didn't control the wires, but we had to use their facilities. At first they refused.' John Reith was still at the helm in Broadcasting House, and thoroughly disapproved of the whole abdication episode; he thought it 'awful that all this crisis was caused by a miserable, second-rate American woman'.

But once the story became public in Britain, in early December 1936, even the BBC had to go with the flow, and Murrow was famously determined. Over the ten days of the Abdication Crisis that month, he managed to broadcast – via the BBC's studios – thirty-nine programmes of news and analysis dedicated to the unfolding drama. On 11 December he even authorized the interruption of a programme sponsored by Heinz (of baked beans fame) to bring the audience the news that the king had given up his throne for 'the woman I love'. The episode persuaded Murrow's ratings-hungry bosses that there was money in news, but it also demonstrated the strength of the rival network NBC. NBC was able to call on the services of a British-born reporter who – as Murrow's biographer A. M. Sperber tells the story – consistently managed to 'get to the studio and broadcast over the one circuit available a quarter of an hour before CBS had its booking'. The young man's name was Alistair Cooke, and he would later become something of a national institution in Britain with his weekly *Letter from America* on Radio Four.

Two months after the Abdication Crisis, Murrow was despatched to London himself – not as a correspondent, but as the European director. His task was to sharpen up the CBS operation in preparation for the great European drama everyone was by then expecting. Ed and his wife, Janet, were given a comfortable berth across the Atlantic and arrived in London by train at Waterloo, where they were welcomed by a representative of the BBC. Murrow was just shy of his twenty-ninth birthday.

His anti-fascist credentials were already well established. He had graduated from Washington State College in 1930 and, after a spell as a paid official in the National Student Federation of America, had been hired in an administrative job by the Institute of International Education, which was founded after the First World War to encourage international student exchanges. Just after he began work at its New York offices, the IIE suddenly acquired a new focus: when Hitler took power in Germany the organization's founder, Stephen Duggan, established a programme to provide American sanctuary for German academics who had lost their jobs as a result of Nazi purges. Murrow had the job of administering the work of the Emergency Committee in Aid of Displaced German Scholars, and he is credited with arranging for over 300 refugee intellectuals to move to new posts in the United States. One of them was the great German novelist Thomas Mann, author of *The Magic Mountain*, who later became a stalwart of the BBC's German Service.

Murrow's anti-Nazi instincts were reinforced by the company he kept when he arrived in Britain. One of his closest friends was Ronald Tree, an American-born Conservative MP and plutocrat (his mother was the daughter of a Chicago department-store magnate and his wife was Nancy Astor's niece), who was to become a significant figure at the Ministry of Information. Tree was a committed anti-appeaser, and a supporter of Churchill and Anthony Eden. His grand home at Ditchley Park, in Oxfordshire, became a centre for anti-appeaser gatherings, and the Murrows were frequent weekend guests. (Ditchley was later used as a retreat by Churchill when Chequers, which was in the path of German bombers, became too dangerous, and it now hosts influential foreign policy conferences.) Tree recorded that 'there was nothing that made him [Murrow] happier than a day in the fields with my keeper, a gun, and a dog, coming back with a brace of partridge and a pheasant or two'.

Murrow had grown up in relative poverty – he worked as a lumberjack in the forests of Washington State to earn the money for his degree course – and, like many American intellectuals of the era, he despised the British class system. But that did not prevent him from enjoying high society. The Savile Row suits are central to the Murrow legend, and one of his biographers has written of 'invitations from the social elite' flowing in to the Murrows: 'Lady Rhondda asking them to dinner at the Ivy restaurant, Lord Stragboli wanting Ed to set aside an evening for dinner and political discussion, the Countess of Listowel wishing they would join her at her home for dinner'.

The team of broadcasters Murrow recruited to CBS reflected both his anti-fascist instincts and his passion for good writing. Eric Sevareid, perhaps the greatest of those who would become known as the 'Murrow Boys', had arrived in Europe as a newspaper journalist after a radical career as an undergraduate at the University of Minnesota. He was taught there by the British socialist Harold Laski (who would later become one of Murrow's close friends in London), and he established an informal 'Jacobins Club', a group of like-minded students with a penchant for the revolutionary methods of 'large-scale organisation, of mass meeting and protest parade'. Their politics were defined by anti-fascism. 'We continued to hope against hope that Hitler could be killed by organised pressure from the democracies of Europe,' Sevareid wrote in his autobiography. 'We put great hopes in German Socialists and Communists, believing with naivete that the truth is strong in itself and cannot lose in the end.' After a spell in campaigning journalism in the American Northwest, he was drawn to Europe, where the century's next great drama had begun to unfold, and he settled in France.

Eric Sevareid of CBS News
– one of the 'Murrow Boys'.

In the summer of 1939 Sevareid was supporting himself by 'working at the Paris *Herald* by day and the United Press by night', when Murrow called him from London with the offer of a job. The two hardly knew one another, but Murrow had been impressed by Sevareid's work. 'I don't know much about your experience,' he said, 'but I like your ideas and I like the way you write . . . There won't be pressure on you to provide scoops or anything sensational. Just provide the honest news, and when there isn't any news, why, just say so. I have an idea people might like that.'

Like Priestley and Dimbleby, Murrow understood that writing for radio required a new set of craft skills. 'What Murrow wanted was for the Boys to imagine themselves standing by a fireplace back home, explaining to the local editor or college professor or dentist or shop-keeper what was going on,' wrote Stanley Cloud and Lynne Olson in *The Murrow Boys*. 'But imagine too, he said, that a maid and her truck-driver husband are listening at the door. Use language and images that are as informative and compelling to them as to the guests around the fireplace. Avoid high-flown rhetoric and frenetic delivery. Focus on the concrete, the specific, the telling detail.'

One of the Murrow Boys was in fact a woman, the clever, rich

Mary Marvin Breckinridge, who by her early thirties had established a significant reputation as a journalist and film-maker. When Murrow stationed her in Amsterdam he told her, 'When you report the invasion of Holland, or I report the invasion of England, understate the situation. Don't say the streets are rivers of blood. Say that the little policeman I usually say hello to every morning is not there today.' Murrow advised her to 'talk like yourself', and when he heard her trying to suppress a cough during a broadcast he rang with the instruction, 'If you feel like coughing, go ahead and cough.'

The BBC was central to everything Murrow did. The CBS offices were just across the road from Broadcasting House (in the course of the war the team had to move three times because of bomb damage, but they never strayed far from BH) and the Murrows rented a flat a short walk away at 84 Hallam Street (which now proudly sports its Blue Plaque in memory of Ed's time there). All CBS broadcasts were made live via the studios in Broadcasting House, and because of the time difference between London and the United States, Murrow often spent much of the night there. He was particularly close to R. T. Clark, the news editor who so famously declared that 'the only way to strengthen the morale of the people whose morale is worth strengthening, is to tell them the truth, and nothing but the truth, even if the truth is horrible.' During the Blitz, Clark, a scholarly figure, installed a camp bed in his underground office just off the wartime newsroom, and the two of them often whiled the night away in earnest conversation. 'Ed would be sitting on the bed,' one of the newsroom subs recalled, 'R.T. in the only chair, sitting there until you couldn't see across the place for the tobacco smoke, leaning forward, old pals having a chat.'

Murrow's transition from an executive who hired other talents to being a broadcaster himself came about almost by accident. He arrived in Vienna during the 1937 Anschluss, Germany's absorption of Austria, so he was the man on the spot when New York commissioned a special programme on this dramatic milestone in the Nazi story. In September 1938, during the Munich Crisis, he for the first time began his broadcast with the words that were to become such a ringing signature: 'This is London.'

The following June, Murrow spoke at a meeting of the English Speaking Union at the organization's Mayfair headquarters, and the minutes give a sense of the way his ideas about wartime reporting were taking shape. The meeting was called to discuss how American reporters could be helped 'to create a sympathetic understanding for this country' in time of war, an objective which everyone present, Murrow included, seemed to accept without question as a proper journalistic ambition. Murrow argued that the key lay with minimal censorship, stressing 'the cardinal importance to American newspapermen and radio commentators that they should be given maximum freedom'. Without this, he said, they would be unable to persuade their readers and listeners to trust them, and he warned that a tough censorship regime might force the networks to transmit their broadcasts from neutral capitals like Dublin or Ankara.

To bring home the value of uncensored broadcasting he cited an incident 'when he had been about to broadcast from a bank in Whitehall overlooking Downing Street and was surprised to hear an American commentator in New York describing the scenes of disturbance outside the Prime Minister's residence'. The minutes record that 'Mr Murrow had been able on that occasion to tell American listeners that such reports of disturbance in Downing Street were false since he was actually looking down on the street and could report to them that the small crowd outside No 10 was absolutely orderly.' This apparently went down very well with his audience: 'It was felt that if an American commentator, even in times of war, could be given the opportunity of making uncensored and even extemporaneous comments of this kind, they could do far more to correct immediately false reports which might be spreading in America than could be done in any other way.'

Murrow laid out the censorship regime for his listeners as Britain moved on to a war footing on 1 September 1939, and he made it sound remarkably benign. 'You will have heard that a degree of censorship or control has been established on communications from London to the United States,' he said. 'Let me explain the position as far as broadcasting is concerned. We are not permitted to divulge military information calculated to be of value to a possible enemy. We have been assured that is the sole purpose of the existing regulations. Within those limits we are to have freedom of expression. If that situation changes, we shall let you know. That means there are certain matters of a military nature which we shall not be permitted to discuss; it does <u>not</u> mean that anyone is telling us what to say.'

He was not alone in disseminating this rose-tinted view. In early October 1939, NBC broadcast a discussion programme comparing wartime life in Britain and France, and the American radio pioneer Frank Gunther told the listeners 'that censorship on the radio in London was very unassuming. All that was required was that the commentator arrive at the station half an hour before the broadcast. The censor arrived and the half hour was spent in going over the material to be used on the air, the censor making polite suggestions here and there.'

The relationship between the American press corps and British censors was not quite as harmonious as these generous public reviews suggest, but, as the Americans were all too well aware, they were beneficiaries of what we today call the 'special relationship'. The BBC and the Ministry of Information readily accepted the conclusions of that summer debate at the English Speaking Union; it was in the national interest that American correspondents should portray the Old Country in a favourable light, and it was therefore essential that the censorship regime should be applied with the lightest of touches.

The BBC had formal responsibility for passing American scripts in the same way that it was responsible for censorship of its own news bulletins, and there was a BBC finger on the 'switch' button whenever Murrow and his colleagues delivered a live report from the studios in Broadcasting House. But the BBC staffers on the American Liaison Unit were left in no doubt about the spirit in which they should go about their duties. A BBC memo shortly after the outbreak of war recorded that 'the M O I [Ministry of Information] take the view that in keeping in with America, we might be prepared to relax a little more than we might for "Home" broadcasting'.

The first principle in the unit's censorship guidelines for American broadcasts was that 'The rules under which the work is carried out [should] allow freedom of speech to a great degree, therefore only matter which might be thought prejudicial to the interest of the nation or allies (military information is dealt with separately) should be censored.' And switch censors were enjoined to remember that 'The cut-off switch should only be operated as a last resort. It is difficult to conceive of any inadvertent indiscretion which could be more disastrous to the interests of this country than the deliberate cutting off of one of the American speakers in the middle of a talk.' And the American Liaison Unit's files reflect Auntie's special affection for Murrow among the American correspondents; less than two months after the outbreak of war one of the Corporation's mandarins was worrying, in a very auntly way, that Murrow 'works himself too hard and worries too much about things'.

≈

During the first few months of war not everyone in Whitehall or the Services understood how important the Americans were to British foreign policy. Roger Eckersley, the BBC official in charge of the American Liaison Unit at Broadcasting House – and therefore the man with overall responsibility for censoring American broadcasts – spent much of his time and energy not censoring but lobbying for greater access, 'knocking on Ministerial doors, begging for facilities, whereas ... the reverse should be the case'. But Dunkirk galvanized the Whitehall machine: 'In the end it was not the hard-pressed armed services or the persistence alone of Murrow and Bate [Fred Bate, Murrow's counterpart at NBC], the BBC, or the MOI that forced the issue,' concluded Murrow's biographer A. M. Sperber, 'but the post-Dunkirk atmosphere itself, imparting an overriding sense of urgency, at decision-making levels, to the question of radio coverage and American opinion.'

Even more importantly, perhaps, the view that American correspondents could be used as a tool of British diplomacy was shared by the new tenant in Downing Street. Churchill understood from very early on that Britain's survival depended on American help. The climax of his defiant Dunkirk speech is remembered for its promise to 'fight on the beaches', but it is just as striking for its tacit recognition of American power; 'even if, which I do not for a moment believe,' he declared, 'this Island or a large part of it were subjugated and starving, then our Empire beyond the sea, armed and guarded by the British Fleet, would carry on the struggle until, in God's good time, *the New World, with all its power and might, steps forth to the rescue and the liberation of the old*' (my italics). And he sent his first direct appeals for help to Washington within days of taking office. At about the same time as the Dunkirk speech, he wrote personally to President Roosevelt: 'I trust you realise, Mr President, that the voice and force of the United States may count for nothing if they are withheld too long. You may have a completely subjugated Nazified Europe established with astonishing swiftness, and the weight may be more than we can bear.'

But Roosevelt was facing a presidential election (in November 1940). The American public was skittish about 'foreign entanglements' and there were two powerful voices warning of the risk that America would be drawn into another European war. The glamorous aviator Charles Lindbergh, made famous by his record-breaking 1927 flight across the Atlantic (and later even more famous by the gruesome kidnapping and murder of his infant son, 'the biggest story since the Resurrection', as H. L. Mencken described it), was the isolationists' star turn, and from the autumn of 1940 he addressed dozens of anti-war rallies on behalf of the 'America First Committee', arguing that if the United States entered the war it would be 'the greatest disaster this country has ever passed through'. Equally obstinate in his opposition to deeper American involvement was Washington's ambassador to London, Joseph Kennedy, the father of the future president. Kennedy, who arrived in London in 1938, supported Chamberlain and the appeasers over Churchill and tried, without Roosevelt's authority, to arrange a meeting with Hitler. He was not popular with his hosts; after one of his isolationist outbursts a Foreign Office mandarin described him as 'a very foul specimen of double-crosser and defeatist', and when the ambassador abandoned his Regent's Park residence to escape the Blitz, another Whitehall wag remarked that 'I thought my daffodils were yellow until I met Kennedy.'

But in the summer of 1940, Lindbergh and Kennedy reflected the national mood. Philip Seib writes in his *Broadcasts from the Blitz* that

'When the British ambassador, Lord Lothian, asked Roosevelt to warn Germany that the United States would intervene rather than allow Britain to be defeated, Roosevelt was sympathetic; but he told Lothian such a move was politically impractical. He estimated that he could get just 40 percent of the public and 25 percent of the Congress to support such a declaration, and if he followed such a course before November he would ensure the election of an even more isolationist Congress.' That made American public opinion a critical factor in Churchill's American policy – and, indeed, in Britain's prospects for survival. And Murrow's broadcasts were to have a decisive impact on how the American people saw the war.

Perhaps it is not surprising that the Murrows were soon able to add Winston and Clementine Churchill to their increasingly long list of grand British friends. There is a story that when Ed Murrow turned up in Downing Street to collect Janet after one of her lunches with Mrs Churchill, the prime minister emerged from his study with the words, 'Good to see you, Mr Murrow. Have you time for several whiskies?'

THAT HARD STONY SOUND

THE AMERICAN PRESS CORPS decamped *en masse* to Dover to cover the Battle of Britain. They booked into the Grand Hotel – 'a good second class establishment in a town where clerks spent holidays in the summer', with its potted palms and 'an elevator that worked sometimes and sometimes didn't' – and from Shakespeare Cliff they watched the dog-fights in the blue summer skies, occasionally dodging the bombs and the machine-gun fire themselves. The young Ben Robertson (one of Murrow's companions on that dramatic night of 7 September) recalled a day when the perfect weather tempted them all to walk up the hill rather than calling a taxi: 'We had been on the road about ten minutes and had reached a pub called the King Lear when we heard the Germans coming ... We heard bullets whizzing about and took cover in the pub.'

The fighting raged on and off all day, so fierce that 'the whole of England began to quake', but between the raids Shakespearean high drama gave way to country-house weekend. Robertson recalled the idle moments when 'We pulled weeds from a potato patch belonging to Paddy, an Irish shantyman, who somehow at the end of his life now found himself settled on this cliff at Dover. We lay in the grass among the red currants and the butterflies while the world was decided about us. We had company that morning – Prince Bernhard of the Netherlands came by the cliff with Penelope Atkin, daughter of the British representative at Dublin and niece of Lord Beaverbrook.'

Robertson was much taken with some of the women correspondents who joined the Dover party – like the 'tall and beautiful'
Helen Kirkpatrick – and in his memoir makes special mention of the
Grand's barmaid, the 'attractive, interesting' Josephine, whom he spotted with 'a copy of *The Grapes of Wrath* under one arm' shouting, 'Go
to it Bofurs' at the gunners on the beach. It all sounds rather fun, and
very romantic.

But there was nothing frivolous about the sense of commitment
the Americans brought to their work. Robertson remembered the
days on Shakespeare Cliff as 'wonderful in every way – they changed
me as an individual'. In his short *I Saw England* – which was published
the following year – he wrote that 'I lost my sense of personal fear
because I saw that what happened to me did not matter. We counted
as individuals only as we took our place in the procession of history.
It was not we who counted, it was what we stood for. And I knew
now for what I was standing – I was standing for freedom. It was as
simple as that. I realised the good that can often come from death. We
were where we were and we had what we had because a whole line
of our people had been willing to die.' Eric Sevareid, in the very fine
memoir he published just after the war, reflects on a similar hardening
of his resolve during the Blitz. 'I knew that the change had been
subtly working in me all through the terrible days of London ...' he
wrote. 'The course was quite clear now, and perhaps it was not too
late. The duty was to fight with every means available ...'

Sevareid is generous in his praise of his boss at CBS. 'Of the
American journalists who did more than their technical duty none
reached the stature of Murrow, whose physical, intellectual and moral
performance in those deadly weeks is not likely to be equalled by any
reportorial voice or pen in this generation,' he declared. He understood
that Murrow was a creature of the radio age, and that the new medium
of reporting required a new kind of reporter. There is a passage in his
memoir worth quoting at some length, because it reveals as much
about radio as it does about Murrow:

> It was not his perfect poise, his magnetic face, or even his
> compelling voice that made the first great literary artist of a new

medium of communication. No practice, training or artifice made him the greatest broadcaster by far in the English tongue. He was simply born to the new art. It is his and – I sometimes think – his alone, never to be shared. A perfect artistic creation can rarely be delivered by radio, no matter how flawless the words or the conception, unless the personality and being of the artist himself approaches the stature of the product – because he is a part of the product, mixed up irretrievably in its essence.

Sevareid also makes the acute observation that 'His whole being was enmeshed in the circumstances of those days and events, yet he held his mind above them always.'

Murrow's response to the crisis of 1940 was to push back against the boundaries imposed by censorship and to experiment ever more creatively with the possibilities of the radio medium. So in mid-August, with Roger Eckersley's backing, he put forward a proposal for a live outside broadcast during an air raid – the full-blown Blitz had yet to begin, but the warning siren was already familiar to London ears. Like Penelope Fitzgerald's Mac, Murrow was a man for whom 'everything is possible, except to leave things as they are'.

The obvious objection was the one that had almost taken the BBC off the air altogether – the fear that radio waves could be used as navigational devices by the enemy. But Eckersley argued that by broadcasting from several sites in the course of the programme they could reduce that risk. Everyone understood that it would be more difficult to control what reporters said when they were out on location rather than in the studio, but the broadcast would be relayed through Broadcasting House and the switch censor would be across the feed in the usual way. Most importantly, moreover, Murrow and his colleagues had by now earned the trust of the authorities. Eckersley argued that the time had come to show the Americans 'that we are, for once, in earnest when we say we want to do everything in our power to help them'.

The project was agreed in just three days – a remarkably swift piece of bureaucratic footwork – and the programme was scheduled for Saturday, 24 August. Murrow's Boys were assigned their tasks:

Larry LeSueur would be at an Air Raid Precaution (ARP) station, Eric Sevareid on the dance-floor with Saturday-night revellers, Vincent Sheean at Piccadilly. The ubiquitous J. B. Priestley was recruited from the home team to wrap things up from Whitehall.

The programme was called *London After Dark*, and it began with Murrow himself standing on the steps of St Martin-in-the-Fields; instead of his usual on-air greeting, he began with 'This is Trafalgar Square.' An air-raid siren had just begun to sound, and Murrow paused so that his audience could hear it; even today it sounds eerie on the recordings, and it must have seemed even more sinister to the Americans who heard it live from several thousand miles away. Broadcasters today sometimes talk about 'letting the wires show' – which means being open about what is involved in putting a programme on the air, and letting the viewers and listeners share the difficulties we sometimes face, especially in live programmes. Murrow did it in 1940 to great dramatic effect. 'People are walking along quite quietly,' he reported. 'We are just at the entrance of an air-raid shelter here and I must move this cable over just a bit so people can walk in.' And he played cleverly with the mental images of London many of his listeners would have recognized. 'Here comes one of those big red buses around the corner – double-deckers, they are,' he noted. 'Just a few lights on the top deck. In this blackness it looks very much like a ship that's passing in the night and you just see the portholes.' But above all, like every good radio reporter, he understood the evocative power of sound, bending down to the pavement with his microphone to share with his listeners 'One of the strangest sounds one can hear in London these days – or rather these dark nights – just the sound of footsteps walking along the street, like ghosts shod with steel shoes.'

Once Murrow had said his piece, the broadcasting baton was handed across London, and when it reached Eric Sevareid he delivered his despatch over the unmistakable big-band sound of the 1940s. From the middle of the dance-floor, he reported that since the band leader had announced that there was a raid in progress, 'I don't think more than half a dozen people have left. They simply put up a big cheer and went on with their song.'

The immediacy of a programme like *London After Dark* would of course have been impossible if all concerned had had to stick to the sort of pre-prepared script that was usually required for censorship purposes. Murrow's style of broadcasting depended heavily on the telling ad-lib, and he made the most of opportunities like that conveniently timed air raid. The files of the BBC's American Liaison Unit reveal an intriguing piece of sophistry that allowed its censors to square this kind of programme with censorship rules. The Ministry of Information defined a script as a document made up of 'grammatical sentences with a meaning'. So the BBC ruled that 'Experienced broadcasters in an emergency should be allowed the use of notes only. These notes should always be as full as possible, and should take the form of "grammatical sentences with a meaning" but no objection would be taken to their extension along the lines which their meaning indicates.'

Murrow kept up the pressure. Four days after the success of *London After Dark* he asked Eckersley to investigate whether he could secure permission for a live night-time broadcast from the vantage of a rooftop. The request was duly submitted and was considered at a Ministry of Information meeting on 4 September. Unsurprisingly, it met with stiff resistance – on the grounds both that such a broadcast might give valuable information to the enemy and that, some argued, the British people would resent their suffering 'being made the subject of broadcasts to America'. Murrow was told to produce sample recordings which could be vetted to assess the security risk. Over the following weekend the Blitz began in earnest, so he had to conduct these experiments in the face of the full fury of the Luftwaffe. He duly clambered up to the roof of BH – which of course was a highly prized German target – and produced the required six recordings. The Ministry of Information promptly lost them, and Murrow had to go through the whole process all over again. His persistence bore fruit: Eckersley was told that the Ministry of Information had 'no objection' to such a broadcast going ahead.

On 21 September, Murrow again clambered up on to the roof of BH. 'I am standing on a rooftop looking out over London,' he began. 'For reasons of national as well as personal security, I am unable to tell you the location from which I am speaking.' Because we have become so used to the idea that Londoners reacted to the Blitz with *sangfroid*, it is easy to forget how terrifying it must have been, especially in its early days. By standing on a roof – when most of the city had headed to the cellars – Murrow was taking a real risk, and he managed to convey the sense of danger without showing off. He paused in his commentary to allow the sound of the raid to reach his listeners. 'Earlier this evening,' he began at one point, only to find the next words lost beneath bangs from the sky; a beat or two, and then he went on: '... again, those were explosions overhead ... earlier this evening we heard a number of bombs go sliding and slithering across to fall several blocks away. Just over head now, the burst of the anti-aircraft fire ...'

Most of the language is simple and direct, but every so often he slips in a metaphor (he has the searchlights 'feeling' the sky) and the odd gentle push to guide the emotions of the audience. 'Now you'll hear two bursts [of anti-aircraft fire] a little nearer in a moment ...' he told them. 'There they are. That hard stony sound.'

The following night he was back on his rooftop, 'feeling rather large and lonesome', as he put it, and although there was no raid when he went live, he gave a masterclass in the effectiveness of 'focusing on the telling detail'. 'Just on the roof across the way I can see a man wearing a tin hat,' he reported, 'a pair of powerful night glasses to his eyes, scanning the sky. Again, looking in the opposite direction, there is a building with two windows gone. Out of one window there waves something that looks like a white bed sheet, a window curtain swinging free in the night breeze. It looks as though it were being shaken by a ghost. There are a great many ghosts around these buildings in London.'

Once Murrow had shown that these rooftop broadcasts could work – without a censorship crime being committed and, mercifully, without anyone dying – the other American network correspondents followed his example and the genre became a staple of Blitz reporting. But he was not always so successful in his attempt to blaze a trail. In October he suggested that he be allowed to give a 'completely uncensored talk' because, he argued, there was 'a large body of opinion among American listeners that there is still a lot of unnecessary censorship as regards the news'. The request was forwarded with the BBC's support, but the Ministry of Information turned it down on the grounds that they could not exempt Murrow from the military side of censorship.

The MoI answer came back in a civilized note from Lindsay Wellington, a BBC man on secondment to Senate House, who wrote that Murrow was 'free to criticise, comment and to give and record opinion, provided that he does not contravene requirements of security censorship'. Roger Eckersley encouraged Murrow to pursue the argument further, and promised his support. But on this occasion Murrow took refuge in sardonic humour. 'I am keeping Wellington's memorandum in order that it may occupy a privileged position in my file of documents reflecting the prostitution of the English language,' he told Eckersley. 'It really is a classic and I am very grateful for it. "Without wishing in any way to be unduly restrictive he does not feel able to agree", and I thought there was a shortage of paper! I confess myself beaten.'

Murrow was working in the basement of Broadcasting House on 15 October, the night the building was hit by a bomb. When the editor from New York came across the line he remarked – having no idea what had happened – that Murrow sounded tired. 'I am tired,' came back the reply. 'It's a tired world.' His laconic coolness under fire is very much part of the legend. At night, when he was not broadcasting, he often roamed the streets and the city's shelters, looking for a story. His colleague Elmer Davis remarked that 'The only objection that can be offered to Murrow's technique of reporting is that when an air raid is on he has a habit of going out on the roof to see what's happening, or driving around town in an open car to see what's been hit. That is a good way to get the news, but perhaps not the best way to make sure you will go on getting it.'

His workaholic and insomniac habits became equally notorious. Sometimes, after a long night of broadcasting and debating with R. T. Clark in his subterranean bunker, Murrow would return to 84 Hallam Street to continue the conversation over bourbon and breakfast. His biographer, A. M. Sperber, writes of his Blitz period that 'Throughout those months, Murrow worked like a man possessed. He seemed to be everywhere at once: driving through the air raids in his little Sunbeam-Talbot to check the casualty reports, never working from handouts; talking with cockneys in subway shelters one moment, with cabinet ministers the next; checking with sources in the offices of governments in exile; monitoring the Commons; patrolling as a neighbourhood fire warden, and, of course, broadcasting up to four or five times a night.'

And, as the events of 15 October reminded everyone, Broadcasting House itself was far from safe. In December a parachute mine tore into BH and the Langham Hotel opposite. One of the Murrow Boys, Larry LeSueur, was in mid-broadcast in the subterranean Studio 4B, and was forced out by water and sewage from the shattered pipes. Murrow's NBC colleague Ned Bate was caught outside and made it to the building badly wounded – his ear had been almost severed and his legs were cut about – but apparently still determined to broadcast. Murrow himself was on several occasions knocked down in the street by blast waves from the bombs, and Eric Sevareid recalled: 'One night, Ed, Larry LeSueur, and I filed out of the BBC and around to the side. We heard nothing, but Murrow suddenly stepped into a doorway, and Larry and I immediately followed suit. At that moment a jagged casing from an anti-aircraft shell crashed precisely where we had been.'

Sevareid may not have been Murrow's equal as a broadcaster, but he was a beautiful writer and the memoir in which he lavishes such praise on Murrow also provides a – perhaps unintended – reminder of the limitations of Murrow's broadcasting brilliance. In 1941 another distinguished member of the American journalistic pack, Quentin Reynolds, produced a Blitz memoir called *The Wounded Don't Cry*. In his 1946 book Sevareid wrote, 'the wounded *did* cry, very frequently'. And in what reads like an implicit rebuke to Murrow, he tells his readers: 'You in America were told each day by your press and radio that the people of Britain were heroic in their endurance in those frightful weeks – and so they were. But it would be to make them more than human and thus to do them less than justice to suggest that none of them at any time betrayed stark fear or that there were no individual cases of hysteria and panic.'

His reflections on the Blitz experience are subtler and more complex – and therefore probably closer to the truth – than Murrow's famous radio reports. He was not afraid to admit his own fear. 'To get to the underground broadcasting studio meant a walk of several blocks for me,' he wrote. 'I would shuffle through the inky blackness to each curbing where the guns would make the crossing street a tunnel of sudden, blinding light. When the shrieking came near I would plaster myself upon the nearest wall, and, however sternly I lectured myself, I not infrequently found myself doing the last fifty yards at a dead run.' And he meticulously documented the odd behaviour that prolonged exposure to indiscriminate bombing produced. 'The nerves established a fairly definite behaviour pattern for the muscles. If you were walking in the street when you heard the shriek of a descending bomb,' he recalled, 'you would stop; if you had been standing still, you would begin to walk. If you were sitting down in a room, you would rise, and if you were standing you were likely to sit down.' On one evening he was in the offices of the *Herald Tribune* when a bomb fell close by, and he noticed that 'Every person in the room quietly changed his position.' One journalist reacted by stretching out on the floor, explaining that 'I just thought I would try it that way, once.' Sevareid remembered that 'No one thought her action peculiar.'

But all this was, of course, recollected in post-war tranquillity, and for Murrow the exigencies of the Blitz moment trumped everything. In October 1940, Sevareid, ill and with his nerves shot by the weeks of bombing, decided to return to the United States, and on the day before his departure he talked to Murrow about his feelings. Murrow immediately spotted the radio and – it must be said – propaganda potential of what he said and persuaded Sevareid to make a valedictory broadcast. 'I talked a little about France,' Sevareid remembered, 'about Paris dying in her coma, about the cities which had broken in spirit, about London which had not – London, which "is not England", but which is Britain, which had become a city-state in the old Greek sense – and about a peaceable people who had gone to war in their aprons and bowlers, with their old fowling pieces, with their ketchup bottles filled with gasoline and standing ready on their pantry shelves. I quoted someone there who had written: "When this is all over, in the days to come, men will speak of this war, and they will say I was a

Broadcasting House in December 1940: a parachute mine caught on the lamppost before detonating in Portland Place.

sailor, or I was a pilot; others will say, with equal pride, I was a citizen of London".'

Sevareid was worried that he had been 'mawkish', but Murrow was right about the impact. When he reached America, Sevareid met a businessman who had heard the broadcast while driving and 'had had to stop his car for a moment', and a history professor who 'told me he heard it in his bedroom and had to bathe his eyes before going down to dinner'. Sevareid's valediction was exactly the version of the Blitz that Murrow wanted to project in the United States.

Their colleague Ben Robertson provides a similar insight into the way Murrow thought of his work. Robertson had made a tour of bombed sites in the naval city of Portsmouth, and while he was discussing his experiences with Murrow, Murrow produced a news summary that had just been received from America by the Ministry of Information. It showed that the heavy raids of the previous few days had 'produced surprisingly little comment in the United States'. Murrow said, 'You know what this means – it means that so much has been written about the bravery and courage of the British that the folks at home are beginning to take the raids for granted – the newness of an air raid has worn off for the folks at home.' Robertson continued, 'Ed and I sat down and wrote a broadcast, and that night we went on the air to say that the newness could never wear off an air raid, that each raid existed alone, and each of them was one of the most terrible and brutal and uncivilised particular events ever staged in the world.'

≈

With the presidential election of November 1940 – two months into the Blitz – American politics moved decisively in the direction Murrow was hoping for. The fact that the Republicans had nominated Wendell Willkie, a political neophyte, was itself an illustration of how far the public mood had swung. At the beginning of the year the favourites had been three much better-known candidates – Senators Robert Taft and Arthur Vandenberg and the New York Mafia-buster Thomas Dewey – who were all isolationists, but Willkie was a vocal champion of financial aid for Britain. On the Democratic side, Franklin D. Roosevelt's decision to run for a third term was controversial – George Washington himself had established the two-term convention when he refused an appeal to run again in 1799 – and the president remained vulnerable to the charge that he would embroil America in a war that, despite the new sympathy for Britain, the majority of voters did not want. Willkie accused the president of planning to take America to war secretly – which was, it can reasonably be argued, exactly what Roosevelt was indeed doing.

In the dying days of the campaign, America's high-profile and combative ambassador to London, Joseph Kennedy, came to the president's assistance in a surprising and, as it turned out, critical way.

Kennedy was convinced that Britain could not stand alone, and throughout the Blitz he had been sending pessimistic messages back to Washington. When his ambassadorial tenure came to an end in October 1940, he had the grace to admit he had been wrong about the Blitz – 'I did not know London could take it,' he said, 'I did not think any city could take it. I am bowed in reverence' – but he remained convinced that Britain would lose the war.

Kennedy arrived back in the United States a couple of weeks before polling day, and the Republicans hoped that, now that he was a private citizen again, he would endorse their man – the tensions between the president and his London ambassador were no secret. But Kennedy, perhaps beguiled by political promises made to him in the privacy of the White House, remained a loyal Democrat. In a radio address he declared, 'Unfortunately during this political campaign, there has arisen the charge that the president of the United States is trying to involve this country in a foreign war. Such a charge is false.' Roosevelt followed this up at a campaign rally, appearing with Kennedy at his side and promising the 'mothers and fathers of America' that 'Your boys are not going to be sent to any foreign wars.'

Roosevelt was re-elected with a shade less than 55 per cent of the popular vote, and immediately set about doing exactly what Ambassador Kennedy had advised against. By early 1941 he had persuaded Congress to pass what became known as the 'Lend-Lease' Act, which allowed him to 'sell, transfer title to, exchange, lease, lend, or otherwise dispose of ... any defense article' to any government he judged important to America's security. It was a blank cheque; Roosevelt could now send Britain pretty much anything he wanted without worrying about whether the bill would ever be paid, and in the course of the war Washington authorized the supply of more than $30 billion worth of equipment ($500 billion in today's money) to the British war effort. It was a handsome response to Churchill's famous plea that America 'give us the tools and we'll finish the job'.

≈

In the autumn of 1941 Ed Murrow went home for a three-month break. Just before taking ship he sent an elegant farewell note to the

BBC's American Liaison Unit 'to say that I have occasionally cursed you and invariably enjoyed working with you'. He had become a national figure in his absence and, when he delivered a high-profile address at the Waldorf Astoria Hotel in New York, President Roosevelt himself sent praise. 'Ed Murrow has lived the war from the beginning,' his message read. 'But more important, he has reported the news day by day and, at the same time, kept faith with the truth-loving peoples of the world by telling the truth when he tells the news. I doubt whether in all history there has been a time when truth in the news – when comprehensive and objective news dispatches – have ever been more needed.'

More than a thousand people – many of them big players in the worlds of broadcasting and politics – turned out for the banquet to honour the 'Chief of the European Staff, Columbia Broadcasting', and Murrow's biographer argues that the evening was also a recognition of the new power of radio; it was, he writes, 'emblematic of a subtle change of emphasis . . . a gravitational shift in communications; radio was the undisputed star of the evening.'

Among the guests was Lindsay Wellington, the BBC and Ministry of Information official whose memo refusing an uncensored broadcast had provoked Murrow to such dark humour. On this occasion Murrow was in gentler mood. He told his audience that 'I have often seen British censorship stupid, but seldom sinister.' He also recognized that 'the very speed of modern communications – with the Germans listening to everything broadcast from London – tends to slow down the release of important news', and – an intriguing position for a reporter to take – stated that during a war he would not broadcast from a country with no censorship at all, because 'the responsibility for human lives would be too great'.

Murrow accepted that his personal experiences in London might have influenced his reporting – making the acute observation that 'An individual who can entirely avoid being influenced by the atmosphere in which he works might not even be a good reporter' – but continued to take refuge behind the mask of journalistic objectivity, telling his audience that 'It is no part of a reporter's function to advocate policy. The most I can do is to indicate certain questions facing America.' In his study *Broadcasts from the Blitz*, Philip Seib, an American professor of journalism, comments that 'There was a certain disingenuousness behind his words', as 'His personal opinion was very clear . . .' That is putting the matter mildly.

The New York dinner was held on 2 December. Five days later Japan attacked Pearl Harbor, killing more than 2,400 Americans (most of them sailors) and knocking out eighteen ships, including five battleships. America declared war on Japan the following day, and on 11 December Hitler declared war on the United States. America was now fully engaged in the worldwide war, just as Murrow and President Roosevelt had long believed it must be.

By the oddest of ironies, Ed Murrow and his wife, Janet, were due to have dinner at the White House on the night of 7 December, 'a day which will live in infamy', as Roosevelt famously described it. Despite the crisis, the dinner went ahead and the Murrows were given scrambled eggs by Eleanor Roosevelt, the First Lady. After dinner Janet returned to the couple's hotel but Ed was asked to wait, and at around midnight he was summoned in to see the president. Bill Donovan, the director of the Office of Strategic Services (which would later become the CIA) was also there and, after quizzing Murrow about the mood in London, the president talked freely about the day's events.

By the time Murrow emerged from the White House after a meeting that lasted for more than half an hour, he had journalistic gold: a first-hand insight into the views and mood of the president of the United States on one of the most momentous days in the nation's history. And yet he kept it to himself. Eric Sevareid was covering the White House beat for CBS by this stage, and Murrow dropped into his office before going to bed. All he offered from his exclusive presidential tête-à-tête was 'It's pretty bad' – in the circumstances, a staggeringly banal statement of the obvious. Janet Murrow said later that her husband spent all night agonizing about whether the conversation had been on the record, even though Roosevelt had never suggested it was not. Murrow let the story go, and it remains one of the most puzzling incidents in the career of this inspirational but complex American hero.

And as far as the British government was concerned, a hero is what he was. In 1943 he was offered – at Churchill's behest, according to Murrow's biographer – the job of running all the BBC's programming, home and foreign. He turned the job down, but it was an extraordinary gesture of admiration and trust from a British prime minister.

That same year, broadcasting from London once again, Murrow violated the censorship regulations by adding a few words to a script that had been passed by the Ministry of Information. Admiral George Pirie Thomson, the chief press censor at the MoI, sent him a note to point this out, but added, 'Please look on this merely as a reminder and not as a formal "reprimand" for I am one of the many who derive the greatest interest and pleasure from your broadcasts.' It was the tone that members of the British establishment used when addressing one of their own.

'I DON'T MIND IF I DO'

E LISABETH BARKER, THE FRENCH SERVICE producer who welcomed Charles de Gaulle to the BBC on the evening of his first great broadcast, was given her break at the Corporation because of a family connection. Her father, a Cambridge don, was a friend of John Reith, then the director-general. But there was, she later recalled, 'no question of me joining on anything but a clerical level', so when she was hired in 1934 she was taken on as a 'shorthand/typist clerk in the news department'. She had an Oxford degree and had spent two years driving all over Central Europe as an assistant to her brother Arthur, who was *The Times*'s Vienna correspondent, but the first task that Auntie assigned her was filleting the newspapers and filing the cuttings in boxes under subject headings – the beginning of the News Information Department, which became such an essential part of newsroom life until the internet made it redundant.

Arthur Barker joined his sister at the Corporation on the eve of war, but he was wooed over lunch at the Athenaeum and walked straight into a senior editor's job in the Overseas Services. Nepotism and sexism were both endemic in the BBC of the 1930s.

Interviewed for the BBC archives on her retirement in 1983, Miss Barker remembered all sorts of indignities endured because of her sex. Women, she said, were routinely paid less than men for the same work, and – unless they were very grand or well connected – they were expected to stop working altogether if they married. The incident that prompted her move to the French Service seems especially shocking today. She had been taken on for research work by a senior figure in the newsroom, and 'a rather silly crisis blew up because he had promoted over the heads of older women a very charming young secretary' ('I won't go into more detail than that,' she added discreetly in her interview) and 'this was causing some disturbance' in the ranks. She decided to tackle her boss about the matter. 'He took this as a form of rebellion or even mutiny,' she recalled, 'and told me he was seeing that I should be transferred to the BBC Monitoring Service far from London, which was not my idea of how to spend the war.'

Her good French and knowledge of Central European languages saved her from exile; this was the autumn of 1939, and instead of being despatched to the Worcestershire countryside she was snapped up by the expanding European News Talks section. But another sexist shadow soon fell across her career. During the Phoney War the BBC engaged the services of an Australian actress called Betty Stockbridge, who had studied in Paris and had good enough French to perform in French films. Auntie felt that Miss Stockbridge, who was blonde, pretty and very famous, might seduce a particular section of the French audience, and Miss Barker was given the job of writing her material, 'talks ... of a sexy nature designed to appeal to the warmer feelings of French troops,' as she later put it. The blue-stocking Elisabeth Barker recognized that she had 'absolutely no qualifications' for this line of work, and the French reaction to the broadcasts was, to put it at its politest, mixed. The series was ended with the fall of France, and the actress sent Miss Barker a case of rosé wine to thank her for her efforts.

As the intensity of the war moved up a gear, Elisabeth Barker's career began to take off. As well as dealing with General de Gaulle and the Free French, she was responsible for talks in Czech and Polish and for liaising with the Czech and Polish governments-in-exile. In 1941 she moved across from the BBC to the secret world of the Political Warfare Executive (the successor to Department EH), where she specialized in the Balkans. This often meant negotiating between different arms of government about the messages disseminated by both the BBC and the so-called 'black propaganda' stations run by the PWE. 'I spent most of my time trying to argue with the Foreign Office on one side and the Special Operations Executive, responsible for subversive activities in enemy occupied Europe,' on the other, she recalled. Sometimes these arguments revolved around extremely complex and sensitive policy questions, such as the proper balance of British support between the conflicting claims of Tito's communist partisans and General Draža Mihailović's royalist Chetniks in Yugoslavia. Dilys Powell, a Greek specialist and later the long-standing film critic of the *Observer*, worked alongside her in the Balkans section, which gives one an idea of the intellectual firepower brought to bear in the field. Elisabeth Barker rejoined the BBC after the war and went on to enjoy a very successful career. As she observed in her retirement interview, 'The war did a great deal for the feminist cause.'

That, of course, is not to say that Auntie had gone through a feminist conversion. Elisabeth Barker's career flourished simply because the Corporation was, suddenly, in desperate need of talent; the Armed Services were greedy for men, and the pool of people with the intellectual abilities and skills needed for BBC war work was limited. In 1937 John Reith's BBC employed 3,500 people, and it was, according to the BBC veteran Gerard Mansell, 'still possible for the Director General to know personally a high proportion of the programme staff'. By the summer of 1941 the staff establishment had risen to nearly 9,000. The expansion was especially marked in Elisabeth Barker's field of foreign broadcasting, where the numbers rose from just over 100 in 1939 to nearly 1,500 two years later.

The Monitoring Service was growing like Topsy too. It began life on a hill above the requisitioned mansion of Wood Norton, where the Corporation's engineers erected a series of aerials to capture foreign broadcasts; these were recorded in a wooden shed on wax records, which the monitors would take away in their bicycle panniers to transcribe and translate. The material was devoured in Whitehall, and the operation quickly extended its reach. By 1941 the monitoring staff had grown to 500 – most of them, of course, language specialists – and they were listening in to nearly 250 news programmes in 30

Listening in to the world – the Monitoring Service.

languages. The *Daily Digest* that resulted from their labours routinely ran to 100,000 words or more. Auntie was growing at a giddy pace.

≈

After her uncertain start in 1939, Auntie was also settling into her role as the nation's comforter and entertainer through its darkest hours, broadcasting a rich mix of variety, comedy, music, drama and factual programmes on the Home and Forces Services. Some of the shows became classics and were continued after the war. Perhaps the most famous, *It's That Man Again*, or *ITMA* as it became known, lasted until 1949 and was taken off the air only because its star, Tommy Handley, died suddenly of a brain haemorrhage.

ITMA began life as a pre-war attempt to recreate an American radio format, but its subversive, goonish humour turned it into a very British wartime institution. Its title was taken from a *Daily Express* headline about Hitler, and much of the humour was directed at the

Nazis, but it also poked fun at fussy British officialdom. In the first wartime series, Tommy Handley starred as the Minister of Aggravation and Mysteries, housed next door to the Office of Twerps. Here is a flavour:

> *Tommy Handley*: Heil folks, it's *Mein Kampf* again. Sorry, I
> should say 'Hello, folks, it's that man again.' That was the
> Goebbled version, a bit doctored. I usually go all goosey
> when I can't follow my proper-gander ... *(Phone rings)*
> 'Hello – yes ... no, sorry, the pigeon post is late today,
> the postman ate the express messenger, feathers and all. I
> haven't had a word from any of my spies. When I get
> those spies *(those pies?)* here I won't mince my words, I
> can tell you. Ring me up again when I am out.
> Goodbye, or, as they say in Pomerania, 'arf window-
> screen.' Now where's my new secretary?
> *Vera Lennox*: Here I am Mr Handtorch.
> *Tommy Handley*: Well, puncture me with a portfolio. Are you
> my new secretary?
> *Vera Lennox*: Yes, I'm Dotty.
> *Tommy Handley*: I am a bit barmy myself. My last secretary
> was Cilly and you're Dotty.

In the course of the war Handley appeared in all sorts of guises – including mayor of a seedy seaside resort called Foaming-at-the-Mouth and squire of Much-Fiddling – and the bizarre cast of characters that peopled the show – Funf the German spy, Mona Lott the laundry woman, Ali Oop the saucy-postcard seller, Colonel Chinstrap, the dipsomaniac Indian Army man – became part of the nation's daily life. 'Public conversation was stitched together by their catch-phrases,' writes Tom Hickman in his book *What Did You Do in the War, Auntie?* 'People found excuses to ring each other up just so they could say "This is Funf speaking." They left each other's company with either "Ta-ta for now"; or "TTFN", like *ITMA*'s second char, Mrs Mopp, whose very name passed into the language as a synonym. Pub barmen served customers with her "Can I do you now sir?" Virtually everyone

ITMA *in recording: Mrs Mopp (Dorothy Summers) and Tommy Handley are in the foreground.*

invited to have a drink would accept with Chinstrap's "I don't mind if I do".'

Another big – and perhaps more surprising – hit was *The Brains Trust*, which was first broadcast under the title *Any Questions?* on New Year's Day 1941. The original – and very simple – idea was, as the chairman, Donald McCulloch, a former public relations officer at the Ministry of Agriculture, put it, to 'encourage men and women in the services to ask questions and to hear experts dealing with their questions'. The programme was completely unscripted, and the panel were given no notice of what they would be asked. In the early days the questions were factual; the first, which was submitted by an RAF sergeant, was 'What are the seven wonders of the world?' (no one on the panel was able to answer it). But as the programme developed, the questions became broader, participation was opened up to the public more generally, and the panel members were allowed to stretch their intellectual legs a little. 'What is the secret of a happy marriage?' a young WAAF wanted to know, and a farmer from the West Country wrote in with, 'After the last war farmers had a very hard time, does the panel think the same will happen this time?' The panel also considered the questions 'What is the meaning of life?', 'What is an inferiority complex?' and (from an RAF pilot) 'How can a fly land upside-down on the ceiling?'

The BBC certainly was not expecting the programme to take off in the way it did. The 1942 *BBC Year Book* noted that 'One of the surprises for wartime radio is that five men discussing philosophy, art and science should have a regular audience of at least ten million listeners ... the popularity of *The Brains Trust* became almost embarrassing.' The key to the programme's success lay in the strange chemistry between the panel members, especially the original trio who began the series and remained regulars when the size of the panel was increased. Julian Huxley (later Sir Julian) was an evolutionary biologist, a Fellow of the Royal Society and brother of the novelist Aldous Huxley; Cyril Joad was a pacifist philosopher with Fabian tendencies and a somewhat colourful personal life; and Commander A. B. Campbell was, or at least claimed to be, a retired sailor. It was said that Campbell had been included in the first show at the last minute when a panel member failed to turn up, and the art historian Kenneth Clark, who joined as an occasional guest later in the war, described him as a 'genial imposter who had in fact been to sea and was said to have been a purser'. Campbell often managed to enrage the other two. 'Julian Huxley took the whole thing seriously,' Clark wrote, 'and was irritated to the point of peevishness by foolish answers,' especially if they came from Campbell. Clark recalled an edition of the programme when 'we were asked to define the word "allergy".' Campbell, he related, 'got in before Huxley and said "I suffer from an allergy. If I eat marmalade my head steams." Huxley and Joad were furious, but next week Commander Campbell said, "I've had 200 letters from people whose heads steam when they eat marmalade."'

The Brains Trust format became, the *BBC Year Book* reported, 'a new way of spending a social evening ... there were dozens of army brains trusts, Rotary brains trusts and village brains trusts. America cabled for copies of the recordings. A *Brains Trust Book* went into print'. Like *ITMA*, *The Brains Trust* gave the English language new catchphrases (Joad's 'It all depends on what you mean by ...' and Campbell's 'When I was in Patagonia ...'), and both programmes were popular with the Royal Family. There was a Royal Command performance of *ITMA* at Windsor Castle on Princess Elizabeth's birthday in 1942, and the *News Chronicle* reported that the queen sent a question in to the *Brains Trust*. 'Why,' she apparently wanted to know, 'do they call the Italians "Wops"?' (At a private lunch I once heard the queen mother – as she had by then become – refer to our European partners as 'those huns, wops and dagos', so the report has the ring of truth.)

Even some worthy programmes designed to help with the war effort became popular hits and created new stars. It was estimated that there were nearly 2,000 broadcasts on food in the course of the war, and *The Kitchen Front*, which was produced with the cooperation of the Ministry of Food to advise housewives struggling with rationing on 'what to eat and how to cook it', attracted audiences of over 5 million listeners.

When the Ministry of Agriculture urged people to 'dig for victory' in September 1940, the campaign was taken up by C. H. Middleton in his weekly gardening talks; *In Your Garden* went out after Sunday lunch and became another national institution. The BBC's 1945 *Year Book* judged that Middleton had 'for four years guided a new national movement towards self-sufficiency' and claimed that 'it would be hard to write a social history of the war years without mentioning Mr Middleton'.

In 1942 his efforts were buttressed by *The Radio Allotment*, a programme based around a patch of land dug out at Royal Crescent, not far from Holland Park. Each week a group of distinguished BBC broadcasters, including the great war correspondent Wynford Vaughan-Thomas, reported on their labours in this elegant setting.

Another unlikely star was the 'Radio Doctor', who broadcast five-minute segments after the 8.00 a.m. news and was described by one paper as 'the doctor with the greatest number of patients in the world'. Because doctors were not allowed to advertise their services, Charles Hill could not use his name, but the programme launched him on a public career and he later became a Tory Cabinet minister (as Lord Hill he was to have an extremely fractious and sometimes bitter relationship with the post-war BBC).

Some of these programmes have echoes in the Radio Four schedules seventy-five years later. Today's *Any Questions?* is more topical than *The Brains Trust*, but it is still unscripted and tests a similar-sized panel with unseen questions, and you can still pick up horticultural tips after your Sunday lunch on *Gardeners' Question Time*.

≈

By the end of 1940 the government – so often criticized by Priestley and others for its failure to understand the importance of broadcasting – finally seems to have woken up to the power of this new player in a total war. After a meeting of the War Cabinet on 30 December, the BBC was invited to put forward proposals for nothing less than 'a possible trebling of present output' of its Overseas Services. The Corporation duly put together a hugely ambitious plan to increase its foreign programming from just under 50 hours a day to over 150, and laid out equally sweeping propaganda aims: 'to convey to all parts of the world truthful news and a prompt, clear and insistent exposition of British policy ... counter and discredit the enemy cause within the enemy countries and among populations subject to enemy occupation', and to 'bring Britain closer to the various parts of the Empire, to British forces serving abroad, to British ships at sea and to the United States'.

Everyone understood that a plan of this kind involved formidable financial and logistical challenges; it was estimated that the BBC would have to build another eighteen transmitters and recruit an extra 2,750 new staff. When the plans were submitted to the Ministry of Information, the BBC stressed that 'if the programme expansion were to be adequately carried out the fullest priorities would be required in the matter of cash, men and material'.

The first obstacle was a shortage of suitable buildings. By early 1941 Broadcasting House – which a decade earlier had seemed to Val Gielgud such a magnificent temple to modernity – was bursting at the seams. Bomb damage did not make life there any easier. Jean Oberlé of the French Service recalled that the *Français parlent aux français* team turned up for work at BH one morning to find their office 'demolished and burnt'. They piled their papers and typewriters into a taxi and moved up the road to Bedford College, a women's higher education institution in Regent's Park which had been requisitioned for the duration. A few weeks later, Oberlé wrote, 'the same morning surprise; half the college in pieces'. Sometimes, he said, the scripts had to be written sitting on the grass in the park. So throughout 1941 Auntie was grabbing any piece of property she could; at almost every meeting that year the Board of Governors were required to approve leases and purchases on hotels, office blocks, boarding houses and theatres.

In January 1941 the first European Services moved into Bush House, and by March the bulk of the Overseas Services were established there – the building was to remain the headquarters of the World Service for more than seventy years. This magnificent edifice, which sits at the bottom of Kingsway between Aldwych and the Strand, was built in the 1920s to serve as an international trade centre. It was designed by an American architect – there is a whiff of Chicago or New York about the place – and it cost some $10 million, earning it the soubriquet 'the most expensive building in the world' in 1929. But it was built for companies wanting to show off their products, not for broadcasting. The floor-space was divided into over 900 'suites', and the BBC's efforts to create a working broadcasting centre there were hampered by the way it had to negotiate with individual leaseholders like Parker Pen, the lawyers Slaughter and May, and the advertising agency J. Walter Thompson. It also took them weeks to persuade the Air Ministry to relinquish a substantial chunk of the building. Asa Briggs records that in the immediate aftermath of the move, 'Accommodation at Bush House ... was so over-crowded that it impaired health and efficiency, while recording facilities were so inadequate that they prevented proper programming.' One of those who worked at Bush House then told Briggs – by way of an illustration of the *ad hoc* nature of the arrangements – that 'the first fortnight's menus consisted entirely of coffee and kippers'.

In the summer of 1941 the Labour MP Philip Noel-Baker took up the cause of BBC staff in the House of Commons, condemning the 'slum conditions' of what he called – Bush House could not be named in public for security reasons – 'the Black Hole of Tooting Bec'. It was, he said, 'the scandal of London'. He told the House, 'There is still a room, not large, in which 40 people have to try to work, and I was told that one man who went there to telephone came out gasping for breath. There are far too many people for the cubic space available ... It is very bad for the health of the staff. One key man has just resigned because he could not stand the strain. The conditions adversely affect output. I do not believe anybody doing that kind of work in such conditions could give more than 50 per cent of what he ought to do.'

Noel-Baker also identified the other big obstacle to the BBC's ambitions to expand: the difficulty of finding qualified staff at a time of manpower shortages. 'The Army will not exempt people for this vital work,' he said. 'I know of one man whom the B.B.C. found after great difficulty, an expert in a special group of languages, who could not be replaced. He was graded C.3 [fit for home service only], but the Army kept him.' Like others before him, Noel-Baker contrasted

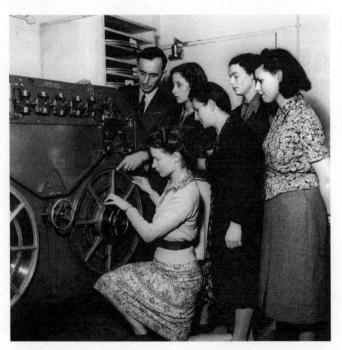

Preparing a steel-tape recording machine for use, 1941. The shortage of manpower forced the BBC to recruit and promote more women.

the efficiency and enthusiasm of Dr Goebbels with the failings of British officialdom.

Asa Briggs stresses that 'it is important to note how little many employees of the BBC, let alone people from outside who broadcast regularly, knew about the *haute politique* of the Corporation'. Most of those we have met in the preceding chapters were too busy writing and producing programmes to worry about what the Board of Governors were up to, or to trouble themselves with the precise details of the constitutional relationship between the BBC and the Ministry of Information. And on the whole the BBC–government relationship worked pretty well through the great national emergencies of Dunkirk, the Battle of Britain and the Blitz – everyone was pulling together in the same great existential struggle for the survival of the nation and its values. But behind the scenes there were important structural changes going on, and the institutional settlement that was worked out between the end of 1940 and early 1942 came to have a significant bearing on the climate in which the programme-makers worked. A mixture of common sense, good luck and the happy involvement of some remarkable individuals allowed the government and the BBC to reach a *modus vivendi* that served Britain well for the rest of the war.

The first big change came after a period of particularly ill-tempered relations between senior figures at the BBC and the Ministry of Information. For a brief period in 1940 the director-general of the Ministry was Frank Pick. He was in many ways an inspired bureaucrat – he was the first chief executive of the London Passenger Transport Board and was responsible for, among many other things, the graphic roundels that are still the Tube's distinctive badge – but he appears to have got on very badly indeed with Frederick Ogilvie, his opposite number at the BBC, and kept threatening that the government would wind up 'taking the BBC over'. At the same time, the Cabinet set up a committee under the chancellor of the exchequer, Kingsley Wood, to consider doing exactly that. The committee came up with a clever compromise which, they believed, would ensure greater government control over Auntie, but avoid the kind of unedifying public battle that might be caused by a straightforward takeover. Two government 'advisers' were to be appointed, one, known as the 'general adviser', to oversee the coverage of home affairs, the other to perform the same task for foreign broadcasting.

Both the BBC's director-general and its Board of Governors objected vigorously. The governors saw it as a threat to their role as the guarantors of the BBC's independence, and Frederick Ogilvie was suspicious of the title 'general adviser', which he felt would allow the government's man to interfere wherever he chose. But the government was determined to push the changes through. At a meeting in January, Duff Cooper, the minister of information, told the BBC that the advisers would represent 'the minister's wartime suzerainty in the broadcasting field', and on 6 February he confirmed in the House of Commons that there would be 'two advisers to the B.B.C., one on general topics, and home policy more particularly, and one on foreign policy', and that these two would 'be officers of the Ministry of Information under the control of the Minister of Information'.

The curious way Cooper formulated his reasoning reflected the eternal tension between the government's instinct to control and its fear of being perceived as over-controlling. 'When, as Minister of Information, I endeavoured to ascertain what my relation would be to the B.B.C, I consulted with those in authority at the B.B.C., and they said, quite frankly, that they were prepared, as far as possible, to do anything I wished. I really could ask nothing more than that,' the Minister explained in the Commons, but, he added, '. . . there has not been that complete liaison which we desired between Government advice and the independent conduct of the B.B.C' – which sounds like a way of saying that Auntie was not doing what she was told. There was a similar ambiguity in the way he spoke of the new plan in answer to a Commons question the following month. It would, he said, 'no doubt, increase the control exercised by the Government', but at the same time he took care to add that, 'The Government's policy has been to maintain the independence of the B.B.C, and I think that decision has general approval.'

It was a Janus-like and muddled way of expressing the government's objectives, but as things turned out the new arrangement had unexpected and, for the BBC as a whole, largely benign results. The two men chosen for the advisers' jobs 'went native', and both turned out to be extremely effective champions of the BBC ethos – indeed they often had to stiffen the spines of their more timorous BBC colleagues in the face of government pressure.

The 'home' or 'general' adviser so feared by Ogilvie was in fact already a native: A. P. Ryan was a BBC man through and through. He had been working at BH since the mid-1930s and had been BBC controller (home) since March 1940. As we saw in Chapter 13, he had shown his mettle as one of Priestley's defenders during the first *Postscripts* series. Asa Briggs records that Ogilvie had to 'release Ryan from duty with the BBC so that he could be seconded to the Ministry of Information in order that he could in turn be seconded as General Adviser to the BBC.'

The foreign adviser, however, was a Foreign Office man, and his arrival was greeted with great suspicion by some BBC insiders. Ivone Kirkpatrick had an impressively colourful background. Severely

A. P. Ryan was forced on the BBC by the government as a 'general adviser', but he proved a doughty defender of BBC values.

wounded in action in the Gallipoli Campaign in 1915, he had spent much of the First World War working in the shadows – first in propaganda, and then as a spymaster running a network of resistance agents in German-occupied Belgium. He began his diplomatic career immediately after the First World War and served as first secretary in Berlin during the crucial years 1933–8. He was, in fact, just the kind of tough-minded and unsentimental government servant the Foreign Office felt they needed to keep the BBC in line.

The BBC veteran Harman Grisewood – who was appointed Kirkpatrick's deputy – includes this vivid sketch of a Whitehall warrior in his autobiography:

He [Kirkpatrick] had the wiry resilience of the physically diminutive. He was quick-witted and sure-footed like a mountain animal, with

Ivone Kirkpatrick, the BBC's foreign adviser: regarded as a Foreign Office plant, he 'went native' and was one of the true heroes of the BBC's war.

a good head for heights, and well-used to rough weather. Despite his manicured 'Mayfair' appearance there was very little of the diplomat in his manner. He thought the arts of flattery were all very well for foreigners, but for the British were a waste of time. Military brusqueries came easier to him than urbanity.

The 'manicured' appearance masked a formidable taste for hard work. Grisewood discovered that in times of real pressure his boss would spend nights in a row sleeping on his desk. Kirkpatrick believed Grisewood had been appointed as his deputy to keep an eye on him; he told his new assistant 'the BBC felt ... that if they were to have a Foreign Office man foisted upon them ... then they must have their own Assistant Controller'. But the Corporation bosses really need not have worried. Kirkpatrick very quickly absorbed traditional BBC values and, as we shall see, fought hard for them. Grisewood, who came to admire him greatly, quotes his pragmatic but also principled view on the risks of putting out lies for propaganda purposes: 'This country must be careful not to sacrifice long-term credibility unless the advantage was considerable – say the equivalent of the destruction of a Division [a military unit generally made up of 10,000–30,000 troops].'

Like Ryan, Kirkpatrick understood the power of truth. Though initially regarded with fear and loathing in the corridors of Broadcasting House as government stooges, these two are, in fact, among the true heroes of the BBC's wartime story.

A SIGH OF RELIEF

WHILE DUFF COOPER TRIED to reshape the government's relationship with the BBC, he was fighting another very bruising turf war behind the scenes – one that brought him into a direct confrontation with Churchill. The service ministries still controlled the way war news was released; they could decide what stories the Ministry of Information could and could not publicize, and sometimes they simply kept information about important military developments to themselves. In May 1941 two of Duff Cooper's most senior officials threatened to resign, complaining that the system made it impossible for the Ministry to fulfil its role in the propaganda war. 'Its [propaganda's] raw material is news and information,' they wrote, 'but the Ministry of Information is so constituted by the Government that it has no control over either of these. It can decide neither *what* to make public nor *when* to make something public nor *what* line or shape to give such information as it is made public.' He conceded to them – in an unattractive metaphor we would probably not use today – that the 'M.O.I. is a misbegotten freak', and promised to raise the issue with the Cabinet.

The following month several newspapers published leaks suggesting that all was not well at Senate House. 'It is now an open secret that Mr Duff Cooper is not prepared to continue on the basis of his present powers,' the *Daily Herald* reported with an air of authority. 'The Minister of Information has found himself repeatedly in an impossible position owing to the restrictions imposed by other State departments on the release of news.' The leaks – which very obviously originated from Senate House – not unnaturally made the service ministries even more reluctant to hand control over the release of news to the Ministry of Information.

On 24 June Duff Cooper laid out his demands in a blunt paper for the Cabinet. 'An important weapon in the conduct of political warfare is the presentation of news,' he wrote. 'The responsibility of deciding what news should be released and the manner in which it should be presented should rest with the Minister of Information.' Therefore, he argued, 'It should be the duty of his Cabinet colleagues, especially the Foreign Secretary and the Service Ministers, to keep the Minister fully supplied with the information at their disposal.' This bold bid to secure control over the Whitehall news machine proposed one modest concession: that the minister of information's actions could be 'subject to the veto of any of his Cabinet colleagues pending reference to the Cabinet for decision'.

Duff Cooper had used the ministerial equivalent of a nuclear weapon, gambling his own job on success. He argued that without the changes he was pressing for 'it would be difficult to justify its [the Ministry of Information's] continuance as a separate government department under a Cabinet Minister', and he suggested that in those circumstances either the minister's role should be downgraded to that of a civil servant or 'the Ministry could be allowed to disintegrate into its component parts'. It is perhaps also worth noting that the paper went in two days after the German invasion of the Soviet Union, one of the turning points of the war, and perhaps not the best moment to attempt a Whitehall putsch.

The memo that bounced back from Downing Street a couple of days later gave Duff Cooper almost nothing at all. Churchill insisted that, 'In general the supply of news from the aforesaid Departments [the fighting ministries and the Foreign Office] will be the responsibility of the Department concerned', and 'operational communiqués from the Service Departments or from the Commanders on the war fronts may not be altered, even in form, without the consent of the Departmental Minister concerned'. Moreover, 'nothing must . . . prejudice the right of

Departmental Ministers to veto or require the publication of any particular fact or statement', and 'Departments which have Public Relations Branches and Press Officers should be at liberty to preserve their existing contacts with the Press for the purpose of dealing with enquiries about their day-to-day work'. Cooper was to be given none of the new powers he wanted, and Churchill simply ignored his huffy talk of abolishing the post of minister of information and dissolving the Ministry.

It was such a humiliating rejection that it made Duff Cooper's resignation inevitable, and he must have known it, but there was one final act to be played out. Just over a year earlier, in his first week as prime minister, Churchill had urged Cooper to find a way of 'establishing more effective control over the BBC'. He clearly did not feel that the appointment of home and foreign advisers had done the trick, and he now returned to the fray. Buried away in Point 9 of the prime minister's paper was the most direct challenge to the BBC's independence the Corporation had faced since war began. 'The Ministry of Information will take full day-to-day editorial control of the B.B.C.,' the memo stated starkly, 'and will be responsible for both initiative and censorship.' The next sentence reveals just how little weight Churchill gave to the principle, which Auntie held as dear as dogma, that the BBC's governors should guarantee its independence. 'It will be the duty of the Minister of Information,' the prime minister declared, 'to carry with him *so far as possible* [my italics], the Board of Governors, who stand as umpires and sureties to Parliament for the spirit in which the B.B.C. propaganda is conducted.'

Churchill's belief that the BBC needed to be cut down to size long pre-dated the war; as long ago as 1933 he had told the Commons that 'These well-meaning gentlemen of the British Broadcasting Corporation have absolutely no qualifications and no claim to represent British public opinion. They have no right to say that they voice the opinions of English or British people whatever.' In a memorable and expressive – if somewhat mysterious – phrase, he condemned the BBC's political commentary as 'this copious stream of pontifical anonymous mugwumpery with which we have been dosed so long'. His visceral antipathy to the Corporation was still strong when, eight years later, he was presented with a draft honours list which included several BBC names, including an OBE for an announcer. 'What's this?' Churchill is reported to have demanded. 'OBE for an announcer! Do you want to make the whole of the honours list a joke and farce? I'll see this never happens as long as there is an England.' And as prime minister in a national emergency, he clearly felt he had the power to bend Auntie to his will.

On 10 July Duff Cooper obediently trotted along to Broadcasting House to inform the Board of Governors that the government was taking 'full day-to-day editorial control of the BBC'. The minutes of the meeting suggest he was in peevish spirits, complaining that 'a week ago his Private Secretary had rung up to ask the name of the person who had been responsible for the decision not to broadcast a script in the Home Service prepared by a Russian connected with the Tass Agency, and that he had not had an answer', and that, more generally, 'the present arrangements in regard to the advisers were not working well, that there were many instances which could be given – some twenty in number – when there had been a failure to carry out Ministry directives'.

For all the bluster, Cooper's proposal for taking 'full day-to-day editorial control' of the BBC was oddly modest; he suggested that the director-general, Frederick Ogilvie, should become a member of his own staff at the Ministry of Information. It makes one wonder whether he really believed in what he was being asked to do.

The response from the chairman of the governors, Sir Allan Powell, was robust. He pointed out that 'it was not apparent that the proposal with regard to the Director General would overcome any of the major difficulties', and he challenged Duff Cooper over his complaints, countering that he 'had been unable to obtain any cases of the failures mentioned', and that any difficulties between the BBC and the Ministry of Information were 'due to the fact that many different persons of differing ranks at the Ministry were giving instructions to BBC staff'. When the governors suggested that they should seek a face-to-face meeting with the prime minister to bring home 'the full recognition of the part broadcasting should play in the war', Cooper 'said he had no objection, but suggested the governors should be very certain of their ground before they went'. The meeting broke up with an agreement to resume the discussion the following week, and the BBC asked for details of the occasions when it was accused of failing to 'carry out Ministry directives'.

When Duff Cooper returned to Broadcasting House on 17 July he was forced to admit that the cases of these failures were 'fewer than he thought' – just two in fact, and they had occurred the previous year. And his proposal to take the director-general on to his own staff was met with a flat 'no'; the governors simply told him that 'they were unanimously of the opinion that the proposal in question would be unworkable and would therefore be unacceptable'. He tried quoting the exact terms of the Churchill memo, but this sally was buried in the best tradition of BBC meetings – by being talked out; 'discussion ensued as to the precise meaning of this decision and as to the steps necessary to give effect to it', the minutes tell us, 'and eventually it was agreed that further consultation should take place between representatives of the Ministry and the BBC on the subject'.

It seems likely that Duff Cooper was running out of puff by this stage, and who can blame him? He had lost his battle for control over the Whitehall information system, and he was now being required to pursue a policy he did not really believe in and could not work out how to implement. Three days later he resigned with, in his own words, 'a sigh of relief'.

≈

If anyone could have been expected to make the prime ministerial dream of BBC control a reality, it was surely the man brought in to replace Duff Cooper. The new minister of information, Brendan Bracken, had bound his career and life fortunes to Churchill so closely that he was widely – but inaccurately – rumoured to be the prime minister's illegitimate son, conceived, it was said by some, during an affair the young Winston had had in South Africa during the Boer War.

Bracken's true past was even more unlikely. He was born into a family of Irish nationalists in County Tipperary in 1901, and proved such a troublesome teenager that in 1916 he was exiled into the care of a priest cousin in the Australian state of Victoria. The good Father secured him a job maintaining boundary fences on a ranch owned by a local Catholic, but he was sacked for spending too much time reading books, and took off across the continent, educating himself as he went and paying his way with odd jobs in teaching and journalism. At the age of nineteen he returned to the British Isles and taught at a school in Liverpool, then presented himself at Sedbergh, the public school in Cumbria, claiming to be four years younger than he was and spinning a completely untrue yarn about his parents having died in an Australian bush fire. The headmaster of Sedbergh was persuaded to take him on as a pupil, and Bracken acquired the Old School Tie he needed to ease his passage into the Establishment.

Election to Parliament came in 1929, and throughout Churchill's wilderness years in the 1930s Bracken gave the future prime minister his unwavering support; the veteran Tory Stanley Baldwin called him Churchill's 'faithful chela' – the Hindi word for a disciple – and when Churchill moved into Number 10 in May 1940 Bracken became his parliamentary private secretary. The prime minister insisted – in the face of objections from the king – that he should be given the rank of privy councillor.

As Bracken's biographer Andrew Boyle noted, 'Since it was plain that Churchill had ... invested his alter-ego, Bracken, with full powers to treat the BBC according to its deserts, the misgivings among the governors and senior executives there ran deep.'

But – once more against the odds – Bracken turned out to be one of the BBC's most effective allies, and not at all the threat to Auntie's independence some feared he might be. The colourful manner in which he had lied his way into respectability suggests he was no great enthusiast for the truth, but by the time he entered Parliament he had a successful career in newspaper and magazine publishing behind him, and he knew how to deal with journalists. He also had a business leader's ruthlessness and efficiency; one aide told Andrew Boyle that 'he moved through the Ministry during that opening week like a dose of salts. No sooner had he decided who should go and who should stay than he followed up the decision in person. His tours of inspection were abruptly dramatic. From one office to another he went, introducing himself and saying: "Ah yes, you're Mr so-and-so. Well, you're out. The letter terminating your employment is on its way." Then on to the next, more lucky individual: "I know what you do, Mr X. I want you to stay and really put your back into it."' Harold Nicolson, who lost his own position as a parliamentary secretary when Duff Cooper went (he was given a seat on the BBC Board of Governors as a consolation prize) noted in his diary, 'I had a talk with Brendan Bracken. He seems to be sacking everyone in the Ministry.'

Once Bracken had sorted out the staff at Senate House he turned his attention to the BBC, and in early September he attended a meeting of the Board of Governors. After an exchange of pleasantries he told them – no doubt to their great delight – that his predecessor's plans were being consigned to history. 'He said,' the minutes record, 'that, while some parts of the [BBC] Charter were in cold storage during wartime consequent on the necessity for the government having power to give direction to the Corporation in matters affecting the war effort, he was satisfied that it was undesirable in the national interest for the BBC to be taken over by the Government, and that the more freedom the Corporation could have in the conduct of its affairs, the better it could serve the national interest.'

Bracken also poured oil on the waters that had been so troubled by Duff Cooper's imposition on Auntie of the two government advisers, recognizing that it was 'unsatisfactory that two permanent officials not on the Corporation's staff should be in a position to give directions to the Corporation that it must carry out'. You can almost hear the smooth whirring of a truly mandarin mind in his solution. 'He adumbrated for consideration,' the minutes tell us, 'a plan by which the advisers might be on the Corporation's staff, yet at the same time holding a rank in the Ministry of Information, a plan which was not without precedent.'

The next governors' meeting duly approved the appointment of Ivone Kirkpatrick as 'Controller (Overseas) A and BBC Adviser for Foreign Affairs' (there was also a 'Controller (Overseas) B', but we need not be detained by this curlicue on the baroque management flow-charts Auntie liked to create) and at the same time A. P. Ryan,

Winston Churchill crossing Horse Guards Parade with Brendan Bracken, his 'faithful chela'. Bracken served as minister of information from 1941 until the end of the war.

yoyoing back to a staff job at Broadcasting House, became 'Controller (News Co-ordination) and BBC Adviser for Home and Empire Affairs'.

≈

The one requirement Bracken did insist upon – very much with Churchill's backing – was that the BBC should appoint an adviser on English to catch some of the grammatical howlers which were apparently offending the prime ministerial sensibilities. G. M. Young was an Oxford historian – perhaps most famous for *Portrait of an Age*, his masterly essay on the Victorians – and he seems to have gone about his duties by locking himself away in his study in the Wiltshire countryside with a pile of scripts, rather as if he were marking a set of undergraduate essays. The results were deliciously donnish. He was provoked into apostrophe rage by a reference to 'reservists of the

Philippines Army', and subjunctives were an equally touchy subject; the sentence 'During the Committee stage, the House agreed to a Government amendment that no woman would be compelled to use a lethal weapon' attracted ferocious underlining beneath 'would' and a furious 'No – this is how Scotchmen draft amendments but Whitehall, thank God, has not yet sunk so low.' A reference to 'Germany's alleged blockade of Great Britain' gets a pencilled box around the word 'alleged' and three exclamation marks, followed by 'This is not a police court story.'

The BBC's governors were irritated when the adviser on English passed comment on the content rather than the style of news programmes – he hated anything that smacked of 'speculation' and what he described as 'gossipy' material – and sniffily noted that this was outside his remit. But his marginalia can hardly be described as a serious threat to the BBC's editorial independence.

Young's oddest contribution was a note, written in October 1941, about the 'difficulty in ... getting the written word to sound well when it is spoken' and the importance of what he called 'cadence'. 'The best example in English of the written word intended to be spoken is of course the Prayer Book,' he declared, adding, 'The compilers had in their ears from childhood the *clamulae* of the Latin service.' This leads him to a disquisition on the rhythmic qualities of the *'cursus planus ... cursus velox ... cursus tardus'* and, apparently his own coinage, the *'cursus Angelicus'*. These classical categories are, it turns out, surprisingly useful in analysing BBC news bulletins: 'industrial centre of Kharkov' was cited as a good example of the *cursus planus*, and 'larger supplies of sugar' as an equally illuminating use of the *cursus tardus*.

This extraordinary document arrived on A. P. Ryan's desk, and he forwarded it to the Ministry of Information, noting dryly that 'you will perhaps agree that Mr Young's suggestions are not easy to translate into language that would be understood by the rank and file of news men engaged in the hurly-burly of issuing six bulletins a day. I am afraid it would be as easy to equip every sub-editor with a tonsure and a surplice as to get him to make head or tail of *clamulae* and *cursus*'. Ryan was something of a classical scholar himself (his BBC leaving present was a complete set of Plutarch) and added, 'We shall have to await a simpler version of the *Quicunque vult servari* for broadcasters, according to Mr Young, before we move from faith to works. In plain English, I look forward to Mr Young coming in next week to tell us what he is talking about.'

The BBC could afford to indulge eccentricity in those days, and Mr Young was kept on as an adviser at £200 a year for the duration of the war.

≈

Brendan Bracken realized that the real threat to the BBC's future was not prime ministerial displeasure, but the chaotic state of its administration and finances. In 1941 the cost of the war was really beginning to squeeze the public purse, and both the Public Accounts Committee of MPs and the Treasury had become concerned about the way Auntie was spending public money. Bracken, though a dedicated defender of the BBC's broadcasting, shared the view that 'not even the BBC possessed a prescriptive right to squander cash like a drunken sailor'. Things were brought to a head by a shattering memo – marked 'Secret' – which arrived from the Ministry of Information on 10 September 1941. The pressure on public spending had reached such a crisis point that, the memo explained, Downing Street was instructing 'all Departments . . . to examine their building programmes with a view to the drastic curtailment of projects which, however important in themselves, can be dispensed with'. Proposals for cutting infrastructure spending were required that very day, and the memo destroyed any hope that the BBC could complete its 'triple expansion' programme by the end of 1941.

It also drew attention to a horrible hole in Auntie's sums. At the beginning of the year the Corporation's accountants estimated that the programme would involve a capital outlay of £2.3 million, but the figure seems to have been arrived at in a somewhat arbitrary manner, and in the earliest draft proposals for 'triple expansion' it is simply scribbled in a margin in pencil. By May the BBC managers involved were clearly in a flap about it, as they were searching somewhat frantically for paperwork to back the figures up. And by

September that estimate had increased to over £5 million, largely because £2.8 million was required for new buildings. The yawning gap – more than £140 million in today's money – was symptomatic of a deeper problem; the organization and management of the BBC was creaking horribly under the strain of the rapid expansion the Corporation was struggling to achieve in 1941, and systems that had been appropriate to the days when John Reith ran the place like a family firm were no longer adequate.

The man Bracken called in to sort things out, Robert W. Foot, was the chairman of the Gas, Light and Coke Company. Foot had no experience of broadcasting, but he understood where the BBC was heading, judging that 'there is little doubt that ... the BBC was drifting nearer and nearer to control by the government, and if the change had not been made the drift would undoubtedly have continued simply because the BBC's own internal organisation was not sufficiently strong and efficient to manage its own affairs, whether financial or otherwise, without considerable interference'. Foot very quickly identified several areas of hair-raising overspending, and set out plans for a complete overhaul of the way the Corporation was run and the way it accounted for its money. Before his arrival, the Treasury had complained that BBC estimates of its expenditure needs were 'very wild indeed', but his reforms were so successful that by January 1942 the Treasury judged the Corporation's financial predictions to be 'very reliable'.

Someone had to pay for the mess Foot had uncovered. The director-general, Frederick Ogilvie, had never been very much interested in management systems – indeed, as we saw in an earlier chapter, he felt the BBC had become too big and impersonal even when he took over a much smaller organization before the war. He had also become bogged down in ill-tempered arguments with some of his managers about issues – like the pros and cons of moving the Monitoring Service from Warwickshire to bigger quarters in Berkshire – which now seem trivial. His fate was decided at a meeting of the Board of Governors on 21 January 1942. 'It was agreed that for some time past the Governors have been concerned about certain weaknesses in the organisation of the Corporation,' the minutes begin.

'The Governors discussed these matters fully ... They came to the unanimous decision that the chief executive control of the BBC under wartime conditions, with the great growth in the number and variety of staff employed and of the financial problems involved, called for different qualities and experience from those suited for peacetime control.'

This was BBC high politics at its most brutal. The governors noted the 'great strain which wartime conditions had imposed on the Director General', and 'asked the Chairman to convey their views to Mr Ogilvie as soon as possible, and authorised him to say that in the event of his placing his resignation in their hands they would make the most liberal financial provision possible for him in his retirement'. Ogilvie was out within a week, and he was replaced by two joint-directors-general – Foot himself, and Sir Cecil Graves, one of the oldest and crustiest of the Corporation's Old Servants. Foot was to be responsible for finance and administration, Graves for programmes.

It seems highly likely that Brendan Bracken was behind the coup against the director-general ('Mother Ogilvie', as Bracken liked to call him), although no smoking gun has come to light. Harold Nicolson, now sitting as a BBC governor, recorded in his diary 'We have decided to retire Ogilvie, and put Graves and Foot as joint Directors-General in his place. I am sure this is right, as Ogilvie is too noble a character for rough war work. Yet I mind deeply in a way. This clever, high-minded man being pushed aside. I hate it. But I agree.'

The commentary on Ogilvie's departure in the 1942 *BBC Year Book* was brief and restrained, noting merely that he had 'carried a heavy burden for over three years' and 'never spared himself in the service of the Corporation'. It was a mealy-mouthed way to thank a man who had been at the helm while Auntie made so much history. Ogilvie was knighted later that year, became the principal of Jesus College, Oxford, towards the end of the war, and died at the age of fifty-six in 1949.

THE SWEET, SMOOTH
SQUEEZE OF A TRIGGER

S IR CECIL GRAVES HAD joined the BBC as an administrator, not a
programme-maker, and his BBC career had begun right back in
1926, the year before the British Broadcasting Company acquired its
Royal Charter and became a corporation. He had founded the Empire
Service in 1932, and he had been Reith's candidate for director-
general when Ogilvie got the job in 1938. His programme views
were decidedly 'Reithian' and his arrival in the top job was followed
by a campaign to clean up the BBC's dance music by eliminating
what one of his lieutenants described as 'crooning, sentimental numbers, drivelling words, slushy innuendos and so on'.

Graves appears to have been particularly repelled by the work of
Vera Lynn. Her programme *Sincerely Yours* was broadcast for the first
time a couple of months before his appointment as joint-director-
general. It was produced by Howard Thomas (who was also the
producer of *The Brains Trust* and clearly had a Midas touch) and the
mix of song requests and messages to British troops serving abroad
proved an immediate success. But the BBC governors did not approve
at all; the minutes of their meeting on 4 December 1941 noted tersely,
'*Sincerely Yours*; deplored, popularity noted'. The new joint-director-
general shared their reservations and reported to a programme meeting
that he had listened with 'shocked surprise' to the music the BBC was
pumping out. 'How could men fit themselves for battle with these
debilitating tunes sounding in their ears,' he demanded, according to

Harman Grisewood's account. 'The BBC ... could not avoid some responsibility for making this lady popular and so for depreciating the morale of fighting men. Besides, the theme of these songs was sentimental sex, and this mood at the best of times was not to be encouraged.'

The admirable A. P. Ryan came to Ms Lynn's rescue. He had just returned from a tour of front-line camps, he told the meeting, and he confirmed that Vera Lynn's photograph was indeed appearing everywhere. 'The strange thing was that the morale of the men was not adversely affected at all,' he reported. 'On the contrary, Vera Lynn seemed to cheer them up ... some might find it shocking,' he agreed, but the fact was that 'if the BBC put a stop to Vera Lynn we would be doing harm to the troops – and in their eyes look very foolish.' So Vera Lynn was allowed to 'let rip', and Grisewood describes this battle as 'the first defeat of many for the old guard'.

Indeed, the 'old guard' were being outflanked all over the place. Throughout 1941, while the energies of the BBC High Command were concentrated on their jousting with Duff Cooper and Churchill, the junior officers and foot soldiers of the European Services had been caught up in an almost accidental but most dramatic broadcasting experiment; it demonstrated the power of the radio medium more vividly than anything that had gone before, and at the same time took the Corporation stumbling into policy and ethical challenges that were altogether more complex and difficult than the straightforward threat of a government takeover.

The inspiration behind what became known as the 'V Campaign' was provided by a Mr Victor de Laveleye, a former Belgian justice minister who had been recruited as the BBC's Belgian programme organizer. Struck by the fact the letter 'V' begins the French word for 'victory' and the Flemish word for freedom (*vrijheid*), he decided to broadcast the suggestion that sympathetic Belgian listeners should chalk it up in public places. The message went out in French on 14 January 1941 and in Flemish the following day.

During the previous autumn and winter weeks the BBC's intelligence assessments had reported a growing sense of frustration among the peoples of Occupied Europe about their impotence in the face of the Nazis, and an intelligence report in December suggested that 'leadership from London in the form of leaflets and radio instructions is expected'. But there was very little evidence of active 'resistance' to the Germans in Occupied Europe at this stage of the war, and the occupiers were certainly not facing any serious military threat from the civilian populations they controlled. In France, for example, early resisters concentrated on circulating polemical tracts and underground newspapers. As the historian Julian Jackson put it in his study *France: the Dark Years, 1940–1944,* 'cast aside romantic images of groups feverishly deciphering messages from London, unpacking parachute drops or sabotaging trains. In 1940–41 there were no contacts with London, and no parachute drops; most early resisters had no idea how to sabotage a train or the means to do it. Equally, the hackneyed phrase he or she "joined the Resistance" is entirely inappropriate to 1940–41. Before it could be joined, the Resistance had to be invented.'

A nugget tucked away in the BBC files of the period provides a clue to how Auntie understood the idea of 'resistance' in January 1941. 'In answer to an official inquiry by the Occupying Authority as to how much milk his cow supplied each day,' the script reads, 'a Breton peasant replied "8 pints." "Nonsense" replied the Authority, "I had better come and watch you do the milking, as you obviously do not know how to get the most from your cow." The cow was duly milked in the presence of the self-constituted expert but the result, much to his chagrin, was only six pints. The cow had of course been carefully milked half an hour before he arrived.' It was scarcely the kind of thing that would make Hitler quake in his jackboots.

So the reaction to Mr de Laveleye's suggestion caught everyone by surprise. People responded not just in Belgium but in France, where Belgian Service programmes could also be heard, and a week after that first broadcast the BBC received a letter from one of the Channel ports with information that Vs had begun to appear all over the place. A listener from Normandy then reported that 'As soon as the Belgians gave their friends the "V" as a rallying sign I went and chalked "V" on the walls,' and more and more stories of V-sightings found their way to London throughout February and March. On 22

March the French Service launched an appeal for Vs to honour King Peter of Yugoslavia for refusing to surrender to the Germans; 'the instruction was instantly followed ...,' writes the French Resistance historian Jean-Louis Crémieux-Brilhac, 'and in Marseilles it provoked a spontaneous demonstration by several thousand patriots'.

By early April letters from as far apart as Rouen in Normandy and Tarbes in the Pyrenees reported that Vs were even being painted on German military buildings and cars, and there was overwhelming evidence that they were 'growing like mushrooms everywhere' in both the German-occupied and the Vichy-run zones of France. A letter from Provence reflected the frustration that was driving the campaign. 'Many speak of revolt,' wrote the anonymous correspondent, 'but what can we do? We have no weapons ... It is true that we do still have chalk, which allows us to draw "V"s and the Cross of Lorraine [de Gaulle's chosen symbol] everywhere ...'

The wits of the French Service began to have fun with this 'thorn in the side of the Nazis', playing on the V theme in ditties they encouraged people to hum and sing. 'Slogan V' was to be sung to a rising scale. It went:

> V ...V ...V ...V ...V ...V ...V ...V ...
> On the walls and on the pavements,
> You can see Vs blossoming everywhere,
> It drives the Boches berserk,
> As for us, it lets us dream.
> V ...V ...V ...V ...V ...V ...V ...V ...

The German reaction was indeed gratifying. On 1 April the collaborationist Radio Paris announced that those guilty of chalking up graffiti would face prosecution, and on 5 April the newspaper *Le Petit Parisien* reported that 6,200 notices had been sent to concierges, property-owners and others, holding them responsible for what were described as 'idiotic calligraphists'. There were similar reprisals all over Occupied Europe, and these angry reactions from the Germans only added to the delight of the team at Bush House. 'The letter "V". Just a single letter, but with a wealth of meaning,' declared one of that spring's programme directives. 'A letter that German soldiers all over Europe are every day getting to know better and better by sight. Drawn with a finger in the dust on the back of an army lorry. Chalked on the door of a billet or company office. Daubed in tar on a tree or wall by a roadside. Cut with a sharp knife on a *Wehrmacht* poster. You do not have to look very far for this letter "V". In the streets of Trondheim and Brussels, along the Flanders roads, in Polish farms, on army vehicles all over Europe. Written by unseen hands, hands that one day will hold something more dangerous than a paint-brush. The finger that writes "V" in the dust will know again the sweet, smooth squeeze of a trigger. The letter V. Symbol of defiance. Symbol of hate. And above all Symbol of final Victory . . .'

The V Campaign began as a BBC initiative, and it was a BBC man who took it to the next level. Douglas Ritchie was the assistant news editor in the European Services – like his boss Noel Newsome he had joined the BBC from the *Daily Telegraph* at the beginning of the war and the two men were close allies. On 4 May Ritchie circulated a remarkable document called 'Broadcasting as a Weapon of War', which laid out a plan for capitalizing on the spontaneous success of the V Campaign in a more organized manner. In some ways it is a chilling document to read today; it marks the moment when the BBC finally caught up with the Nazi understanding of the raw power of radio. But it is also a recognition that the BBC had earned something its German competitors could no longer lay claim to: the trust of the listeners.

Ritchie began with two propositions:

> 1) After twenty months of war it is now clear that there are in Europe an enormous majority of people who wish to see the Allies win the war. In almost every enemy-occupied country people are showing that they bitterly resent the presence of the occupying troops and, at great personal risk, are committing acts of hostility and sabotage.
>
> 2) It is equally clear, from the evidence of intelligence reports, of neutral observers, and of the Press and Radio of all countries, that the BBC's broadcasts to the occupied countries are listened to by a remarkably high percentage of the population.

Ritchie argued that 'It is almost impossible to exaggerate the significance of these two facts. We have here, if we develop it and make use of it, a weapon of war of an entirely new kind. No such power has ever been in the hands of man before. The Germans have no such weapon.' Drawing on the experience of the previous weeks, he then lists the kind of action he believes that his 'V Army' could be mobilized to undertake:

> The Germans are short of certain metals. In households all over Europe there are innumerable metal articles which have not yet been requisitioned. Most of these can be buried in the ground at a word broadcast from London.
> The Germans are short of oil. At a word from London sugar can be slipped into petrol tanks all over Europe and buildings where oil and petrol are stored can be set on fire.
> The Germans are short of rubber. At a word from London, motor tyres can be slashed all over the Continent . . .

The list rolls on, culminating in the bold promise that 'When the British government gives the word, the BBC will cause riots and demonstrations in every city in Europe.' Most of the document is focused on Ritchie's proposals for economic and civil disruption, but it looks forward to the possibility of creating a more directly military role for the 'V Army' at a future date. And Ritchie recognized that his ambitions could not be fulfilled by the BBC alone. 'To turn this possibility into reality we have to do two things,' he wrote. 'We have to sharpen the weapon and practise its use and we have to convince the British government by demonstration, if necessary, that the weapon has all the striking power that we claim and that it must be used to bring the war to a rapid conclusion.'

At the end of May the BBC established a committee to put Ritchie's ideas into practice; its objectives included broadcasting propaganda that would make the listeners 'feel themselves part of a great army', and giving this army instructions that would 'be good for its morale and bad for the morale of the German garrisons' and 'greatly increase Germany's economic difficulties'.

Ritchie himself took the lead. Casting himself as 'Colonel

Britton' – his true identity remained a closely guarded secret until the end of the war, and when he was interviewed by an American reporter the 'Colonel' remained 'concealed behind a lofty partition' – he began a series of regular talks on the European Services. At first his exhortations to trouble-making were restrained; he told people to hide their small change, for example, so that the Germans could not use spare *sous* to boost their supplies of nickel, but his repertoire of ways to annoy the Nazis was greatly enhanced when a bright spark at the Ministry for Economic Warfare made an inspired connection between the V sign and Beethoven's Fifth Symphony. '[H]ere is the letter "V" – the sign of Victory – in Morse,' Colonel Britton told his audience on 27 June 1941. 'Three short taps and a heavy one. When you knock on the door, there is your knock. If you call the waiter in a restaurant, call him like this – "*Eh, garçon* (tap tap tap TAP)". Tell all your friends about it and teach them the "V" sound. If you and your friends are in a café and a German comes in, tap out the "V" sign all together.' The Colonel then played the first few bars of the Fifth. 'Beethoven's V symphony, his Victory and Freedom Symphony,' he continued. 'You'll notice that Beethoven is playing in the rhythm of the "V" sound – the Morse signal for the letter "V". This Symphony is called "Fate knocking on the door . . ." and the "V" rhythm – the rhythm of fate – is heard throughout Beethoven's Fifth Symphony. He uses it again, this time triumphantly, in the Scherzo. The Germans sometimes play this symphony (they don't know what it means), but when you hear it you'll hear Beethoven playing out the rhythm of victory and freedom.'

Flush with these early successes, the BBC planned a 'V Campaign Gala Day' in July, and to prepare for it they ratcheted up the pressure through the European Services. An edict went out that 'all news bulletins to the occupied territories should, until further notice, include a special section containing one or more resistance stories under the heading of "Europe against the Germans".' Editors were told that 'Stories will be circulated in preparation for a systematic campaign to discredit German finance and destroy all belief in the currency of any country tied to the New Order,' and instructed that 'special prominence' should be given to stories about inflation in Germany and the occupied territories.

The BBC was not exactly lying – indeed it is clear that the programme teams were acutely conscious of the danger of losing the trust of their audiences if they crossed the line into full-blown untruths. But Auntie was certainly crafting a selective news agenda for propaganda purposes.

On 17 July the French Service broadcast a new V ditty, this one to be sung to the tune of '*Au clair de la lune*':

> Yes right across France
> Free and occupied
> Everyone is singing
> The V song.
> V on every lip
> V in every heart,
> V is for Victory
> V is for Valour.

The date set for the V Gala was 20 July, and at the last moment, in an extraordinary twist, the Germans tried to pre-empt it. Clearly frustrated by their inability to control the V virus, Goebbels and his propaganda team decided they would simply appropriate the V symbol for the Nazis. German V signs now began to appear all over Europe, and the Berlin newspapers were filled with stories claiming the V as a symbol of German victory. A monster V was hoisted on to the Eiffel Tower in Paris; one of Prague's streets was renamed Viktoria Street; and a vast V banner was hung from the balcony of the royal palace in Amsterdam.

At the BBC this stratagem was taken as the greatest possible compliment. 'This is a victory for the peoples of Europe, who have dictated this move to the Nazis,' declared Noel Newsome. Newsome had his own radio programme called *The Man in the Street*, and the news from the V front provoked a scathing riff on the symbols of resistance across Europe: 'The Nazis could not suppress the "V", so they have been compelled to adopt the hollow pretence that it is theirs . . . Soon, perhaps, the Germans will be forced to pretend that the letters RAF stand for the Luftwaffe, that the Cross of Lorraine is a new type of Swastika, that Queen Wilhelmina's portrait is really that of Hitler, that

King Haakon's photograph is one of Goering, in younger and slimmer days, and that the Czechoslovak slogan "Truth Prevails" is Goebbels' family motto ... but there are limits to propaganda, limits to the credulity and forgetfulness of what Hitler contemptuously describes as the sheep-like masses.'

The icing on the cake came in the form of a prime ministerial endorsement for the V Campaign – and, after all the difficulties with Downing Street, this must surely have been especially prized at the BBC. Churchill's support was secured by Ivone Kirkpatrick and his government contacts, and the prime minister's message was broadcast as the climax of the V Gala. 'The "V" sign,' he declared, 'is the symbol of the unconquerable will of the occupied territories and a portent of the fate awaiting the Nazi tyranny. So long as the people of Europe continue to refuse all collaboration with the invader, it is sure that his cause will perish and that Europe will be liberated.'

Thereafter Churchill adopted the V sign as his own trademark – often with a cigar between the fingers that formed his V– cheerfully taking over this clever BBC creation at almost exactly the time of his most sustained assault on the Corporation's independence. The BBC also marked the gala by broadcasting a special programme on the Home Service telling the V Campaign story, and public reaction was almost universally enthusiastic. The *Daily Express* had already described Colonel Britton as the 'Scarlet Pimpernel of the Radio', and Brendan Bracken, who took over as minister of information on the day of the V Gala, told the Commons that the campaign was 'a sort of *Lift Up Your Hearts* signal to the oppressed people of Europe' – *Lift Up Your Hearts* being an early-morning religious programme, a distant ancestor of *Thought for the Day*.

But simply by being so successful the campaign began to run into trouble, and even in the dizzy days of July there were signs of the forces that would eventually lead to Douglas Ritchie and his Colonel Britton being grounded. The main worry was that the campaign was encouraging unrealistic expectations, mobilizing a 'V Army' before anyone knew what to do with it. D-Day was still three years away, and the British government was not even close to the point at which it could capitalize on Ritchie's promise to 'cause riots and demonstrations in every city in Europe'. At a meeting of the V Committee immediately after the gala of 20 July, 'it was urged by members of the Committee that Colonel Britton's broadcasts should in the coming weeks be less dramatic in tone and substance; that they should be directed less towards exciting an emotional response from listeners and more to carry out small, practical suggestions; and that the "mobilisation" campaign should for the moment be allowed to fall into the background'.

≈

Because it had gained such a high profile, the V Campaign became caught up in broader political currents. The V Gala was originally planned for 14 July, Bastille Day, but there were now fourteen exiled European governments resident in London, and some of them objected to the idea of such a high-profile propaganda effort being directly linked with France. To deal with this 'complicated policy tangle', the date was put back to the 20th and Colonel Britton had to resort to some fancy on-air footwork to explain the change. This in turn encouraged the involvement of the Foreign Office, which had finally woken up to the political and diplomatic significance of the V Campaign and wanted to exercise its own controls over Colonel Britton's messages.

The obsessive secrecy and jealous turf-guarding that were such a feature of British official life during the war – especially in the spookier bits of Whitehall – added to the muddle. Both the main sections of the Special Operations Executive – SO1, which dealt with propaganda, and SO2, which dealt with sabotage – felt that the BBC was poaching on their territory, but at this stage of the war SOE was wrapped in so much official mystery that very few people knew about it.

One of the best guides to this murky world is *The Secret History of PWE: The Political Warfare Executive 1939–1945*, a book which itself has an intriguing history. The government commissioned David Garnett, the Bloomsbury novelist and publisher, to write it in the immediate aftermath of the war, but it was considered so sensitive that it was not published until 2002. Garnett suggests that at the time

Ritchie wrote his manifesto on 'Broadcasting as a Weapon of War', 'the persons to whom he circulated his paper were ignorant of the existence of many secret SO1 activities and for that matter equally ignorant of the existence of SO2'. If the BBC did not know about the organization that was officially in control of this turf, they could hardly be blamed for trespassing there; but SOE saw Douglas Ritchie's broadcasts as a particular threat. 'Unless controlled,' Garnett wrote, 'Colonel Britton was likely to direct attention to some place, or incident, to which it was of vital importance not to refer for fear of jeopardising the safety of SOE agents.'

Garnett himself was part of the propaganda team operating out at Woburn Abbey, and they too complained that the BBC was straying on to their patch. As an example of amateurish BBC meddling, Garnett cited a Douglas Ritchie proposal that ordinary members of the public in Britain should be encouraged to send messages over the Channel attached to toy balloons. 'This would . . . have led to a flood of uncoordinated propaganda reaching the Continent,' Garnett complained. It might also, he worried, have drawn attention to balloons that his own organization was using to send over 'Black printed matter' as part of their secret propaganda campaigns. These bureaucratic battles were fought with all the ardour of men fired with the belief that they were part of a great ideological and existential struggle, but every so often they drop pleasingly into farce.

The formation of the Political Warfare Executive, or PWE, as a successor to Department EH was supposed to put a stop to precisely this kind of rivalry. Churchill signed it into existence in the summer of 1941, just after Brendan Bracken's appointment to the Ministry of Information, and Robert Bruce Lockhart, a former spy (he had served in Russia during the revolution there), was recruited as the new body's director-general. 'It is the plain truth which will be denied by no honest person inside our various propaganda organisations,' Bruce Lockhart wrote, 'that most of the energy which should have been directed against the enemy has been dissipated in inter-departmental strife and jealousies.' But at first the new organization only made things worse.

The PWE was run by a committee of the three ministers with

departmental interests in propaganda: the foreign secretary, Anthony Eden; the minister for economic warfare, Labour's Hugh Dalton (whose department controlled SOE); and Brendan Bracken as minister of information. But Bracken and Dalton loathed one another (Dalton referred to his Cabinet colleague as 'simply a guttersnipe', and Bracken returned the compliment by telling Churchill that Dalton was 'the biggest bloodiest shit I ever met') and both felt they should be in sole control of the propaganda machine. They fought bitterly until Dalton was moved to the job of president of the Board of Trade in early 1942. Anthony Eden was not greatly interested in this area and was, for the most part, happy to give Bracken a free hand in the field thereafter.

It did, however, help that the two key players involved in day-to-day management of the V Campaign – Robert Bruce Lockhart of the PWE and Ivone Kirkpatrick on the BBC side – were old friends, and managed to remain good-humoured even while sparring with one another. Bruce Lockhart's diaries are full of references to plots being hatched at Woburn Abbey to do down Kirkpatrick and his BBC colleagues, but they are also peppered with references to club lunches and late-night beers with 'Kirk', as he affectionately called him. The tone of their relationship is nicely caught in a memo from Kirkpatrick to Bruce Lockhart in August 1941, when Colonel Britton was encouraging factory workers in occupied countries to undermine the German war effort with a 'Go Slow' campaign. 'You said you thought you could get someone to draw a tortoise on a factory wall,' Kirkpatrick reminded his PWE colleague. 'What we should like is a tortoise with a "V" on it and underneath the inscription – "The Tortoise Wins". Do you think you could possibly ask your Czechs to get this done? I know it sounds ridiculously trivial, but it makes quite a good peg to hang a story in the other language broadcasts.'

In September Bruce Lockhart and Kirkpatrick established yet another V Committee ('Oh! These meetings,' complained Bruce Lockhart in his diary), which met in a PWE building away from the BBC, and had a brief to 'ensure the V campaign received the necessary guidance in relation to the policy of the Government Departments and the Fighting Services'. Bruce Lockhart stated that he 'felt that, like a military campaign, the "V" campaign must have its periods of offensives alternating with quiet periods, and that it was now desirable that the movement should be continued on a more subdued note', and Kirkpatrick agreed, proposing that in Colonel Britton's next talk 'a sentence should be inserted making it clear that the talk dealt with a long term plan, so that listeners might not be led to look forward to landings in occupied territories or other exceptional activities'. Ritchie and his colleagues accepted the new limits on their agenda, but the system inevitably choked off some of the spontaneity and originality that had marked Colonel Britton's earlier sallies.

≈

The sniping between newsmen and propagandists went on behind the scenes throughout the autumn of 1941, and the despatches that tell the story of their battle are rich in irony. The propagandists became positively po-faced about the need to protect the BBC's purity, because that was an argument for containing Auntie's ambitions and keeping her off their territory. The team at Bush House, meanwhile, tried to shore up their position as truth-tellers on the moral high ground, even though they had, with the V Campaign, certainly crossed the line between pure news and propaganda. 'We must give the truth as we see it,' Noel Newsome declared, 'not from some bogus propaganda angle. If our case is genuine and honest, the news will present it without being doctored. I cannot agree to giving news content entirely according to an estimate of what it would suit us for Europe to regard as the proper degree of importance.' Colonel Britton's talks routinely used selective reporting and colourful language to make a case, but that did not stop Newsome circulating a paper in which he stated that 'the best Political Warfare is that waged with the weapons of responsible journalism, not that carried out with the instruments of the clever advertiser'. Several senior members of the PWE had been recruited from J. Walter Thompson, and they inevitably took this jibe personally.

Despite the carry-on behind the scenes, the V symbol remained as popular as ever out in the field. RAF pilots flying over northern France reported that fishermen were holding up their oars in V signs, and pilots operating over the Netherlands spotted men running across fields to greet them with their arms held up to form the same symbol. And Colonel Britton continued to exercise his great talent for annoying Nazis. In early November he devoted a large part of a talk to food and drink. 'One thing the Germans like very much is food,' he told his audience. 'And they like drink. And they prefer your food and drink to their own. You should make sure that the food and drink are suitable to people who are uninvited guests.' The next passage has been crossed out in the copy of the script kept in the BBC Archives, perhaps because Ritchie was judged to have gone over the top. 'I had a letter from a café proprietor who said he could never restrain his chef from spitting on food ordered by German guests,' he had written. 'And "why should I restrain him?" wrote the café proprietor. "I do it myself when he has a night off." I had another letter from the owner of a beer hall in one of the occupied countries. This man said he always kept a bottle of dirty liquid under the counter to pour into German beer.' Other forms of 'mild persecution' suggested by the Colonel included asking German soldiers 'apparently friendly but highly disturbing questions', such as 'Where do you think the German High Command will stop the Russians in their advance on the Russian front?' and 'When are you going to invade Britain and finish the war?'

On 26 December 1941, less than three weeks after the Japanese attack on Pearl Harbor, Winston Churchill addressed a joint session of the two Houses of Congress in Washington. Alluding to recent Allied victories in Russia and Libya, and to America's entry into the war, the prime minister said, 'All these tremendous facts have led the subjugated peoples of Europe to lift their heads again in hope. They have put aside forever the shameful temptation of resigning themselves to the conqueror's will. Hope has returned to the hearts of scores of millions of men and women and, with that hope, there burns the flame of anger against the corrupt and brutal invader, and still more fiercely burns the ardent hatred and contempt for the filthy quislings he has suborned.' Vidkun Quisling was the Norwegian leader who had collaborated with the Nazis during the German conquest of his country, and his name had become synonymous with collaboration – 'a new word', as Churchill himself had put it on an earlier occasion, 'which will carry the scorn of mankind down the centuries'.

As he left the podium on Capitol Hill – to thunderous applause on all sides – Churchill flashed his V sign, and his speech was a gift to the V campaigners. The time, he seemed to be saying, was nearly ripe for the mobilization of the 'V Army', the 'subjugated peoples of Europe' who were now stirring under the Nazi yoke. Ritchie's V sub-committee – the one at the BBC that proposed ideas, not the one at the PWE that vetted them – took the view that 'This passage sets the tone and temper of "V" broadcasts in coming weeks. It brings the underground front into perspective with the general strategy of the war. It suggests the "V Army" is ready and expectant and that our propaganda should be moving gradually towards a call for more direct action at a later stage.' And to follow up the prime minister's attack on quislings, the committee decided that Colonel Britton should announce that 'from time to time the names and records of individual traitors will be broadcast'.

In early January 1942 he duly called the soldiers of the 'V Army' to their new duties. 'You are asked to memorize the crimes of your enemies,' he said. 'They brought the world to war. Their plan is to make members of the Nazi Party overlords of Europe, Asia, Africa and the whole world. They conducted the war with an excess of brutality which you know only too well. Think of what they have done to you. To your family, to your towns, to your fellow countrymen and women, to your country, to your Church – to your God. God will avenge, but He has given you the right to meet force with force for the purpose of re-establishing peace, freedom and justice.'

David Garnett and his friends begged to differ. One of the strangest but most important of their dark arts was the use of bogus radio stations. These transmitted from the grounds of Woburn Abbey, but presented themselves as underground stations broadcasting from within Occupied Europe itself and, in keeping with the addiction to code and acronym that was rife at the time, they were referred to as Research Units, or RUs. Colonel Britton's assault on quislings, David Garnett declared, 'was likely to result in compromising RUs which were running similar features'. He added that 'the naming of quislings was disliked because it was widely felt that a British colonel had not the necessary authority to attack individual foreign nationals in this way. For these reasons Colonel Britton was eventually stopped from naming Quislings and the embarrassment ceased.'

Unable to settle their differences, the protagonists in the great V Campaign debate turned to the creation of yet more committees in the hope of keeping this new 'weapon of war' alive. A 'sub-committee on operational propaganda' was set up to 'report on the extent to which operational propaganda, with special reference to sabotage, could be used in open broadcasting'. This sub-committee in turn recommended the creation of a 'permanent co-ordinating committee' with representatives from the 'PWE, MEW [Ministry of Economic Warfare], SOE, the BBC', but the members were in such violent and evident disagreement with one another that the chairman simply cancelled its first meeting before they even began work.

David Garnett neatly sums up the factors which, by the first months of 1942, had made the demise of the V Campaign inevitable: 'The fact was that if Colonel Britton's campaigns were suitable for one part of Europe, they were unsuitable for another; that the Allied plans for a landing on the Continent would not be ready for years, that the Allied governments preferred to give their own instructions to their own peoples and disliked a British spokesman doing so, and that PWE and SOE were carrying out their own methods of bringing "Secret Armies" into being, and encouraging resistance by secret broadcasting.'

On 8 May 1942 Bruce Lockhart wrote to Douglas Ritchie to tell him that he had decided to suspend the V Campaign because it 'must either advance or retreat. An advance in the desired direction is not yet possible, and I think you will agree that it is better to stop than to go back.' It was a generous note, devoid of the rancour that had sometimes marked the campaign's progress. 'You have done a remarkable piece of work which will have its place in the history of this war,' Bruce Lockhart told Ritchie, promising to ensure that the foreign secretary and Brendan Bracken were made aware of his achievements.

After the war Ritchie was appointed the head of the BBC's Publicity Department. At the age of fifty he suffered a severe cerebral haemorrhage, and enjoyed a second, very different celebrity as the author of the book – called simply *Stroke* – that he published in 1960 about his recovery. His V Campaign had illustrated how powerful and disruptive radio could be, but it also brought home the medium's limitations. Radio might well, as he argued in his seminal paper on 'Broadcasting as a Weapon of War', be used to help shorten the war, but it could not do it on its own.

TAKE THE SECOND ALLEY
ON THE RIGHT

RESISTANCE MOVEMENTS IN THE occupied countries of Europe were developing at very different speeds and, as David Garnett rightly identified, that was one of the factors that undermined the V Campaign. But just as the campaign began to run out of steam, resistance in France was taking off in ways that made radio a bigger player in the game than ever.

The first member of the German armed forces to be killed in Paris was called Alfons Moser, and he was shot on the morning of 21 August 1941 at the Barbès-Rochechouart metro station. The assassination was carried out by a small group of Communist Party members in revenge for the execution of two young communists in a wood near Verrières-le-Buisson, south of Paris, a couple of days earlier. It was a watershed for resisters, a huge step up from anything that had gone before. Albert Ouzoulias, a young Communist Party activist who had been involved in planning the operation, recognized that he and his comrades were crossing a Rubicon; 'it was not easy,' he wrote, 'to progress from underground leafleting, organising strikes and even cutting cables and sabotage to guerrilla action. You have to imagine what it was like for an 18-year-old – or indeed for anyone – to go into a Paris street one evening and wait alone for a Nazi officer or soldier in order to execute him'.

The man who fired the fatal shot at Alfons Moser had a personal motive; twenty-year-old Samuel Tyszelman, one of the party members executed at Verrières-le-Buisson, had been his friend. But there were bigger political forces at play too. The French Communist Party, a powerful presence in the country's pre-war politics, had been traumatized by the 1939 Molotov–Ribbentrop Pact, the non-aggression agreement between Moscow and Berlin which gave Hitler a free hand to invade Poland and later Western Europe. When Hitler turned on Stalin and invaded the Soviet Union in June 1941, the ideological battle lines suddenly became clear again, and the move to direct action against the Nazi occupiers was part of a more general party determination to take on fascism.

Moser was chosen as a target at random – the hit squad arrived at the metro station looking for a suitable victim and spotted what one of them later described as 'a magnificent naval commandant strutting on the platform'. Moser was in fact – despite all his gold braid and shiny buttons – only a cadet, and his killing marked a watershed for the occupiers too. The German authorities responded with an announcement that 'from August 23rd all those French nationals under arrest . . . are to be considered hostages', and that 'In the event of another incident of this kind hostages will be shot – the number corresponding to the gravity of the crime.' Six French communists were executed immediately, and a cycle of assassinations and reprisal executions began.

In Nantes on 20 October, two Communist Party commandos killed Lieutenant-Colonel Karl Hotz, the military governor, as he crossed the city's cathedral square. Two days later the Germans shot forty-eight 'hostages' in reprisal. Twenty-seven of them were communists interned at Châteaubriant in Brittany, and they included a seventeen-year-old boy called Guy Mocquet, who had been arrested a year earlier for distributing Communist Party literature on his bicycle. The young man's last letter to his parents remains one of the most quoted documents of France's war years. 'I am going to die!' he wrote. 'What I ask of you, and especially you, my beloved mother, is that you are brave. I am – and I want to be as brave as those who have gone before me. Of course I would have preferred to live. But I hope with all my heart that my death will do some good.' The letter is especially poignant because of its childish touches: Guy hopes that his clothes will be sent back to the family and that his brother will be 'proud to wear them one day', and signs off with the full affection of 'my child's heart'. His father was a Communist Party activist, and Guy added a message for him: 'Know that I have done my best to follow in your footsteps.' France had a new martyr, and the armed struggle was well and truly joined.

But it was, as far as de Gaulle was concerned, far too early for this phase of the struggle against the occupation, and the fact that the attacks on the Germans were being carried out by communists only made the news from France more unwelcome. From London the party's new, aggressive resistance tactics looked very much like a bid to assume the leadership of the anti-Nazi movement, and de Gaulle understood all too well that whoever controlled resistance during the war was likely to dominate French politics in its aftermath. So he turned to what remained his most powerful means of controlling – or at least influencing – events in France: the BBC.

On 23 August, in the aftermath of the Moser killing, de Gaulle's spokesman, Maurice Schumann, broadcast an appeal for calm. In keeping with the message that was being pumped out by Colonel Britton at this period, Schumann urged would-be resisters to focus on economic disruption rather than violence. 'I know how hard it is to contain oneself when a reasoned, indeed a holy rage suffocates you,' he declared. 'But controlling yourself is not the same as resignation – quite the opposite, in fact. At the moment it should mean a hidden struggle in the workshop, on the factory floor, in the office, everywhere, a struggle that is fought at every moment and over every bolt and every cog of the enemy's war machine; the true battle station for a worker saboteur, that is to say a patriotic worker, is the factory, nowhere else.'

On 23 October, after the reprisal executions following the Nantes attack, de Gaulle himself took to the microphone. He told his audience that it was 'absolutely natural and absolutely justified that Germans should be killed by the French', but he warned them sternly that 'The French war must be waged by those in charge, that is to say by me and by the National Committee. It is necessary that all fighters, both those within France and those outside, should follow my orders. And the order I give for the occupied territory is that Germans should not be killed there.' And he assured his audience that 'as soon as we are in a position to attack together – from within and without – you will receive the orders you want'.

De Gaulle's efforts to assert his authority over the resisters inside France preoccupied him for the next year and more – it was, apart from anything else, essential that he persuade his British hosts that he was the authentic leader of opposition to the German occupation. The Gaullist version of history – which the general and his supporters managed to sell so successfully after the war – drew a clear, direct connection between de Gaulle's *Appel* of 18 June 1940 and the armed groups of *maquis* fighters who helped to drive out the Germans after the D-Day landings four years later; the first, according to this narrative, made the second inevitable.

But the way resistance developed in France was in fact much messier and more complicated. Many of the resistance groups that had begun to blossom in 1941 were spontaneous, home-grown affairs without any allegiance to the general in Carlton Gardens, where de Gaulle had established his London headquarters. And they were a disparate and often fractious bunch. Politically, they were coloured every hue of the rainbow; they ranged from communists, trade unionists and anti-clerical republicans to Catholic nationalists and monarchists, and their ranks even included representatives of far-right groups like the *Croix de feu* and *Action française* which had flourished in France before the war. They were divided by bitter personal as well as ideological rivalries, and many of them, especially those operating under the Nazi jackboot in the German-occupied zone, resented the idea of being told what to do by a leader enjoying the early Victorian elegance of the St James's area of London.

The man who turned France's various groups of resisters into a single movement worthy of the name 'Resistance' was called Jean Moulin. At the outbreak of war he had been the *préfet* responsible for running the Eure-et-Loire department south-west of Paris – so he was a senior civil servant and not a politician, which made him more acceptable to some of the more ideologically minded resisters. In the aftermath of the German victory he was arrested and beaten up by the invaders for refusing to go along with false accusations against a group of Senegalese troops. He showed his mettle while in custody. Fearing he might crack under pressure, he tried to slit his own throat with a shard of glass. The Germans patched him up and reinstated him – only for the Vichy regime to fire him a few months later because he had headed the private office of a socialist minister in the mid-1930s. For most of 1941 he lived quietly in southern France, and in October he slipped out of the country via the Pyrenees and made his way to London.

Moulin's character and background made him an ideal emissary, and he evidently impressed de Gaulle; as the historian Robert Gildea has put it in his book *Fighters in the Shadows*, 'Discreet, cool-headed, relatively free of political attachments, Jean Moulin was just the man London was looking for to undertake its mission to draw together the various resistance movements under the authority of London.'

Moulin was parachuted back into France on New Year's Day 1942, and he spent the next sixteen months cajoling the leaders of the various resister groups to unite and – which proved even more difficult – to accept de Gaulle's leadership. A full year after his arrival he succeeded in bringing the three main resistance organizations in southern France together in the *Mouvements Unis de la Résistance*, or MUR, with a unified military structure known as the *Armée secrète*, and at the end of May 1943 he convened the first meeting of the *Conseil National de la Résistance*, which united the resistance movements of both the north and the south. Not long after this milestone, Moulin was betrayed, arrested and killed (the precise circumstances are not clear, but he may have been beaten to death personally by Klaus Barbie, the notorious local Gestapo chief of Lyons).

But the benefits of coordinated action were, by then, very evident. On 1 May 1942, for example, all the main resistance groups – including the Communist Party and the trades unions – lent their support to one of de Gaulle's BBC appeals for Labour Day protests. On 29 April Maurice Schumann instructed people that 'from 18.30 on 1st May' they should walk 'silently and individually' past their town halls, and all over the Vichy-run zone they did just that. In the Occupied Zone peaceful public protest of this kind was impossible, but the day was marked by what one Resistance historian has called 'an unprecedented number of acts of sabotage against railways and industrial plant', while in the Normandy port of Caen resisters managed to derail a train, killing ten Germans and wounding twenty-two.

≈

Jacques Duchesne's team at the French Service, meanwhile, were making hay with the reputation of the new Vichy prime minister, Pierre Laval. Laval began his political life as a socialist, but the way he acquired a substantial fortune in the late 1920s gave him a reputation as a greedy and possibly corrupt opportunist. Throughout the 1930s he moved steadily to the right in his politics, and by the time of the German victory in France in 1940 he was sympathetic to fascist ideas. So when Pétain appointed him as his prime minister on 18 April 1942 he was a highly controversial figure.

In Bush House, van Moppès was quick off the blocks with a satirical nursery rhyme, sung to the tune of a cautionary tale about a rich old woman who uses her fortune to seduce a young husband:

> Leading the dance in Paris
> Of all the German agents
> There is still that old dog Laval
> Who never feels he has enough money.
> Ah Laval, Laval, Laval,
> Who so much loves the Germans,
> Ah Laval, Laval, Laval,
> Who so much loves money . . .

And *Les Français parlent aux français* made enthusiastic use of letters the BBC had received about Laval during the previous weeks. In many of them he was linked with Marcel Déat, another former socialist, who, in February 1941, had formed a party advocating active collaboration with the Nazis; 'the people are grinding their teeth in anger', ran one of the letters read out on the air, 'and when they abandon themselves to the full force of their rage, it will be an ill-wind for traitors. Laval and Déat already realise this. But this is only the beginning. I wish I had killed those two with my own hand, and I am surely not alone in that.'

In June, Laval himself made the propagandists' work a great deal easier. In a speech towards the end of the month he declared that he hoped for a German victory over Britain and the United States, and at the same time launched the *Relève*, a system designed to provide the German war machine with French labour. The *Relève* programme was sold on the basis that French workers would leave for Germany in return for the release of French prisoners of war, but it quickly became highly unpopular and was to prove an immensely costly mistake for Laval and his Vichy government. At the French Service, Pierre Bourdan was quick to spot how damaging it would be; he declared on the air that it was the first piece of good news for two weeks (the British had surrendered to General Rommel at Tobruk the day before, with 25,000 British soldiers being taken prisoners of war, so it was a bleak time), saying, 'We hadn't expected such a clear and flagrant admission of Germany's difficulties.' 'Laval the slave-trader,' declared *Les Français parlent aux français* on the day after Laval's speech. 'From now on those two words will be inseparable, the description will stick to his name like an indelible stain. Wait and see. The name Laval must never be spoken without this immediate echo: slave trader.'

It was against this backdrop that de Gaulle decided to make Bastille Day 1942 a demonstration of his power – and in particular of the threat he posed to Pétain, Laval and the Vichy regime. On 13 July Maurice Schumann delivered a dramatic call to action in the *Honneur et Patrie* slot at 9.25 p.m.:

> In full agreement with General de Gaulle and the French National Committee, the three main resistance movements leading the struggle on our nation's soil against the invader and his accomplices make the following appeal to French men and women in the so-called non-occupied zone.
>
> July 14th offers you all the opportunity to show your feelings as you wait to impose your will. It is a festival of freedom. Celebrate it with greater fervour than ever now, when our country has been sold down the river and liberty is suppressed.
>
> French men and women of the non-occupied zone, bring out the bunting around your homes – who would dare to criticise you on our national festival? French men and women of the

non-occupied zone, walk the main streets of your towns in the afternoon and show the tricolour.

Finally and above all, at 18.30 on the evening of July 14th, gather in great numbers to sing the *Marseillaise* and to throw flowers at the feet of symbolic monuments.

This injunction was followed by a list of rallying points in the main cities of the Vichy-controlled zone, from Grenoble at the foot of the Alps to Avignon in the Midi and Toulouse in the south-west. The Resistance in the Unoccupied Zone was now sufficiently well organized and equipped to send information to London via hidden radio transmitters, so within a very short time the BBC was able to broadcast back news of a huge response to the appeal for Bastille Day protests, tightening the screw of truth on the Vichy regime another notch. On 17 July Schumann read out a communiqué stating that in Lyons 'There was a vast crowd flowing through the streets from four in the afternoon. Moving from the station to the Places des Terraux [the city's magnificent main square] the demonstration lasted until nine in the evening. Many more than a hundred thousand patriots took part.' The communiqué reported that the crowds came out despite a massive military and police presence ordered on to the streets by Laval, and defiantly chanted slogans like 'Laval, Pétain and Darlan [Admiral François Darlan, another senior Vichy figure] – to the stake!'; 'We want bread and guns'; and '*Vive de Gaulle!*' There was similar news from the Savoie city of Chambéry. Schumann reported that when a group of pro-Vichy militiamen of the SO [*Service d'ordre légionnaire*] there tried to get up a chant of '*Vive Pétain! Vive Laval!*' the crowds turned on them with such ferocity that the police had to bundle them into the police station. Broadcasts like this made it impossible for Vichy to keep the lid on what was really happening.

In Marseilles the 14 July protests led to outright violence and indeed death. Street fighting broke out between Gaullist demonstrators and Vichy supporters, and members of the fascist French Popular Party (widely known by its French acronym, PPF) opened fire on the crowd, wounding five men and killing two women. On 16 July the BBC announced that these 'martyrs' would be buried the following day and broadcast details of the funeral procession – so the city authorities, fearing another demonstration, cancelled the funerals and arranged for the two women to be buried in secret.

But, in the final play of this cat-and-mouse game, the BBC was able to broadcast the location of their graves. At 1.15 p.m. the following Sunday, 19 July, the French Service put out an appeal for people to gather at the main entrance to the St Pierre cemetery at five that afternoon, and the message was delivered with a level of detail which must have been most unsettling to the Vichy authorities who had tried to hush up the two women's funerals. 'As you enter the cemetery,' the broadcast instructed, 'take the second alley on the right, the one called the Tree of Heaven Alley. Follow it round to the left as far as the twentieth tomb, and behind that you will find the graves of Madame Simon and Madame Krebs.'

At the appointed time, less than four hours after the broadcast, a 'huge crowd' gathered at the gate, and for an hour people processed past the graves, covering them with flowers in the colours of the tri-colour. When he went on the air to report all this on 21 July, Schumann was even able to give the story what journalists call 'colour': '[H]ere's a poignant and powerfully symbolic detail,' he said. 'One of those who joined the cortège in this moment of national mourning was a vet-eran, blinded in battle, escorted by two young women, one of them wearing a cross of Lorraine across her chest.'

Later in the same broadcast, Schumann provided further news that had reached London of Bastille Day demonstrations (40,000 people on the streets in Toulouse, 10,000 in Carcassonne) and, in a sally he must have relished, revealed that there had even been protests in Vichy itself. Not only could those 'voices of freedom' from London conjure up a crowd; they were, it seemed, all-knowing about what was happening in France.

THE HORSE SENDS HIS
LOVE TO POLYDORUS

JEAN MOULIN'S HEROIC EFFORTS to unite the Resistance did not altogether put an end to the rivalries that divided it, and the bad feeling between different groups operating in France was sometimes reflected in unseemly squabbles about airtime in London. The BBC's French Service became embroiled in French politics precisely because it was such a powerful influence on events in France.

Fernand Grenier, a hard-line and pro-Soviet member of the French Communist Party, was sent to London in January 1943 to cement the party's relations with de Gaulle – he was escorted by de Gaulle's most famous agent, 'Colonel Rémy', and a British ship collected the two of them off the Brittany coast, depositing them at Falmouth. Grenier had impressive Resistance credentials. He had been arrested and interned in October 1940, and for a while was held in the same prison as the young communist hero Guy Mocquet, but he escaped in the summer of 1941 and went underground. He broadcast on the BBC as soon as he reached London, introducing himself on the air on 15 January 1943 with a sentence of heroic length: 'After having shared, in Paris itself, the daily dangers faced by Resistance fighters, after having known the same privations, the same mental suffering, the same hopes as our oppressed but indomitable people, I have come to London, on the instructions of the Central Committee of the French Communist Party, to pledge to General de Gaulle and the National Committee of France the loyalty of tens of thousands of our supporters who, despite fear, in factories as much as in the ranks of irregulars and partisans, in universities as well as the Reich's camps, from Nantes to Strasbourg, from Lille to Marseille, daily risk their lives to sustain the struggle against the hated Hitlerian invader.'

It was a hugely important moment for de Gaulle, a public declaration that he had broad popular support and that the two wings of resistance – that within France and that beyond her borders – would fight as one. The collaborationist French media in France paid Grenier the compliment of characteristically hysterical criticism. 'We should not be surprised,' declared the fascist PPF's *Le Cri du Peuple* 'that he has rallied to the cause of the criminal general, who is paid with Jewish gold,' and the official Vichy paper, *Le Journal des débats*, wrote of the 'bolshevisation of the Gaullist movement'. Grenier was delighted; 'these themes were repeated in angry radio rants over the following days,' he wrote. When he returned to France after the war, party comrades told him how important the broadcast had been for them; 'all of them listened to Radio-London,' he recalled, 'and now, for the first time in two years, they heard the voice of a communist on the air'.

The broadcast also provided one of those striking pieces of anecdotal evidence of the level of audience penetration the BBC had achieved. The following day, between six and eight in the morning, Grenier's parents-in-law back in France were visited by some twenty friends and neighbours who had heard it and wanted to pass on their congratulations.

But Grenier felt the broadcasts on the BBC failed to reflect the realities of life in Occupied France. By this stage of the war the Germans controlled the whole country – they had moved into the southern, Vichy-controlled zone in response to the Allied landings in North Africa in November 1942. This made it even more difficult for the Vichy government to resist German demands for French labour and, at the time of Grenier's flight, Laval and his ministers were preparing the hated law known as the STO, or *Service du travail obligatoire*, which would lead to thousands of young French workers being deported to Germany. At his first meeting with de Gaulle, Grenier told him that

'Many of them [the workers] would prefer to stay in France and play a part in the struggle, but not enough is being said on Radio-London to encourage them not to go.' De Gaulle, it seems, was unenthused and told Grenier to take the matter up with one of his deputies. And when Grenier prepared a talk directed at those threatened with deportation under the STO regulations, it was held back from transmission for nearly a month.

Grenier became a regular on the BBC, but he complained that he was always given slots when the audience was small, and his request to be allowed to speak in Schumann's prime-time *Honneur et Patrie* segment was turned down. His choice of subject matter was heavily influenced by his communist ideology, and he complained about the way it was censored. When he broadcast a talk in praise of 'The miners of the Pas-de-Calais region', for example, he was told to cut out a passage celebrating Charles Debarge, a communist miner turned Resistance leader who had carried out a series of bold attacks before being fatally wounded in a shoot-out with German troops the previous September. In his script, Grenier rather cleverly enlisted the help of that giant of French literature Victor Hugo, quoting the great man's appeal to the guerrilla fighters who took on the Prussians in the war of 1870–71: 'Oh you irregulars, cross the market halls, swim the torrents, use the twilight, move like snakes in the ravines, slip, creep, aim and fire, exterminate the invasion! Defend France with heroism! Be terrible in your patriotism.' But Victor Hugo or not, this was far too extreme for current policy on direct action, and out of the script it came!

Grenier's relationship with the BBC reached something of a crisis in March when two of his talks were turned down on policy grounds. In a piece he had written about a group of communist *résistants* who had been executed at Rennes, he was asked to add a plea that people 'should avoid premature action' and to remove the term '*franc-tireur*' from the text. The word can be translated as 'sniper' or 'guerrilla fighter' (or, indeed, in a more peaceful context, a freelance journalist), and the Communist Party had adopted it for the title of its Resistance militia, who were known as the *Francs-tireurs et Partisans*, or FTP. The term had a special resonance because it was first used to describe the irregular soldiers of the 1870 Franco-Prussian War so powerfully apostrophized by Victor Hugo. Grenier erupted. 'I may not even use the word "*franc-tireur*" when I speak of these heroes?' he demanded of the BBC official concerned. 'As if we were talking about something shameful, actions of which the BBC disapproves and seeks to hide? The German Tribunal itself ruled that they were condemned to death "for acting as *francs-tireurs*", and within France their sentence was promulgated in those terms, by the Nazis themselves.'

There was a good deal more in this vein, and the letter arrived on the desk of one Colonel Lewis Gielgud, a senior official at the French Service. He was Val Gielgud's brother, and his response was in keeping with the suave family style: he asked Grenier to dinner. Over the meal Gielgud told Grenier that the cuts in his text had been made at the request of de Gaulle's Free French, who particularly objected to the way he had used his BBC broadcast to make a recruiting appeal on behalf of the FTP. Grenier put this version of events to one of de Gaulle's aides, who flatly denied it, and claimed that the objections had come from the British. Grenier was so disgusted by this episode that for a while he refused to do any more broadcasting. A couple of months later his wife was smuggled out of France and joined him in London, and she told him that his friends and comrades missed hearing him on the air, so he relented.

For all his doubts about some aspects of BBC policy, the way Grenier wrote about Auntie in his war memoir, *C'était ainsi* [That's How It Was], helps explain why the Corporation became so much a part of Resistance mythology. In August 1943 he broadcast a talk under the title 'The Hell of Auschwitz', based on information about conditions in the camp which had reached London via Resistance sources in France. The piece was widely picked up by the papers in Britain and the United States. After the war he was told by Marie-Claude Valliant-Couturier, a prominent communist resister who had been deported to Auschwitz early in 1943, that the regime under which she and other French deportees were being kept was relaxed in the immediate aftermath of the broadcast, making it possible for them to survive their ordeal. Whether there really was any connection between the two things is, in a way, immaterial. Valliant-Couturier was an important and high-profile Resistance figure and she believed, rightly or wrongly, that a BBC broadcast had helped to save her life.

Fernand Grenier was also responsible for a poignant broadcast built around a collection of letters and articles that had been smuggled out of detention centres in France. They were written by Communist Party members being held as 'hostages' by the Germans – 'men', as he put it, 'who face every day the chance that they will be shot on the morrow' – and they included two poems by a nineteen-year-old party member. The first was a salute to another young man who had faced the firing squad:

> Goodbye C ... my old friend
> At seventeen these assassins took your life
> Savagely, and without pity for your youth.
> You faced death without fear
> And fell valiantly.
> And the cry 'Vive la France'
> Were the last words on your lips.
> Your fine smile has gone,
> And we who are in prison
> Will leave here to avenge you.
> Goodbye, my old friend.

After quoting the poem, Grenier picked up the story like this: 'But R ... did not emerge from prison to avenge his "old friend". Instead he left his comrades to face a fire-squad himself. A few hours before he died he wrote these clumsy but heart-rending lines:

> We are all communists
> And for having proclaimed that at the top of our voices
> We are on that dark list
> Of those put up against the wall.
> O you who are free!
> O our brothers in arms!
> We are always at your side,
> And not one of us will falter.

For us, the moment of our passing approaches,
Death already holds out his embrace,
But we will be avenged,
And that task rests with you.'

Over the course of the war BBC broadcasts like this became a way of memorializing France's dead. The Resistance historian Jean-Louis Crémieux-Brilhac performed the heroic scholarly task of producing an extensive anthology of French Service broadcasts, and in his preface he lists some of those whose memories were immortalized on the airwaves: 'Du Fretay, Hackin, Bingen, Brosset, Danielou, Brosselette, Leclerc, and many others who died for a free France, can be found alive, for a moment, in these pages, along with Gabriel Péri, Guy Mocquet, and so many martyrs who fell in obscurity on their native earth; the BBC had the sad privilege of making their last words known to France.'

≈

Listening in secret to the words of young men speaking from beyond the grave must have been an eerie experience. But what on earth was the audience supposed to make of a broadcast like the following, which went out at 1.30 p.m. on New Year's Day 1943?

The crab will meet snakes. We say: the crab will meet snakes.
With dreamy steps I have followed the lonely way. We say: with dreamy steps I have followed the lonely way.
Maurice spent a good Christmas with his friend and is thinking of the two mimosas which will flower.
Edith, the daughter of Christine and James, her husband and their five children send their love to their families.
The beautiful cat sends her love to Pauline and also to Patou and Paquin.
From the horse to Polydorus: the horse sends his love to Polydorus, his god-daughter and his friends.

The idea of using the BBC to send coded messages to Resistance groups in France is generally credited to Georges Bégué, a young

French reservist who had been evacuated from Dunkirk. He considered joining de Gaulle's Free French after the *Appel* of 18 June, but the general was away the day he turned up at their headquarters in London and Bégué was thoroughly unimpressed by the officers he dealt with. He had a British wife and an engineering degree from Hull, and in August 1940 he applied to join the British Army instead. Bégué was assigned to the Royal Signals and sent – to his disgust – to learn how to run a telephone exchange at Catterick Camp in North Yorkshire, but in January 1941 SOE identified him as a potential secret agent and he was offered the chance of undercover work in France. After a couple of months of training as a radio operator, he was dropped into the central French department of Indre on the night of 4 May 1941, and he has gone down in history as the first SOE agent on French soil.

Bégué based himself in the town of Châteauroux and made his first radio transmission from there on 9 May. Over the next six months he succeeded in building a network of agents, but he also, very quickly, understood the risks involved in radio communication with London: his signals were easily jammed, German radio-detection vans posed a constant threat, and he put himself in danger whenever he went on the air. Thus – according to SOE legend – was born the idea of communicating with agents in the field by code inserted in the BBC personal messages.

But Maurice Buckmaster, the spymaster who took over the French section of SOE (F Section, as it was known), also claimed authorship of this wheeze. In the 1970s he told the French writer Dominique Decèze, '[W]e were looking for ways of keeping the use of clandestine radios to a strict minimum, because it was extremely dangerous to the operators ... we knew that since the surrender of France the BBC had been sending messages to the families of those who had been evacuated at Dunkirk or had fled the country, and in May 1941 I had the idea of using this service ...'

The first coded message – 'Lisette is well' – is thought to have been transmitted in September that year and, whoever thought of the idea first, Bégué and Buckmaster together worked it up into an extremely sophisticated system. Bégué was captured by Vichy police in October 1941, but he escaped and managed to get back to London via the Pyrenees, serving for the rest of the war alongside Buckmaster as SOE's signals officer.

Like many of the best ideas, the system had the great virtue of simplicity. Even before it was formally introduced, the BBC's personal messages included some which fell between the innocent and the operational; for example, those transmitted on 20 February 1941 (before Bégué had even been dropped into France) included one that was clearly directed at the underground escape network known as the Pat Line, which smuggled people over the Pyrenees. 'The Scottish officer who left Marseille on 27th December has arrived in London,' it ran. 'He thanks Lulu, Odette and all the others who lived with him. He sends his very best wishes to his friends in Marseille.'

Since everyone who left France for Britain was putting them-selves on the wrong side of the law in their home country all personal messages, even the most innocent, tended to be slightly cryptic, so it could be difficult to distinguish between genuine greetings intended to reassure friends and family and those planted by SOE. The coded phrases contained a clue that would – so the theory went – be intel-ligible only to the intended recipient, so they could be transmitted, as the code-makers have it, *en clair*. What was more, it could be fun; when there was nothing to report, SOE sometimes inserted blank messages to confuse the listening Germans. Buckmaster considered himself something of a whizz at crosswords (he claimed to be able to solve the *Times* puzzle on the bus going to work) and enjoyed com-posing these quasi-poetic sallies.

The system could be used to confirm details of a planned drop of arms or an agent (the call on BBC airtime tended to be especially heavy at periods of full moon) and to trigger or delay a sabotage operation – these 'operational messages' were generally quite short, between three and eight words. But the system could also be exploited in a more sophisticated way to help agents in the field establish their bona fides. If they needed to convince a local contact that they really were from London, they could instigate the transmission of a pre-arranged message on the BBC. Sometimes agents even used the system to persuade people to help them financially, organizing BBC announcements which effectively served as a British government IOU. These 'recognition messages' could be as much as fifty words long.

The experience of an agent called Gaston Tavian illustrates how heavily agents came to depend on the system. A career NCO who made his way to London in April 1942, he was landed back in France by Lysander a month later with a mission to make contact with Resistance groups in Corsica. His introduction to the local Resistance leader on the island was a BBC message that 'In my aunt's garden there are three beehives.' The apicultural theme was chosen because he had been interested in the subject in his youth, and when another agent was sent to join him his arrival was signalled by 'Gaston is going to eat honey.' From Corsica, Tavian moved back to mainland France, and in Chambon in the Loire region he again had recourse to the BBC, this time to persuade a local man to allow his house to be used for clandestine radio transmissions. 'To reassure him I asked him to choose a "control phrase",' he remembered, 'and his wife said, "On Sunday we were at Perthuiset, on St Etienne beach, and had a very pleasant swim." The message that came over the BBC was, "A swim at Perthuiset is pleasant."'

For a period in November 1942 London became concerned that Tavian had been arrested, so the BBC was asked to broadcast a question that only he could have understood: 'For Gaston and Georges – Georges Descroisette of the "Ali" network. What colour was Korigan's coat?' Tavian understood this was a reference to a bay mare he and a fellow soldier called Descroisette had helped to look after during the Phoney War, so he broke radio silence to transmit the correct answer back to London. And when the time came for him to be picked up by Lysander again, the horsey theme continued: '[T]he message announcing the arrival of the plane to take us back to London was "the Red is on",' he remembered, 'a well-known racing phrase, as it refers to the red flag put out when the race begins.'

≈

The use of the BBC to send coded messages to resistance groups has long been celebrated as an example of the wartime wizardry of the

British secret services. Rather less well-known is the fact that the Germans were also using Auntie as a channel of communication with agents they sent to Britain. The details are laid out in a 1942 MI5 document which was not opened for study until 2005.

The Security Service investigation was in part prompted by the arrest of one Lucien Jules François Lecoq, who flew across the Channel from Le Havre in a private plane on 7 December that year. Everyone who turned up from the Continent in unusual circumstances during this period was – unsurprisingly – screened, and, under questioning, Lecoq admitted that he was a German agent. His mission was to join the Royal Air Force, steal a Typhoon (a single-seat fighter-bomber) and fly it back to German-occupied territory. As an agent he was being run from the Avenue Foch (the Gestapo headquarters in Paris) by a German officer called Schmidt of the SS Security Service, the *Sicherheitsdienst*, or SD. Schmidt was already known to MI5 and Lecoq revealed that 'If he had arrived safely . . . he had arranged with Schmidt to send a message to the BBC. This message was intended for the Germans and also for his wife. The text of the message was "Coq tells his wife that he's got through successfully."'

The episode was still under investigation at the time the MI5 document was drawn up, and it became part of a more general Security Service inquiry into controls over the BBC messaging system. The officer responsible looked back at the lessons of previous incidents of this kind, most notably that of an agent identified as Pelletier. This man had been dropped into France as a British agent in early 1941 (even earlier than Bégué, if the MI5 dates are right), but had been captured and 'turned' by the Germans before returning to Britain in April 1942. The MI5 report is a model of narrative clarity:

> 2. In the early stages of his interrogation by the Fighting French [de Gaulle's organization] and prior to his confession, PELLETIER had asked that the following message should be sent over the BBC '33 333 would like to let his friends know that all is well'. In deference to the Fighting French scheme that PELLETIER might be run as a XXX agent [a triple agent, or one who had been twice turned] this message was accordingly sent by MI5.

3. At a later stage when PELLETIER had been completely broken, the following account of the matter was arrived at. After consenting in Paris to work for the *Abwehr* [German military intelligence], and agreeing to their instructions, he himself suggested that he should announce to them his safe arrival by the above coded message. The Germans were pleased with the idea, which they appeared to view as something of a novelty. At the same time PELLETIER intended that the message should afford aid and comfort to his family as well as to the *Abwehr*, and to this end he instructed a friend in Paris to listen to the message. He had no intention of approaching any specific individual in the BBC, nor did the Germans make any such suggestion. He intended simply to make his request to the Personal Message Service, in the normal way, in which, provided his cover here as a loyal ally held, he did not anticipate the slightest difficulty.

4. The truth of PELLETIER's statement that his message was primarily intended for German ears is confirmed by a report from a Fighting French source in Paris that the Germans had been listening for PELLETIER's message with impatience, and were very pleased with themselves when it arrived.

The Security Service concluded that the Pelletier episode in fact gave no great cause for concern, as he was 'a marked man from the moment of his arrival', and was allowed to transmit his message only because of the plot to run him as a triple agent. And the MI5 verdict on BBC security was, by and large, benign. The rules for personal messages were indeed strict. All were subject to a minimum delay of fourteen days before they were sent ('to eliminate the possibility of secondary meaning messages of immediate importance being sent in circumstances in which they would be of use to the enemy'); no one was allowed to send more than one message every three months; and all messages were subject to 'postal censorship', which meant that 'if the message is, on the face of it, suspicious, it may be rejected or modified at the discretion of the censor'. Crucially for the BBC, MI5 found no evidence that its staff had been infiltrated by agents employed to facilitate the transmission of coded messages.

This intriguing episode did not interrupt the BBC practice of sending personal messages to comfort families in Occupied Europe –

'Soon . . . They're coming!' David Low, Evening Standard.

which undoubtedly provided a valuable humanitarian service – and the use of the system for clandestine purposes grew in importance right up until D-Day.

Today we would worry about the contradictions thrown up by a broadcaster which claimed a unique status as the champion of openness and a purveyor of truth, while at the same time operating as part of a war-fighting intelligence network. It was, of all people, the SOE spymaster Maurice Buckmaster who identified the community of interest between these two aspects of Auntie's wartime life. 'We needed to build total confidence in the BBC,' he wrote, 'so that, when the moment came, French patriots would accept, without hesitation or demur orders transmitted over its wavelengths.' Trust, in other words, was everything. To be a good spy, Auntie had to remain honest.

DER CHEF

I N EARLY JUNE 1942 the Tory backbencher Sir Waldron Smithers sent Brendan Bracken a list of twenty-two people he considered suitable for 'intelligence, broadcasting and propaganda purposes', and on 10 June he followed up his initiative with a question to the minister of information in the Commons. 'In view of this wealth of expert knowledge,' he demanded, 'will my Right Honourable Friend use these gentlemen to replace aliens in the BBC and the Ministry of Information, and thus stop German infiltration?' Bracken squashed this ugly eruption of xenophobia elegantly and firmly. 'I resent that suggestion very much,' he replied. 'It is a great pity that this House should be used as a sounding board for this new campaign against decent Germans who left their country because of their opposition to Hitler, and who can and are playing a most worthy part in the war effort.'

Sir Waldron Smithers had inherited his Chislehurst seat from his father in 1924 and was almost a parody of the Tory backwoodsman. A fellow Conservative described him as 'an extreme Tory of a vanished age' who was 'not insensitive to the consoling effect of alcohol', and he later made headlines by campaigning for a 'Committee on un-British Activities' along the lines of Senator McCarthy's notorious American model. But in 1942 he was not alone in his anxieties about 'German infiltration', and his question touched on a real dilemma: should the BBC use German broadcasters in the way it used exiled nationals of the occupied nations of Europe? Behind that question lay a deeper set of questions about the proper ambitions and means of broadcasting to an enemy.

The contrast between the BBC's French and German Services brings home Auntie's dilemma. The British government – and therefore the BBC – never regarded the people of France as enemies; official attitudes towards the Vichy regime of course hardened as its collaborationist instincts became clearer, but all BBC broadcasting to France was based on the premise that most of the audience was friendly towards Britain and wanted to be liberated; the BBC and the French people were, it was assumed, on the same side. That made it possible to recruit the brilliant cast of *émigrés* who made the French Service so sparkling, and it also meant that the French Service team could be allowed the freedom to take risks.

But the Germans *were* enemies. In the summer of 1940, at exactly the time the French Service began to flourish, anti-German feeling in Britain was running at its highest, and that of course had an impact on BBC broadcasting. In his short book *Propaganda*, Lindley Fraser, one of the most successful German Service broadcasters, describes the change like this: 'In the initial months of the war there was an optimistic tendency to believe that it was worthwhile to make a sharp distinction between the National Socialists and the military clique on the one hand and the great mass of the German people on the other. The BBC at the time, reflecting perhaps the general trend of public opinion, felt not merely that there was no need for bitterness towards Germans as such but also that by stressing this point it might persuade some of them at least to join in the struggle against the common enemy . . . This was however a naïve approach and once the war was brought home to Britain, in the summer and autumn of 1940, it was replaced by a more realistic tone. British propaganda accepted (again reflecting public opinion in general) that even though there were Germans wholeheartedly opposed to Hitler and his war machine yet they represented a tiny minority . . .' Thereafter the propaganda message became more aggressive, stressing 'the growing strength and the determination of Britain and her allies'.

But finding the right people to get any message across proved a challenge, because, just as Jacques Duchesne of the French Service was attracting the best and brightest French exiles to his office at Broadcasting House, the German Service was going through a 'crisis in morale'. With the real threat of an imminent German invasion, even those Germans who had fled the Nazis fell under suspicion. Refugees from Germany – 'enemy aliens', to use the eloquently revealing phrase of the time – were being interned, and there was a sometimes hysterical campaign against them in the press. When refugees were deported to Australia and Canada, the *Daily Herald* greeted the story with the inflammatory headline: 'Country saved from Fifth Column Scab'. The BBC's policy towards German refugees was – unsurprisingly in this context – extremely restrictive; they could be used on air only as announcers (reading someone else's words), never as commentators. And Asa Briggs records that when the king and queen visited Broadcasting House, 'even refugee broadcasters who had been fully screened were not allowed near the royal visitors'. During the visit, Leonard Miall of the BBC's European Services summed up the distinctive culture of the German Service succinctly in an aside to the queen; it was, he told her, 'where we do the dirty work; where our colleagues try to raise the morale of their listeners, we try to lower it'.

That background explains why the wartime stars of the German Service were – again in marked contrast to the French Service – British intellectuals with a good understanding of German culture. Hugh Carleton Greene – brother of the novelist Graham Greene and later BBC director-general – was appointed as the service's editor in October 1940. He had been the *Daily Telegraph*'s chief correspondent in Berlin during the 1930s. Lindley Fraser began broadcasting at the request of his friend Frederick Ogilvie, who was then the BBC's director-general. He was a brilliant academic (who had taught Harold Wilson at Oxford) with a superb command of the German language. The appeal of his talks was increased by the slight Edinburgh accent with which they were delivered, and after the war he gave up academia and devoted himself to German broadcasting full time, becoming something of a celebrity in the German-speaking world. Another prominent member of the team was the future Labour Cabinet minister Richard Crossman. He had travelled extensively in Germany before taking up his fellowship at Oxford, and his first wife was a German Jew.

The BBC's policy against native German broadcasters also reflected a calculation that German listeners would regard most refugees as traitors and would therefore be reluctant to listen to their views. The only refugee judged grand enough to command an audience was the great novelist Thomas Mann. His anti-Hitler talks were recorded in Los Angeles, where he was living in exile, and flown over to London for transmission.

An internal Foreign Office review of the German Service concluded that the policy of keeping Germans off the air came with a price tag. While praising the 'good, clear and genuinely "German"' enunciation of the announcers, it complained that most British speakers 'completely disregard the German rules' of good delivery and were guilty of creating 'an intolerable atmosphere of tedium'. Even Fraser and Crossman were accused of the 'sin' of 'reading a sermon' rather than addressing their audience directly. The same – unsigned – memorandum also advised that 'People with a Jewish accent should be rigidly excluded from the microphone.' This, the anonymous author claims, is 'nothing to do with anti-Semitism'. 'German ears are very sensitive to this accent,' he writes, 'even when an English ear would not detect the difference. It is <u>always</u> unpleasant.'

The anti-refugee hysteria of the summer of 1940 faded as the threat of a German invasion receded, but the debate identified by Lindley Fraser – about whether Britain was at war with the German people or the Nazis – became a settled feature of wartime British public life. Another way of framing the question was whether it was possible to separate the two, and there were plenty of people who believed that it was not. Prominent among them was the veteran civil servant Sir Robert Vansittart, who had run the Foreign Office for most of the 1930s. In 1941 he published an influential set of essays under the title *Black Record: Germans Past and Present*, which argued that Nazism was simply the latest manifestation of a centuries-old German habit of bestial behaviour, and that Hitler's barbarity and aggression represented 'the extension and popularisation of the old imperialism and militarism'.

Vansittart provided the Nazis with a long pedigree. He had enjoyed the benefits of a classical education at Eton. 'I learnt the beginning of the truth at school,' he wrote, 'from having to construe Julius Caesar. Julius Caesar says that in Germany two thousand years ago: "Robbery has nothing infamous in it" when committed upon a neighbour; indeed, it was even thought to keep youth fighting fit for the annual war. It never occurred to the Germans that there should *not* be a war every year. It was only a question of *who* was to be attacked and devastated – for in those days they destroyed towns and townlets as thoroughly as they did in Flanders and northern France in 1914 or in Poland in 1939; and they killed and burned everything they could see, including animals, just as today they machine-gun cows if they can't find children.' The Roman historian Tacitus was also called as a witness ('a further observation of Tacitus on their habit of murdering their slaves would be endorsed by the poor Czechs and Poles of our own day') and all sorts of evidence from German history – the torture instrument known as the Iron Maiden of Nuremberg, Bismarck's faith in 'blood and iron', the duelling tradition of German students – is cited in the case for the prosecution.

Sir Robert charged those who took a more benign view of Germans with what he called 'Illusionism'. 'The difference between them and me is simply this,' he wrote. 'They believe that, so soon as the Nazi system has been liquidated, a decent, Christian, *effective* German government will emerge, in which you can have full confidence. This is most dangerous nonsense; the German character makes anything of the kind definitely impossible. I do not say that every German is bad; I do say that so vast a majority of Germans in the plural has been made bad by centuries of misteaching, that it will follow *any Fuehrer*, cheerfully and ferociously, into any aggression. Germans in the plural have got to be completely regenerated and retaught – and this can only be achieved by force and time.'

Although he had given up his formal government role, Vansittart remained an extremely influential figure in government circles, and he was made a peer in the year his book came out. *Black Record* proved so popular that it went through fourteen editions in 1941 alone, and Robert Bruce Lockhart, the veteran diplomat and spy who became the director-general of the Political Warfare Executive, arranged for miniature copies to be smuggled into Occupied France, writing the preface himself. Vansittart's extreme anti-German views earned him his own 'ism' – 'Vansittartism' became shorthand for the idea that the German character was, in some fundamental way, corrupted, and that this reality should dictate Britain's policy towards Germany. A Foreign Office memo written in the summer of 1942 quotes Bruce Lockhart's view that 'the principal controversy . . . dividing England in two and even the Cabinet was what is called Vansittartism – namely, are Nazis and Germans to be regarded as identical or were there good Germans as well as Nazis?'

As the document points out, the Vansittartist policy, 'which would lump all Germans together in a common condemnation', made life difficult for the propagandists, because it precluded any attempt to seduce potentially sympathetic members of the audience. If 'good Germans' were a tiny and irrelevant minority, it made little sense to waste energy trying to reach them. And the controversy over Vansittartism put the BBC in an awkward position. As Crossman explained it in a memo to Bruce Lockhart in November 1941, 'HMG has not yet defined in any detail its policy to Germany after the war. Moreover the attitude of various ministers has varied considerably, some viewing the German people as potential allies now, some warning that they can only be cured of National Socialism by a prolonged period of discipline after the war. In this situation it would be improper for our BBC broadcasts to give either a precise message of hope, or a precise message of general retribution to the German people.'

Lord Vansittart even faced accusations from some quarters that he had given unwitting aid and comfort to Germany's propaganda machine. The *New Statesman* reported that *Black Record* had been translated into German and widely distributed with a foreword by Dr Goebbels himself. Questions were asked in the House, and his lordship's secretary despatched a violent letter of protest to the editor of the *New Statesman*, demanding evidence. Robert Bruce Lockhart and Ivone Kirkpatrick at the BBC instigated an investigation and they established that the story, while not entirely untrue, had been overwritten. Goebbels had indeed quoted from the book in propaganda material, but it had not been circulated in its entirety.

≈

Because broadcasting to Germany was such a sensitive area, the government's propagandists were much more closely involved in the BBC's German Service than they were in the other European services. Both Lindley Fraser and Dick Crossman were recruited by the organization which began as Electra House (or Department EH) and became the Political Warfare Executive, or PWE (although both men also continued to broadcast on the BBC). Crossman understood the propaganda value of the BBC's reputation for truth-telling, and he made the use of facts something of a fetish. At the end of 1940 Hitler declared that 1941 would be the year of total victory. On Crossman's advice, the BBC's German news bulletins on 1 January began with the announcement 'This is London with the news on the first day of the year in which Hitler has promised you final victory.' The BBC kept the gag going, and on 31 December reminded its German audience that 'This is the last day of the year in which Hitler has promised you final victory.' By that stage Germany was at war with both the Soviet Union and the United States as well as Britain. Recordings of speeches by Hitler and other senior Nazis were carefully analysed and filed so that they could be used as reality-checks when events turned out rather differently from the promises and predictions Germany's leaders had made.

In the early days, the spooks out at Woburn Abbey shared many of the objectives and techniques of the BBC itself. In his official PWE history, David Garnett records that in 1940 and 1941 one of their aims was to 'attract an audience by providing a reliable news service'. Goebbels' lack of honesty about the Luftwaffe's failure during the Battle of Britain had, Garnett argued, 'led many Germans to listen to the BBC'. And he recorded that the one slip made by the Corporation – inaccurately claiming that Berlin's Potsdamer station had been hit in an early RAF raid – was still quoted against it three years later. 'The fact that this single instance was always quoted and no other could be found,' he wrote, 'was a tribute to the accuracy of the BBC.'

A campaign dreamed up by Dick Crossman's team in 1941 illustrates the way the PWE believed they could exploit the BBC's reputation. The objective was 'to widen the fissure between the Gestapo and the German Catholic and Protestant Opposition'. It was inspired by Clemens von Galen, the aristocratic Bishop of Münster, who, Lord Vansittart's views notwithstanding, clearly qualified as a 'good German'. In the summer of 1941 he delivered three powerful sermons attacking the Nazi regime for the systematic killing of elderly and disabled people, the tactics of the Gestapo and the persecution of the Church. The texts of his homilies were secretly printed and illegally circulated among German Catholics, and the PWE men felt the episode 'revealed a deep conflict in the hearts of sincere German Christians'. It was an obvious propaganda target. The PWE believed there was a 'hard core' of between 10 and 20 per cent of Christians who could be 'driven to the point of refusing to continue making compromises'.

The PWE plan for exploiting this was based on the BBC's standing as a trusted source of information. 'At first sight, the problem that the voice of the enemy advising German Christians not to deny God on earth would be "taken with a pinch of salt", seems insoluble. But it is not,' the planning document argues. 'The first essential is that as far as possible we should get over our emotional appeals to them from the London radio, but as the <u>reporting</u> and quoting of world Christian opinion. In this way the German listener overhears, rather than being preached at.' The document proposed a *World Comment* feature after the lunchtime news, which would include a digest of what the Christian world was saying about Germany, and two Christian programmes – one Catholic and one Protestant – each Sunday afternoon.

So far, so BBC-ish, but the way the document suggests these pro-grammes should be filled involves a phrase that would surely have given Auntie the vapours: 'news creation'. The PWE team argued that '[I]f our plan is to succeed, we must undertake the creation of news, by getting the kind of material that fills the needs of our plan uttered by Christian leaders throughout the world, or published in the press. It is probably true also that it would further lull any feeling the

German might have that the enemy was trying to get at him, if such opinions were expressed by the religious leaders and press of America, rather than England' (the plan was drawn up before Pearl Harbor and America's entry into the war). The document gives very precise instructions for what the American bishops must be persuaded to say: 'News created on this theme should be an expression of opinion by Christian leaders, that inevitably Germany will lose the war if the Gestapo continues in power, because God's love will be withdrawn from Germany.' They must also drive home 'to German Christians that, if by word and deed they fail to protest both in private and in public against the pagan doctrines of the race theory, pagan education, "mercy killings" etc. they are denying Christ on earth, and will surely be denied by him in heaven.'

The document does not explain how the leaders of world Christianity would be persuaded to collude in this clever wheeze, and it seems unlikely that the plan to use the BBC in this way got very far. But a campaign along these lines did feature on one of the PWE's so-called Research Units, or RUs, the secret radio stations it ran from the grounds of Woburn Abbey. David Garnett records that here too 'the object was to widen the breach between the forty million German Catholics and their Nazi rulers'. The station was code-named G7 and it was 'run by a Catholic priest who spoke five or six days a week with two transmissions on the 49 metre band. The priest wrote and spoke his own scripts; had a S German voice and purported to be inside Germany. He kept his views closely in line with the pronouncements of the German Catholic bishops.' Garnett notes with satisfaction that 'the station was clearly heard in Sweden where it was believed to be in Germany'.

As the war developed, the PWE relied more and more on their RUs, and it became a common shorthand to refer to the BBC's broadcasts as 'white' propaganda in contrast to the 'black' propaganda pushed out by the secret radio stations. The difference between the two grew as the 'black' experts got into their stride. Not everything transmitted on the black stations was a lie, but the PWE regarded skilful deception as one of its main weapons; as one senior official put it, 'We must never lie by accident, or through slovenliness, only deliberately.' And the PWE took particular pride in those lies that were so convincing that they managed to deceive their BBC colleagues.

The most imaginative member of the PWE team was Sefton Delmer, who was recruited from the *Daily Express*. He spoke good German – he was born in Berlin – and early in the war he had been booked to give a series of BBC talks. The first, on 19 July 1940, coincided with Hitler's speech in the Reichstag celebrating his victory in France, in which he famously made his 'final peace appeal' to Britain. Delmer went on the air half an hour after Hitler had sat down. He had met the German leader in the course of his work for the *Express* and addressed him directly. 'Let me tell you what we here in Britain think of this appeal of yours to what you are pleased to call our reason and common sense,' he said. 'Herr Führer and Reichskanzler, we hurl it right back at you, right in your evil-smelling teeth . . .' The BBC thus rejected Hitler's peace offer two days before the British government gave its formal response (which was the same, although less colourfully expressed) and Sefton Delmer became part of BBC history.

But in his approach to journalism and propaganda he was as 'un-BBCish' as it was possible to be. 'I longed to show the BBC the difference between the stodgy news presentation of the old-fashioned journalism to which the BBC bowed down, and the sharp and vivid style of Fleet Street which I hoped to adapt to Radio,' he wrote. 'I wanted to demonstrate the mass appeal of the significant "human story", until now absent from the air, the technique of "personalising" the news.' He complained about the 'the spinsterish insistence of the BBC on its freedom from government control', and he lied with unashamed zest. Delmer believed that to 'stimulate Germans into thoughts and actions hostile to Hitler they would have to be tricked'.

His first venture into the field of 'black radio' was a station that 'undermines Hitler, not by opposing him, but by pretending to be all for him and his war'. It involved the creation of a character called Der Chef, who purported to be the leader of a clandestine military organization, and the station – its call-sign was '*Gustav Siegfried Eins*', 'signallers' German for George Sugar One' – was designed to sound as if it was a private communications network rather than a public broadcasting operation. Delmer hoped that the German listener would discover the waveband by chance while tuning his radio, thus being led to believe that he was 'eavesdropping ... on radio talk not intended for his ears'. Der Chef's 'caustic and salaciously outspoken views' were interspersed with coded messages to give the impression that he was communicating with members of his secret group, and his opinions reflected the views of some of the traditional German officer class who were loyal to Hitler but repelled by the more radical aspects of Nazism. When, for example, Hitler's deputy, Rudolf Hess, flew to Britain on a peace mission in 1941, Der Chef let rip like this: '[T]his fellow is by no means the worst of the lot. He was a good comrade of ours in the days of the Free Corps. But like the rest of this clique of cranks, megalomaniacs, string-pullers and parlour Bolsheviks who call themselves our leaders, he simply has no nerves for a crisis. As soon as he learns a little of the darker side of the developments that lie ahead, what happens? He loses his head completely, packs himself a satchel full of hormone pills and a white flag, and flies off to throw himself on the mercy of that flat-footed bastard and drunken old Jew Churchill. And he overlooks completely that he is the bearer of the Reich's secrets, all of which the [obscenity] British will now suck out of him as easily as if he was a bottle of Berlin White-Beer.' Delmer was especially proud of 'flat-footed bastard and drunken old Jew Churchill', which he felt would immediately confirm Der Chef's bona fides.

David Garnett recorded that 'Delmer did not scruple to introduce passages of extreme indecency which undoubtedly did much to attract an audience quickly'. The use of pornography as 'Listeners' Bait' got him into trouble, because the signal from *GS1* (*Gustav Siegfried Eins*) could sometimes be picked up locally in Bedfordshire, leading to complaints from members of the public. These reached the distinguished ears of Sir Stafford Cripps (then serving in the government as Lord Privy Seal), who took Robert Bruce Lockhart, PWE's director-general, to task over the matter. The puritanical Cripps was especially put out by 'very lurid descriptions of a German admiral's orgy with his mistress and four maritime sailors', which were broadcast in December 1941, and told Bruce Lockhart that 'he has heard of one house where people listened to this account. Two young women had been there and had been physically sick'. Bruce Lockhart notes in his diary that 'This is typical of Cripps' extravagance of views; he is very near to being a religious maniac.' Cripps told him, 'even if [it was] good propaganda he would rather lose the war than win by such methods, but he was sure it was bad propaganda'.

The part of Der Chef was played by Peter Seckelmann, an author of detective novels who had fled from Berlin in 1938 and enlisted in the British Army. He was joined on *GS1* first by a German journalist who had also left the Fatherland just before the outbreak of war (he had a Jewish wife) and then by Max Braun, a prominent socialist who had led anti-Hitler groups in the Saarland. The BBC restrictions on employing German refugees did not apply to black broadcasting and, according to the PWE's official history, 'Delmer always had the greatest contempt for the BBC staff, but maintained there were excellent refugees to be had if you knew how to find them.' Delmer's

Sefton Delmer, master of 'black' broadcasting.

team of exiles was later beefed up with volunteers from PoW camps. They were all put up in a large Victorian house called The Rookery in the Bedfordshire village of Aspley Guise, with Sefton Delmer, assisted by his wife, in the role of 'housemaster'.

Delmer liked boasting about his ability to lie convincingly, and it is difficult to judge when this unreliable narrator is spinning a line in his autobiography. But he paints a convincing picture of a jolly communal life at The Rookery. The boarders lived well by wartime standards; they were provided with venison from the grounds of Woburn Abbey, there was a gardener to grow vegetables and they had their own chickens. Delmer was an oenophile and kept the wine cellar well stocked, and romance, he tells us, blossomed among the inmates. One of the prisoners of war, a 'Bavarian monarchist with a name known throughout Europe since as long ago as the fifteenth century', became engaged to a beautiful Jewish girl, scandalizing one of his fellow officers. And on the anniversaries of *GS1*'s first broadcast Delmer threw birthday parties for his brain child. The priest broadcaster of *G7* evidently enjoyed these as much as anyone. An American officer visited The Rookery while the celebrations were in full swing and afterwards remarked that he had been prepared for almost anything in this strange world, 'but never, never did I expect to see a priest in a Conga line!'

Word of this high living reached the ears of Delmer's old colleagues on the *Sunday Express* and a reporter was sent up to Aspley Guise to sniff around. The paper could not print anything until the war was over, but the story was eventually published in 1946 under a headline that speaks eloquently of the standards of luxury in austerity Britain: 'Fat-of-the-land Life of German PoWs. Mushrooms Cooked in Wine'.

THE WINTRY CONSCIENCE OF
A GENERATION

THE BBC BEGAN BROADCASTING in Hindustani on 11 May 1940, the day after the German offensive in Western Europe began. The timing was a coincidence, but, as Whitehall saw the war, every aspect of this global conflict was linked; Churchill believed there was a very close connection between Britain's security in Europe and the politics of the Indian sub-continent.

At the outbreak of war, the pro-independence Congress Party was

George Orwell: 'All propaganda is lies, even when one is telling the truth.'

running eight of India's eleven provinces under the limited self-rule provisions introduced by the Government of India Act of 1935. India declared war on Germany along with Britain in September 1939, but the viceroy, Lord Linlithgow, made the announcement without troubling to consult Congress leaders, and all the party's provincial ministries resigned in protest. The political crisis made the 'jewel in the crown' a natural target for enemy broadcasts. 'German propaganda to India was asking why Indians should die for Britain and pointing out that while the British talked of democracy India remained a subject nation,' writes the BBC historian Gerard Mansell. India was, as another historian has put it, 'a jewel, as all could see, that was loosely fixed'.

Quite why George Orwell was considered just the man to anchor it firmly in the imperial diadem is not immediately obvious. Indian-born himself, he was pro-independence and, after his experience as a colonial police officer in Burma, a committed anti-imperialist. He was also a notorious member of the awkward squad and is remembered today as the author of the dictum 'All propaganda is lies, even when one is telling the truth.' But the record of his interview at the BBC in the summer of 1941 suggests that, as the BBC jargon has it, he could 'do a good board'. 'I was much impressed with him,' recorded the BBC official who conducted the interview. '... His past experience and his interest in India and Burma, his literary abilities and contacts, and his personality, which seemed to me to be strongly marked and attractive in spite of the very diffident and not very impressive manner in the initial stages of our interview, all marked him out as a very suitable person to work in English talks etc. intended for Indian listeners, particularly Indian students.'

Orwell himself appears to have raised the issues of his left-wing past and his time fighting with the Republicans in Spain, but he evidently dealt with them well; 'when I questioned him closely about his loyalties and the danger of finding himself at odds with policy, his answers were impressive,' wrote Auntie's man. 'He accepts absolutely the need for propaganda to be directed by the Government, and stressed his view that in war-time discipline in the execution of government policy is essential.'

The memo notes that Orwell's appointment would need to be approved by a mysterious body known as 'the College', and a couple of impatient handwritten notes in the margin suggest that 'the College'

310

(the phrase is always used with inverted commas) took a while to give its blessing. An entry in Orwell's wartime diary confirms that 'the College' was BBC slang for MI5. On 28 August he recorded in the diary, 'I am now definitely an employee of the BBC'. The same day's entry concludes with a prescient observation: 'We are in for a long, dreary, exhausting war, with everyone growing poorer all the time. The new phase which I foresaw earlier has now started, and the quasi-revolutionary period which began with Dunkirk is finished. I therefore bring this diary to an end, as I intended to do when the new phase started.' The six-month gap in his diary that follows means we have to rely largely on other sources for an account of his early days with Auntie.

Orwell's employment began with a training course at Bedford College in Regent's Park, briefly the home of the French Service before the bombs drove them to Bush House. 'On the day when a stranger offered me his hand and said "I am George Orwell",' remembered the literary critic William Empson, 'we were both students at the start of a six-week course in what was called the Liars' School of the BBC.' This seems an unnecessarily harsh soubriquet, as the course involved a great deal of a grittily practical nature (the class titles included 'Practical acoustics and microphones' and 'Exercises in making running commentaries and use of recording vans') and some sessions sound mind-numbingly tedious ('Administration of the BBC', a talk given by the BBC 'Controller – Administration', and 'Organisation and Problems of the Overseas Division' among them). Orwell told Empson that he been ruled unfit for military service. 'I have what half the men in this country would give their balls to have,' he was accustomed to remark, 'a yellow ticket [or whatever colour it was, meaning he could not be conscripted], but I don't want it.'

Orwell's formal BBC title was talks assistant, later talks producer, in the India Section of the Eastern Service, and for most of his time with the Corporation he was based at 200 Oxford Street, yet another of the buildings colonized for the BBC's wartime use. Much of his work sounds thoroughly enjoyable. Laurence Brander, the India Section's intelligence officer (all the BBC overseas services had such persons), argued that the output should be high-brow stuff aimed at educated Indians, 'the very best all-British product', which was 'sensible, cultivated, gracious and interesting'. To this end Orwell recruited what Brander later described as 'impressive processions of literary men and professors ... hurrying through the BBC broadcasting to India'. The glittering list included his friend Cyril Connolly, the poets Stephen Spender, T. S. Eliot and Dylan Thomas, the China scholar Joseph Needham, the novelist E. M. Forster, the writer Naomi Mitchison, and the political scientist Harold Laski.

In August 1942 he launched a radio magazine called *Voice*, which consisted largely of poetry readings and critical conversation. 'It may seem a little dilettante to be starting a magazine concerned primarily with poetry at a moment when, quite literally, the fate of the world is being decided by bombs and bullets,' Orwell conceded in the first 'Editorial'. 'However our magazine ... isn't quite an ordinary magazine. To begin with it doesn't use up paper or the labour of any printers or booksellers. All it needs is a little electrical power and half-a-dozen voices.' Orwell's cultural broadcasts feel like a dry run for the Third Programme, which was founded after the war and, under Harman Grisewood, became a by-word for cultural elitism (morphing eventually into today's Radio Three).

But Orwell's duties also included writing newsletters – which were translated into Gujarati, Marathi, Bengali and Tamil for broadcast – and news commentaries, most of which were read on the air by his boss in the India Section, Zulfiqar Bokhari (who later became the first director-general of Radio Pakistan). This took him into grubbier territory, the contours of which were clearly drawn in a 1942 BBC policy document on the Empire Service:

> The primary purpose of news commentaries is propaganda. They make it possible to 'put across' the British view of the news, without sacrificing the reputation that has been carefully built up for veracity and objectivity in news presentation. The commentary can, by its selection of particular events for emphasis and its explanation of tendencies, supply the perspective that is needed, in close proximity to the news bulletins, especially when news as revealed in official communiqués is bad, or fluctuating rapidly. Moreover, it achieves this objective in a radio form that is popular not only in North America but throughout the world.

The document lays down that, in drawing up scripts, 'the commentator takes his line from the daily "directive" written by the Empire News Editor', which in turn reflected the views of the foreign adviser (Ivone Kirkpatrick), guidance from the Foreign Office and the Ministry of Information, and 'occasional suggestions and requests from the Dominions, Colonial and India Offices'.

The question of why George Orwell applied for this kind of work is perhaps even more puzzling than the question of why the BBC hired him to do it. His BBC obituary described him as 'the wintry conscience of a generation', yet his propaganda work seemed, on the face of it, a betrayal of everything he stood for.

Orwell's logic, which he in fact followed through with characteristic integrity, emerges in an extended debate – much of it conducted in the pages of the radical American quarterly the *Partisan Review* – about pacifism. Orwell fired the first shot in a 1941 book review of *No Such Liberty*, a novel by the pacifist and conscientious objector Dr Alex Comfort (later famous for his 1972 illustrated manual *The Joy of Sex*). 'The fact is that the ordinary short-term case for pacifism, the claim that you can best frustrate the Nazis by not resisting them, cannot be sustained. If you don't resist the Nazis, you are helping them, and ought to admit it ... The notion that you can somehow defeat violence by submitting to it is simply a flight from fact.' Orwell regarded pacifism as a moral cop-out; in May 1942, again in the pages of the *Partisan Review*, he declared, 'Nor is there any real way of remaining outside such a war as the present one ... The idea that you can remain aloof from and superior to the struggle, while living on food which British sailors have risked their lives to bring you, is a bourgeois illusion ...' There is no reason to doubt Orwell's declaration to William Empson that he did not want his 'yellow ticket'; he had, after all, shown in Spain that he was willing to risk his life for his beliefs. His final attempt to join the army was rebuffed by the Willesden Medical Board with a Grade 4 National Service Card, which ruled out any kind of military service.

That in turn meant he had to find some other way of participating in the war effort, and in that context BBC propaganda work did not seem so very wicked. In the course of the pacifism controversy in the

Partisan Review, he was accused of 'conducting British propaganda to fox the Indian masses'. He replied that 'most of our broadcasters are Indian leftwing intellectuals, from Liberals to Trotskyists, some of them virulently anti-British. They don't do it to "fox the Indian masses", but because they know what a Fascist victory would mean to the chances of India's independence.'

In late 1942 Orwell corresponded directly with one of his opponents in the *Partisan Review* debate, and he explained his position like this: 'As to the ethics of broadcasting and in general letting oneself be used by the British governing class. It's of little value to argue about it, it is chiefly a question of whether one considers it more important to down the Nazis first or whether one believes doing this is meaningless unless one achieves one's own revolution first. But for heaven's sake don't think I don't see how they are using me. A subsidiary point is that one can't effectively remain outside the war and by working inside an institution like the BBC one can perhaps deodorise it to a certain extent.'

In the course of his work Orwell had access to all the BBC Monitoring Reports of enemy broadcasting, and he argued that, judged by the general standard, his own programmes 'aren't as bad as they might be'; at the end of the letter he writes, 'To appreciate this you have to be as I am in constant touch with propaganda Axis and Allied. Till then you don't realise what muck and filth is normally flowing through the air. I consider I have kept our little corner fairly clean.'

He could not, of course, keep his corner completely clean, and he was forced to adopt some positions he must have found uncomfortable. Orwell's experiences in Spain and the evidence of Stalinist purges in the years immediately preceding the war had left him with a deep hatred of the Soviet Union, and it is reflected in the private thoughts he recorded when he resumed his war diary in March 1942. Commenting on the way communists in Mexico were hunting down Trotskyite refugees from Europe, he wrote, 'Just the same tactics as in Spain. Horribly depressed to see these ancient intrigues coming up again, not so much because they are morally disgusting as from this reflection: for 20 years the Comintern [the Soviet-inspired international movement dedicated to worldwide communist revolution] has used these methods and the

Comintern has always and everywhere been defeated by the Fascists, therefore we, being tied to them by a species of alliance, shall be defeated with them.'

A week earlier he had noted that, 'From studying the German and Russian wireless I have long come to the conclusion that the reports of Russian victories are largely phony [*sic*].' Yet he was perfectly happy to trumpet the USSR's military successes in his news commentaries, and he was, in keeping with British government policy towards this hugely important ally, even willing to praise the virtues of Soviet society. A little over a month after those disobliging comments in his diary, he had Bokhari tell his listeners, 'Since the Soviet power was established, the prime significance of May Day for the Russian people has been a patriotic one, and since Stalin told the Stakhanovite workers seven years ago that "life is growing better, life is growing happier", the day has been the occasion of a temporary relaxation from the strain and effort demanded of Soviet workers, and has something of the quality of the fourteenth of July in France . . . It is the firm belief among Russian workers that it is because their land is a socialist one that it has withstood Hitler's attempts to disrupt it politically.' Eighteen months after that broadcast Orwell began work on *Animal Farm*, his enduring satire on Stalin-style socialism.

Commentaries which dealt with India were, of course, a particular problem for Orwell; he handled it partly by limiting the scope of his comments, and sometimes by ignoring the story altogether. In March 1942 Sir Stafford Cripps, the senior Labour politician and former British ambassador to Moscow, was sent to negotiate with India's leaders in the hope of securing their support for the war effort. Orwell, who genuinely believed that India had more to fear from a Japanese invasion than from continuing British rule, gave Cripps a terrific puff in his weekly *News Review*, calling him 'the ablest man in the British Socialist Movement', praising his austere way of life ('So simple are his manners that he is to be seen every morning having his breakfast in a cheap London eating house, among working men and office employees') and claiming that 'Everyone in Britain is delighted to see such an important mission as the one Cripps is now undertaking, conferred upon a man who even his critics admit to be gifted, trustworthy and self-sacrificing.'

Cripps promised Nehru, Gandhi and the other Congress leaders post-war self-government and Dominion status for India, but he failed to convince them (Gandhi called Cripps's offer a 'post-dated cheque drawn on a crashing bank'), and despite the BBC's cheering from the touchline, his mission ended in failure.

Orwell put the best construction he could on the story. 'It is clear from the reports that have come in from many countries that only the supporters of Fascism are pleased by the failure of Sir Stafford Cripps' mission. On the other hand, there is a general feeling that the failure was not complete, in so much that the negotiations have clarified the issue and did not end in such a way as to make further advances impossible,' he wrote in a *News Review* on 18 April. He then resorted to the old propagandist's trick of playing the man and not the ball: 'Axis broadcasters are attempting to represent the breakdown as a refusal on the part of India to defend herself, and an actual Indian desire to pass under Japanese rule. This is a direct lie, and the Axis broadcasters are only able to support it by deliberately not quoting from the speeches of Mr Nehru and other leaders.' But in a diary entry written on the same day he reveals that he and his colleagues in the Empire Service were guilty of precisely the same economy in their reporting. 'Nehru is making provocative speeches to the effect that all the English are the same,' he wrote. '... At the same time he reiterates at intervals that he is not pro-Japanese and Congress will defend India to the last. The BBC thereupon picks out these passages from his speeches, and broadcasts them without mentioning the anti-British passages, whereat Nehru complains (quite justly) that he has been misrepresented. A recent directive tells us that when one of his speeches contains both anti-British and anti-Japanese passages, we had better ignore them altogether. What a mess it all is.'

In August 1942, at a meeting in Bombay, Gandhi launched the 'Quit India' movement, demanding an immediate British withdrawal, and the following day he was arrested along with Nehru and several other Congress leaders. This time Orwell kept his thoughts to his diary. 'Nehru, Gandhi, Azad [a nationalist Muslim leader] and many others in gaol. Rioting over most of India, a number of deaths, countless arrests,' he recorded on 10 August. 'Ghastly speech by Amery

[Leo Amery, Churchill's secretary of state for India] speaking of Nehru and Co. as "wicked men", "saboteurs" etc. This of course broadcast on the Empire Service and rebroadcast by AIR [All India Radio]. The best joke of all was that the Germans did their best to jam it, unfortunately without success.'

The official directive on how this news from India should be covered on the Empire Service landed on Orwell's desk within a couple of days. 'Appalling policy handout this morning about affairs in India,' reads his diary entry on 12 August. 'The riots are of no significance – the situation is well in hand – after all the number of deaths is not large etc etc. As to the participation of students in the riots, this is explained along the "boys will be boys" lines, "We all know that students everywhere are only too glad to join in any kind of rag" etc. etc. Almost everyone utterly disgusted. Some of the Indians when they hear this kind of stuff go quite pale, a strange sight.'

Orwell understood the ambiguities of his position all too well. His famous dictum about propaganda always being lies is from a diary entry in March 1942, around the time of the Cripps mission. The next sentence is less often quoted: 'I don't think this matters, so long as one knows what one is doing, and why.' And if he was ever in any danger of forgetting the moral murkiness of the world he was working in, his own past was there to remind him. The writer Cyril Connolly asked for permission to quote from *Homage to Catalonia*, Orwell's account of his Spanish Civil War experiences, in one of his broadcasts. Orwell 'opened the book and came on these sentences: "One of the most horrible features of war is that all war-propaganda, all the screaming lies and hatred, comes invariably from people who are not fighting . . . It is the same in all wars; the soldiers do the fighting, the journalists do the shouting, and no true patriot ever gets near a front line trench, except on the briefest of propaganda tours . . ."' Orwell notes bitterly in his diary: 'Here I am in the BBC, less than five years after writing that. I suppose sooner or later we all write our own epitaphs.'

His immediate BBC bosses appear to have been, on the whole, sympathetic over Orwell's moral dilemmas, and to have managed him intelligently. In October 1942 Laurence Brander suggested that Orwell should broadcast his commentaries on the news himself, allowing the

BBC 'to "cash in" on the popularity of "George Orwell" in India'. Orwell responded with a memo to the Eastern Service Director, L. F. Rushbrook Williams. 'If I broadcast as George Orwell I am as it were selling my literary reputation, which as far as India is concerned probably arises chiefly from books of an anti-imperialist tendency, some of which have been banned in India,' he pointed out, adding, 'If I gave broadcasts which appeared to endorse unreservedly the policy of the British government I should quite soon be written off as "one more renegade" and should probably miss my potential public, at any rate among the student population ... clearly we should defeat our own object in these broadcasts if I could not preserve my position as an independent and more or less "agin the government" commentator.' He therefore asked for a guarantee of 'reasonable freedom of speech' before agreeing to go ahead with the broadcasts. Rushbrook Williams referred the matter to his boss, R. A. Rendall, the assistant controller of the Overseas Service, with a recommendation that Orwell's condition should be accepted, which it was. Rushbrook Williams's handwritten note to Rendall suggests that Orwell's memo should not be shown to 'the Establishment side' – roughly what today we would call the HR department – because 'to people who do not know him as you and I do it might be misleading'.

And there were indeed plenty of BBC bureaucrats who did not understand Orwell and seemed determined to make his life difficult. When the Empire Service talks manager noticed that Orwell had booked a talk on 'Plastics' not long after another programme on the same subject, he circulated a memo complaining that 'it certainly seems extravagant from the point of view of the corporation that we have paid for two talks on the same subject within less than a week', and that 'Blair [Orwell's real name] is working rather too independently of the existing regime'. A Miss B. H. Alexander from the Copyright Department engaged him in a vigorous exchange of memos about the proper protocol for approaching writers with a view to quoting from their works, driving him closer to distraction. 'The thing that strikes one in the BBC,' he erupted in the summer of 1942, '... is not so much the moral squalor and the ultimate futility of what we are doing, as the feeling of frustration, the impossibility of getting *anything* done, even any successful piece of scoundrelism'.

He then gives this devastating account of the programme-making process: 'When one plans some series of talks, with some more or less definite propaganda line behind it, one is first told to go ahead, then choked off on the grounds that this is "injudicious" or "premature", then told to go ahead, then told to water everything down and cut out any plain statements that may have crept in here and there, then told to "modify" the series in some way that removes its original meaning; and then at the last moment the whole thing is suddenly cancelled by some mysterious edict from above and one is told to improvise some different series in which one feels no interest and which in any case has no definite idea behind it.' More dispiriting than all this, however, was the conclusion that not many people were listening anyway: 'Except, I suppose, in Europe, the BBC simply isn't listened to overseas, a fact known to everyone concerned with overseas broadcasting.'

The picture was not quite that bleak; in the course of the war the BBC built up a significant following in several non-European markets, including, notably, the Middle East and Latin America (the head of the Latin American Service was able to claim that by the end of 1944 'the majority of Latin Americans automatically turn to the BBC for accurate war news, and for the confirmation or refutation of unofficial rumours'). But Orwell did have a point about India; radio simply had not caught on in the sub-continent in the way it had in Europe and North America. At the outbreak of war, the population of Britain was 47,680,500, and 8,893,582 radio licences had been issued. For the United States the figures were a population of 131,669,275 and 57,000,000 radio licences. But India's 389,000,000 people had bought only 100,388 radios between them. As an Empire Service internal report pointed out, this meant that while in Britain there was one radio for every 5.36 people and in the United States one radio for every 2.3 people, 'in India there was one radio for every 3,875 people'.

In October 1942 Orwell had a frank talk with Laurence Brander, the India Section intelligence officer, who had just returned from a six-month tour in the field. 'His conclusions,' Orwell confided to his diary, 'so depressing that I can hardly bring myself to write them down. Briefly – affairs are much worse in India than anyone here is allowed to realise, the situation is in fact retrievable but won't be

319

retrieved because the government is determined to make no real concessions, hell will break loose when and if there is a Japanese invasion, and our broadcasts are utterly useless because nobody listens to them.' Brander later recalled that 'I found that our programmes were at a time of day when no one was listening and that they could hardly be heard because the signal was so weak,' and that 'very few students had access to wireless sets'. He also concluded that some of Orwell's talks were heard by 'no one except Japanese monitors'.

In the end it was frustration rather than moral self-loathing that drove Orwell from his job at the BBC. The story of wartime broadcasting to India is, in a way, the flip-side of the French Service story; the second was a success in ways no one could have predicted, the first was an equally unexpected failure.

≈

For more than four decades Orwell's wartime broadcasts were thought to have been lost, but, acting on a hunch, the writer and literary sleuth W. J. West eventually tracked them down in the BBC's Written Archives at Caversham, and they were published in 1985. They of course do not stand in the first rank of the Orwell *oeuvre* – and they probably tell us more about Auntie's mind than about Orwell's. But Orwell's time at the Corporation was to pay dividends in the greatest and most enduring of his works, the dystopian novel *Nineteen Eighty-Four*. In a 1948 letter about the book to his publisher, Fredric Warburg, he states that 'I first thought of it in 1943.' Orwell finally left the BBC in November that year.

The way he borrowed material for the novel from his BBC experience is well documented. Room 101 has entered the English language as shorthand for the home of our greatest fears; policy meetings of the BBC Eastern Service took place in Room 101 of 55 Portland Place, where Orwell worked in his early days with the Corporation. And the description of the Ministry of Truth, or Minitrue, where *Nineteen Eighty-Four*'s protagonist, Winston Smith, is employed, is very clearly influenced by the University of London Senate House which housed the Ministry of Information.

But Orwell's war diaries also suggest a deeper connection between his frustration with 'the moral squalor and the ultimate futility' of his BBC work and the unredeemed pessimism of parts of *Nineteen Eighty-Four*. After reading the manuscript for the first time, Fredric Warburg wrote a report for his production and promotion teams in which he describes it as 'amongst the most terrifying books I have ever read'. He ends the memo with the judgement 'it is a great book, but I pray I may be spared reading another like it for years to come'. One of the central themes that makes *Nineteen Eighty-Four* such a bleak read is the way the human spirit can be forced to acquiesce in the defeat of truth.

Orwell's angriest diary reflections on this subject are – this should be recorded in fairness to the British authorities – usually inspired by the torrent of Axis propaganda that flowed across his desk in the BBC Monitoring Reports, rather than by directives from the Ministry of Information. In April 1942, for example, he quotes an Italian broadcast which made such extravagant claims about food shortages in London ('Five shillings were given for one egg yesterday ... peas have become the prerogatives of millionaires') that no one could possibly believe them. This, Orwell argues, should be considered 'stupid propaganda', but, 'You can go on telling lies, and the most palpable lies at that, and even if they are not actually believed, there is no strong revulsion either.' He goes on, 'We are all drowning in filth. When I talk to anyone or read the writings of anyone who has any axe to grind, I feel that intellectual honesty and balanced judgement have simply disappeared from the face of the earth. Everyone's thought is forensic, everyone is putting a "case" with deliberate suppression of his opponent's point of view, and, what is more, with complete insensitiveness to any sufferings except those of himself and his friends. The Indian nationalist is sunk in self-pity and hatred of Britain and utterly indifferent to the miseries of China, the English pacifist works himself up into frenzies about the concentration camps on the Isle of Man and forgets about those in Germany etc. etc ... Everyone is dishonest and everyone is utterly heartless towards people who are outside the immediate range of his own interests.'

He returned to the theme two months later following the assassination of the senior Nazi Reinhard Heydrich in Prague. Heydrich was fatally wounded in an attack led by two British-trained

Czech agents, and the Germans responded by wiping out a village called Lidice, which had a population of some 2,000. The official announcement of the reprisal was picked up by BBC Monitoring and Orwell kept a copy:

> The search and investigation for the murderers of SS Obergruppen-führer Gen. Heydrich has established unimpeachable indications that the population of the locality of Lidice, near Kladno, sup-ported and gave assistance to the circle of perpetrators in question. In spite of the interrogation of the local inhabitants, the pertinent means of evidence were secured without the help of the local population. The attitude of the inhabitants to the outrage thus manifested, is manifested also by other acts hostile to the Reich, by the discovery of printed matter hostile to the Reich, of dumps of arms and ammunition, of an illegal wireless transmitter, of huge quantities of controlled goods, as well as by the fact inhabitants of the locality are in active enemy service abroad. Since the inhabit-ants of this village have flagrantly violated the laws which have been issued, by their activity and by the support given to the murderers of SS Obergruppenführer Heydrich, the male adults have been shot, the women have been sent to a concentration camp and the children have been handed over to the appropriate educational authorities. The buildings of the locality have been levelled to the ground, and the name of the community has been obliterated.

Orwell commented in his diary, 'It does not particularly surprise me that people do this kind of thing, nor even that they announce that they are doing them. What does impress me, however, is that other people's reaction to such happenings is governed solely by the political fashion of the moment. Thus before the war the pinks believed any and every horror story that came out of Germany or China. Now the pinks no longer believe in German or Japanese atrocities and automatically write off all horror stories as "propaganda". In a little while you will be jeered at if you suggest that the story of Lidice could possibly be true. And yet there the facts are, announced by the Germans themselves and recorded on gramophone discs which will no doubt still be available.'

History has not been quite that brutal – at the time of writing the Heydrich story has just been retold in a successful film with a star-studded cast. But Orwell's contention that truth is at the mercy of political fashion rings true again almost seven decades after the completion of his masterpiece: sales of *Nineteen Eighty-Four* spiked suddenly in January 2017, when President Trump's adviser Kellyanne Conway introduced the world to the very Orwellian concept of 'alternative facts'.

One of the very few hints of hope in *Nineteen Eighty-Four* is provided by the singing of a prole woman, which Winston Smith hears outside the room he rents for his affair with Julia. The proles are the uneducated working classes of the novel's world, and Orwell tells us – in a characteristic aside – that the songs 'were composed without any human intervention whatever on an instrument known as a versificator', but this woman 'sang so tunefully as to turn the dreadful rubbish into an almost pleasant sound'. Winston and Julia listen as 'her voice floated upward with the sweet summer air, very tuneful, charged with a sort of happy melancholy'. Winston is struck by the fact that 'he had never heard a member of the Party singing alone and spontaneously'.

The singing is a clever, subtle metaphor, and Orwell's first biographer, Bernard Crick, thinks the writer found it at the BBC. The scene in the novel takes place in June, and in the same month in 1942 Orwell noted the following in his diary: 'The only time when one hears people singing in the BBC is in the early morning, between 6 and 8. That is the time when the charwomen are at work. A huge army of them arrives all at the same time, they sit in the reception hall waiting for their brooms to be issued to them and making as much noise as a parrot house, and then they have wonderful choruses, all singing together as they sweep the passages. The place has quite a different atmosphere at this time from what it has later in the day.'

If Crick is right, perhaps the BBC years were not quite as 'futile' as Orwell feared.

OXFORD IS HELD BY THE GERMANS

GEORGE ORWELL'S RESIGNATION LETTER was handsome. 'I have been treated with the greatest generosity and allowed very great latitude,' he told L. F. Rushbrook Williams. 'On no occasion have I been compelled to say on the air anything that I would not have said as a private individual.' There was, however, one occasion on which he had tacked very close to what he would, with his hatred of euphemism, have called an outright lie.

On 19 August 1942 Allied forces mounted a raid on the northern French port of Dieppe, the first serious assault on Occupied Europe since the fall of France more than two years earlier. Here's how Orwell reported the episode in one of his commentaries:

> On Wednesday of this week there took place the largest combined operations raid of the war, on Dieppe on the French coast, about 60 miles from the coast of Britain. British, Canadian, Free French and American troops took part, the whole force evidently numbering 5,000 or 10,000. They remained on shore for about 10 hours, successfully destroyed batteries of artillery and other military objectives, before re-embarking. Tanks were successfully landed, and took part in operations. This is probably the first time in this war that tanks have been landed from small boats on an open beach. It is known that there were heavy casualties on both sides and very heavy losses of aeroplanes. The Germans are known

to have lost about 90 planes destroyed for certain and a large number were reported as probably destroyed, so 130 would be a conservative figure for their total loss. The British lost nearly 100 planes. These losses are much more serious for the Germans than the British, as the great part of the German airforce are now on the Russian front, and any large loss of planes means that others have to be brought across Europe to replace them.

But in his diary on that same day he recorded a very different picture painted by his friend David Astor (later editor of the *Observer*), who was serving with the Royal Marines and so saw the Dieppe raid 'at more or less close quarters'. He told Orwell that it had been 'an almost complete failure'. 'Only trivial damage' had been done to Dieppe's defences, according to Astor, and only one of the three main assault parties had reached its objective, while 'the others did not get far and many were massacred on the beach by artillery fire'. As for those tanks, about thirty or forty had, by Astor's account, been landed, but 'none got off again', and the 'newspaper photos which showed tanks apparently being brought back to England were intentionally misleading'. Astor took the view that 'the affair was definitely misrepresented in the press'.

Almost everyone lied about the Dieppe Raid and it has been described as 'one of the most blatant examples of disinformation of the entire war'. Even Frank Gillard, the BBC man on the spot, admitted later that he was 'almost ashamed' when he read back his own report. The fact that his eyewitness account pulled in huge audiences and attracted enthusiastic reviews from the public and some of his colleagues only made things worse. 'I read in BBC literature about my "memorable report" from Dieppe,' he remembered. 'To me it's memorable in all the wrong ways. It's memorable with shame and disgrace that I was there as the BBC's one and only eyewitness and I couldn't tell the story as I ought to have told it.'

The raid was driven by a mixture of political and military factors. Stalin was pushing hard for the opening of a western front to relieve the pressure on the Soviet Union, and Roosevelt had – somewhat unwisely – personally promised Vyacheslav Molotov, the Soviet foreign minister, that the Allies would attack in Europe in 1942. Churchill vetoed that on the grounds that Britain was not ready, and a high-profile raid seemed a good way of showing willing without committing too many resources. In military terms, it offered the possibility of a 'dress rehearsal' for the full-scale invasion that would one day come (that is why tanks were involved) and the RAF saw it as a way of drawing the Luftwaffe into a pitched battle which they felt confident of winning. Finally, it was seen as an opportunity to give Canadian troops – many of whom had been cooped up in camps in southern England for months of frustrating inaction – the chance to fight. The bulk of the assault troops who arrived off Dieppe on the morning of 19 August were Canadian – the British troops involved were specialist commandos, and the Americans and Free French provided no more than token contributions.

Dieppe has been described as 'the blackest day in Canadian military history'. Five thousand Canadian troops were engaged in the action, and 3,400 of them were killed, captured or wounded. The Canadian Army lost more men as prisoners of war that day than they did in all the rest of the European campaign. Dieppe was much better defended than the Allies had believed, and the terrain proved more difficult than their intelligence assessments had suggested; the planners had been forced to estimate the gradient of the beaches by looking at pre-war holiday snaps. Those troops that made it ashore endured what one historian has described as 'seven long and fear-filled hours on the smoke-shrouded beaches, where disciplined formations were, in a few minutes, reduced to scattered groups of badly shocked individuals, blind and deaf to all but the primeval need to survive'. In *Dieppe: August 19*, Eric Maguire writes that 'From junior officers to Company commanders, to Brigadiers, to Force Commander, the chain of command was reduced to a state of paralysis.' The raid began at 4.50 a.m., and just before 11.00 Allied commanders were forced to call a retreat. Almost none of the raid's objectives had been achieved.

Attempts to cover up the scale of the disaster only made things worse. At 6.15 a.m. an announcement on the BBC French Service alerted the world to the fact that an attack on Dieppe had begun. The broadcast was intended as a warning; it stated that this was only a raid, not a full-scale invasion, and advised French civilians to stay out of harm's way, avoiding any action that might provoke German reprisals. But the mere mention of fighting on the French coast was, of course, enough to excite interest at home.

Nothing else went out until late that evening, when a communiqué stated that heavy fighting was in progress (it had long since been over) and that it involved an unspecified number of Canadian troops. At midnight the BBC news reported 'According to a communiqué released by the Combined Operations Headquarters a short while ago reports received from the force commanders … show that as a combined operation the raid was a successful demonstration of coordination of all three services,' which may have been true as far as it went, but was scarcely the full story.

Reporters who had been on the scene found that their despatches were first held up, then heavily censored. 'There was an immediate stop put on all reports about fighting on the beaches,' Gillard

Frank Gillard with his 'Midget', the equipment used for recording in the field.

remembered. 'We were not allowed, for twenty-four hours, to say a word about that. "Deferred another six hours, deferred another six hours." Finally, the report I was allowed to go with concerned almost entirely the air action that was going on above our heads. Everything else was heavily censored and I was not able to tell the true story of Dieppe.' His despatch did include a reference to a landing craft with its sides smeared with blood, 'a grim sight in the morning sun', but that is as close as it comes to describing the terrible reality of what had happened.

On the French Service on the evening of the raid, Jean Marin's commentary made no mention of casualties and described the events of the day only in the most general terms. He stated that the surprise attack, 'in its scale, the numbers involved and the military methods deployed constituted a new stage in Allied strategy', and the broadcast ended by celebrating the fact that 'for the first time since June 1940 French soldiers have attacked the German enemy on French soil'. There were in fact only fifteen Free French commandos involved, and they were attached to a British unit.

The vagueness of the official Allied version of events left plenty of room for the German story to fill the airwaves. 'After a quiet start their propaganda machine got into gear,' wrote Eric Maguire, 'the principal line being that the British had been forced into a hasty and badly organised invasion attempt by pressure from Russia. This theory was pressed home by the enemy over a period of several weeks, and with the seed of doubt already planted in people's minds it is little wonder that the Dieppe raid came to be regarded both at home and abroad as an invasion attempt which had a deserved and bloody ending. British propaganda had simply no answer to that.' It was, it seemed, right back to the bad old days of the Scapa Flow attack, when the papers complained that 'a lie gets half-way round the world before truth can get its boots on'.

Writing after the war, Churchill claimed that Dieppe provided invaluable lessons for the D-Day landings almost two years later. 'Dieppe occupies a place of its own in the story of the war,' he argued, 'and the grim casualty figures must not class it as a failure. It was a costly but not unfruitful reconnaissance in force.' But in propaganda and reporting terms it was one of the darkest chapters in this story.

≈

'Safe home. Glad to see you back' – those, according to the broadcaster Jonathan Dimbleby, were the words with which the commissionaire at Broadcasting House greeted his father when in August 1942, the same month as the Dieppe raid, Richard Dimbleby returned after a three-year stint abroad. He had reported from France, North Africa, Greece, Turkey and the Middle East and, as he was to discover when he went on a speaking tour that autumn, his despatches had made him famous.

Within the BBC he had also earned a reputation for good living at Auntie's expense. Edward Ward – the Old Harrovian son of a viscount, so presumably no stranger to the finer things of life himself – was greatly impressed by the Dimbleby style when he was sent to cover for him in Cairo in 1941. 'Richard Dimbleby met me,' he recalled in his autobiography. 'After we had talked for a while he asked me what I was going to do about expenses. "Oh, I think I'll charge a flat rate of £2 a day," I said.' Dimbleby replied, 'My dear chap, you'll find you can't possibly live on that!' Dimbleby kept, as Ward observed, 'a large houseboat on the Nile with a staff of servants. He had a big Chrysler car with a chauffeur who looked like a Turkish admiral. Naturally he could not live on £2 a day.'

By the time Dimbleby returned to London, Ward had been captured at Tobruk and Charles Gardner, his other partner in the pioneering days of radio reporting, had left the BBC to join the RAF. With the honourable exceptions of Frank Gillard – who, his Dieppe performance notwithstanding, was a fine reporter – and Godfrey Talbot, who took over from Dimbleby in the Middle East, there were very few in Broadcasting House capable of doing the job; despite the popularity of Dimbleby's front-line reporting, the BBC had done little to build a corps of war correspondents. An assessment by the Foreign News Committee that winter lamented, 'We all share . . . feelings of disappointment, indeed of shame, that British radio should still be failing, after three years of war, to exploit its unique possibilities as a medium for reporting,' and concluded that the handful of BBC correspondents (or 'observers', as they were known) had 'made no impact on the public mind'. The director of outside broadcasts, Michael Standing, was equally damning; 'it is undeniable that the Corporation has so far failed almost dismally to exploit the unique broadcasting possibilities of the war,' he wrote.

The BBC bosses felt that some of the blame for this sorry state of affairs could be laid at the government's door, arguing that the Ministry of Information and the armed services were still giving preferential treatment to newspaper correspondents. In October 1942 Cecil Graves wrote formally to the Ministry of Information warning of dire consequences unless the government 'backs the BBC and puts its case at least as high as that of the Newspaper Proprietors Association'. His joint-director-general, R. W. Foot, returned to the fray in a note to Brendan Bracken. 'I don't care twopence about the prestige of the BBC or anything of that sort,' he declared, 'but I do care, as I know you do, that broadcasting should really be used to serve the country to the full extent of its possibilities, and until we can get away from the complete fallacy that broadcasting is a competitor to the Press, and therefore must be treated as if it were just another newspaper, the country must inevitably fail to receive from broadcasting the service to which it is obviously entitled.'

Five months after returning to Britain, Dimbleby provided everyone with a vivid illustration of what radio war reporting could do. On 6 January 1943 he became the first BBC correspondent to fly with the RAF on a bombing raid over Germany. His pilot was Wing Commander Guy Gibson, who would later become famous for leading the 'Dambusters' raid on the Möhne dam, and their target that night was Berlin. The flight got off to a bad start – Dimbleby managed to put a kink in his oxygen tube and passed out as the Lancaster climbed over the south coast of England. But he was revived in time for his first sight of anti-aircraft fire, and reported what he saw with his characteristic precision: 'It was bursting away from us and much lower. I didn't see any long streams of it soaring into the air as the pictures suggest: it burst in little yellow winking flashes and you couldn't hear it above the roar of the engines. Sometimes it closes in on you, and the mid – or tail – gunner will call up calmly and report its position to the captain so that he can dodge it.'

When they reached the German capital the ack-ack became so intense that 'for a moment it seemed impossible that we should miss it, and one burst lifted us into the air as though a giant hand had pushed up the belly of the machine.' Dimbleby described the 'great incandescent flowerbeds' spreading across Berlin as incendiary bombs hit the city, and the 'dull, ugly red as the fires of bricks and mortar and wood spread from chemical fires'. Looking down on the burning capital of the Nazi regime filled him with 'a great exultation', a revealing moment of emotion and a reminder that the BBC reporting ethic of the day was very far from 'impartial'. On the way back to Blighty, Dimbleby vomited in the cockpit. It cannot have been a comfortable flight, and he later wrote a note to Guy Gibson saying he had been 'paralysed with fright'.

He had good reason to be terrified, as the casualty rates among Bomber Command crews were shockingly high; at one point in 1942 it was estimated that they had no more than a 10 per cent chance of surviving a full tour of duty (the two BBC correspondents who lost their lives during the war, Guy Byam and Kent Stevenson, were both killed on bombing missions). But, as Dimbleby put it in his note to Gibson, the night 'gave me a unique chance to see for myself what is being done night after night in the name of Freedom', and because of his skills as a reporter he was able to share that experience with the audience. The piece only ran in the news, and that was cited in an internal BBC document as an example of the way the Corporation was failing to exploit what was 'surely unique broadcasting material'.

The RAF was delighted by Dimbleby's report and, according to Jonathan Dimbleby's biography of his father, 'the Air Ministry sought in future to deal with the BBC only through Richard Dimbleby'. He flew another twenty RAF missions in the course of the war.

≈

Two months after Dimbleby's flight over Berlin, the BBC as a whole had an opportunity to demonstrate how effective its reporting could be. In March 1943, in one of the odder and less well-known military adventures of the Second World War, Allied troops invaded Oxford-shire, mock-battling their way through the English countryside from London to Oxford over six days. It was another important stage of the planning for the fighting to come in France, and the BBC was allowed to cover the exercise (code-named Spartan) with a view to persuading the services that radio reporters could play a valuable role on the battlefield.

As S. J. de Lotbiniere, one of the BBC's 'team leaders' during the exercise, put it, 'Newspapers were restricted by the tradition of "one newspaper, one correspondent", and we were challenged to prove our case for a large team.' The BBC was given permission to deploy full teams, including recording cars, with both the friendly and the 'enemy' forces. The Corporation's men (and there were certainly no women involved at this stage) were told to report to Paddington Station on the morning of 6 March, equipped with helmets, camping equipment and return tickets to Oxford.

They were to operate under an 'as real' censorship regime, which was extremely tough and was explicitly designed with propaganda as well as security considerations in mind. 'The primary object of the Exercise is to practise the advance from a bridgehead and the control of air forces operating with the Army,' declared the 'Censorship Rulings for Operation Spartan'. 'It is particularly desirable that the offensive nature of the Exercise should be stressed ... The Exercise should not be described in any way as a "full dress rehearsal".'

Correspondents were instructed to be careful about detail: 'No indication may be given of the total numbers involved or of the total or relative strength of either force,' the 'Rulings' continued. 'It may, however, be said that the Exercise is the "biggest ever".' Some of the instructions make obvious sense in security terms: Section 8, sub-section e, for example, stated that, 'No reference to the extent, nature, success, or lack of success of decoys, dummies, or deception methods will be allowed.' Others are more puzzling. The press photographers who were also allowed on the exercise were advised that 'No formation signs may be shown other than the Giant Panda and the signs of the Guards Armed Division and the Canadian Army Tank Brigade.'

The censorship regulations did not, however, prevent the use of what today we would call 'colour', and the BBC's correspondents responded by painting the kind of word pictures that work so well on radio. Here is Wynford Vaughan-Thomas speaking on the evening of 7 March, at an early stage of Spartan:

> I am speaking to you from the Front Line – or, at least, from that vague No-Man's Land that's the Front Line in modern mobile warfare. I am crouched actually in a ditch beside the camouflaged anti-tank guns – right on top of Bald Hill, and I'm looking out over the Valley of the Thames, and right in the centre of the picture – looks absolutely lovely in the cold spring sunshine – just about five miles away from us is Oxford. At the moment Oxford is held by the Germans. It gives one a strange feeling looking across this country to know that you are looking right into hostile territory. I've got a young Canadian captain with me – he comes from Winnipeg – and he and his company of the Royal Winnipeg Rifles have had a tough time getting here. They had a thirty miles route march and then they had hardly any sleep; in fact they're looking pretty rough, with a three days' growth of beard, and dirty, and bleary-eyed, but they're in good spirits because we've got the high ground overlooking Oxford and the enemy. And I'm lifting up my head for a minute from the shelter – not that we can see much of the enemy – he seems to have gone to ground; our own boys have done the same. They're camouflaged in woods to the right of us, in hedges and ditches, and you can't see a thing of them, but I am just going to borrow the captain's binoculars and look out now and see if I can see something of the Nazis.

Vaughan-Thomas then interviewed his Canadian captain, and asked him whether he had 'seen anything of the Nazis?' The young man from Winnipeg played along magnificently. 'We have nothing but reports from forward "Recky" elements,' he said. 'They claim to have traced them down to that rear of the high hill here on our left. They seem to be in quite some force; it's not worrying us a great deal though; I feel certain – through the boys – that we have the situation well in hand.'

The great trick of this style of reporting was that it evoked the atmosphere of front-line life without giving away the sort of detail that might worry the military censors; Vaughan-Thomas brought the listener into his ditch without any need to mention Giant Pandas or troop numbers.

Since it was possible that engineers and correspondents might, in a real battle, be killed or injured, the BBC encouraged them to learn one another's skills. T. Vizard, the broadcast assistant who recorded Vaughan-Thomas's despatch, also interviewed a couple of residents of Henley-on-Thames himself, and they gamely told him that rations had improved since the 'Germans' left. Vizard had the wit to add in his despatch, 'They are both English-speaking, luckily.' He finished by asking his interviewees (who were introduced as a shopkeeper and a housewife) to sum up the reaction of the people of Henley to the arrival of British troops. 'Well I should say hurrah for Tommy,' said one, and 'It's hurrah for Tommy and Henley-on-Thames,' added the other.

The Southland forces – as the Allied troops were code-named – pushed ahead and moved into Oxford itself. At noon the following day Dimbleby took up the story. 'I am talking at a street corner in Oxford,' he said, 'which was entered by our forces last night after the enemy had evacuated the city. We have paused here to make this report before driving through the city and out northeast – the general direction in which our Canadian infantry are advancing.' The exercise planners had appointed Field Marshal Gerd von Rundstedt as the commander of German forces (he was the real German commander-in-chief in Western Europe at the time) and Dimbleby allowed himself a little strategic speculation. 'Von Rundstedt . . . is a wily man, and we can only believe that his withdrawal and swing northeast is designed to give him a better chance of resisting us at some later point, or even counter-attacking,' he mused. 'Whether the reported approach of some of his tanks at Headington is a counter-attack of significance, I don't yet know – I may be able to say more about that tonight.'

Like Vaughan-Thomas, Dimbleby included some imaginative local colour: 'The people of Oxford are taking it all with admirable calm. While the enemy was withdrawing from the city, they remained inside their houses, hearing the crashing explosions as the lovely old

Richard Dimbleby after a mission with the RAF.

bridges of the city are destroyed one after another. When our people appeared on the banks of the river, the people were already gathered on the far bank to welcome them.'

More than ninety despatches were filed in the course of Operation Spartan, and the BBC teams came back fizzing with enthusiasm. The features man put up a list of suggested broadcasts, including 'The Fall of Aylesbury', 'Street Fighting in Towcester' and 'The Great Tank Clash'. On 23 March the BBC played the best of the recorded material – linked by the distinctive tones of the great John Snagge – to a high-powered group that included Sir James Grigg, the civil servant whom Churchill had unexpectedly promoted to the post of secretary of state for war the previous month; Sir Ronald Adam, the adjutant general; and Sir Bernard Paget, the commander-in-chief of Home Forces. This 'bumper audience' gathered in the office of R. W. Foot, the joint-director-general, and they were mightily impressed by what they heard, especially by what was described as the 'sound photography' recorded by some of the BBC teams. The military men advised that 'the less we tried to deal with strategy, interviews with Commanders in Chief etc., and the nearer we got to actual operations, interviews with regimental commanders, down to the fighting soldiers, the greater the interest and the greater the freedom from censorship troubles'.

As a direct result of the Spartan experiment, Paget agreed to take BBC correspondents on attachment with the regular army to, as an Auntie memo put it, 'train our people in general military routine and practice; to give them a chance of really getting to know the modern British soldier'.

The BBC had already begun to work on the creation of a specialist team of war reporters, and with the positive official reaction to the coverage of Spartan the final piece of the jigsaw fell into place. There was some debate about what the new breed of broadcasters should be called; there was talk of a 'Radio Commando Unit', a 'Front Line Reporting Unit' and even a 'Warcasting Unit'. In May, A. P. Ryan came up with the term 'War Reporting Unit' and it stuck. Ryan added a characteristic postscript: 'Personally it seems that all that matters is to have a handy name and get on with it.' One of the greatest adventures in broadcasting history had begun.

The one really stuffy review of the Spartan episode came not from the military but from Richard Dimbleby. His generally thoughtful report on the lessons of the exercise included a passage which reflected the grandee who required his chauffeur to dress like a Turkish admiral rather than the inspired watcher and wordsmith who had flown over Berlin a couple of months earlier: 'I have learnt how to conduct myself in the field and at formation Headquarters by three years of hard practice. Last week I was given as engineer and travelling companion a young man who had never worn a uniform in his life until two days before, and who would most certainly never have passed the eliminating test of officer cadetship. He wore his field cap at a rakish angle and had a cigarette drooping from his lips from early morning until he went to sleep at night. He addressed private soldiers, military policemen and

'This is the B.B.C. Could you arrange to capture an island for the 6 o'clock news?' *NEB*, Daily Mail, 14 June 1943.

sentries as "old boy". At least on one occasion, in my presence, he addressed an elderly War Office General by calling at him "I say", again the cigarette dangling. He kept it there while he talked, and when he had finished gave a friendly wave and turned away. The cigarette was still there.'

THE CRUSADING SPIRIT

STEWART MACPHERSON WAS THE son of a tractor-factory manager in the Canadian midwest, 'plough jockey country', as he liked to call it. In 1936 he took ship to Britain and found his first BBC berth as an occasional ice-hockey commentator, playing heavily on the happy accident of his childhood familiarity with the game. In 1942 he was offered a permanent job in the Outside Broadcasts Unit, and when the War Reporting Unit (WRU) was formed his 'compelling objective was to become a member'. He was selected alongside his fellow Outside Broadcasts specialist Wynford Vaughan-Thomas, who had made his name as the Welsh-language commentator at the Coronation of George VI and earned his war-reporting spurs during the Blitz.

Guy Byam (or Byam-Corstiaens, as he appears in the BBC's administrative files) had already seen action by the time he joined; he had served in the Royal Naval Volunteer Reserve and when his ship was sunk in 1940 he managed to swim to safety. He had suffered 'flash-blindness' from an explosive shell during the engagement and had lost the sight of one eye permanently. He was working as a sub in the French Service (he had studied at the Sorbonne before going up to Cambridge) when he was talent-spotted for the WRU.

Frank Gillard had been a teacher before the war, Howard Marshall was an Oxford rugby Blue and former sports commentator, and Pierre Lefèvre had been broadcasting on the French Service as an actor and impressionist. Chester Wilmot, one of the greatest of them, was poached from the Australian Broadcasting Corporation (he came in on a star salary of £1,000 a year, which put him on a par with Dimbleby). The BBC's ambition was a corps of correspondents 'strong enough in numbers and quality to aim at covering adequately all major battles on land and sea'. Auntie wanted men who could 'add much needed distinction' to the coverage, and she cast her net wide.

The jobs were eagerly sought after, despite the dangers. When Frank Gillard was informed that his salary had been increased to £680, he wrote a jaunty note back to the administrative officer, News Division: 'This is excellent news, I only hope that I live to enjoy it.' There was a strong *esprit de corps*, and the team was animated by a real sense of mission. 'The BBC is the last refuge of truth in a world that has lost its standards and values,' Howard Marshall wrote to the director-general. 'There is a hunger for truth ... The BBC must meet it.'

Selection for this elite group did not, however, mean freedom from BBC bureaucracy. Vaughan-Thomas was pursued across Europe over two stop-watches he failed to hand in when he left Outside Broadcasts and was sent a memo about this urgent matter the day before he covered the Allied entry into Rome. The administrative officer responsible had the grace to add, in a handwritten PS, 'Have heard a lot from you recently, with interest!'

One of the lessons drawn from the Spartan exercise was that correspondents needed a basic understanding of military strategy and tactics. 'It was pretty clear that those lacking military knowledge were apt to flounder for fear of making errors,' wrote the Outside Broadcasts director Michael Standing, 'and also were unable to appreciate the full significance of local developments. It is imperative, therefore, that anyone accompanying the Army on actual operations should be thoroughly versed in this subject.' Correspondents were duly given a reading list of military books, and most were sent on the attachments offered by the army.

They were to be given the honorary military rank of captain. The army opposed granting the same privilege to BBC engineers, but they were eventually designated 'engineer correspondents' and accepted at the same rank as their on-air colleagues, although their pay was based on that of first lieutenants. The War Office regulations stated that 'it must be accepted as a guiding principle that an accredited war correspondent is entitled to be treated in all respects as an officer, until he has shown himself to be unworthy of such trust. Complete frankness on one hand; loyal discretion on the other; and mutual co-operation in the great and almost sacred task of leading and steadying public opinion in times of national stress or crisis.' The regulations laid down, with heraldic precision, that all correspondents should wear a 'Cap badge in gilt worsted the letter "C" in relief on a half-dome, surrounded by an endless cable – worn on a disc of green cloth', and carry the words 'British War Correspondent' as their shoulder title. And the BBC advised its men to adapt their behaviour to army customs; 'be scrupulously careful about giving and returning salutes,' the guidance read.

In the class-bound British Army of the 1940s, Dimbleby's concerns about the importance of proper military bearing and behaviour made more sense than they do today. The country boy Stewart MacPherson was horrified to find himself seconded for training to the Grenadier Guards, the senior regiment of the Guards Division – even Dimbleby recognized that troops of the Royal Household had 'unnecessary mannerisms' and took 'longer to thaw' than most of the army. 'I complained bitterly,' MacPherson wrote in his autobiography. 'I was a Canadian and wouldn't fit in at all. I wouldn't have a chance.' He was picked up at Thetford station in Norfolk by 'four of the tallest soldiers I had ever seen' and tried to engage them in conversation, but 'the only reply I could squeeze from any of them was the word "Sir".' When he arrived at their camp he made a hash of saluting the sergeant major, almost knocking his own cap from his head, and 'When I arrived at the Adjutant's office I found he was wearing a monocle. Well this ties it! I thought.'

MacPherson's Grenadiers really put him through his paces. 'Their training involved climbing hills, wading rivers, sleeping in the rain,' he wrote. 'I did all of it including carrying my recording gear.' The shared physical hardship helped overcome social barriers, and MacPherson bonded with the grand guardsmen. On his last night in camp a couple of officers suggested 'a walk before dinner', and when MacPherson agreed he discovered that 'the intention of these gentlemen was to cover six miles in an hour which was faster than I could travel on a

Training for D-Day: Stewart MacPherson of the War Reporting Unit.

bicycle'. He was left well behind, and eventually the monocled adjutant sent a despatch rider to pick him up. MacPherson felt his honour was being tested. 'I looked at the lad, who was grinning, and I said, "You tell the Adjutant to take your motor cycle and ..."' It was reported to him later that his defiance had won the regiment's commanding officer a £4 bet with the adjutant, and when he finally staggered into camp his arrival was greeted with 'shouts of delight'.

The bonding process was to prove as important as the physical fitness. In 1946 the BBC published *War Report*, a collection of the best despatches broadcast by members of the WRU, with an introductory history of the unit by the writer Desmond Hawkins (who made his mark after the war by developing the BBC's natural history programmes in Bristol). 'Perhaps that was the greatest benefit of the months of training,' he wrote, 'the winning of the army's respect and friendship. When invasion came, the correspondents were no longer meddlesome civilians in a kind of khaki fancy-dress; they knew the army jargon and the army ways. They were men of the army who happened to have an unusual and specialist job.'

Today most BBC journalists would feel queasy about such a close relationship with their military minders; during the Falklands War the BBC's editorial guidelines famously stated that 'We should try to avoid using "our" when we mean British. We are not Britain. We are the BBC.' But the bond between the men of the WRU and their military hosts was a natural consequence of the BBC's understanding of its wartime role, and no one then questioned the Corporation's patriotism in the way they did during the Falklands campaign. The foreword to *War Report* was contributed by no less a military figure than Field Marshal Montgomery, who had commanded Allied ground forces on D-Day. 'I think it is right to say that the key-note of this campaign was the Crusading Spirit, which inspired all ranks of the Allied Expeditionary Force,' he wrote, 'and which enabled them to face up to the great and often continuous demands that were made on their energy and enthusiasm and courage. This Spirit had many and deep sources, and the BBC was one of the means by which this Spirit was fostered. In this way these Correspondents made no mean contribution to victory.'

The spirit of cooperating fully with the military even extended to the area of censorship. WRU correspondents were sent on a course at the School of Military Intelligence at Matlock in Derbyshire to learn 'how to avoid trouble' – in other words, how to censor themselves. This involved being taken to a mock German headquarters where a 'Nazi' intelligence officer played a collection of recordings made by a 'British correspondent'. The intelligence officer then analysed these to show how 'innocent-seeming remarks' could be converted into 'significant military information'. The Matlock course also included information on German military organization and how to protect secrets under interrogation as a prisoner of war. It was followed by a further week's training with censors at the Ministry of Information in London. Successful self-censorship was, as Desmond Hawkins pointed out in his official history, much more important for radio correspondents than it was for their colleagues in print. 'It is easy enough to cancel a word here or there in a written despatch,' he wrote, 'easy enough for a sub-editor to re-write a phrase or a sentence. In a recording the only person who can rewrite even a single word is the original speaker; and deletions are much more difficult to handle once they are on disks than they would be in print.'

In his review of the Spartan exercise, Richard Dimbleby raised the practical question of transport. 'The Austin saloon I had during *Spartan* was grossly overloaded and rendered top-heavy by a wire mattress spread over its roof,' he reported. 'I doubt if its springs would hold much more than a week or two on the roads of Europe.' He argued that an observer's 'whole efficiency depends on rapid mobility', so a 'fast or utility' vehicle was 'essential'. Dimbleby also put in a plea for jeeps; 'these fast little vehicles,' he wrote, 'ample for conducting officer and observer, are ideal for use well forward'.

An even more decisive factor in determining a correspondent's ability to move around the battlefield was the weight of his recording equipment. The BBC had made huge strides in recording techniques in the course of the war, but the location recordings made by Dimbleby and his colleagues in France and North Africa all required equipment installed in trucks or cars. As late as January 1943, as the plans of the WRU were being laid, the BBC's superintendent of sound recording was arguing that 'battery operated recording equipment of any kind was something of a freak' and that the task of producing equipment light enough to be carried into battle by one or even two men was more or less hopeless.

The engineers worked on the problem throughout 1943 and eventually produced what became known as 'the Midget'. 'This portable recording unit, weighing only 40 lb., was the lightest in the world,' wrote Desmond Hawkins, with more than a dash of BBC pride. 'It carried twelve double-sided disks giving a total of more than one hour's recording; a microphone on a spring clip could be attached to anything from the branch of a tree to the rim of a steel helmet, and the detachable dry-battery unit was ready wired to put in with a single connector. Operation was so simple that anyone could use it without the assistance of an engineer – unlike a truck unit, which needed a technician.'

Those who used the Midget remembered it rather differently. One member of the WRU described it as 'cumbersome and difficult to hump around ... from slit trench to slit trench under enemy fire'. It had to be set down on level ground and cranked into motion with a handle – like an old-fashioned car – and there was no play-back facility, so correspondents could never be quite sure whether their recordings had taken. But Frank Gillard, who waded ashore on the Normandy beaches carrying his Midget above his head, said later that 'most of the really vivid and historic and memorable actuality recordings of World War II ... were actually made on these little Midgets, and without them the sound record of World War II would be a very poor thing indeed.' The success of the War Reporting Unit owed every bit as much to this technical advance as it did to journalistic enterprise.

≈

In November 1943 there was another reshuffling of the cards at the top of the BBC pack, and this time it was to have a direct and lasting effect on the BBC's journalism. Sir Cecil Graves surrendered to the ill-health that had plagued him throughout his time as joint-director-general and resigned. R. W. Foot became the sole director-general, but created the new job of editor-in-chief and appointed William Haley, a director of the Reuters news agency, to the job. Haley was an experienced newspaperman – he had begun his career as a reporter on *The Times* and had a long association with the *Manchester Guardian* – and when Foot himself resigned in March 1944 he became the first journalist to be appointed BBC director-general, combining the role with his original position of editor-in-chief.

Haley had strong editorial views, and fostered the journalistic culture that flourished at the BBC after the war. His view of the way the BBC reported bombing raids was characteristic. 'The BBC policy regarding the bombing of Germany is that it is a scientific operation,' he ruled in April 1944, 'not to be stunted, to be gloated over or to be dealt with any other way than the most objective factual reporting arising from the communiqués and from material obtained from Air Headquarters or Bomber stations.' He probably would not have approved of the 'great exultation' that Richard Dimbleby had felt on his first sortie over Berlin a year earlier.

THE BIGGEST ASPIDISTRA
IN THE WORLD

T HE QUESTION OF WHETHER the BBC should regard all Germans as enemies was never entirely resolved, and the tensions between 'black' and 'white' propagandists became more and more acute as the campaign to liberate Europe drew closer. Sefton Delmer's second big venture into black broadcasting brought him into direct conflict with the BBC. And it was – as he tells the story – partly inspired by Auntie's prissy ways.

The Admiralty had established a psychological warfare department of its own – Naval Intelligence Department 17 – and asked Delmer to train its officers in propaganda techniques. In their offices overlooking Horse Guards Parade, Ian Fleming (then working in Naval Intelligence under the code-name 17F) introduced Delmer to his friend Robert Harling, a typographer and novelist who in post-war life became the editor of *House and Garden*, and Donald McLachlan, a former teacher at Winchester, later the founding editor of the *Sunday Telegraph*. These two became Delmer's star pupils, and between them they cooked up a plan for undermining the morale of German naval crews. It involved, however, the cooperation of the BBC, and here they hit resistance. Hugh Carleton Greene, the German Service editor, allowed Harling and McLachlan to produce a special naval programme for broadcast, but 'he would not let them write a special naval news bulletin. The news had to be written by the BBC and no outsiders were allowed to interfere with it.' This was, in Delmer's judgement, a serious setback, because 'in my view, and that of Donald McLachlan, carefully selected news items, skilfully presented are the most subversive propaganda force of all'. Delmer added, 'The result of this BBC obstinacy was that the Admiralty turned more and more to Black.'

This gave him a powerful new ally in an ambition he had nurtured for some time: the creation of a black news operation. His efforts in this direction had until then been frustrated by the restricted broadcasting facilities at his disposal; Der Chef's fulminations were recorded in a basic studio rigged up at a country house, and then transmitted from the grounds of Woburn. Delmer believed that to produce a convincing news channel he needed a more sophisticated studio and the facility to broadcast live. And that meant a land-grab on one of the most fought-over pieces of secret kit Britain acquired in the course of the Second World War: the giant 650-kilowatt radio transmitter known as 'Aspidistra'.

Aspidistra was ordered secretly from the United States on Churchill's personal authority in May 1941. The cost is recorded by David Garnett at the oddly precise figure of £111,801.4s.10d – some £5.7 million in today's money. The prime minister was persuaded by a technical report claiming that 'This apparatus would create a raiding Dreadnought of the Ether firing broadsides at unpredictable times at unpredictable objectives of the enemy's radio propaganda machine,' and its code-name was taken from a popular Gracie Fields song that began:

> For years we had an aspidistra in a flower pot
> On the whatnot, near the 'atstand in the 'all
> It didn't seem to grow 'til one day our brother Joe
> Had a notion that he'd make it strong and tall
> So he's crossed it with an acorn from an oak tree
> And he's planted it against the garden wall
> It shot up like a rocket, 'til it's nearly reached the sky
> It's the biggest aspidistra in the world
> We couldn't see the top of it, it got so bloomin' high
> It's the biggest aspidistra in the world.

Churchill's interest in propaganda was fitful – his attempt to take control of the BBC was almost absent-minded – but he seems to have been fascinated by the power and sophistication of this enormous gadget and asked almost obsessively for progress reports on its erection. On 7 September 1942 Robert Bruce Lockhart recorded in his diary: 'A busy day which began with a typical minute from the P.M.; "Please state what advantages Aspidistra can give us (8 lines) and report every three days what day it will be ready to function."'

By early October installation work on the masts at Crowborough in Sussex was well advanced and the first tests at full power took place on 12 October to 'great excitement'. But there was a delay in securing extra valves for the system. 'Another minute – a tiresome one – from the P.M. on valves,' Bruce Lockhart wrote on 16 October. 'He wants to know if we have built this vast machine without making proper provision for spares. Answer is – of course we did, but there is a bottleneck for radio equipment in Washington. Also wanted to know how long a valve will last!' The 'very fine' new studios linked to Aspidistra were built at Milton Bryant, near the PWE's offices at Woburn, and on 21 October Bruce Lockhart noted with relief, 'Heard today that tubes for Aspidistra have arrived.'

The rows over how Aspidistra should be used began even before it was declared operational and continued right up until the end of the war. They eventually drew in the Political Warfare Executive, the BBC, the chiefs of staff, the Americans at the Supreme Headquarters of the Allied Expeditionary Force in Europe, the foreign secretary and the minister of information. There were some notoriously ill-tempered exchanges between senior figures who should have known better, and the emotions that swirled around seem out of all proportion to the issues at stake. The PWE had been made financially responsible for the deal, and the decision to buy the transmitter had been kept secret from the BBC, so the spooks understandably believed they would have first call on its use. But the BBC had to be let in on the secret when it emerged that this 'Dreadnought of the Ether' might interfere with the Corporation's own transmissions.

The BBC's head of engineering, Sir Noel Ashbridge, immediately raised several objections to the project, complaining that 'the scheme had been carried out extravagantly', and that 'there had been no previous consultation with BBC engineers'. More importantly for the future, however, he also argued that 'firing broadsides at unpredictable times at unpredictable objectives of the enemy's radio propaganda machine' would constitute jamming, and that the Cabinet had, as a matter of policy, decided against jamming on the grounds that 'we did not stand to gain in a radio war. If we jammed German broadcasts they would jam the BBC Home Service.' It would be much more sensible, the BBC argued, to use Aspidistra to boost the BBC's own overseas broadcasting.

History handed the BBC a convenient coincidence. As Aspidistra came on stream in November 1942, the Allies were preparing for Operation Torch, the invasion of French North Africa. Morocco, Algeria and Tunisia were controlled by Vichy, but the Americans and British believed that many of the troops in the colonies were sympathetic to de Gaulle and the Free French, and could be won over. So propaganda was an important element in the Torch strategy. The main propaganda objective during the operation was identified as 'to make known the official proclamations by President Roosevelt and the Prime Minister to the population of France and North Africa', and it was agreed that the BBC French Service – with its established reputation – was the right medium for doing this. Aspidistra could supply the extra power needed to ensure that its transmission reached North Africa clearly – it was estimated that it increased the effective range of French Service transmissions by 175 per cent – and it was duly called into service for the first time.

'We come among you only to destroy and eliminate your enemies,' Roosevelt told the French forces. 'Give us your co-operation . . . Long Live Eternal France,' and his words came clearly over the air. Round One in the great Aspidistra war thus went to the BBC, although David Garnett claimed the credit for PWE; 'thanks to Aspidistra,' he wrote in his official PWE history, 'PWE was able to overcome the jamming of the BBC French Services at this crucial moment in the formation of French opinion . . . Aspidistra had done all that it had been allowed to do with triumphant success on its first trial.'

The spooks could not quite resist the temptation to dabble in a little black broadcasting during this episode. For a couple of quarter-hour periods they retuned Aspidistra to take over the wavelength of a

Vichy-controlled station broadcasting from the Moroccan capital, Rabat; this had the unfortunate consequence of briefly convincing the British Admiralty that Rabat had fallen to Allied forces. It was, Garnett conceded, 'an early example of the difficulty of carrying out counterfeit operations without informing all on our own side who might be misled by them. This difficulty dogged the Aspidistra plans until the end.'

≈

Sefton Delmer's claim for broadcasting rights on Aspidistra was cooked up over a champagne-fuelled lunch with Donald McLachlan just before Christmas 1942, when the Dreadnought of the Ether had been doing its stuff for the BBC for a couple of months. The idea was to create a full-blown German radio station, mixing news and entertainment programmes, which would present itself as an official Nazi broadcaster. The black propagandists could then slip unsettling pieces of created news into the bulletins to undermine German morale. Delmer sold the idea to an enthusiastic Robert Bruce Lockhart, who went in to bat on his behalf. 'Bruce,' Delmer wrote in his autobiography, 'was too old a hand in Whitehall politics not to be aware that a live news bulletin, complete with music, greetings from home and all the other attractions of a German forces radio, was going to bring us slap up against the BBC. For just as the Church of England regards the British heaven as its established monopoly, so did the BBC, in those days before Commercial Television, regard the British ether as theirs.'

Early in 1943 Delmer took possession of the smart new studios at Milton Bradley and found 'everything ... the last word in up-to-dateness and efficiency'. He eventually managed to secure permission for not one, but two full-dress black radio stations, and his admirers regarded them as the masterpieces of his propaganda work. *Deutscher Kurzwellensender Atlantik* (German Shortwave Radio Atlantic) was aimed at the navy, especially U-boat crews, and *Soldatensender Calais* (Soldiers' Radio Calais), which was broadcast on medium wave and went on the air in November 1943, was directed at German land forces. Both followed a similar formula, mixing entertainment and music with news and comment in a way that suggested the stations were legitimate Nazi organs. Some of the music was specially performed by a German band which had been captured by the Eighth Army while touring North Africa and sent back to Britain, and the Americans obligingly provided 'the latest and best American dance music' to leaven the mix. News and comment items drew heavily on intelligence gleaned from interviews with German PoWs, which helped make the programmes sound authentically 'German'.

The most useful material came from none other than Dr Goebbels himself. Goebbels had established a system for disseminating news information to the offices of the official Nazi news agency, the *Deutsches Nachrichtenbüro* or DNB, through teleprinters known as *Hellschreibers* (after Rudolf Hell, the German inventor who developed them in the 1920s). The DNB's London correspondent left his behind when he abandoned ship at the outbreak of war, and it was found in his office in the Reuters building. The *Hellschreiber* ensured that Delmer's radio stations received official Nazi announcements and news flashes as fast as their legitimate counterparts in Germany and Occupied Europe.

Delmer's guiding principle was 'Cover, dirt, cover cover, dirt, cover, dirt'; he and his team tried to introduce unsettling news and information in ways that would not undermine the stations' apparent authenticity. They would, for example, broadcast alarming stories about imaginary epidemics, framed as if they were evidence of the wonders of life under the Nazis. The following news item related to conditions in the 'KLV camps' to which German children had been evacuated to escape allied bombing: 'Dr Conti, the *Reichsführer* for Physicians, has congratulated the medical officers at the KLV camps in the Gau Wartheland for the selfless devotion with which they are fighting the diphtheria epidemic among the children in their care. He has expressed his satisfaction at their success in overcoming the tragic lack of medicaments, and reducing deaths by an average of sixty a week.'

British intelligence also helped with material. A German military order circulated in August 1942 stated that those on active service were eligible for leave if their homes were bombed, and a copy was discovered in a stash of captured documents. Delmer's black stations regularly reminded the audience of the contents of 'OKW [Wehrmacht High Command] order 967/42g' and helpfully provided regular updates on which German streets had recently enjoyed the attentions of the RAF.

Another favourite theme, aimed in particular at the German troops garrisoning France, was that the German High Command regarded France as a much less important theatre than the Eastern Front – with the implication that the occupying forces in France could therefore expect no reinforcements when D-Day came. There was an extra twist to this message. 'Units which show themselves smart and efficient,' Calais claimed, 'are drafted to the Eastern Front' – or, as Sefton Delmer put it, 'Promotion in France is a sure way to death in Russia.'

It was of course extremely difficult to assess the effectiveness of these tricks; the kind of fan mail that arrived at the BBC from France was unlikely to find its way to The Rookery from grateful listeners in Germany. But Delmer was able to point to the evidence of a number of captured German documents which expressed concern about the impact of his stations. An SS report about Calais in the spring of 1944 stated that 'the chief effect of the station's news transmissions, which have been described as psychologically excellent, arises from the practice of giving absolutely unexceptionable information, which has been carried verbatim in the German News Service, and mixing in with it a number of isolated, more or less tendentious items'. The result, the document concludes, had been just what Delmer would have hoped for; 'since New Year,' it states, 'observers in Munich and the provinces point out with all urgency that the transmitter has caused the greatest unrest and confusion among the population by news concerning the situation at the fronts and at home, and that the population is showing ever increasing trust in the station's news service as its reports have shown themselves more or less correct'.

After the war an even more treasured review from Dr Goebbels himself came to light. He noted in his diary that the Calais station 'does a very clever propaganda job and from what is put on the air, one can gather that the British know exactly what they have destroyed in Berlin and what they have not'.

Delmer's successes were not always welcomed at the BBC. 'Although Aspidistra had only been lent to them by our department, long possession had made the BBC regard it as theirs by right. That it should be transferred to those rough, vulgar fellows of the "Black" was unthinkable,' Delmer wrote. When, in July 1943, Delmer first proposed using Aspidistra's medium-wave capability to broadcast the Calais station and to increase the reach of *Atlantik*, the idea met stiff BBC resistance. Ivone Kirkpatrick, who represented the BBC at PWE meetings, argued that 'Black is alright on short wave, but if you get on the medium wave with all your lies and distortions, you will undermine the whole currency value of British propaganda as a purveyor of truth.'

The arguments advanced in support of this were sometimes contradictory. The BBC contended that, 'With a powerful transmitter there would be no secrecy about this news service which would be monitored everywhere. Thus the Allies would be as easily deceived as the Germans,' but also that 'within some short period listeners would realise that it was not a German station and would therefore assume it was of British origin and that British propaganda would stand convicted of acting a lie'.

Nevertheless, the BBC managed to persuade both Bruce Lockhart and Brendan Bracken into what Delmer and his allies regarded as 'the fantastic standpoint that to deceive our friends on shortwave was perfectly admissible, but to do so on medium wave would be criminal and dangerous'. Delmer put his case in a minute to Bruce Lockhart, who was his immediate superior: 'I am entirely unable to accept the view – which I know has been put forward to you very forcibly this weekend in my absence by some of my colleagues – that there is something in itself dishonourable and damaging about deceptions.' The wrangling went on for nearly four months before the Calais station (which, because it was so close to a real German station, was sometimes described as 'grey' rather than 'black') was allowed on to the air.

Aspidistra was not the only source of friction between the BBC and the Political Warfare Executive. The PWE's attempts to influence the BBC's overseas broadcasts were constantly frustrated, and in a lecture given after the war Bruce Lockhart reflected that 'practical experience proved very soon that control of the BBC is quite futile unless the controllers are next door to the microphone. Not unnaturally the BBC resent interference by people who were buried in the country ...'

The main burden of fighting these battles on the BBC's side fell on the shoulders of Ivone Kirkpatrick. After his bureaucratic skirmishes at meetings of the PWE, Kirkpatrick would drop into Harman Grisewood's office to gossip about the day's events, and Grisewood came to think of many of the people we have met in these chapters 'like characters in a long Tolstoyan novel which I was being compelled to study like a book for an exam'. Ivone Kirkpatrick, he recalled, 'was rather different. He was a character in the novel, but he was becoming a "real life" character too. In more and more detail he would talk over with me episodes and highlights which amused or exasperated him.'

Grisewood summed up the culture clash that lay at the root of Kirkpatrick's trials: 'The main structure of the "novel" was the tension between the PWE people, with headquarters at the ducal mansion at Woburn, and the BBC people at Bush House. The tension was basically a power struggle in which the men at Woburn wanted to dominate and direct the BBC's service in detail. The Woburn people operated several secret broadcasting stations which were meant to be deceptive. These were called "black" stations, whereas Bush House was "white" and open. The black operators developed their own psychology which was aggressive and superior. The Bush House people were defensive and suspicious. PWE were responsible for the policy, both of the black and white stations, but the BBC had the right to refuse any detail which conflicted with its reputation or harmed its credibility.'

In early 1942, the PWE's London headquarters was moved to Bush House, the home of the BBC's European Services, in an attempt to deal with some of these tensions. But the move brought the culture clash between the two into even starker relief. One lift in the building led to a world where truth was king, another to a world dedicated to deception and trickery. Kirkpatrick was a figure of calm authority amid the feuding tribes, 'omnicompetent and always active'. Grisewood describes how 'his fine gold pencil would flash across the page in correction of a news bulletin or a talk to the French about their naval establishments or a satirical dialogue in German'. He 'showed no self-conscious pride in these accomplishments', Grisewood tells us, but 'did what he did in order to keep the thing going'. He adds that

Kirkpatrick 'in the Tolstoyan drama was, for me, a hero of dutifulness which I came to admire very deeply'.

≈

Early in 1944 a new front was opened in Kirkpatrick's struggles with the secret services: the Special Operations Executive was making such heavy demands on the airwaves for the coded messages it sent to its agents that it threatened to overwhelm regular BBC programmes altogether.

SOE had come a very long way since Georges Bégué was para-chuted into France in May 1941. Its original offices were at 64 Baker Street, but by the final stages of the war they had spread across 6 acres of Marylebone and stretched all the way to Portman Square. So many grand country houses had been requisitioned for training that it was waggishly suggested that SOE stood for 'stately 'omes of England'. Sabotage was taught at Stevenage, black propaganda at Watford and 'field craft' and guerrilla tactics in the Highlands. In the course of the war nearly 300 agents were deployed, and SOE's field of operations spread right across the European theatre. France remained a priority, and of course became even more of one as D-Day approached; that secret army that Colonel Britton had dreamed of mobilizing would finally be called to arms, and SOE's agents were to be given the task of coordinating Resistance action as the Germans faced the Allied forces in Normandy.

Despite some notorious failures – most notably the penetration of the Prosper network by German military intelligence – Maurice Buckmaster, the leader of SOE's F (French) Section, had, by 1944, built a substantial and sophisticated organization in France. There were some sixty networks operating across the country – with code-names including Detective, Archdeacon, Physician, Stockbroker and Musician, so that the list reads a little like an excerpt from the rules of the board game Cluedo. And the system for dropping arms and other supplies was well developed (4,000 tons of material was dropped into France in the three years between the springs of 1941 and 1944).

But running all these networks inevitably involved greater communication between London and the field, and that in turn put pressure on BBC airtime. In the autumn of 1943, BBC officials were already urging SOE to 'prune' its messages because the volume was 'seriously interfering with the BBC's news service'. MI6 – SIS, as it was commonly known – was also using the BBC to communicate with its agents by this stage, and the BBC complained that the failure of the two secret organizations to coordinate their messages made life even more complicated.

The pace of arms drops picked up as D-Day approached, and that of course meant yet more coded messages. An internal SOE memo on 7 February 1944 noted that 'Our requirements for this month are approximately double the previous month; peak day for instance was 4th February, with 71 messages on the 19.30 and 21.15 programme'. Those 71 messages took 8½ minutes to read out, in a programme that was only 15 minutes long. A simple sum illustrated the scale of the problem to come. 'An increase of 100% in March would,' the memo warns, 'mean that we require transmission time of 17 minutes; two minutes in excess of the normal programme.' Even that piece of arithmetic took no account of MI6's needs; 'we have left out of consideration messages sent by SIS [MI6],' wrote the SOE planner. 'This number is quite likely to increase, which would make the programme even longer than 17 minutes.'

SOE's D-Day plans raised the prospect of an even greater increase in the volume of coded traffic. They involved three separate sabotage targets: 'Green' action would be aimed at railways; 'Tortoise' was the code for action against main roads; and the 'Purple' plan was designed to disrupt communications. SOE had divided France up into regions identified by a letter and a number (A1–4 covered the area around Calais, for example, while the south – the area controlled by Vichy before the German occupation of the whole country in November 1942 – was split between R1, 2, 3, 4, 5 and 6), and proposed to transmit messages that would indicate which plan should be activated in which region. 'The Fox loves grapes,' for example, would tell groups operating in the northern A zones to attack railways, while 'The voice of the Kraut is far away' was an instruction to disrupt communications in R3, along the coast in the south-west. What was more, there would need to be two rafts of messages: the first set to put

Resistance groups and SOE agents on alert, the second to spring them into action. SOE estimated that 'for a day or two before D–Day to a day or two after D–Day' they would need to 'send out signals to over a thousand groups throughout France to attack their allotted targets'.

Ivone Kirkpatrick was confronted with SOE's demands for airtime at a meeting on 9 February 1944, and he erupted. An SOE minute of the meeting records that 'Kirkpatrick, in some indignant tones, replied that we must have been aware in the last two years that this emergency would arise and that we had sufficient time to make the necessary arrangements to overcome these difficulties . . . He failed to see why we had not built our own equipment and why we should get into this jam and ask or demand the facilities of the BBC.' Kirkpatrick sarcastically suggested that SOE demands were so extreme they might bump the Supreme Allied Commander himself off the air; the minute goes on to record that 'Various arguments arose, one of which was whether Eisenhower's proclamation to the French would be more important than the requirements of SOE. He [Kirkpatrick] rather thought that Eisenhower might come first.' Kirkpatrick refused to give ground and roped in Brendan Bracken to fight the BBC's corner. SOE had to appeal to Churchill before they were able to secure the airtime they wanted.

While this row boiled merrily away, SOE were discreetly using their BBC privileges to engage in a little pre-D–Day psychological warfare. 'We hit upon a small plan to divert the German attention from the Normandy area where the attack was, in fact, to take place,' wrote Maurice Buckmaster. SOE's agents in France were encouraged to leak out the information that any reference to soup in BBC broadcasts was a reference to the area around Calais. Once they were confident that this false trail had found its way to German counter-intelligence, 'we broadcast endless sentences of the order of '*Monsieur Gerard aime le potage*' [Mr Gerard loves his soup], '*Caroline demande bouillon*' [Caroline asks for broth], and so forth'. Buckmaster claimed a good result; 'the Germans moved a division to the Pas de Calais,' he wrote in his autobiography.

FRONT-PAGE STUFF

ONE OF THE ENJOYABLE legends that has grown up around D-Day
is that the BBC announced the Normandy landings by
broadcasting some lines from the nineteenth-century French poet
Verlaine. In fact, the stanza was part of two great waves of code that
swept over the air on the evenings of 1 and 5 June 1944. The first
three lines of Verlaine's 'Song of Autumn' went out among the 160
messages d'alerte that were broadcast on the 1st. They translate as 'the
long sighs of autumn's violins' and are wonderfully onomatopoeic in
the original: '*Les sanglots longs/Des violons/De l'automne*'. The next
three lines, which included a small mistake, were among the 187
messages d'exécution broadcast on the eve of D-Day. Verlaine wrote
'*Blessent mon coeur/D'une langueur/Monotone*' (Wound my heart with
monotonous languor), but the word '*Bercent*' was substituted for
'*Blessent*', so in the BBC's version the poet's heart was being 'lulled'
by those autumnal violins rather than hurt by them. Whether or not
that change had any literary significance is unclear, but the burden of
the coded message was precise: it was a signal to the Ventriloquist
network operating around Tours to start attacking railways.

Guillaume Mercader, a Resistance leader in Normandy, was
waiting for a rather less poetic piece of code – 'It is hot in Suez'
followed by 'The dice have been thrown' – and later recalled that he
was overwhelmed with emotions of 'joy and hope' when, on a radio
hidden in the cellar of his bicycle shop in Bayeux, he heard the

invasion signal come through. 'The day we had longed for so ardently had arrived,' he remembered, 'and what was more it was to unfold along our own coast.' Every Resistance leader who picked up one of these D–Day warnings must have been powerfully moved, and, in an unexpected way, the strange-sounding messages seem to have caught the heightened mood of the moment.

After the war, the real codes dreamed up by SOE in Baker Street were sometimes augmented by romanticized memories. There is, for example, still a legend in the Vercors, in the foothills of the Alps, that the area's *résistants* were instructed to rise with the phrase '*Le chamois des Alpes bondit*' [The Alpine mountain goat leaps], but, as Paddy Ashdown notes in his history of the Vercors uprising, 'There is no evidence whatever in any of the very comprehensive records held by the BBC Archives that any such phrase was either on the list of messages prepared for this night or among those that were actually broadcast.'

≈

There were powerful emotions at play on the English side of the Channel too. On the eve of D–Day, Churchill and de Gaulle locked horns in a most spectacular row, which came to a head over a BBC broadcast.

De Gaulle had left London for Algiers in May 1943, settling in the French colony to consolidate his control over the opposition to the Vichy regime. By the spring of 1944 he and his colleagues had, in the words of his biographer Jonathan Fenby, 'put in place the structure of the Republic they intended to install after the Liberation of France'. On 3 June 1944 his National Committee in Algiers proclaimed itself the provisional government of the French Republic, and that same day de Gaulle flew back to Britain to be briefed by Churchill on the D–Day plans. Churchill lent de Gaulle a plane, just as he had done when the general fled Bordeaux in June 1940, but this was a very different journey from that furtive escape four years earlier. This time de Gaulle arrived with a staff of 140. He was driven to London in a Daimler from the royal fleet, and the British government put up his entourage at Claridge's. De Gaulle ensconced himself in his favourite London hotel, the Connaught.

The following day Churchill entertained him to lunch in the train carriage he had had stationed near Portsmouth to serve as his field headquarters during the great campaign to come. The prime minister gave de Gaulle the D-Day date and outlined the Allied strategy; de Gaulle wrote that 'at this moment of History, the same spirit of mutual esteem and friendship animated all those who were there, whether they were French or English'. But when Churchill suggested that de Gaulle should fly to Washington to persuade President Roosevelt that he should be allowed to take power in post-liberation France, the atmosphere soured. De Gaulle, who had had to put up with months of sniping from Washington, exploded, demanding of Churchill, 'Why do you seem to think that I need to place my claim to power in France before President Roosevelt?' He added that he had, to his irritation, discovered that troops landing in France would be carrying 'so-called' French money, which he had not approved. 'How can you imagine that we British would take a position different from Washington's?' Churchill shot back. 'We are going to liberate Europe, but only because the Americans are with us.'

The prime minister then – according to de Gaulle – made a revealing declaration which was to haunt Anglo-French relations for decades to come: 'Every time we have to choose between Europe and the open seas, we shall choose the open seas. Every time I have to choose between you and Roosevelt, I shall choose Roosevelt.'

Matters became even more uncomfortable when the Supreme Allied Commander, Dwight D. Eisenhower – who, unlike his president, rather admired de Gaulle – showed him the text of the proclamation he planned to read on the BBC on D-Day. De Gaulle did not like what he saw. 'He [Eisenhower] was behaving as if he would take over our country, even though he was merely an allied general, skilled at commanding troops but without the least right to intervene in the government of France.' De Gaulle was offered the opportunity to amend the text, only to discover that copies had already been printed for distribution in France.

There was even worse to come. On 5 June he was informed that the following day the BBC's airwaves would be given over first to the exiled leaders of Occupied Europe – the king of Norway, the queen of the Netherlands, the grand-duchess of Luxembourg and the prime minister of Belgium – and then to General Eisenhower. Only then would de Gaulle be allowed to broadcast, his subordinate status underlined by this humiliating running order. De Gaulle erupted again at this affront to his dignity – and, as he saw it, the dignity of France – and refused to broadcast.

De Gaulle spent the night of 5–6 June at the Connaught, and Churchill was at Number 10. These two great leaders passed most of those history-laden hours raging about one another's duplicity; the head of the Foreign Office, Sir Alexander Cadogan, wrote later, in a damning if politically incorrect judgement, that they behaved 'like girls approaching the age of puberty'. At one in the morning Churchill told de Gaulle's ambassador, Pierre Viénot, that his leader was guilty of 'treason at the height of battle'. A British envoy was despatched to the Connaught, and at two in the morning de Gaulle confirmed that he would not join what he called the 'oratorical chain' on the BBC. However, he did agree to broadcast if his outing on the airwaves could be clearly separated from the addresses given by Eisenhower and the European leaders. Churchill was still breathing fire – from his bed he dictated an instruction that de Gaulle should be flown straight back to Algiers, but it was never followed through.

The foreign secretary, Anthony Eden, then took charge of the broadcast. Robert Bruce Lockhart, who, as head of the PWE, would be responsible for the details, had decamped to the Savoy for the night to be near Bush House – he was checked in under an assumed name for security reasons, which meant that Eden could not, at first, track him down and accused him of having been 'on the binge'. It took Bruce Lockhart most of the rest of the night to agree the time and protocol for de Gaulle's address and the announcements that would promote it. At some point during the small hours Brendan Bracken rang him to say that Churchill, apparently in more emollient mood, wanted de Gaulle to be treated with 'every deference' when he turned up to broadcast. Eden, however, insisted that de Gaulle's text should be vetted by the Foreign Office to ensure that it would be acceptable to the Americans.

Bruce Lockhart finally got to bed at 6.00 a.m., and was woken at

7.00 with the news that German radio was already broadcasting news of the Normandy landings. This seems to have been a strange moment of what one might call propaganda 'howlround'. The first news of the invasion was broadcast by Sefton Delmer's black Calais station, and Delmer (who of course worked for Bruce Lockhart) claimed he put it out not because he was tipped off by his own side, but because the news came through from the German news agency DNB courtesy of the *Hellschreiber* which its correspondent had abandoned in London at the outbreak of war.

As thousands of Allied troops poured on to Normandy's beaches, de Gaulle was still playing coy over his broadcast. A Foreign Office meeting was convened and then abandoned without sight of his script. When the general turned up at Bush House at 12.30 he found several senior American officials in the welcoming party, and 'was frigidity itself, shook hands limply and stalked on'. He still had not produced a script, and tried to insist that he be allowed on to the air at 1.00 p.m., on the grounds that the Germans were about to cut off electricity to the area around Paris. Ivone Kirkpatrick eventually managed to persuade him to let everyone *hear* his text by explaining that this important address would need to be translated into several European languages and so would have to be recorded.

When de Gaulle finally sat before the microphone he recorded, Bruce Lockhart wrote in his diary for that day, a 'very fine broadcast – nice reference to England as the "sole bastion of freedom and now the base of liberating armies".' The text was typed up and circulated to the Foreign Office, who approved it (despite the fact that de Gaulle included a reference to the 'government of France' without the qualifying word 'provisional'), and it was played out at 5.30 p.m. There was, Bruce Lockhart added, 'No mention of Yanks', even though American soldiers were, at that moment, dying to liberate France. The diary entry also records that 'BBC Bush House, who thinks it made de Gaulle as a broadcaster, turned out in great numbers to welcome him. He himself was very nice to the French team.' There is a certain symmetry in the way his years in exile were book-ended by BBC broadcasts.

De Gaulle's address included a call for restraint directed at the

Resistance; he stressed that the fight against the occupying forces must be carried out 'in good order' and that 'our action in the enemy's rear must be co-ordinated as closely as possible with the frontal attack by the Allied and French forces'. That message, however, ran contrary to the spirit of many of the instructions sent out in the coded messages broadcast on the BBC a day earlier. In addition to the carefully directed disruption campaigns against railways, roads and communications (codes Green, Tortoise and Purple), the SOE instructions included calls for straightforward 'guerrilla' activity against the Germans, even in the southern regions R1–6, many miles from the fighting in Normandy.

This was the result of a decision taken by Eisenhower on 3 June; he ruled that in order to confuse the Germans about Allied intentions, the Resistance must be called out right across France. Those who had waited in frustration for so long to take the fight to the enemy were only too eager to respond, but it meant that those BBC calls to arms turned out to be death sentences for many of them. The Germans still regarded Resistance fighters as terrorists, not soldiers, and in the ten weeks between D-Day and the liberation of the whole of France in mid-August, they responded to Resistance attacks with – in their eyes – appropriate severity. The uprising in the Vercors was brutally suppressed – the Germans killed 840 French men and women and burned 500 houses to the ground. In the Corrèze region in the south-west a *maquis* group fighting under the name of Guy Mocquet, the young communist executed by the Germans in 1941, succeeded in killing 40 German troops; the Germans promptly hanged 95 civilians in the departmental capital of Tulle. In the Ardennes a force of *maquisards* was surrounded by 3,000 German troops who shot more than 100 of them and shovelled the bodies into a mass grave.

Guillaume Mercader, the Resistance leader who heard the call to arms in his Bayeux bicycle shop, was more fortunate. The Allied lines were very close, and by the evening of 6 June he had managed to make contact with a British intelligence officer. His Resistance network was engaged to provide information about German troop movements, and the following day the first British forces arrived in Bayeux. Maurice Schumann, de Gaulle's BBC spokesman, was with them and turned up at the bicycle shop, which had been designated the local Resistance command post. Within little more than a week of picking up that coded reference to the weather in Suez, Mr Mercader was among the welcoming party for the general himself.

In his *Mémoires de guerre*, de Gaulle described his return to French soil with some emotion, slipping into his odd habit of third person reminiscence. 'We moved from street to street on foot,' he wrote. 'In the opinion of General de Gaulle, a kind of wonder gripped the inhabitants [of Bayeux], who burst into cheers or melted into tears.' The people gathered in the park known as the Place du Château (soon to be renamed the Place Général de Gaulle) to hear the general's address. 'For the first time in four terrible years,' he wrote, 'this French crowd heard a French leader declare before them that the enemy was the enemy, that duty called them to fight him, and that France too would be victorious. In truth, this, surely, was a "national revolution".'

And at this pivotal moment of French history, there was a reminder of the BBC's role in building what we might today call the de Gaulle 'brand'. Maurice Schumann introduced his leader with the call-sign he had used at the beginning of de Gaulle's broadcasts from London: '*Honneur et Patrie* – here is General de Gaulle!'

≈

At the end of the nine o'clock news on D-Day, listeners to the BBC's Home Service heard the following announcement:

> War report! Night by night at this time this programme will bring you news of the war from correspondents and fighting men; it will contain live broadcasts and recordings made in the field, special broadcasts made from forward areas, and dispatches and expert comment; to give the latest and fullest picture of the war on all fronts. Here is John Snagge to introduce tonight's *War Report*.

War Report was to stay on the air right up until VE Day in May the following year. There was a six-week break early in 1945 when the pace of the Allied advance slowed, but 235 editions were broadcast over eleven months of fighting – and regularly attracted audiences of

10–15 million listeners. It was a milestone in the history of broadcasting, breaking new ground in the way it 'took the microphone to places where things were happening. And let it listen – to the sounds of battle, to the voices of men just returned from the fighting line, to observers who had spent that day touring the scene of action.' And the logistical organization behind it provided a template for covering big news stories that would still be familiar to anyone working in the broadcasting industry today.

The news-gathering operation was formidable. Auntie may have been slow to put resources behind her war-reporting effort, but she made up for it now. Twenty correspondents were deployed on the eve of D-Day, and they covered every branch of the fighting services – Guy Byam was with the paratroopers; Chester Wilmot with the glider-borne troops; Howard Marshall, who combined managerial responsibility for the War Reporting Unit with his reporting duties, with the British Army; and Richard Dimbleby with the RAF. The United States Army and Navy were covered too.

Frank Gillard, on standby at Broadcasting House, had put together holding scripts to cover any delay in getting stories back. 'They won't let you go in the first wave – as a rule,' read one. '"No," the force commander says firmly. "It's going to be a pretty bloody five minutes, and every man I take in has got to be effective. We can't carry one spare body, and if we did take you you'd probably get hit and become a liability to us." So you are obliged to take a seat in perhaps the first follow-up wave. At any rate, that gives you a full view of what happens to the first assaulting parties.' In a note attached to the script in the BBC archives, Gillard scrupulously records that his despatch was based on his experience of landings during the Italian campaign the previous year.

A. P. Ryan sent each of the correspondents an individually addressed note. 'You handful of men have been chosen to undertake the most important assignment so far known to broadcasting,' he told them. His advice was full of good sense – indeed it reads like a manifesto for the very best kind of BBC values. 'Describe the events of which you are an eye-witness as accurately as you can,' he instructed. 'Give credit of course for gallantry and generalship. Let pride in the achievements of our armies come through. But never seek to "Jazz-up" a plain story. Events will have their own drama. You are not dramatists. The play and the persons in the play are ready-made for you. You are broadcast reporters sent out to observe and tell us what you have seen.' It is still a common grouse among foreign correspondents (especially when they are taking risks) that their material is sometimes given only cursory attention by those comfortably ensconced back at base (especially, in the old days at least, when the London-based editors had had a good lunch) and Ryan met that concern head-on. 'Every word of yours comes into the limelight here,' he reassured them. 'Whatever else goes wrong, your stuff won't suffer from not being looked at properly.' But he also warned that 'We shall edit hard at this end and kill everything that is not worth using ... There are no back pages in a broadcast. Everything we put out is in the nature of front-page stuff.' It was a stirring call to arms.

Ryan also laid down the law on the perennial BBC problem of internal rivalry. 'All BBC men in the field are serving the Corporation as a whole,' he wrote, '... from the point of view of war reporting the normal distinctions between news, features, O.B.s [Outside Broadcasts], and between Home, Overseas and European do not exist. We have a world audience and we mean to give it the most accurate, the fullest and the most vivid and alive account of coming operations that we can.'

War Report was the jewel in the broadcasting crown, but the War Reporting Unit was there to serve the whole BBC machine, and, indeed, the world beyond it. It was estimated that 725 of the 914 radio stations then broadcasting in the United States carried the BBC's programmes on 6 June 1944.

In Britain seven transmitting stations had – in great secrecy – been established along the south coast, in an arc running from Plymouth in the south-west to Ramsgate on the Kent coast, with lines back to Broadcasting House in London. Discs recorded on Midgets in the field were to be flown or couriered by ship back to Britain. The editing process was, by today's digital standards, almost unimaginably cumbersome; 'from the disk which you wish to edit you take the first passage you want to hear, and record it on a second disk; from the same original master disk you make a copy of the next passage you want to use, recording it on a third disk; then you play the desired passages consecutively on to a fourth disk'.

To help sort, judge and cut down the stream of material pouring into Broadcasting House, and sometimes to have it censored if that had not been possible in the field, correspondents were asked to phone in their despatches by what was known as the 'Telediphone'. Their words were recorded on to another set of wax discs at Broadcasting House, typed up by an army of secretaries and distributed around the various editorial departments. In the *War Report* office, a former Green Room for guests in the basement of Broadcasting House, the scripts were laid out on a long walnut table, 10 foot by 2 foot, which stretched down the centre of the room. The scriptwriters were ranged along another table placed at its end, forming the top of a capital T, and worked their way through the piles, cutting back the great chunks of raw history that had come down the line and shaping the night's programme.

At dawn on D-Day Howard Marshall was with the British Second Army just off the Normandy coast, and despite Frank Gillard's cautious warnings, he *was* allowed in with the first wave. 'I was in a barge which was due to pick up the brigadier of an assault group,' he reported in his despatch, 'and we were going in with the first assault wave. So we circled round with the various types of vessels opening fire on the beach, which we could see quite plainly in the dim morning light.' Once they had collected their brigadier they faced the obstacles the German defenders had dug in along the waterfront; 'the wind was driving the sea in with long rollers,' he reported, 'and the enemy had prepared anti-invasion, anti-barge obstacles sticking out of the water – formidable prongs, many of them tipped with mines, so that as your landing-barge swung and swayed in the rollers, and they are not particularly manageable craft, it would come in contact with one of these mines and be sunk.' Marshall's barge duly struck a mine, and as the water poured in he and the rest of the assault team waded ashore in 5 feet of water.

Marshall was twice capsized in the course of the day, and his report began with the words 'I am sitting in my soaked-through clothes with no notes at all: all my notes are sodden – they're at the bottom of the sea.' He managed to get back to the British coast by early evening and, still dripping wet, sent his report up the line to Broadcasting House at 7.15, in good time for the first edition of *War Report*.

Guy Byam took a little longer to get his story back, but then he was parachuted behind enemy lines. On the evening of 8 June he gave the *War Report* audience a vivid description of the experience. 'In the plane we stand pack to breast,' he began. 'I am jumping one but last in my stick. And as we stand in the plane, for there is no room to sit, we feel the tremendous vibration of the four motors as we start down the runway. And all around in the coming darkness are other great planes and row upon row of gliders.'

His unit was due to rendezvous at a copse, but he could not find it in the darkness. 'It's a tricky business, this moving about the enemy countryside at night. But we are well in hand and at most I shall only meet my own patrols. I find the unit after being sniped at once and challenged a number of times. They are assembled under a hedge. Like a tentacle into the air was the radio-set aerial, and the major was signalling. Allied soldiers talking to each other through the night.' And later, as the troops moved through the countryside, he added one of those telling details that really count in a good report. 'The people are pleased to see us. We apologize for the bringing of war to their homes. But in little ways they show they are glad to see us. A dead paratrooper is laid out in the best bedroom covered from head to foot with flowers. This is the story up to the early hours of the first day.'

Individual reporters like Gillard and Godfrey Talbot had been pioneering this kind of reporting during the Italian campaign in 1943, but no broadcaster in the world had attempted anything on this scale. The 1946 anthology of *War Report* broadcasts has been republished several times, and even today it is impossible not to be impressed by the strategic sweep of the material as well as the strength of individual despatches. As a clear and evocative account of the fighting from D-Day until the Allied victory on 5 May 1945, it is still hard to beat.

And the BBC's technical teams had good reason to be proud of their contribution; the Midget stood up remarkably well in battlefield conditions. Chester Wilmot memorably pushed its capabilities to the limit and beyond during an offensive near the port city of Caen. The hedgerow where he had taken cover came under fire from what were known as *Nebelwerfers*, German mortars that made a wailing sound when fired, earning themselves the nicknames Moaning Minnies, Wailing Winnies and the Sobbing Sisters. So he clipped his microphone to a hedge and 'dived for the bottom of the ditch, shoving as much of myself as possible into an old German dugout'. After the first salvo he found that the sapphire recording head had been jumped by the force of the explosions, cutting into his recording disc so deeply that it stopped revolving. So he tried again: 'I just had time to wind the Midget and fit a new sapphire and another disk before the next wailing sound. I set the recorder going and sought early refuge in the bottom of the ditch. The Midget recorded perfectly right through the bursting salvo, for the mortars landed a little further away; and so, for the first time, we had a recording of the German weapon our troops most disliked.'

The BBC's first mobile transmitter, mounted on a 3-ton truck and code-named Mike Charlie Oboe, or MCO for short, arrived at Arromanches in a gale on the night of 17 June. Like Howard Marshall, it was plunged into several feet of water before it made it to the beach, but the BBC's engineers, working by the light of 'bomb blasts and ack-ack fire', had it up and running within a matter of hours. The official *War Report* history records that 'In spite of its rough passage across the Channel, and the enforced haste with which it was put into operation, MCO's debut was a great success. The transmitter at Broadcasting House flashed back the words "Reception quite satisfactory".'

The following day the BBC was allowed to take over one of the towers of the ancient Château de Cruelly outside Bayeux, and a stone-flagged room with slit-windows (the building had been used by both sides during the Hundred Years War) and a vaulted ceiling was transformed into one of the Corporation's busiest studios. Field Marshal Montgomery established his headquarters in the grounds nearby, and the correspondents who piled in to file their reports (sometimes queuing on the chateau terrace as they waited for their

Camouflaging one of the mobile transmitters positioned along the south coast for D-Day.

turn at the microphone) looked down on the Allies' military nerve centre from a studio window.

Two more high-powered transmitters – Mike Charlie Nan and Mike Charlie Peter – were shipped over a couple of months later, and they shadowed the Allied forces as they advanced. It is not entirely fanciful to identify this as the moment when 'rolling news' was born. When MCN and MCP were in the right place at the right time, 'if important news "broke" just as a London programme was going on the air, it was possible – given reasonable conditions – to relay the correspondent's voice in any programme to any part of the world'.

When correspondents got too far ahead of the hardware they used some imaginative techniques to get their material back to base. Just after the liberation of Brussels, Chester Wilmot transmitted his despatch from a device hidden in a suitcase that had been dropped into Occupied Belgium for the use of the local Resistance movement; the army picked it up and obligingly passed it on to the BBC.

The close cooperation between the BBC and the fighting services during the campaign was apparent on D-Day itself, in the very first edition of *War Report*. At the end of the programme the BBC broadcast Montgomery's morale-boosting message to the men under his command. 'We have a great and righteous cause,' he told them. 'Let us pray that the Lord, mighty in battle, will go forth with our armies and that His special providence will aid us in the struggle ... Good luck to each one of you – and good hunting on the mainland of Europe.'

Little over a month after D-Day, however, there was a sharp reminder of who was in charge. On Sunday, 16 July, Montgomery visited the 6th Airborne Division to award medals to some of the troops and Chester Wilmot was there to cover the story. He asked Montgomery for permission to record his address, thinking – according to his version of events – that he could, if nothing else, give copies to the soldiers as a memento of the occasion. Montgomery agreed, but stipulated – according to *his* version of events – that the speech should never be broadcast. When sections of his speech *were* broadcast on the following night's *War Report*, there was a 'tremendous row'.

It is not clear which part of the speech Montgomery considered sensitive, but it included an anecdote which no doubt went down well with the troops in the field but which might have been thought in poor taste at home. Montgomery praised the paratroopers for their successes, but warned that some of the troops they were facing were 'fanatical Nazis'. To illustrate the point he told a story about a young German soldier who was being treated for his wounds in a British field hospital. 'They [the medical staff] said "We're going to give you a blood transfusion," and they made the arrangements to give it,' Monty explained. 'And he saw the bottle of blood – an ordinary bottle of blood which you have put into you. And he said "Is that British blood?" and they said "Yes, good British blood." And he said "No British blood for me." And they said "If you don't have this blood you will die." And he said "Alright I will die." And he did.' The script records that at this point there was 'laughter' from the troops.

When Montgomery heard that sections of his speech had been transmitted, he was so angry that he simply closed down BBC broadcasting from Normandy. Howard Marshall, who was Auntie's senior man at the Cruelly headquarters, was told to send an urgent message back to Broadcasting House. 'Vitally important that no despatch from this sector Normandy Front, from whatever source, agency, services, or any other, be used in 9 o'clock news or War Report Tonight,' it read. 'No contributions from here tonight. This based on positive ruling given to me personally by Commander-in-Chief. Regard it imperative [for] our future operations abide absolutely by decision.'

Wilmot was sent back to Blighty on Montgomery's personal instructions, and allowed to return to the front only when it emerged that he was largely blameless in the affair – an internal BBC inquiry concluded that Howard Marshall himself had failed to label the offending disc properly before sending it back to London. No one seems for a moment to have questioned Montgomery's right to close down the BBC's operations on his personal whim.

While Auntie was still smarting from this episode, there was another sharp reminder that the Corporation's freedom was circumscribed by bigger political considerations. On 20 July 1944 the aristocratic German war hero Colonel Count Claus von Stauffenberg tried to assassinate Hitler by leaving a bomb in a conference room where the Führer was studying intelligence material at his Wolf's Lair headquarters in eastern Prussia. The plotters against Hitler, many of whom were tradition-minded Prussian Army officers, apparently wanted to make peace with Britain and to save Germany by abandoning Nazism, and the incident should have been a propaganda gift; here was clear and dramatic evidence of significant German opposition to Hitler. But Vansittartism – the idea that the Nazis and the Germans were, to all intents and purposes, one and the same – had now become official Allied policy; President Roosevelt had declared in January 1943 that only the 'unconditional surrender' of Germany would be accepted.

This made it impossible for the BBC's German Service to broadcast material that might have capitalized on the 20 July plot. 'Any hopes they might have cherished of splitting the Germans and inciting the generals to further rebellion were crushed,' Sefton Delmer wrote. 'For Crossman and Carleton Greene were not only stopped from saying anything to encourage the rebels, they were specifically ordered to announce that His Majesty's government was not prepared to absolve the army of its responsibility for the war or to differentiate in any way between Germans and Germans. All were responsible. The only terms on which Germany could have peace were – as before – unconditional capitulation.' Delmer noted with some relish that as a result of this position 'the task of dividing the Germans was therefore right back in the laps of the "Black" men.'

THE WHOLE WOOD
SMELT OF THE DEAD

IN SEPTEMBER 1944 HOWARD MARSHALL left the BBC for a secondment to the Ministry of Reconstruction and Frank Gillard took over as the senior man on the Western Front. As he followed the advancing Allied armies, Gillard encountered so much praise for the BBC that it must have felt, from time to time, like a royal progress. 'There's always a tremendous personal welcome for us, as representatives of the BBC, when we go into newly liberated towns,' he reported. 'People crowd in upon us to express their thanks, and they invariably say, "We listen to the BBC, and we trusted the BBC, because it always told the truth."'

In mid-September he broadcast from the newly liberated Dutch city of Eindhoven, which was the home of the Philips radio works. Gillard reported that 'The Germans long ago confiscated all wireless sets belonging to the people of Eindhoven, but it was a futile thing to do in a city where almost every other man is a radio engineer. The Philips workers turned out thousands of clandestine sets – in fact they practically mass produced them, made in tiny biscuit boxes out of parts they took from the works when the Germans weren't looking.'

He was surprised by a local man who approached him with the question, 'Tell me, has Mrs Davis sent Chester Wilmot a new typewriter yet?' Wilmot had tacked a request for a replacement typewriter on to the end of one of his despatches, and the man had picked it up on his wireless as it was being fed back to Broadcasting House. 'You really have to meet these allies of ours in France, Belgium and Holland to realise what the London radio has meant to them in the last four years,' Gillard told his listeners back at home. 'Their whole lives have revolved around it, the broadcasts from London have been everything to them. Thousands of them say they couldn't have kept up their hopes and resistance without them . . . they turn their dial, anxious not to miss a single word, even when it's just Chester Wilmot asking for typewriter reinforcements.'

While Gillard was celebrating liberation in Eindhoven, Chester Wilmot himself was, together with Guy Byam, some 50 miles closer to the German border – but they were caught up in a very different story. They were part of what became known as Operation Market Garden, deployed with the troops of the 1st Airborne Division and the Polish Independent Brigade who were dropped on 17 September near the city of Arnhem to secure bridges across the Lower Rhine. It was the largest airborne assault in history, but Allied intelligence had underestimated the strength of the German opposition (especially the number of tanks the Germans could call on) and the paratroopers were soon bottled up in a small corner north of the river. After nine days of fierce fighting, they were ordered to withdraw. The original force was nearly 12,000 strong, but only 3,900 of them made it back across the Rhine, the rest being either killed or captured. It was the last big British defeat of the Second World War, and the story was memorably told in the classic film *A Bridge Too Far*.

Both Byam and Wilmot were among those who escaped, and Byam, who had already had to swim for his life once (when his ship sank), got away by plunging into the Rhine. The despatches filed by both men were among the most powerful broadcast by the BBC in the course of the whole war. Here is a flavour of Byam's:

> At about ten o'clock we slowly groped our way through the woods, while the artillery on the other bank poured fire into the surrounding countryside to make the Hun believe we were attacking further along the river. And in the drizzle and the wet the men felt their way through the dense trees where the foliage was split and where one could hear the Germans talking as they sat somewhere in the darkness crouching in their slit trenches, and

we groped our way on and the whole wood smelt of the dead, and the farms and little houses were on fire. And then we came out of the wood into a field and crept in long lines down to the Rhine. The mortars were bursting in what seemed like a spray of sparks, almost amongst us now, and we lay on the ground, pressing our faces into the wet grass. It was then that I decided to have a go at swimming the river. The men themselves patiently waited their turn to get into a boat, and if a man floundering in the dark got ahead of someone else, there would be a quiet 'Come on, chum, take your turn.' And the boatloads got over the Rhine, and swept down by the current I at last managed to get to the other bank. The hell was behind us.

A note in Byam's personal BBC file from his time as a sub in the French Service suggests he caught the eye of his bosses early in his BBC career; the European director of production described him as a 'script writer of outstanding promise', and added, 'I have a constant fear that some film company who can outbid the Corporation financially will one day find out more about him'. And a report card signed by A. P. Ryan on 11 January 1945 adds – no doubt with the Arnhem despatch in mind – that 'He is exceptionally keen and has been responsible for some outstanding broadcasts.' Three weeks after that was written, Guy Byam was dead, killed while reporting an American bombing raid on Berlin.

On 21 October 1944, Gillard, still broadcasting from the Netherlands, where the front had stabilized for a while, sent in a despatch on the subject of 'Radio Propaganda'. 'The Germans are picking up the BBC on powerful receivers,' he revealed, 'and re-transmitting the programmes out here locally, in the battle areas, in great strength. It's not done out of kindness, you can be sure of that. There's a purpose behind it all. They run the BBC uninterruptedly for an hour or more, and then suddenly the programme breaks off and an announcer in English slips in a little German propaganda. Then back to the BBC again.' He had just heard a re-broadcast of the popular programme *Music While You Work*, which was followed by a bogus news programme that 'gave the Nazi version of what's happening on the war fronts', complete with convincing-sounding Allied sources like a report from a Reuters

correspondent and a communiqué from General Eisenhower. Other techniques he recorded included the broadcasting of personal messages from troops who 'have passed from your ranks to swell the numbers of the fortunate prisoners of war'. The objective, Gillard said in his despatch, was to 'catch the ears of British and Allied soldiers by making them think that they're listening to a BBC station, and then pump in propaganda before the listeners realise what is happening; and the propaganda is all designed to unsettle the troops, to soften them, to stimulate a longing to be out of the war, to make them think of home'.

Gillard cannot have known this, but his account of the German campaign mirrored exactly the propaganda techniques his own side would use during the final months of the war. This kind of thing was right up Sefton Delmer's crooked and curious street and, as Delmer himself had noted after the plot against Hitler in the summer of 1944, the task of influencing German opinion and morale was 'right back in the laps of the "Black" men.'

The Aspidistra transmitter was designed to 'capture' enemy broadcasts in just the way the Germans were hijacking BBC wavelengths, but its use in this way was, even at this late stage, still controversial in official London. Not long before the assault on Arnhem, a spectacular Whitehall turf war blew up over an operation code-named Braddocks II.

Its forerunner, Braddocks I, had been dreamed up by Churchill himself, apparently after reading a book called *The Moon Is Down* by the American novelist John Steinbeck. Steinbeck's story, published in 1942, is set in a German-occupied country which is unnamed but bears a great similarity to Norway, and it includes an episode in which the local resistance movement is helped by British drops of small sticks of dynamite to use against the Germans. Churchill, it seems, read the book at Chequers and was much taken with the idea of arson as a weapon of war, so he ordered the development of an incendiary that could be used by resistance movements throughout Europe. The devices were code-named 'Braddocks', and some three million of them, packed with gelignite and fitted with a delaying detonator, were duly manufactured. But the RAF was reluctant to deliver them; according to Sefton Delmer, Sir Arthur 'Bomber' Harris declared, 'I am not going to have my aircrews risking their lives for some damn novelist's fancy toys.' The scheme was put on ice.

It was revived in the autumn of 1944, but Braddocks II was designed as more of a 'psy-ops' campaign than a straightforward sabotage operation. The idea was to drop Braddocks in areas of Germany where foreign workers were concentrated, at the same time as pumping out a black propaganda campaign suggesting that the incendiaries were much more dangerous than they actually were, and that hordes of foreigners were itching to get their hands on them. Aspidistra would be used to hijack a German radio wavelength and then broadcast fake police instructions, ordering the public to go out at night in large numbers to find and collect these terror weapons from particular places. This, it was hoped, would produce general fear and chaos.

Sefton Delmer claims to have dreamed up the wheeze, and it was, more importantly, backed by Eisenhower himself. But no one consulted Brendan Bracken about the plan, and when he learned of it (from Robert Bruce Lockhart) he 'blew up at once', demanding to know why he had not been consulted and claiming to be 'the sole arbiter of the uses for which Aspidistra was to be employed'. Bruce Lockhart (who, in his diary, fingers Dick Crossman as the main brains behind the scheme) did his best to calm Bracken down, but was forced to listen as the minister of information berated Hastings 'Pug' Ismay, Churchill's closest military adviser, over the telephone, telling him to 'Shut up, you chutney-eating general' when Ismay tried to interrupt his flow. Bracken then dictated a 'rude and, in parts inaccurate letter to the Foreign Secretary', rebuking the chiefs of staff for signing off the scheme with the Americans without consulting him.

As matters threatened to get completely out of hand, news came through that Paris had been liberated, and it appears that the row was interrupted by celebrations; Bruce Lockhart spent an evening drinking champagne with Lord and Lady Vansittart. But Braddocks II had to go ahead without the direct use of Aspidistra. The PWE dropped leaflets instead, and Delmer put out 'alarmist messages' about the incendiaries on his Calais station. The Americans gave up dropping

Braddocks altogether in the spring of 1945, and a huge stockpile had to be destroyed at the end of the war.

Bracken may have won that round in the Aspidistra wars, but in the aftermath of the Braddocks affair he was, according to David Garnett in his official PWE history, forced to accept the principle of 'the use of Aspidistra in connection with future military operations'. As a result, Sefton Delmer was finally given full licence to play with the technical toy he liked to call 'Big Bertha'. As he tells the story, his opportunity came following another Churchillian intervention. While staying as a guest at Eisenhower's headquarters, the prime minister is said to have noticed a piece in the American military magazine *Stars and Stripes* which reported that the Allies were broadcasting a 'stay put' order to German civilians; Eisenhower had decided that large numbers of refugees on the country's roads would cause difficulties for the advancing Allied armies. Churchill, however, thought a bit of chaos on the roads was just the ticket and persuaded Eisenhower to change the strategy. 'The fun,' as Sefton Delmer put it in his autobiography, 'was about to begin.'

Big Bertha – let us now fall in with Delmer's nomenclature, since we are in his hands for much of the telling of this episode – had the capacity to 'squat' on a radio wavelength, ready to take it over at a moment's notice. The Germans – like the British earlier in the war – had developed the technique of turning off some of their transmitters if they feared they might be used as navigational aids during a raid, and, with the help of the RAF bombing planners, Delmer was able to predict which stations might be taken off the air on any given evening. Radio Cologne was selected as a target. It had been regularly interrupting its normal programmes with emergency public-safety messages, and Delmer trained up a couple of Germans (a PoW and the actress wife of a member of his repertory company at Aspley Guise) to play the parts of the station's announcers.

A suitably chaos-causing message was then crafted on Sefton Delmer's instructions. In his autobiography he states that the people of Cologne were to be told that 'women and children must leave their homes at once, this very night, taking only fifteen kilograms of their most essential belongings with them', because enemy tanks were approaching the city, while men were to be instructed to stay put and defend home and hearth. His memory must have played him false – and he was never one to worry too much about the facts in the telling of a good story – because the PWE records show that the actual text he and his team came up with sent out precisely the opposite message; it informed the population that *only* men of fighting age were to be evacuated, as they could carry on the battle to save the Reich. Everyone else must shift for themselves. 'Folk comrades,' the emergency announcement began, 'the enemy has reached the gates of our *Gau* [district]. His intention to destroy the *Reich* and exterminate the German people will meet with fanatical resistance ... on account of enemy penetration in the eastern side of the Rhine, our population is open to all the effects of modern weapons and threatened with complete destruction. The utmost discipline must therefore be maintained in this hour. Since the evacuation measures originally planned have become impossible ... only those compatriots who are suited to carry out the decisive struggle ... will be evacuated. The evacuation of a great number of our compatriots will, for the time being, be impossible. Their duty, therefore, is to stick it out and, if need be, face death bravely.'

On the appointed evening, Radio Cologne duly went off the air during a bombing raid – as the RAF had predicted it would – and Aspidistra took over the wavelength for around an hour. The programmes were interrupted by Delmer's two fake announcers, who read their scripts 'without a fluff and in the exact rhythm and intonation of the genuine Cologne team'.

The Cologne operation was followed by similar Aspidistra 'intrusions' directed at the people of Frankfurt and Leipzig, and a document later captured by the advancing Americans suggested that Big Bertha had 'pooped', as Delmer liked to put it, with some success. A Nazi party official in Westphalia reported that 'considerable misunderstandings and great unrest were caused among the population by the intrusion of enemy wireless announcements on the German radio. The enemy wireless propaganda broadcasts cleverly formulated announcements and orders from the *Gauleiter* in the Western District, or terrifies whole neighbourhoods by the announcement of the approach of enemy tanks and scouting cars, evacuation orders etc. – and for only two clear reasons: the creation of chaos in the transport system, targets for terror attacks, and panic.' There was nothing Delmer enjoyed more than a good review from the opposition team.

≈

The opposition's most effective propagandist, Lord Haw-Haw, went on churning out his broadcasts until the bitter end. By late April 1945 everyone knew that the game was up, but William Joyce was still in Hamburg with his wife, Margaret, who had by then established something of an on-air reputation of her own. On 28 April Mussolini was killed by Italian partisans, and his body was hung upside-down in a Milan square alongside that of his mistress. Lady Haw-Haw noted, 'BBC confirm Mussolini rumour and gave gloating description of how he was hung and then his body was thrown in a Milan square and riddled with bullets. The BBC call these people patriots.'

On 30 April Hitler and Eva Braun, who had just become his wife, committed suicide in the Führer's bunker in Berlin. On the same day, William Joyce gave his last broadcast and, his words plainly slurred by alcohol, said his farewells. That distinctive delivery which had helped to make him so famous was now distorted by a drunk's random speech rhythms:

> You have heard something about the Battle of Berlin. You know that, there, a tremendous, world shattering battle is being waged. Good. I will only say that the men who have died for the Battle of Berlin have given their *lives* to show that whatever happens, Germany *will* live. *No* coercion, *no* oppression, *no* measures of tyranny that any foreign foe can introduce will shatter Germany. Germany *will* live because the people of Germany *have* in them the secret of life: *endurance*. *Will* and *purpose*. And therefore I say to you these last words – you may not hear from me for a few months – I say *Es lebe Deutschland* [Long live Germany]. Heil Hitler, and farewell.

He and his radio colleagues had, as Mary Kenny puts it in her biography of Joyce, 'plundered the cellars of the Hamburg *Funkhaus* [broadcasting centre]; they ate and drank everything in sight. This was not "Twilight over England", as William had predicted, but the *Götterdämmerung* of *Germany Calling*, half tragedy, half farce.'

Wynford Vaughan-Thomas played it for laughs — albeit sardonic ones — when he found his way to Haw-Haw's studio with British troops four days later. 'This is Germany calling,' he began, 'calling for the last time from Station Hamburg, and tonight you will not hear views on the news by William Joyce, for Mr Joyce — Lord Haw-Haw to most of us in Britain — has been most unfortunately interrupted in his broadcasting career, and at present has left rather hurriedly for a vacation, an extremely short vacation if the Second British Army has anything to do with it, maybe to Denmark and points north. And in his place this is the BBC calling all the long-suffering listeners in Britain who for six years have had to put up with the acid tones of Mr Joyce speaking over the same wave-length that I am using to talk to you now.'

Vaughan-Thomas delivered his despatch sitting in front of Lord Haw-Haw's microphone; he had rummaged through the desk and found that in his diary Joyce had pencilled in some time to 'collect my wits'. Vaughan-Thomas was clearly enjoying himself; 'Well, he and the citizens of Hamburg have now got plenty of time to collect their wits,' he said, 'for tonight the sturdy soldiers of the Devons, the famous Desert Rats, are on guard over Haw-Haw's studios . . .'

Vaughan-Thomas was right about Joyce's destination after his hurried departure from Hamburg. Lord Haw-Haw and his wife had indeed headed to 'points north', settling in Wassersleben, a resort on the Baltic coast near Germany's border with Denmark. They lived peacefully under assumed names for nearly a month, making themselves popular with local people and even entertaining the British soldiers who were, by then, stationed in the town. On 28 May 'Wilhelm Hansen' bumped into two British officers collecting firewood in the forest and could not, it seems, resist the temptation to engage them in conversation. Eventually one of them asked, 'You wouldn't by any chance be William Joyce, would you?' Joyce reached for his false passport and the officer, thinking he was going for a gun, shot him through the buttocks. The wound was superficial and Joyce survived to face charges of treason. He argued that, since he was not really British, he owed no allegiance to the Crown, but he was convicted. He was hanged at Wandsworth Prison in January 1946.

≈

The final days of the war unfurled in a dizzying blaze of BBC scoops. Auntie was the first news organization in the world to break the news of Himmler's suicide; she flashed the German surrender in Italy within fifteen minutes of the news coming through; and, on the night of Vaughan-Thomas's broadcast from Haw-Haw's den, Chester Wilmot recorded Montgomery's acceptance of the German generals' capitulation. The tone of the reports was, perhaps inevitably, sometimes coloured by triumphalism, but the correspondents of the WRU found plenty to prompt sober commentary too. Germany was on its knees, and, even in his report from Haw-Haw's desk, Vaughan-Thomas reflected on the sombre scenes they found. 'We thought Bremen was bad,' he declared, 'but Hamburg is devastated. Whole quarters have disintegrated under air attacks. There are miles upon miles of blackened walls and utterly burnt out streets, and in the ruins there are still a million people and 50,000 foreign workers living in the cellars and the air-raid shelters.'

On 5 May 1945, *War Report* included an interview with the signals sergeant responsible for transmitting the armistice order to German troops. 'Their operator was very obedient and correct,' he said, 'but I could tell he knew the importance of the message he received.' Wilmot asked him how. 'His Morse was all over the place when he repeated the message back to me,' came the reply. 'His hand was obviously very shaky. My hand was shaky too – but that's off the record! And today we've been sending the Germans orders. For my wireless operators this has been the greatest morning of the war. They've been sending messages from the Field Marshal [Montgomery] himself to the German Command we've been fighting for five and a half years – just the job!'

John Snagge signed off that night's programme with the announcement that with victory on the Western Front, *War Report* was coming off the air.

≈

Writing twenty years later, Wynford Vaughan-Thomas described the first months of 1945 as 'a strange and frightening spring for the BBC war correspondents'. No one, he pointed out, 'wants to take risks in the last minutes of a battle'. He and Richard Dimbleby covered the crossing of the Rhine, the last big set-piece action of the war; Vaughan-Thomas made it over the river in a Buffalo, an amphibious assault craft developed by the Americans, and Dimbleby was dropped with the gliders through 'a furious storm of flak'. When the two met after the battle, Dimbleby told his colleague, 'I don't think I want to see much more of war. I've had five years of reporting it, and that's enough for any man.'

But the war had one more great reporting task in store for him. One April morning, 'which had a deceptive promise of warmth in the air', a rumour reached the press that British troops had discovered a camp where typhus had broken out. Vaughan-Thomas assumed it was just another prisoner of war camp and declined to follow up the story. Dimbleby, with a true reporter's instincts, took his jeep up to a place called Belsen.

'I picked my way over corpse after corpse in the gloom, until I heard one voice raised above the gentle undulating moaning,' he began his despatch. 'I found a girl, a living skeleton, impossible to gauge her age because she had no hair left, and her face was only a yellow parchment sheet with two holes for eyes. She was stretching out her stick of an arm and gasping something, it was "English, English, medicine, medicine."'

It cannot have been easy to find the words to describe a concentration camp. Dimbleby's report succeeds because he simply told the listeners what he found, without fuss or hysteria. He uses adjectives sparingly, and the metaphors are rare and carefully chosen. Of a huge pile of bodies ('perhaps 150,' he estimated) he says, '[T]heir yellow skin glistened like stretched rubber on their bones ... They were like polished skeletons, the skeletons that medical students like to play practical jokes with.' And he delegates the job of guiding the listeners' emotions. 'One woman, distraught to the point of madness, flung herself at a British soldier who was on guard at the camp on the night that it was reached by the 11th Armoured Division,' he reported;

'she begged him to give her some milk for the tiny baby she held in her arms. She laid the mite on the ground and threw herself at the sentry's feet and kissed his boots. And when, in his distress, he asked her to get up, she put the baby in his arms and ran off crying that she would find milk for it because there was no milk in her breast. And when the soldier opened the bundle of rags to look at the child he found it had been dead for days . . . I have never seen British soldiers so moved to cold fury as the men who opened the Belsen camp this week.'

A group of Dimbleby's colleagues published a memorial book after his death from cancer in 1965. It included the Belsen despatch, and Vaughan-Thomas described meeting his colleague immediately after his visit to the camp. Dimbleby was driving his jeep along a narrow road through one of those 'gloomy pine woods that dot the level north German plain', and the promise of spring had given way to the threat of rain. 'Richard got out and said to me at once, "It's horrible; human beings have no right to do this to each other," Vaughan-Thomas remembered. '"You must go and see it, but you'll never wash the smell of it off your hands, never get the filth of it out of your mind. I've just made a decision . . . I must tell the exact truth, every detail of it, even if people don't believe me, even if they feel these things should not be told."'

POSTSCRIPT

WHEN RADIO FOUR CAME into being in 1967, replacing the Home Service which had broadcast since 1939, one of the programme strands that survived the transition was called *The Time of My Life*. It encouraged well-known figures to dilate on the subject of a period when they had been especially happy and engaged with the business of being alive, and in early 1968 the Oxford historian Alan Bullock chose his time as a wartime editor in the BBC's European Services. Explaining his choice, Bullock said, 'I always think, looking back, that we were very lucky, those of us who went in late 1939/early 1940, to be in on the ground floor of something which was quite new, where nobody had any experience to go on, where we had to work it out for ourselves ...'

The way he described the experience helped me understand why this has been such a challenging but enjoyable book to write. For most of the war, the BBC's European Services were broadcasting to people who were cut off by the terrible reality of Nazi occupation. To talk to their audience in a way that would make sense to them, Auntie's men had to make a huge imaginative leap; Occupied Europe was, Bullock told his interviewer, a 'shadowy world', and 'you were shut off from this. You had to try and guess what it was. You had to try and reconstruct it.' This, he reflected, describes precisely the work of a professional historian, 'trying to imagine what it must be like to be somewhere you couldn't go'. Wartime Europe felt 'as remote from us, broadcasting to it, as, say, the sixteenth century' from the twentieth.

While reading back the record of Auntie's war, I have done my best to forget everything I have learned during my three decades as a broadcaster; a sense of the freshness of the world 'where we had to work it out for ourselves' is essential to understanding the scale of the BBC's wartime achievement. I am sure I have sometimes distorted the wartime reality by looking at it through today's prism, but I have seen it clearly enough to feel what a thrilling time it must have been.

Bullock was sent to Germany in the summer of 1945 and had the privilege – from a historian's perspective – of seeing 'the dissolution of a society, the actual . . . disappearance of a great and powerful state'. He tried to get a sense of whether his wartime work as a broadcaster had made any impact on the course of the conflict, and, travelling through a traumatized Europe, he was, like Frank Gillard during the closing months of the war, reminded repeatedly of the reputation the BBC had established. 'Wherever you went in Europe for years after the war, and certainly in Western and Central Europe, the word "BBC" was an absolute passport,' he said. He found Auntie's 'reputation for reliability . . . most movingly demonstrated again and again.'

Reflecting on the BBC's relationship with the government, he added, 'The BBC didn't ever think of itself as conducting political warfare. It thought of itself as broadcasting news bulletins.' That is a golden gloss on the struggles fought by men like Ivone Kirkpatrick, but Bullock's verdict on the almost accidental nature of Auntie's war record of relative independence rings true. 'I think it was a conscious decision with very little understanding of its implications,' he said, 'but it worked out extremely well.' Auntie herself, Bullock's interview suggests, had 'the time of her life' during the Second World War.

If is, of course, tempting to look back to the period for lessons about today's broadcasting culture, but the differences are more striking than any similarities. It is, for example, almost impossible to overstate how much easier the BBC's life was made by the eclipse of party politics between the formation of Churchill's Coalition government in 1940 and the General Election of 1945. Party rivalry did not disappear altogether, and when domestic political battles broke out the BBC almost always found itself being forced on to the defensive.

Bullock knew this at first hand. He was the European news talks editor when the Beveridge Report was published in November 1942 and, believing that this great statement of the principles of a welfare state had propaganda potential in Europe, he pushed it hard on the air, commissioning a series of talks. The BBC was promptly accused by a right-wing Tory MP of trying to force the government into adopting the report's recommendations, and the Conservative MP for Cambridge University, Captain Kenneth Pickthorn, complained in the Commons that 'repeated exposition of the Beveridge Report on overseas broadcast programmes' might give the world the impression that Britain suffered from 'excessive preoccupation with our own standards of comfort'. After Churchill had given a broadcast about the report, Beveridge himself wanted to respond on the air; the BBC governors considered the issue so sensitive that they insisted he must first clear his script with the government (faced with that restriction, Beveridge gave up on the idea of broadcasting).

But episodes like this were the exception rather than the rule. For the most part Auntie was able to focus on her wartime mission of truth-telling without worrying too much about the complicating obligation to achieve political balance.

In my introduction I quoted from *Human Voices*, Penelope Fitzgerald's wonderfully evocative novel about the wartime BBC, and her words bear a second visit. 'Without prompting,' she wrote, 'the BBC decided that truth was more important than consolation, and, in the long run, would be more effective. And yet there was no guarantee of this. Truth ensures trust, but not victory, or even happiness. But the BBC had clung tenaciously to its first notion, droning quietly on, at intervals from dawn to midnight, telling, as far as possible, exactly what happened. An idea so unfamiliar was bound to upset many of the other authorities, but they got used to it little by little, and the listeners had always expected it.'

Reading the passage back at the end of this journey, I realize that it strikes one false note: in the early days, many of the listeners did *not* expect the BBC to tell the truth. Indeed the evidence – some of the reaction to Charles Gardner's Battle of Britain broadcast, for example, and Marjorie Redman's suspicions about the way Priestley was treated – suggests that people were much more inclined to believe that the BBC would lie to keep the nation's spirits up, and would always do what it was told by the government. The idea that 'truth is the first casualty of war' was common currency by the 1930s. One of the more influential books of the inter-war years was *Falsehood in Wartime, Containing an Assortment of Lies Circulated Throughout the Nations During the Great War*. Written by the Labour MP (and later peer) Arthur Ponsonby, it listed some of the lies told about the Germans during the First World War. The BBC had to earn the trust of its audience.

But Fitzgerald was right about the way the authorities 'got used to it little by little'. Alan Bullock made a similar point in his *The Time of My Life* interview. Speaking of the relative independence enjoyed by the European Services, he said, 'I think it meant we were a livelier service, and the people who might have ended that situation saw there were advantages in it and left it alone.' The change in the tide of war of course helped; it is much easier to tell the truth when that truth reflects victories, not defeats. Churchill's failed attempt to take 'day to day editorial control' of the Corporation coincided with Russia's entry into the war, and the story might have had a very different ending if Britain had been forced to soldier on under the sort of pressure it faced in 1940 and early 1941.

But pragmatism is at a premium in a total war; the BBC was allowed to go on telling what Dimbleby called 'the exact truth, every detail of it' because it worked, and it helped Britain win. Far from being the 'first casualty' of war, the habit of truth-telling grew into a strapping lad, and Auntie deserves credit for the way she nurtured him.

SOURCES

M UCH OF THE MATERIAL for this book – including BBC memos, scripts, internal reports, public statements and confidential correspondence – has been gathered from the BBC's Written Archives at Caversham in Berkshire, which can be visited by appointment by academics and writers doing research. Quotations from parliamentary debates are from Hansard – Hansard online (https://hansard.parliament. uk/) is a joy to use. I have also drawn on government papers held at the National Archives at Kew, which has a helpful online search facility (http://www.nationalarchives.gov.uk/).

I am grateful to copyright holders of books and papers for permission to use quoted material. My publisher and I have made every effort to obtain permissions to use copyright material and apologize for any omissions here. We will be pleased to make appropriate acknowledgements in any future edition.

Full details of books in the notes below are provided where they are first mentioned; the place of publication is London unless otherwise stated. Where I have quoted several times from the same book within a chapter I have identified the book the first time – other quotations from the same author within that chapter are from the same source, unless otherwise stated. Translations from the French are, for the most part, my own.

Introduction

1 'The Pope . . .': Harman Grisewood, *One Thing at a Time: An Autobiography*, Hutchinson and Co., 1968.

2 'in a small bedroom . . .': Wilfred Pickles, *Between You and Me*, Werner Laurie, 1949.

2 'a flavour both of undue influence ...':Val Gielgud wrote two memoirs covering this period of his life: *Years of the Locust*, Nicholson and Watson, 1947; and *Years in a Mirror*,The Bodley Head, 1965. I have drawn on both.

4 Asa Briggs, *The History of Broadcasting in the United Kingdom*,Vol. III: *The War of Words*, Oxford University Press, Oxford, 1961.

5 'In this Hall ...': Freddie Grisewood, *The World Goes By*, Secker and Warburg, 1952.

5 'I did not like ...': Douglas Ritchie, *Stroke: A Diary of Recovery*, Faber and Faber, 1960.

5 'The first heroic or primitive ...': Penelope Fitzgerald, *Human Voices*, Collins, 1980.

7 'is a land of snobbery and privilege ...': From his 1941 essay 'England Your England'. For quotations from Orwell I have relied on Peter Davison's *George Orwell: The Complete Works*, published by Secker and Warburg, 1998.

8 'I must say that ...': Charles Gardner, *A.A.S.F.*, Hutchinson and Co., 1940.

12 'I owe so much to you ...': The incident is recalled in John Simpson's introduction to the 2014 edition of *War Report*, published by BBC Books.

15 'Well, that was one ...':This is among the memorable despatches collected in *War Report: A Record of Dispatches Broadcast by the BBC's War Correspondents with the Allied Expeditionary Force*, first published by Oxford University Press, Oxford,1946.

1 The Cellist and the Nightingale

17 'There she would sit ...': Grisewood, *One Thing at a Time*.

20–21 There is a good account of the Nazis' radio propaganda campaign in M. A. Doherty's *Nazi Wireless Propaganda: Lord Haw-Haw and British Public Opinion in the Second World War*, Edinburgh University Press, Edinburgh, 2000.

21 'Many years later the authenticity ...': The most controversial of Rauschning's books was *Hitler Speaks: A Series of Political Conversations with Adolf Hitler on His Real Aims*,Thornton Butterworth, 1939.

22 'Spreading with the speed of light ...': Charles Rolo, *Radio Goes to War*, Faber and Faber, 1943. This book has some rich detail of Nazi radio campaigns.

22 Asa Briggs, *The History of Broadcasting in the United Kingdom*,Vol. II: *The Golden Age of Wireless*, Oxford University Press, Oxford, 1965.

23 'Siân Nicholas, who has written . . .': *The Echo of War: Home Front Propaganda and the Wartime BBC*, Manchester University Press, Manchester, 1997.

23 'anxious to hear a sports broadcast . . .': from E. S. Turner, *The Phoney War on the Home Front*, Michael Joseph, 1961.

24 'Val Gielgud . . .': I have again drawn from both Val Gielgud's memoirs.

27 'I was just enough of a gentleman . . .': Vernon Bartlett, *This Is My Life*, Chatto and Windus, 1937.

2 There Must Be Experts Somewhere

32 'The historian Philip Taylor suggests . . .': in 'If War Should Come: preparing the Fifth Arm for Total War 1935–39': *Journal of Contemporary History*, Vol. 16, No. 1, 1981.

34 'One modern historian . . .': Ian McLaine, *Ministry of Morale: Home Front Morale and the Ministry of Information in World War II*, George Allen and Unwin, 1979.

37 'for a day or two buoyed up by . . .': Ian McIntyre, *The Expense of Glory: A Life of John Reith*, HarperCollins, 1993. Reith's autobiography, *Into the Wind*, Hodder and Stoughton, 1949, and *The Reith Diaries* (ed. Charles Stuart), Collins, 1975, are also valuable sources for this episode.

39 'Patience and a willingness to listen . . .': Briggs, *The Golden Age of Wireless*.

40 'Reith left the BBC . . .': Grisewood, *One Thing at a Time*.

40 'I believe that . . .': quoted in Jack Payne's autobiography, *Signature Tune*, Stanley, Paul and Co., 1947.

3 The Bomber Will Always Get Through

41 'London had had some experience . . .': There is a good account of the raids on London in Jerry White's *Zeppelin Nights: London in the First World War*, The Bodley Head, 2014.

44 'Wood Norton Hall is . . .': Gielgud, *Years in a Mirror*.

46 'It is my impression . . .': The letter is quoted by Jonathan Dimbleby in *Richard Dimbleby: A Biography*, Hodder and Stoughton, 1975.

47 'an ordinary saloon car . . .': Gardner, *A.A.S.F.*

50 'That theme was taken up in the *Listener* . . .': The *Listener* was founded in 1926, the year the BBC became a corporation, and closed in 1991. The archive has now been digitized and is available to researchers.

4 The Sound of Ripping Paper

53 'Joyce's biographer, Mary Kenny ...': Mary Kenny, *Germany Calling: A Personal Biography of William Joyce, 'Lord Haw-Haw'*, New Island, Dublin, 2003.

54 'more ideas about broadcasting ...': Briggs, *The Golden Age of Wireless.*

56 'The work of Department EH ...': David Garnett, *The Secret History of PWE:The Political Warfare Executive 1939–1945*, St Ermin's Press, 2002.

57 'the office messenger arrived ...': Gielgud, *Years of the Locust.*

58 'Lady Grigg said ...': quoted in McLaine, *Ministry of Morale.*

5 *Cette Drôle de Guerre*

61 'My plane for "destination unknown"': Gardner, *A.A.S.F.* This chapter draws heavily on Charles Gardner's lively and near-contemporary memoir of his time with the RAF in France.

62 'Their subject matter was concerned mainly with ...': Noël Coward, *Future Indefinite*, Heinemann, 1954.

66 'no heating, little hot water ...': Jonathan Dimbleby, *Richard Dimbleby.*

67 'outside the houses ...': Richard Dimbleby's scripts are held by the BBC Written Archives, but a number of them, including this one, are quoted in Jonathan Dimbleby's *Richard Dimbleby*. Others are reproduced in *War Report* and *Richard Dimbleby, Broadcaster, by his Colleagues*, a commemorative volume edited by Leonard Miall and published by the BBC in 1966 after Dimbleby's death the previous year from cancer.

68 'Notoriously, at the start of the war ...': Turner, *The Phoney War on the Home Front.*

70 'Tom Hickman, in his book ...': Tom Hickman, *What Did You Do in the War, Auntie?*, BBC Books, 1995. The origin and date of the nickname remain a matter of debate. The first known reference in print is a 1953 Leslie Illingworth cartoon in the *Daily Mail*, in which a character looking like Oscar Wilde's 'Aunt Agatha' is seen welcoming the birth of commercial television with the words 'Just like her old Auntie'. The following year it crops up in a letter to *The Economist* in a way that suggests it was, by then, common currency. In 1959 the BBC's director general, Hugh Greene, took the view that the term harked back to the pre-war days of John Reith's reign, but Lord Reith himself told the *Daily Express* in 1963 that 'I can never understand this "Auntie" business. Nobody ever dared to call the BBC "Auntie" in my day.'

71 'The BBC correspondent Frank Gillard ...': Quoted in Hickman's book.

6 My Eton Grandsons Told Me . . .

73 'At Stuttgart . . .': William Shirer, *Berlin Diary: The Journal of a Foreign Correspondent, 1934–1941*, Hamish Hamilton, 1941.

74 'Coward remarked that . . .': Coward, *Future Indefinite.*

75 'In no other war had the British . . .': Turner, *The Phoney War on the Home Front.*

77 'kind of left-wing Fascist . . .': Kenny, *Germany Calling.*

79 'On 5 December 1939 . . .': All the correspondence that follows is preserved in the BBC Written Archives.

7 Mr Churchill Should Sleep in His Boots

87 'The Opposition is getting . . .': Harold Nicolson, *Diaries and Letters* (ed. Nigel Nicolson), Weidenfeld and Nicolson, 2004. The full archive of the diaries is held at Balliol College, Oxford, and is available for researchers.

87 'mostly . . . consists of . . .': Evelyn Waugh, *Put Out More Flags*, Chapman and Hall, 1942.

88–9 'Kenneth Clark, the art historian . . .': For an account of Clark's time at the Ministry of Information, see James Stourton's biography, *Kenneth Clark: Life, Art and Civilisation*, Harper Collins, 2016.

92 'The most notorious example . . .': The story is vividly told in McLaine, *Ministry of Morale.*

93 'The newspapers like the word . . .': Rear Admiral George Thomson, *Blue Pencil Admiral: The Inside Story of the Press Censorship*, Sampson, Low, Marston and Co., 1947.

100 'complaints against the BBC . . .': Garnett, *The Secret History of PWE.*

8 So Many Goodbyes

102 'Captain David Strangeways . . .': The story is told in Andrew Roberts, *The Storm of War: A New History of the Second World War*, Allen Lane, 2009. I have frequently relied on this book for general information about the progress of the Second World War.

102 'Good morning, sir . . .': James Langley, *Fight Another Day*, Collins, 1974.

103 'there was no earthly chance . . .': Gardner, *A.A.S.F.*

110 'The German air force had . . .': Nicholas Harman, *Dunkirk: The Necessary Myth*, Hodder and Stoughton, 1980. More recent additions to Dunkirk literature include Hugh Sebag Montefiore's *Dunkirk: Fight to the Last Man*, Penguin, 2015, and Sinclair McKay's *Dunkirk: From Disaster to Deliverance – Testimonies of the Last Survivors*, Aurum Press, 2015.

112 'At a meeting of the War Cabinet . . .': The meeting is described in John Lukacs, *Five Days in London, May 1940*, Yale University Press, 1999.

113 'We are creating . . .': Nicolson, *Diaries and Letters*.

9 A Better Margate

117 'knobbly backbone of England . . .': J. B. Priestley, *The Good Companions*, Heinemann, 1980.

117 'the clogs and shawls . . .': J. B. Priestley, *Margin Released: A writer's reminiscence and reflections*, Heinemann, 1962.

118 'Although he was . . .': David Cannadine, *Aspects of Aristocracy: Grandeur and Decline in Modern Britain*, Yale University Press, 1994.

118 'Priestley learned his love of country . . .': There is a good account of this period of Priestley's life in Neil Hanson's *Priestley's Wars*, Great Northern Books, Bradford, 2008. Judith Cook's *Priestley*, Bloomsbury, 1997, is also a valuable source.

120 'The BBC's *Postscripts* . . .': The first run of broadcasts proved so popular that they were almost immediately issued as a book, which I have used as the source for my quotations from the scripts; J. B. Priestley, *Postscripts*, Heinemann, 1940.

123 'became in the months . . .': Graham Greene, 'A Lost Leader', in *Reflections* (ed. Judith Adamson), Reinhardt Books, 1990.

129 'Churchill first learned . . .': For an account of the early rhetorical influences on Churchill, see Richard Toye, *The Roar of the Lion: The Untold Stories of Churchill's World War II Speeches*, Oxford University Press, Oxford, 2013.

130 'I was asked once . . .': Charles Eade (ed.), *Churchill By His Contemporaries*, Hutchinson, 1953.

132 'How I wish Winston . . .': Nicolson, *Diaries and Letters*.

10 War Noise, Bells, Guns, Sirens etc

134 'For now the Germans . . .': A transcript of Charles Gardner's report is held at the BBC Written Archives, but it is also available online, as is the Listener Research survey of public reaction.

138 'there were things . . .': Priestley, *Postscripts*.

139 'spent all of one day . . .': Gielgud, *Years in a Mirror*.

143 Marjorie Redman's diaries are held at the Imperial War Museum. They have been published as *Consequently This Country Is at War with Germany*, AMS Educational Ltd, Leeds, 2009.

146 'by Ursula Bloom . . .': This prolific novelist and biographer turned out more than 500 books. I have been unable to track down the one referred to here.

11 Irrevocable Words

148 'French faces . . .': Eric Sevareid, *Not So Wild a Dream*, Alfred Knopf, New York, 1947.

149 'I was nothing . . .': Charles de Gaulle, *Mémoires de guerre*, Plon, Paris, 1955. There is an English edition translated by Jonathan Griffin, Collins, 1955.

149 'The Underground resistance . . .': Edward Tangye Lean, *Voices in the Darkness: The Story of the European Radio War*, Secker and Warburg, 1943.

150 'De Gaulle was appointed . . .': I have drawn on two de Gaulle biographies for this chapter: Jean Lacouture, *De Gaulle, the Rebel, 1890–1944* (trans. Patrick O'Brien), Collins Harvill, 1990; and Don Cook, *Charles de Gaulle: A Biography*, Secker and Warburg, 1984.

152 'they found an "overwrought" de Gaulle . . .': Sir Edward Spears, *Assignment to Catastrophe*, Heinemann, 1954.

153 'As our country . . .': Pierre Bourdan (real name Pierre Maillaud), *Carnet des jours d'attente*, Editions Pierre Trémois, Paris, 1945.

153 'a woman, an English journalist . . .': Jean Oberlé, *'Jean Oberlé vous parle': Souvenirs de cinq années à Londres*, La Jeune Parque, Paris, 1945.

155 'a huge man . . .': Elisabeth Barker later gave a number of accounts of the evening, including an interview held in the BBC Written Archives. She is also quoted by Asa Briggs in *The War of Words*.

156 'The BBC's engineers . . .': Because no recording of the speech exists, there is some dispute about the text de Gaulle actually broadcast. I have used the script reproduced in Jean-Louis Crémieux-Brilhac, *Ici Londres, 1940–1944: Les Voix de la liberté*, La Documentation Française, Paris, 1975. I am grateful to the historian Julian Jackson – who, at the time of writing, is working on a new biography of de Gaulle – for his advice about this episode. De Gaulle's wartime speeches and broadcasts were collected in *Discours et messages pendant la guerre, juin 1940–janvier 1946*, Librairie Plon, Paris, 1970.

156 'as Asa Briggs puts it . . .': in *The War of Words*.

158 'according to the French historian Dominique Decèze …': Dominique Decèze, *Ici Londres: La Lune est pleine d'éléphants verts,* J. Lanzmann & Seghers, Paris, 1979.

12 *C'est Moi, Churchill, Qui Vous Parle*

166 'The historian Andrew Roberts notes …': Roberts, *The Storm of War.*

167 'an axe blow …': De Gaulle, *Mémoires de guerre.*

169 'The French historian …': Decèze, *Ici Londres: La Lune est pleine d'éléphants verts.*

169 'he would fulminate …': Oberlé, *'Jean Oberlé vous parle'.*

172 'I don't know whether …': This and subsequent quotations from the French Service programmes are taken from Jean-Louis Crémieux-Brilhac, *Ici Londres, 1940–1944: Les Voix de la liberté.* The four volumes of anthology and commentary trace the development of broadcasts to France throughout the German occupation. They represent an impressive scholarly achievement, and are themselves a reflection of the importance French historians attach to the BBC's role.

174 'Now and then …': Tangye Lean, *Voices in the Darkness.*

177 'French Radio from London …': Introduction to Crémieux-Brilhac, *Ici Londres, 1940–1944: Les Voix de la liberté.*

180 'On 21 October …': Jacques Duchesne's account of this episode was first broadcast as a BBC programme and later published as *Deux Jours avec Churchill*, Editions de l'Aube, La Tour-d'Aigues, 2008.

13 Impregnable Fortress of Stupidity

183–4 'Last night not so bad in Hampstead …': Redman, *Consequently This Country Is at War with Germany.*

186 'A large proportion …': Priestley, *Postscripts.*

191 'sly demagogue …': Nicolson, *Diaries and Letters.*

192 'In his book …': McLaine, *Ministry of Morale.*

14 Fireflies in a Southern Summer Night

201 'The BBC is not exactly …': Terence Dooley (ed.), *And So I Have Thought of You: The Letters of Penelope Fitzgerald*, Fourth Estate, 2009.

202 'find out the reaction of the British people …': Fitzgerald, *Human Voices.*

202 'You burned the city of London . . .': Quoted by Philip M. Seib in *Broadcasts from the Blitz, How Edward R. Murrow Helped Lead America into War*, Potomac Books, Washington DC, 2006.

203 'talk[ing] about the world . . .': Ben Robertson, *I Saw England*, Jarrolds, 1941.

203 'Before eight, the siren . . .': Murrow's broadcasts from the last days of peace in 1939 to the spring of 1941 have been collected in *This Is London* (ed. Elmer Davis), Schocken Books, New York, 1989. There is a wider selection from his broadcasting work in *In Search of Light: The Broadcasts of Edward R. Murrow, 1938–1961* (ed. Edward Bliss Jr), Alfred A. Knopf, New York, 1967.

203 'a tall, thin man . . .': Sevareid, *Not So Wild a Dream*.

205 'Murrow's first encounter . . .': The story is told in A. M. Sperber, *Murrow: His Life and Times*, Freundlich Books, New York, 1985, on which I have drawn for much of the biographical detail in this chapter.

207 'there was nothing . . .': This and the quotation at the end of the next paragraph are from Seib, *Broadcasts from the Blitz*.

208 'What Murrow wanted . . .': Stanley Cloud and Lynne Olson, *The Murrow Boys: Pioneers on the Front Lines of Broadcast Journalism*, Houghton, Mifflin Company, New York, 1996.

210 'The following June . . .': Though the meeting took place at the English Speaking Union, the minutes are preserved in the BBC's Written Archives.

15 That Hard Stony Sound

215 'a good second class establishment . . .': Robertson, *I Saw England*.

216 'I knew that . . .': Sevareid, *Not So Wild a Dream*.

219 'I am standing on a rooftop . . .': Murrow, *This Is London*.

221 'The only objection . . .': quoted in Sperber, *Murrow*.

225 'With the presidential election . . .': There is a good account of the political debate in the United States during this period in Seib, *Broadcasts from the Blitz*.

227 'when he delivered a high-profile . . .': The evening is described in Sperber, *Murrow*.

16 'I Don't Mind If I Do'

230 'no question of me joining . . .': This account of Elisabeth Barker's career is based on her interview held at the BBC Written Archives.

232 'still possible for …': Gerard Mansell, *Let Truth Be Told: 50 Years of BBC External Broadcasting*, Weidenfeld and Nicolson, 1974.

234 '*Tommy Handley* …': This sketch is quoted in Hickman, *What Did You Do in the War, Auntie?*

239 'demolished and burnt': Oberlé, *'Jean Oberlé vous parle'*.

239 'Accommodation at Bush House …': Briggs, *The War of Words*.

244 'He had the wiry …': Grisewood, *One Thing at a Time*.

17 A Sigh of Relief

246 'he was fighting another very bruising turf war …': This episode is well described in McLaine, *Ministry of Morale*.

249 'OBE for an announcer …': Sir Robert Bruce Lockhart, *The Diaries of Sir Robert Bruce Lockhart* (ed. Kenneth Young), Vol. 2: *1939–1965*, Macmillan, 1989.

250 'Bracken's true past …': I have drawn on two biographies for Brendan Bracken's extraordinary life story: Andrew Boyle, *Poor, Dear Brendan: The Quest for Brendan Bracken*, Hutchinson, 1974; and Charles Edward Lysaght, *Brendan Bracken*, Allen Lane, 1979.

252 'I had a talk …': Nicolson, *Diaries and Letters*.

255 'not even the BBC …': Boyle, *Poor, Dear Brendan*.

18 The Sweet, Smooth Squeeze of a Trigger

258 'How could men …': This episode is described in Grisewood, *One Thing at a Time*.

260 'cast aside romantic …': Julian Jackson, *France: the Dark Years, 1940–1944*, Oxford University Press, Oxford, 2001.

261 'the instruction was …': Crémieux-Brilhac, *Ici Londres, 1940–1944: Les Voix de la liberté*.

268 'the persons to whom …': Garnett, *The Secret History of PWE*.

268 'It is the plain truth …': Bruce Lockhart, *The Diaries of Sir Robert Bruce Lockhart*.

19 Take the Second Alley on the Right

275 'The first member …': The incident is described in Robert Gildea, *Fighters in the Shadows: A New History of the French Resistance*, Faber and

Faber, 2015. I have also drawn from this book for the account of the reprisals that followed.

275 'it was not easy …': Albert Ouzoulias, *Les Bataillons de la jeunesse*, Editions Sociales, Paris, 1967.

278 'The man who …': For a biography of Jean Moulin, see Alan Clinton, *Jean Moulin, 1899–1943*, Palgrave, 2002.

279–80 'An unprecedented number …': Crémieux-Brilhac, *Ici Londres, 1940–1944: Les Voix de la liberté*.

280 'Leading the dance in Paris …': This and the French Service broadcasts that follow, including those by Maurice Schumann, are collected in Crémieux-Brilhac, *Ici Londres, 1940–1944: Les Voix de la liberté*.

20 The Horse Sends His Love to Polydorus

285 'these themes were repeated …': Fernand Grenier, *C'était ainsi*, Editions Sociales, Paris, 1978.

289 'Du Fretay, Hackin …': Crémieux-Brilhac, *Ici Londres, 1940–1944: Les Voix de la liberté*.

289 'The idea of using …': Georges Bégué's story is well told in Dominique Decèze, *Ici Londres: La Lune est pleine d'éléphants verts*.

292 'The experience of an agent …': Gaston Tavian's account of using the BBC message system also appears in Decèze's book.

295 'We needed to build …': Quoted in Crémieux-Brilhac, *Ici Londres, 1940–1944: Les Voix de la liberté*.

21 Der Chef

297 'In the initial …': Lindley Fraser, *Propaganda*, Oxford University Press, Oxford, 1957.

298 'even refugee broadcasters …': Briggs, *The War of Words*. The comment from Leonard Miall is from the same source.

299 'an influential set of essays …': Robert Vansittart, *Black Record: Germans Past and Present*, Hamish Hamilton, 1941.

302 'David Garnett records that …': Garnett, *The Secret History of PWE*.

305 'I longed to show …': Sefton Delmer, *Black Boomerang: An Autobiography*, Viking Press, New York, 1962.

306 'very lurid descriptions …': Bruce Lockhart, *The Diaries of Sir Robert Bruce Lockhart*.

22 The Wintry Conscience of a Generation

310 'German propaganda to India . . .': Mansell, *Let Truth Be Told*.

310 'All propaganda is lies . . .': All quotations from Orwell's diary are from *George Orwell: The Complete Works* (ed. Peter Davison).

311 'On the day when a stranger . . .': Empson's essay is in *The World of George Orwell* (ed. Miriam Gross), Weidenfeld and Nicolson, 1971.

311 'the very best all-British . . .': Laurence Brander, *George Orwell*, Longmans, Green, 1954.

312 'It may seem a little dilettante . . .': Orwell's wartime scripts for the BBC are held in the BBC's Written Archives, but were edited for publication by W. J. West, in *Orwell: The War Commentaries*, Duckworth/BBC, 1985, and *Orwell: The War Broadcasts*, Pantheon Books, 1986. For the story of how this came about, see page 320.

313 'Orwell's logic . . .': There is a clear analysis of Orwell's attitude to propaganda in C. Fleay and M. L. Sanders, 'Looking into the Abyss: George Orwell at the BBC', *Journal of Contemporary History*, Vol. 24, No. 3 (July 1989).

313 'The fact is . . .': These articles are reproduced in *George Orwell: The Complete Works* (ed. Davison).

319 'the majority of Latin Americans . . .': Quoted in Mansell, *Let Truth Be Told*.

320 'In a 1948 letter . . .': Quoted in Bernard Crick, *Orwell: A Life*, Secker and Warburg, 1980.

323 'were composed without . . .': *George Orwell: The Complete Works* (ed. Davison).

23 Oxford Is Held by the Germans

325 'one of the most blatant . . .': Nicholas, *The Echo of War*.

326 'the blackest day . . .': Eric Maguire, *Dieppe: August 19*, Jonathan Cape, 1963.

329 'Safe home . . .': Jonathan Dimbleby, *Richard Dimbleby*.

329 'Richard Dimbleby met me . . .': Edward Ward, *Number One Boy: An Autobiography*, Michael Joseph, 1969.

330 'It was bursting away from us . . .': This script is reproduced in Jonathan Dimbleby, *Richard Dimbleby*.

24 The Crusading Spirit

338 'plough jockey country ...': Stewart MacPherson, *The Mike and I*, Home and Van Thal, 1948.

339 'They were to be given the honorary ...': There is a good account of the formation and training of the War Reporting Unit in Brian P. D. Hannon, 'Creating the Correspondent: How the BBC Reached the Frontline in the Second World War', *Historical Journal of Film, Radio and Television*, Vol. 28, Issue 2, 2008, pp. 175–94.

341 'In 1946 ...': For publication details, see note on page 390.

25 The Biggest Aspidistra in the World

345 'he would not ...': Delmer, *Black Boomerang*.

346 'This apparatus ...': Garnett, *The Secret History of PWE*.

347 'A busy day ...': Bruce Lockhart, *The Diaries of Sir Robert Bruce Lockhart*.

351 'An SS Report ...': Quoted in Delmer, *Black Boomerang*.

353 'like characters in ...': Grisewood, *One Thing at a Time*.

354 'Its original offices ...': For an account of the growth of SOE, see Max Hastings, *The Secret War: Spies, Codes and Guerrillas, 1939–1945*, William Collins, 2015, and Maurice Buckmaster, *They Fought Alone: The True Story of SOE's Agents in Wartime France*, Odhams Books, 1958.

26 Front-page Stuff

357 'two great waves of code ...': All the messages are listed in Crémieux-Brilhac, *Ici Londres, 1940–1944: Les Voix de la liberté*.

357 'joy and hope ...': Guillaume Mercader's story is told in Marie-Josèphe Bonnet (ed.), *Les Voix de la Normandie combattante – Eté, 1944*, Editions Ouest-France, Rennes, 2010.

358 'As Paddy Ashdown notes ...': Paddy Ashdown, *Cruel Victory: The French Resistance, D-Day and the Battle for the Vercors 1944*, William Collins, 2014.

358 'put in place ...': Jonathan Fenby, *The General: Charles de Gaulle and the France He Saved*, Simon and Schuster, 2010.

359 'at this moment of History ...': De Gaulle, *Mémoires de guerre*.

360 'like girls approaching the age of puberty ...': Sir Alexander Cadogan, *The Diaries of Sir Alexander Cadogan O.M. 1938–1945* (ed. David Dilks), Faber and Faber, 2010.

360 'on the binge …': Bruce Lockhart, *The Diaries of Sir Robert Bruce Lockhart.*

362 'The Germans still regarded …': There is a full account of these episodes in Gildea, *Fighters in the Shadow*, and of the Vercors uprising in particular in Ashdown, *Cruel Victory.*

372 'Any hopes they …': Delmer, *Black Boomerang.*

27 The Whole Wood Smelt of the Dead

377 'I am not going to have …' Delmer, *Black Boomerang.*

378 'the use of Aspidistra …': Garnett, *The Secret History of PWE.*

379 'the PWE records show …': The script is reproduced in David Garnett's book.

380 'as Mary Kenny puts it …': Kenny, *Germany Calling.*

383 'Writing twenty years later …': In *Richard Dimbleby, Broadcaster, by his Colleagues* (ed. Miall). The collection also includes the text of Dimbleby's Belsen broadcast.

Postscript

387 'Without prompting …': Fitzgerald, *Human Voices.*

ACKNOWLEDGEMENTS

I OWE A PARTICULAR DEBT of gratitude to Jeff Walden of the BBC's Written Archives; he responded to my requests for research material with imagination and thoroughness, and was unfailingly courteous and welcoming during my many visits to Caversham. I would also like to record my debt to Robin Barnwell, who produced the BBC television series on this subject and generously shared some of the results of the impressive research work he and his team did while making the programmes. The staff at the Imperial War Museum and the National Archives were efficient and pleasant, and dealing with the librarians at the London Library was, as ever, a delight.

My agent Vivienne Schuster retired while I was writing this book, but she launched me on to the project with such enthusiasm that we were in full sail by the time Gordon Wise took the helm; he guided me safely home. Susanna Wadeson, my editor, gave me just the advice I needed when I found myself in a tangle over chronology, and when I asked for a few months off the book while I pursued a television project she took it in her stride. She has been unfailingly supportive and has made the whole process – from commissioning to publication – enormously enjoyable. The final production process has been completed at some speed, and great credit is due to Lizzy Goudsmit for her dogged pursuit of permission to quote passages from the books I have cited. Caroline Hotblack has come up with a wonderfully evocative set of images in very short order, and I am in awe of the attention to detail and wide knowledge which Brenda Updegraff brought to the copy-edit. My wife, Fiona, read everything first and improved almost all of it.

PICTURE ACKNOWLEDGEMENTS

Front endpapers Copyright © BBC Photo Library

p. vi British Cartoon Archive/Associated Newspapers Ltd/Solo Syndication

p. 2 Photo by Kurt Hutton/Picture Post/Getty Images

p. 14 Roger-Viollet/Topfoto

p. 15 AP/REX/Shutterstock

p. 18 Photo by © Hulton-Deutsch Collection/CORBIS/Corbis via Getty Images

p. 38 Leopold Joseph/Associated Newspapers/REX/Shutterstock

p. 54 Mike Gunnill/REX/Shutterstock

p. 63 © Imperial War Museums (C 806)

p. 69 Daily Mail/REX/Shutterstock

p. 119 Granger, NYC/Topfoto

p. 124 (top) Photo by Felix Man/Picture Post/Getty Images; **(bottom)** Associated Newspapers/REX/Shutterstock

p. 125 (top) © Imperial War Museums (NA 12101); **(bottom)** Photo by Felix Man/Picture Post/Hulton Archive/Getty Images

p. 135 Copyright © BBC Photo Library

p. 156 Copyright © BBC Photo Library

p. 204 Bettmann/Getty Images

p. 208 Photo by Anthony Potter Collection/Getty Images

p. 224 Photo by H. F. Davis/Topical Press Agency/Getty Images

p. 233 Photo by Picture Post/Hulton Archive/Getty Images

p. 235 Photo by Haywood Magee/Picture Post/Getty Images

p. 240 Copyright © BBC Photo Library

p. 243 Copyright © BBC Photo Library

p. 244 Photo by Keystone-France/Gamma-Rapho via Getty Images

p. 253 Photo by Keystone/Hulton Archive/Getty Images

p. 295 British Cartoon Archive/Associated Newspapers Ltd/© Solo Syndication

p. 307 Photo by Kurt Hutton/Picture Post/Hulton Archive/Getty Images

p. 309 Photo by ullstein bild via Getty Images

p. 327 Photo by Leonard McCombe/Picture Post/Hulton Archive/Getty Images

p. 335 Photo by Leonard McCombe/Picture Post/Hulton Archive/Getty Images

p. 337 British Cartoon Archive/Associated Newspapers Ltd/© Solo Syndication

p. 341 Photo by Leonard McCombe/Picture Post/Hulton Archive/Getty Images

p. 369 Copyright © BBC Photo Library

Back endpapers: Copyright © BBC Photo Library

INDEX

INDEX